DIE WITTELSBACHER

Ein Jahrtausend in Bildern

DIE WITTELSBACHER
EIN JAHRTAUSEND IN BILDERN

Herausgegeben von Luitpold Prinz von Bayern

S.K.H. Herzog Franz von Bayern
zum 80. Geburtstag

Inhalt

Vorwort	11
Prolog	15
Die Grafen von Scheyern	18
Herzog Otto I. von Bayern – Pfalzgraf Otto VI. von Wittelsbach	20
Herzog Otto II. von Bayern – Herzog Ludwig II. von Bayern	22
Herzog Ludwig V. von Bayern – Kaiser Ludwig IV. der Bayer	24
Herzog Ludwig I. von Bayern der „Kelheimer"	26
Von 1180 bis zur Zeit der Landesteilungen	29
Ludwig der Bayer	31
Kaiser Ludwig der Bayer	32
Der Hausvertrag von Pavia	42
Herzog Stephan III. von Bayern-Ingolstadt	44
Herzog Ludwig VII. von Bayern-Ingolstadt	46
Die Herzöge von Bayern-München und die Reichen Herzöge von Bayern-Landshut	51
Herzog Albrecht III. von Bayern-München	52
Herzog Christoph „der Starke" von Bayern-München	56
Herzog Albrecht IV. von Bayern-München	60
Die Primogeniturordnung	62
Herzog Ludwig IX. von Bayern-Landshut	64
Herzog Georg der Reiche von Bayern-Landshut	66
Das Konfessionelle Zeitalter	73
Herzog Wilhelm IV. von Bayern	74
Herzog Ludwig X. von Bayern-Landshut	86
Herzog Albrecht V. von Bayern-München	90
Herzog Wilhelm V. von Bayern	98
Kurfürst Maximilian I.	103
Kurfürst Maximilian I. von Bayern	104

Kurfürst Ferdinand Maria von Bayern	132
Max Emanuel, der „Blaue König"	151
Kurfürst Max II. Emanuel von Bayern	152
Kaiser Karl VII. Albrecht, Kurfürst von Bayern	172
Kurfürst Maximilian III. Joseph von Bayern	184
Die Wittelsbacher als Kirchenfürsten	206

Die Pfälzer Linien 227

Alte Pfälzische Kurlinie	228
Linie Zweibrücken-Veldenz	244
Linie Pfalz-Neuburg (I)	246
Linie Pfalz-Simmern-Sponheim	260
Linie Pfalz-Neuburg (II)	266
Kurfürst Karl Theodor von der Pfalz und Bayern	277
Linie Pfalz-Bayern	278
Linie Pfalz-Zweibrücken	300
Linie Zweibrücken-Birkenfeld-Gelnhausen – Herzöge in Bayern	312

Das Königreich Bayern 339

König Max I. Joseph	341
König Maximilian I. Joseph von Bayern	342
Prinz Karl von Bayern	374
König Ludwig I.	379
König Ludwig I. von Bayern	380
König Otto I. von Griechenland	422
Prinz Adalbert von Bayern – Adalbertinische Linie	432
König Maximilian II.	451
König Maximilian II. von Bayern	452
König Ludwig II.	477
König Ludwig II. von Bayern	478

König Otto I. von Bayern	514
Prinzregent Luitpold	**517**
Prinzregent Luitpold von Bayern	518
Prinz Leopold von Bayern	540
Prinzessin Therese von Bayern	546
Prinz Arnulf von Bayern	548
Ludwig III., der letzte König von Bayern	**551**
König Ludwig III. von Bayern	554

Das Königliche Haus nach der Revolution von 1918 — 579

Prinz Franz von Bayern	580
Prinz Ludwig von Bayern	586
Kronprinz Rupprecht von Bayern	592
Herzog Albrecht von Bayern	616
Die Familie heute	628
Exkurs I: Wittelsbacher Könige in europäischen Ländern	**638**
Exkurs II: Der Hausritterorden vom Hl. Georg	**650**

Anhang — 667

Literaturauswahl	668
Bildquellen	673

Foreword

Many demanding historical works have already been composed about the history of our family. Major exhibitions have been produced, such as on the 800th anniversary of the House of Wittelsbach in Bavaria in 1980. In addition, numerous monographs have been published about important personalities of our family.
The long timespan of their governance and the temporarily very extensive branching of the House of Wittelsbach in Bavaria and the Palatinate make it very difficult to trace the connections between the individual lines of the family until this day without profound historical knowledge. For the first time, an attempt has now been made in the present volume, to highlight the development of the various family branches pictorially and thus make them more tangible for our times. Naturally, this book can make no claim to completeness and thus can hardly do justice to all the important persons and events of our family's dynamic past. The objective was rather to awaken interest in deeper study of the many interesting historical details.
For this volume, we have chosen visual language, which conveys impressions more quickly than the written word. It is to create a sustained idea about the characters and dramatic events, that characterised the fortunes of this ruling family in the heart of Europe, a family that has existed for almost one thousand years.

The idea for this work emerged during the more than twenty-year cooperation with Prof h. c. Hannes Heindl, who designed a picture calendar about a member of our family annually during this time. These pictures are the basis of this book. They were supplemented by comprehensive picture research, especially on the succession transition from the Palatinate and on the 20th century. The rich treasure-trove of artworks connected to our family from approximately ten centuries (which was collected only in approximate fashion here) also enabled us to provide targeted information about individual personalities and their significance in the pictorial representation of the various lines of the House of Wittelsbach, which focuses on the rulers of Bavaria and their environment. In the arrangement of the chapters, in cases where there was a splitting-off of important lines of the family, each of them was focused on and dealt with, in order then to continue again with the line of the respective family head. The iconographic programme includes mainly paintings, prints and depictions of monuments; photographs were intentionally not used, as far as possible.

Vorwort

Über die Geschichte unserer Familie wurden viele anspruchsvolle historische Werke verfasst. Große Ausstellungen sind entstanden, wie zum Beispiel im Jahre 1980 zum 800. Jubiläum der Wittelsbacher in Bayern. Zudem erschienen zahlreiche Monografien über einzelne bedeutende Persönlichkeiten unserer Familie.
Die lange Zeitspanne ihrer Regierungszeit und die zeitweise sehr breite Verzweigung der Wittelsbacher in Bayern und der Pfalz machen es ohne tiefer gehende Geschichtskenntnisse recht schwierig, die Verbindungen zwischen den einzelnen Linien der Familie bis zum heutigen Tag nachzuvollziehen. Im vorliegenden Band wurde nun erstmals versucht, die Entwicklung der verschiedenen Familienzweige bildlich sichtbar und damit für die heutige Zeit greifbarer zu machen. Naturgemäß kann dieses Buch keinen Anspruch auf Vollständigkeit erheben und somit kaum allen wichtigen Personen und Ereignissen der bewegten Vergangenheit unserer Familie gerecht werden. Ziel war vielmehr, das Interesse an einem tieferen Einstieg in die vielen interessanten Details der Geschichte zu wecken.
Wir haben für diesen Band die Bildsprache gewählt, die Eindrücke schneller transportiert als das geschriebene Wort. Sie soll eine nachhaltige Vorstellung darüber schaffen, welche Charaktere und einschneidenden Ereignisse die Geschicke dieser seit fast tausend Jahren bestehenden Herrscherfamilie im Herzen Europas prägten.

Die Idee zu diesem Werk entstand während der mehr als zwanzig Jahre andauernden Zusammenarbeit mit Prof. h. c. Hannes Heindl, der in dieser Zeit jährlich einen Bildkalender über ein Mitglied unserer Familie gestaltete. Diese Bilder sind die Grundlage des nun vorliegenden Buches. Sie wurde durch umfangreiche Bildrecherchen, insbesondere zum Übergang der Erbfolge aus der Pfalz und zum 20. Jahrhundert, ergänzt. Der reichhaltige Schatz der mit unserer Familie in Zusammenhang stehenden Kunstwerke aus knapp zehn Jahrhunderten (der hier nur annähernd gehoben werden konnte) ermöglichte uns, bei der bildlichen Darstellung der verschiedenen Linien des Hauses Wittelsbach – mit Schwerpunkt auf die Regenten Bayerns und ihres Umfelds – auch gezielte Hinweise auf einzelne Persönlichkeiten und deren Bedeutung zu geben.
Bei der Kapitelanordnung wurden bei Abspaltung wichtiger Linien der Familie diese jeweils vorangezogen und abgehandelt, um dann wieder mit der Linie des jeweiligen Familienoberhaupts fortzufahren. Das Bildprogramm umfasst vorwiegend Gemälde, Drucke und Abbildungen von Denkmälern, bewusst wurde so weit als möglich auf Fotografien verzichtet.

Above all, I would like to thank Prof h. c. Hannes Heindl for his tireless work in researching the pictures – some of which are very unusual – and their description. He made a significant mark on this work.
Prof Dr Michael Körner contributed the explanations of the large historical framework; he accurately presented key guiding principles of our family. I would also like to thank the C. H. Beck publishing firm in Munich, which allowed the adoption of text extracts from the book "Die Wittelsbacher" (The House of Wittelsbach) by Prof Körner. Johanna Binder and Martina Dolhaniuk added the historical overviews on the Bavarian rulers and the captions in their necessary concise form.

In addition, I would like to thank Dr Gerhard Immler, the head of the Secret Archive of the House of Wittelsbach, who supported us with the captions and the research with his expertise, as well as the management of the art collections of the Wittelsbach Compensation Fund, Andreas of Majewski and Brigitte Schuhbauer, for their competent assistance in the picture research. The Bavarian Department of State-owned Palaces, Gardens and Lakes led by its President Bernd Schreiber and its employees gave us enormous non-bureaucratic help in the procurement of extensive picture material. Furthermore, we received full support from many museums, archives and private collectors from around the world in all enquiries regarding more pictures; they are listed in detail in the appendix of the book.
From my administration department, I would above all like to thank Manuela Meyer, who coordinated the work for this book. My sincere thanks go to the Volk publishing firm for the realisation of this work.

My cousin, Duke Francis of Bavaria, always emphasized the importance of the next generation internalising respect for and understanding of the role of the House of Wittelsbach in Bavaria. I hope that this book, marking his 80th birthday, makes a small contribution to this cause.

Luitpold Prince of Bavaria

Ich darf mich vor allem bei Prof. h. c. Hannes Heindl für die unermüdliche Arbeit bei der Recherche der zum Teil sehr außergewöhnlichen Bilder und deren Beschreibung bedanken. Er hat dieses Werk maßgeblich geprägt. Prof. Dr. Michael Körner trug die Erläuterungen des großen historischen Rahmens bei; er stellte wesentliche Handlungsmaximen unserer Familie treffend dar. In diesen Dank einschließen möchte ich den C. H. Beck Verlag in München, der die Übernahme von Textauszügen aus dem Buch „Die Wittelsbacher" von Prof. Dr. Körner gestattete. Johanna Binder und Martina Dolhaniuk ergänzten die geschichtlichen Überblicke zu den bayerischen Herrschern und die Bildtexte in der gebotenen knappen Form.

Ebenso gilt mein Dank Dr. Gerhard Immler, dem Leiter des Geheimen Hausarchivs der Wittelsbacher, der uns bei den Bildtexten und bei der Recherche mit seinem Fachwissen unterstützte, sowie der Verwaltung der Kunstsammlungen des Wittelsbacher Ausgleichsfonds, Andreas von Majewski und Brigitte Schuhbauer, für die kompetente Hilfe bei der Bildrecherche. Die Bayerische Verwaltung der staatlichen Schlösser, Gärten und Seen unter der Leitung ihres Präsidenten Bernd Schreiber und seinen Mitarbeitern gab uns unbürokratisch enorme Hilfestellung bei der Beschaffung umfangreichen Bildmaterials. Darüber hinaus erhielten wir von vielen Museen, Archiven und privaten Sammlern in aller Welt volle Unterstützung bei allen Anfragen nach weiteren Bildern; sie sind im Anhang des Buches noch einmal detailliert aufgeführt.
Aus meiner Verwaltung möchte ich mich vor allem bei Manuela Meyer bedanken, die die Arbeiten zu diesem Buch koordinierte. Dem Volk Verlag danke ich herzlich für die Realisierung dieses Werkes.

Mein Cousin, Herzog Franz von Bayern, legte immer besonderen Wert darauf, dass auch die nachfolgende Generation Respekt und Verständnis für die Rolle des Hauses Wittelsbach in Bayern verinnerlicht. Ich wünsche Ihm, dass dieses Buch anlässlich seines 80. Geburtstages dazu einen kleinen Beitrag leistet.

Luitpold Prinz von Bayern

Prologue

Information about the life of Countess Haziga and Otto, the rich steward of the see Freising, is sparse. We do know that they lived at the start of the 11th century and they had significant rulership rights in Altbayern. Today, they are considered the progenitors of the counts of Scheyern and their descendents, the House of Wittelsbach. Only vague information is contained about them in the few written sources that have been handed down from that time. However, they started one of the dynasties that co-determined the history of Europe for more than 1,000 years and continue to shape it up until today.

In the fourth painting of the so-called "Scheyern Prince Cycle" in the capital church of the Benedictine Abbey of Scheyern, they are clearly recognisable, or rather, visible. Haziga and Otto appear almost casually, in a group of several people, as the founders of Scheyern Abbey, the former family seat and royal burial ground of the early House of Wittelsbach. The Cycle of Scheyern is considered perhaps the best-known painting sequence on the life and activities of the Bavarian dynasty from its beginnings until the 17th century. Nevertheless, it in no way aims to be what it seems to be at first glance: a representation of historical reality, a faithful chronicle of the family's early history.

The history of the portraits themselves is changeful. First, Duke Friedrich of Bavaria-Landshut had the walls of the capital church furnished with scenes from the family history of the counts of Scheyern and the dukes of Bavaria at the end of the 14th century. In the mid-16th century, these paintings were renewed and revamped, until finally they were transferred onto wooden tablets and supplemented by several new paintings at the behest of Abbot Stephan Reitberger from 1623. The cycle ends with the enfeoffment of Maximilian I with electoral dignity in 1623; in contrast, the first few tablets of the painting sequence deal with events that stretch back to the 10th century.

The creators of the medieval wall paintings and the revampers and remodellers of later centuries had one thing in common: they knew about the power of visual representation, about the power of images to affect the observer, about the precious value of capturing a statement permanently on stone, wood or canvas. The general comprehensibility of what was shown was also a concern in most cases – in some cases, however, only a well-informed group was to be able to interpret certain picture elements according to their intention. Thus, the paintings of the princes of Scheyern served not only to document the past; rather, they were to symbolise the self-conception and legitimisation of the family as a dynasty. "Another's" attention was to be directed to "that which related to himself" and the importance of the House of Scheyern and Wittelsbach was literally to be presented to the observer – even if it was a family member of one's own of future generations.

Prolog

Die Informationen über das Leben von Gräfin Haziga und Otto, dem reichen Vogt des Bistums Freising, sind spärlich. Das Paar lebte zu Beginn des 11. Jahrhunderts, so viel ist bekannt, und verfügte über bedeutende Herrschaftsrechte in Altbayern. Sie gelten heute als Stammeltern der Grafen von Scheyern und deren Nachkommen, der Wittelsbacher. Nur verschwommen treten sie aus den wenigen schriftlichen Quellen hervor, die aus dieser Zeit überliefert sind. Doch stehen sie am Beginn einer der Dynastien, die die Geschichte Europas über fast 1.000 Jahre mitbestimmten und auch bis heute gestalten.

Auf dem vierten Bild des sogenannten „Scheyerner Fürstenzyklus" in der Kapitelkirche der Benediktinerabtei zu Scheyern sind sie klar erkennbar, beziehungsweise: sichtbar. Fast beiläufig, in einer Gruppe mehrerer Personen, treten Haziga und Otto als Stifter des Klosters Scheyern auf, der ehemaligen Stammburg und Grablege der frühen Wittelsbacher. Der Zyklus von Scheyern gilt als die vielleicht bekannteste Bildfolge über das Leben und Wirken des bayerischen Herrschergeschlechts von seinen Anfängen bis ins 17. Jahrhundert, und dennoch will er keineswegs das sein, was auf den ersten Blick naheliegt: eine Wiwedergabe der historischen Wirklichkeit, eine getreue Chronik der frühen Geschichte der Familie.

Die Geschichte der Bildnisse selbst ist wechselvoll: Zunächst ließ Herzog Friedrich von Bayern-Landshut zu Ende des 14. Jahrhunderts die Wände der Kapitelkirche mit Episoden der Familiengeschichte der Grafen von Scheyern und der Herzöge von Bayern ausstatten, zu Mitte des 16. Jahrhundert erfuhren diese Malereien Erneuerungen und Umgestaltungen, bis sie schließlich ab 1623 auf Veranlassung von Abt Stephan Reitberger auf Holztafeln übertragen und durch mehrere neue Bilder ergänzt wurden. Der Zyklus endet mit der Belehnung Maximilians I. mit der Kurwürde im Jahr 1623, die ersten Tafeln der Bildfolge hingegen behandeln Ereignisse, die bis ins 10. Jahrhundert zurückreichen.

Eines war den Urhebern der mittelalterlichen Wandmalereien und den Um- und Neugestaltern späterer Jahrhunderte gemeinsam: Sie wussten um die Macht visueller Repräsentation, um die Wirkmächtigkeit des Bildlichen auf den Betrachter, um den kostbaren Wert, eine Aussage beständig auf Stein, Holz oder Leinwand zu bannen. Auch die allgemeine Verständlichkeit des Gezeigten war meist ein Anliegen – zum Teil sollte es aber auch nur einem eingeweihten Kreis möglich sein, bestimmte Bildelemente gemäß einer beabsichtigten Intention zu deuten. Die Scheyerner Fürstenbilder dienten so nicht nur dazu, Vergangenes zu dokumentieren, vielmehr sollten sie das Selbstverständnis und die Legitimation der Familie als Herrschergeschlecht versinnbildlichen. Der Blick des „Anderen" auf das „Eigene" sollte gelenkt werden, dem Betrachter – und sei es ein eigenes Familienmitglied zukünftiger Generationen – die Bedeutung des Hauses Scheyern bzw. Wittelsbach buchstäblich vor Augen geführt werden.

On a journey through 1,000 years of Wittelsbach family history using visual representations, as undertaken by this volume, paintings of the rulers – kings, emperors, electors, dukes – dominate. They follow certain painting traditions that can be perceived from the time of Roman Emperor Augustus up until today. In the process, the ruler portrait in particular always becomes a code for power, its – mostly divine – legitimisation and all-surpassing uniqueness.

Hence, the pictures collected in this volume are never documentation of historical reality alone. Rather, it can be claimed that they are never this in the first place. For example, a battle painting of the Thirty Years' War appears at first glance to be a depiction of a historical moment that is true to reality. However, at second glance one recognises that three different temporal levels of events are represented simultaneously – advancement of the armies, battle and finally flight of the enemy. The result is a "pre-programmed" statement about the clout and courage of the victors – the expression of a specific historical intention of the artist or client. Many portraits were produced only after the event, possibly after an interval of several centuries – these too are to be appreciated in the context in which they were produced and thus for the particular statement they express about what is depicted. In addition to contemporary representations, the selection in this book also includes such historical paintings in order to make important personalities and noteworthy events of the Wittelsbach family history visible, without, however, considering them as documentary. Naturally, it is also impossible to create a complete chronological painting series of all family members starting from the early Middle Ages and continuing until today. The lack of pictorial sources of the early times of the family history and contemporary art-history and sociocultural facts alone prohibits this. Therefore, the selection remains incomplete; in many places, only a few central figures represent a family line or even an entire age. On the other hand, noticeable emphasis is to be allowed in the places that the publisher considers particularly interesting for today's observer and that evidently illustrate the panorama of a specific epoch in which the House of Wittelsbach as a ruling family played a key role in shaping history. Chapter introductions give the fortunes of individual lines of the family a place in the large historical framework. In addition, short biographies of individual outstanding personalities complement selected paintings in the sequence.

Taken on its own, the Scheyern Prince Cycle is a look at the past, produced to a large degree from the perspective of the temporally distant observer and highly symbolically charged. With this look at the past in mind, this book also aims always to be aware of its own, modern perspective and to invite the observer to discover more than pure historical facts. In a time of digital, unending reproducibility of images, it can barely be imagined anymore what material value alone a painted portrait possessed in times past, not to mention the non-material possibilities of expression that were able to carry the fame of what was depicted into the future beyond its finiteness: a piece of immortality for everyone who could afford to be captured on canvas by an artist's hand.

Auf einer Reise durch rund 1.000 Jahre Wittelsbacher Familiengeschichte anhand bildlicher Darstellungen, wie sie der vorliegende Band unternimmt, dominieren Bilder der Herrschenden – Könige, Kaiser, Kurfürsten, Herzöge. Sie folgen bestimmten Bildtraditionen, die vom römischen Kaiser Augustus bis in die heutige Zeit wahrzunehmen sind. Immer wird dabei vor allem das Herrscherporträt zu einem Code für Macht, ihre – meist göttliche – Legitimation und alles überragende Einzigartigkeit.

Die in diesem Band versammelten Abbildungen sind also niemals allein Dokumentation geschichtlicher Wirklichkeit. Vielmehr ist zu behaupten, dass sie es nie von vornherein sind: Ein Schlachtengemälde des Dreißigjährigen Krieges zum Beispiel zeigt sich auf den ersten Blick als scheinbar wirklichkeitsgetreue Abbildung eines historischen Moments, auf den zweiten Blick erkennt man jedoch, dass gleich drei verschiedene Zeitebenen des Geschehens simultan dargestellt sind – Anrücken der Armeen, Kampf und schließlich Flucht des Feindes. So ergibt sich eine „vorprogrammierte" Aussage über die Schlagkraft und Tapferkeit der Sieger – Ausdruck einer bestimmten historischen Intention des Künstlers oder Auftraggebers. Viele Bildnisse entstanden erst im Nachhinein, womöglich im Abstand mehrerer Jahrhunderte – auch sie sind in ihrem Entstehungskontext und damit in ihrer besonderen Aussage über das Abgebildete zu würdigen. Die Auswahl des vorliegenden Buches bedient sich neben zeitgenössischer Darstellungen auch dieser Historienbilder, um bedeutende Persönlichkeiten und denkwürdige Ereignisse der Wittelsbacher Familiengeschichte sichtbar zu machen, ohne sie jedoch als dokumentarisch zu erachten. Auch kann es naturgemäß nicht gelingen, eine vollständige chronologische Bildreihe aller Familienmitglieder ausgehend vom hohen Mittelalter bis in die heutige Zeit zu erstellen. Schon allein der Mangel an bildlichen Quellen der Frühzeit der Familiengeschichte und zeitgenössische kunsthistorische und soziokulturelle Gegebenheiten verbieten dies. Daher bleibt die Auswahl unvollständig, an vielen Stellen repräsentieren nur wenige zentrale Personen einen Familienzweig oder gar ein ganzes Zeitalter. Andererseits soll eine auffällige Gewichtung an den Stellen erlaubt sein, die dem Herausgeber als besonders interessant für den heutigen Betrachter erscheinen und das Panorama einer bestimmten Epoche, in dem die Wittelsbacher als Herrscherfamilie Geschichte entscheidend gestalteten, sinnfällig veranschaulichen. Kapiteleinleitungen geben dem Schicksal einzelner Linien der Familie einen Platz im großen historischen Rahmen. Dazu ergänzen Kurzbiographien zu einzelnen herausragenden Persönlichkeiten punktuell die Bildabfolge.

Der Scheyerner Fürstenzyklus ist, für sich genommen, ein Blick auf die Vergangenheit, zum Großteil aus der Perspektive des zeitlich fernen Betrachters entstanden und hochgradig symbolisch aufgeladen. Diesem Blick auf die Vergangenheit eingedenk will sich auch dieses Buch stets der eigenen, modernen Perspektive bewusst sein und den Betrachter dazu einladen, mehr zu entdecken als reine historische Fakten. In einer Zeit der digitalen, unendlichen Reproduzierbarkeit von Bildern ist kaum mehr vorstellbar, allein welch materiellen Wert ein gemaltes Porträt in früheren Zeiten besaß, ganz zu schweigen von den ideellen Ausdrucksmöglichkeiten, die den Ruhm des Abgebildeten über seine Endlichkeit hinaus in die Zukunft zu tragen vermochten: ein Stück Unsterblichkeit für all diejenigen, die es sich leisten konnten, von Künstlerhand auf Leinwand gebannt zu werden.

PROLOG
Die Grafen von Scheyern

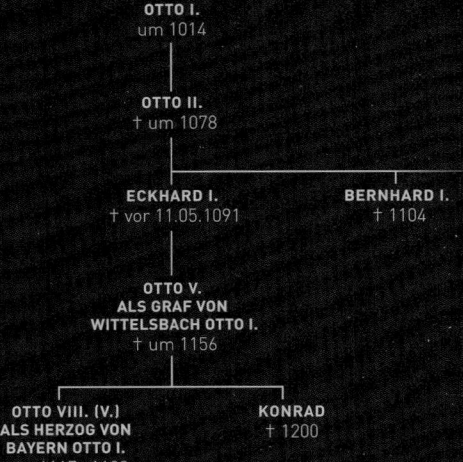

Bestätigung der Gründung der Klöster Bayerischzell und Fischbachau durch Papst Paschalis II. 1203.
Graf Otto und Gräfin Haziga von Scheyern und ihre Söhne Bernhard und Eckard treten als Stifter der beiden Klöster auf.
Diese und die folgenden Abbildungen stammen aus dem Fürstenzyklus der Kapitelkirche des Klosters Scheyern, dessen Ursprung im späten 14. Jahrhundert liegt. Herzog Friedrich von Bayern-Landshut (1375–1393) hatte die Grafen von Scheyern und Wittelsbach dort darstellen lassen. Fortgeführt wurde der Zyklus bis zur Belehnung Maximilians I. mit der Kurwürde durch Abt Stephan Reitberger (1610–1634).
Tafelbild des Scheyerner Fürstenzyklus (Zyklusbild 4), Künstler unbekannt, 1624/25.

Confirmation of the foundation of Bayerischzell and Fischbachau Abbeys by Pope Paschal II 1203.
Count Otto and Countess Haziga of Scheyern and their sons Bernhard and Eckard appear as founders of both abbeys.
These and the following pictures come from the Prince Cycle of the capital church of Scheyern Abbey, which dates from the late 14th century. Duke Friedrich of Bavaria-Landshut (1375–1393) had the counts of Scheyern and Wittelsbach painted there. The cycle was continued until the enfeoffment of Maximilian I with electoral dignity by Abbot Stephan Reitberger (1610–1634).
Panel painting of the Scheyern Prince Cycle (cycle painting 4), artist unknown, 1624/25.

PASC. II. P. M. OTTO. FVNDAT HAZIGA. FVNDATRIX. FILII OTTO. PERINHARDVS ET ECKARDVS F^dTIO MONASTER: IN CELL. ET VISCHBACHAV A PASCHALI II. P.P.M. CONFIRMATA.

PROLOG
Herzog Otto I. von Bayern – Pfalzgraf Otto VI. von Wittelsbach

Herzog Otto I. von Bayern mit seiner Gemahlin Agnes und seinem Sohn Ludwig.
Zum Dank für seine Treue wurde Pfalzgraf Otto VI. 1180 von Kaiser Friedrich Barbarossa mit dem Herzogtum Bayern belehnt. Als Herzog Otto I. brachte er die bayerische Herzogswürde nach der Absetzung des Welfen Heinrichs des Löwen an seine Familie. Der Wappenschild des Herzogs zeigt noch das alte wittelsbachische Wappen (gelber Zackenbalken auf rotem Grund). Die weiß-blauen Rauten kamen erst mit dem Erbe der Grafen von Bogen in die Familie.
Tafelbild des Scheyerner Fürstenzyklus (Zyklusbild 7), Künstler unbekannt, 1624/25.

Duke Otto I of Bavaria with his consort Agnes and his son Ludwig.
In 1180, Count Palatine Otto VI was enfeoffed with the Duchy of Bavaria by Emperor Friedrich Barbarossa as a reward for his loyalty. As Duke Otto I, he brought the Bavarian dukedom to his family after the removal from office of Welf Heinrich der Löwe. The duke's shield still shows the old Wittelsbach coat of arms (a bar of yellow prongs on a red background). The white-blue lozenges came into the family only with the heritage of the counts of Bogen.
Panel painting of the Scheyern Prince Cycle (cycle painting 7), artist unknown, 1624/25.

PROLOG
Herzog Otto II. von Bayern – Herzog Ludwig II. von Bayern

Schönheitengalerie in der Wittelsbacher Grabkirche von Scheyern (I).
Katharina (England), Benedicta (Moosburg), Christina (Castell), Segiret (Burgund), Elisabeth (Bogen), Agnes (Lothringen), Radegundis (Frankreich), Gertrud (Kärnten). Durch die Einheirat Elisabeths von Bogen kamen die heute bekannten weiß-blauen Rauten in das Wappen der Wittelsbacher.
Tafelbild des Scheyerner Fürstenzyklus (Zyklusbild 10), Künstler unbekannt, 1625.

Beauty gallery in the Wittelsbach Basilica of Scheyern (I).
Katharina(England), Benedicta (Moosburg), Christina (Castell), Segiret (Burgundy), Elisabeth (Bogen), Agnes (Lothringen), Radegundis (France), Gertrud (Carinthia). Due to the marriage of Elisabeth of Bogen into the family, the today well-known white-blue lozenges became part of the coat of arms of the House of Wittelsbach.
Panel painting of the Scheyern Prince Cycle (cycle painting 10), artist unknown, 1625.

Herzog Otto II. bringt um 1260 durch seine Heirat mit Agnes die Kurwürde der Rheinpfalz nach Bayern.
Otto II. starb 1253 unter Kirchenbann, wurde aber dennoch in Scheyern begraben. Zwölf Jahre später wurde er durch den Papst vom Bann losgesprochen. Rechts Herzog Heinrich XIII. von Niederbayern mit seiner Gemahlin Elisabeth von Ungarn.
Tafelbild des Scheyerner Fürstenzyklus (Zyklusbild 11), Künstler unbekannt, 1625.

Due to his marriage to Agnes, Duke Otto II brings the electoral dignity of the Rhenish Palatinate to Bavaria, c. 1260.
Otto II died under excommunication in 1253, but was buried in Scheyern nevertheless. Twelve years later, he was absolved of the excommunication by the Pope. On the right, Duke Heinrich XIII of Lower Bavaria with his consort Elisabeth of Hungary.
Panel painting of the Scheyern Prince Cycle (cycle painting 11), artist unknown, 1625.

Herzog Ludwig II. mit seinen Gemahlinnen Maria von Brabant, Anna von Glogau und Mechthild von Habsburg und seinem Sohn Herzog Rudolf I. um 1285.
Herzog Ludwig II. ließ Maria von Brabant wegen eines falschen Verdachts des Ehebruchs enthaupten, zur Sühne stiftete er das Kloster Fürstenfeld. Rechts sein Sohn Rudolf, der Stammvater der Pfälzer Linie, mit seiner Frau Mechthild von Nassau.
Tafelbild des Scheyerner Fürstenzyklus (Zyklusbild 12), Künstler unbekannt, 1625.

Duke Ludwig II with his consorts Maria of Brabant, Anna of Glogau and Mechthild of Habsburg and his son Duke Rudolf I, c. 1285.
Duke Ludwig II had Maria of Brabant beheaded on false suspicion of adultery. To make atonement, he founded Fürstenfeld Abbey. On the right is his son Rudolf, the progenitor of the Palatinate line, with his wife Mechthild of Nassau.
Panel painting of the Scheyern Prince Cycle (cycle painting 12), artist unknown, 1625.

ROMA.PARENS.LIGAVT.SED.SCHYRA.MATER.IN.SACRVM.NOS.TVMVLVM.GRATIOSE.INDIDIT.
HÆC.ENIM.AVITA.ET.PRIMA.NOSTRÆ.VIRTVTIS.EDVCATRIX.ALTRIXQ.IMORTALIS.EST.DDD.

NON.EG.SED.SVSPECTO.IDSCE.PÆRITAS.ET.CAVE.CTO.CREDERE.MAG.V.H.PRINC.RVD.DE.MACIS.AVDISSET.AT.A.LLVORE.SE.DVCI.
PASSVS.EST.ADEOQ.FR.SVO.AVGVSTO.MINVS.FAVIT.NON.SAT.ÆQV.V.POSTERIS.VISVM.EXEMPLVM.

Herzog Ludwig V. von Bayern und sein Vater Kaiser Ludwig IV. um 1350 mit Kirchenmodellen.
Herzog Ludwig V. war zugleich Markgraf von Brandenburg. Zu sehen ist u. a. ein Modell der Kirche von Pfaffenhofen an der Ilm.
Tafelbild des Scheyerner Fürstenzyklus (Zyklusbild 14), Künstler unbekannt, 1625.

Duke Ludwig V of Bavaria and his father Emperor Ludwig IV with model churches, c. 1350.
Duke Ludwig V was also Margrave of Brandenburg. The model churches that can be seen include one of the church of Pfaffenhofen an der Ilm.
Panel painting of the Scheyern Prince Cycle (cycle painting 14), artist unknown, 1625.

Darstellung der Söhne Kaiser Ludwigs IV. des Bayern: Albrecht I., Wilhelm I. und Stephan II. nach 1347.
Nach dem Tode Kaiser Ludwigs des Bayern 1347 wurde das Erbe geteilt. Albrecht I. (links) bekam Niederbayern-Straubing und Holland, Stephan II. (rechts) Niederbayern-Landshut. Hinter ihm seine Söhne Stephan III., Friedrich und Johann II.
Tafelbild des Scheyerner Fürstenzyklus (Zyklusbild 15), Künstler unbekannt, 1625.

Depiction of the sons of Emperor Ludwig IV, the Bavarian: Albrecht I, Wilhelm I and Stephan II, after 1347.
After the death of Emperor Ludwig the Bavarian in 1347, the inheritance was divided. Albrecht I (left) received Lower Bavaria-Straubing and Holland, Stephan II (right) Lower Bavaria-Landshut. Behind him his sons Stephan III, Friedrich and Johann II.
Panel painting of the Scheyern Prince Cycle (cycle painting 15), artist unknown, 1625.

Schönheitengalerie in der Wittelsbacher Grabkirche von Scheyern (II).
Die vier Damen sind die beiden gebürtigen Wittelsbacherinnen Elisabeth von Brandenburg (gen. „die schöne Else") und Sophie von Böhmen sowie Magdalena Visconti von Mailand und Katharina von Görz, die ins Haus Bayern einheirateten. Rechts die Einigung der Kurfürsten Ruprecht I. und Stephan II. von 1339, die gemeinsame Stimme bei der Königswahl abwechselnd auszuüben. Die dritte männliche Person könnte Ruprechts Bruder Rudolf II. sein.
Tafelbild des Scheyerner Fürstenzyklus (Zyklusbild 16), Künstler unbekannt, 1625.

Beauty gallery in the Wittelsbach basilica of Scheyern (II).
The four ladies are Elisabeth of Brandenburg (named "Beautiful Beth") and Sophie of Bohemia, both of whom were born into the House of Wittelsbach, as well as Magdalena Visconti of Milan and Katharina of Gorizia, who married into the House of Bavaria. On the right, the agreement of electors Ruprecht I and Stephan II of 1339 to exercise their joint vote in the election of the king alternately. The third male person could be Ruprecht's brother Rudolf II.
Panel painting of the Scheyern Prince Cycle (cycle painting 16), artist unknown, 1625.

VERES·R͞EG͞VM·EXPRIMVNT·P͞ñ·NOTANT·   ALBERT·DVX·BAV·INF· GVILIELMVS·HOLLAND· STEPHANVS·D·B·SVP·

VIDEN·HOS·HEROES·SVNT·LVD·IV·SACRA·PIGNORA·EIVSQ·SOCER·GENVS·PLANE·REGIVM·
VEL·SI·QVID·REGALI·EST·REGALIVS·IMO·PLVS·QVAM·REGIVM·QVIA·EX·OMNI·PARTE·CÆSAREVM·

BRANDENBVRG· BOEMIA· MEDIOLANVM· GORICIA· RVPERT·RV· STEPHAN·ELEC͞OR·
  B·OPH·ELEC·FIL· LVDOV·IV·FIL·

M·RARIS·ICONAS·HAS·PER·ANN·CCXLIII·HEIC·ANONYMAS·STARE·GNOSCE·ILLVSTRISSIMA·INSIGNIA·
EX·ILLIS·SVNT·RVP·AC·STEPH·HINC·ET·I·D·SEPTEMVIRATV·PER·VICES·OB·EVDO·VTRINQ·A·M·CCCXXXIX·CVNT·M·E·

PROLOG
Herzog Ludwig I. von Bayern, der „Kelheimer"

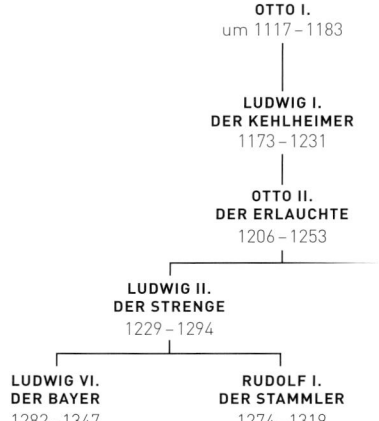

Ermordung Herzog Ludwigs I. „des Kelheimers" 1231.
Herzog Ludwig I. wurde 1231 auf der Donaubrücke in Kelheim von einem Unbekannten erstochen. Von Zeitgenossen wurde vermutet, es habe sich dabei um einen Anschlag des Kaiser Friedrichs II. gehandelt, dem der Bayernherzog zu mächtig geworden sei. Ludwig wurde im Kloster Scheyern beigesetzt. Der Maler verlegt das Verbrechen in einen Innenraum, der Mörder flieht durch die Tür ins Freie, während Ludwigs Gefolgsleute bestürzt zu Hilfe eilen.
Tafelbild des Scheyerner Fürstenzyklus (Zyklusbild 10), Künstler unbekannt, 1625.

Murder of Duke Ludwig I "the Kelheimer" 1231.
Duke Ludwig I was fatally stabbed by an unknown person on the Donaubrücke (bridge) in Kelheim in 1231. Contemporaries suspected it was an attack by Emperor Friedrich II, for whom the Duke of Bavaria had become too powerful. Ludwig was buried in Scheyern Abbey. The painter places the crime in an inside space, with the murderer fleeing through the door into the open, while Ludwig's distraught followers rush to his aid.
Panel painting of the Scheyern Prince Cycle (cycle painting 10), artist unknown, 1625.

LVDOVICVS. OTTONIS. M. FIL. BAIOARIÆ. DVX. COMES. PALAT. RHENI.
LVD. OLIM. F. SED. EX. HOC. INFELIX. QVOD. IN. IPSO. PONTE. KELHEIM. PER. MRIONĒ VVFREDSIERIT.

From 1180 to the time of the territorial partitions

At the great court council of Emperor Friedrich I in Altenburg, Thuringia, on 16 September 1180, Count Palatine Otto of Wittelsbach was enfeoffed with the Duchy of Bavaria. For contemporaries, the real event in this dramatic story was the removal from office of Heinrich der Löwe – combined with the loss of Saxony and Bavaria – while the enfeoffment of the member of the House of Wittelsbach was rather taken for granted. The Duchy of Saxony was annihilated, while only Styria was removed from the Duchy of Bavaria.

Otto I had grown up as a loyal follower of the Emperor; the triad of the first three dukes from the House of Wittelsbach, including dukes Ludwig I and Otto II, managed to stabilise their rulership thanks to their major prestige in the empire and the country, thanks to their origin from the Bavarian tribal nobility, thanks to a loyal ministerial following – and against the massive competition of rival houses of counts and seven old episcopal sees.

The most important and enduring attainment of the House of Wittelsbach outside Altbayern belonged to Duke Ludwig I; he was enfeoffed as Count Palatine of the Rhine in 1214. All members of the House of Wittelsbach of the following centuries bore the title of a Count Palatine of the Rhine just like that of a Duke of Bavaria. Although the fact that this office of count palatine remained with the House of Wittelsbach until the end of the Old Empire is often not really appreciated, it contributed very significantly to the profile and self-evaluation of the dynasty.

After the division of the duchy between the two sons of Duke Otto II had begun, no more did any son of a duke want to forego rulership or become a member of the clergy; with interruptions, Bavaria remained divided for 250 years, with four sub-duchies existing for a time. With its fratricidal wars over rights and titles, this epoch of territorial partitions, which lasts until 1506, has for a long time had an extremely bad press in the historical narrative of the state of Bavaria: the disagreement over imperial policy led to the loss of electoral and imperial dignity; fragmentation in territorial policy threw away opportunities; the high material expense of the individual courts weighed the country down.

On the other hand, recently the positive impact associated with these territorial partitions has been emphasised. The intensity of the exercise of rulership in a small area caused optimised legal development and a sophisticated administrative expansion. Several capitals and residences not only led to higher costs, but in fact meant more life, more business, more culture. Landstände (territorial estates). A great deal was expected of the Landstände, the representatives of the country: they provided advice, acted as arbitrators and provided assistance or resistance; the internal constitution of the sub-duchies was the most modern in the empire at the time. Munich, Landshut, Burghausen, Straubing, Ingolstadt, Amberg, Neumarkt, Neunburg vorm Wald – until now, these places are influenced by the time of the many dukes.

Von 1180 bis zur Zeit der Landesteilungen

Auf dem Hoftag Kaiser Friedrichs I. im thüringischen Altenburg wurde am 16. September 1180 Pfalzgraf Otto von Wittelsbach mit dem Herzogtum Bayern belehnt. Für Zeitgenossen war in dieser dramatischen Geschichte die Absetzung Heinrichs des Löwen – verbunden mit dem Verlust Sachsens und Bayerns – das eigentliche Ereignis, wogegen die Belehnung des Wittelsbachers eher als Selbstverständlichkeit gelten mochte. Das Herzogtum Sachsen wurde zerschlagen, das bayerische Herzogtum nur um die Steiermark verkleinert.

Otto I. war groß geworden als treuer Gefolgsmann des Kaisers; der Trias der ersten drei Herzöge aus dem Hause Wittelsbach, einschließlich der Herzöge Ludwig I. und Otto II., gelang die Stabilisierung ihrer Herrschaft dank des großen Ansehens in Reich und Land, dank ihrer Herkunft aus dem bayerischen Stammesadel, dank einer treuen Ministerialen-Gefolgschaft – und gegen die massive Konkurrenz rivalisierender Grafengeschlechter und sieben alter Bischofssitze.

Die bedeutendste und dauerhafteste Erwerbung des Hauses Wittelsbach außerhalb Altbayerns gelang Herzog Ludwig I.; er wurde 1214 mit der Pfalzgrafschaft bei Rhein belehnt. Alle Wittelsbacher der nachfolgenden Jahrhunderte führten den Titel eines Pfalzgrafen bei Rhein wie den eines Herzogs von Bayern. Dass dieses Amt des Pfalzgrafen bis zum Ende des Alten Reichs beim Haus Wittelsbach verblieb, wird zwar häufig nicht so recht wahrgenommen, trug aber ganz wesentlich zum Profil und zur Selbsteinschätzung der Dynastie bei.

Nachdem 1255 das Teilen des Herzogtums unter den beiden Söhnen Herzog Ottos II. einmal eingeführt war, wollte kein Herzogssohn mehr auf das Regieren verzichten oder geistlich werden; mit Unterbrechungen blieb Bayern 250 Jahre lang geteilt, zeitweise gab es vier Teilherzogtümer. Diese Epoche der Landesteilungen, die bis 1506 reicht, hat mit ihren Bruderkriegen um Rechte und Ansprüche in der bayerischen Landesgeschichtsschreibung lange Zeit eine ausgesprochen schlechte Presse gehabt: Die Uneinigkeit in der Reichspolitik habe zum Verlust von Kur- und Kaiserwürde geführt; die Zersplitterung in der Territorialpolitik habe Chancen vergeben; der hohe materielle Aufwand der einzelnen Hofhaltungen habe das Land belastet.

Demgegenüber werden neuerdings auch die positiven Auswirkungen betont, die sich mit diesen Landesteilungen verbinden lassen. Die Intensität der Herrschaftsausübung im kleinen Raum bewirkte eine optimierte Rechtsentwicklung und einen differenzierten Verwaltungsausbau. Mehrere Hauptstädte und Residenzen führten nicht nur zu höheren Kosten, sondern bedeuteten faktisch mehr Leben, mehr Wirtschaft, mehr Kultur. Die Vertreter des Landes, die Landstände, waren gefordert: Sie berieten, schlichteten, leisteten Hilfe oder Widerstand; die innere Verfasstheit der Teilherzogtümer war die modernste im damaligen Reich. München, Landshut, Burghausen, Straubing, Ingolstadt, Amberg, Neumarkt, Neunburg vorm Wald: Bis in die Gegenwart hinein sind diese Orte von der Zeit der vielen Herzöge geprägt.

Ludwig the Bavarian

The young son of a duke, Ludwig, born in 1282 as the eighth child of Ludwig II of Upper Bavaria, was initially not earmarked for the "career" that caused him to go down in history as the most important member of the House of Wittelsbach of the Middle Ages. Ludwig and his older brother Rudolf were born in the middle of the confusing rulership conditions of the time of the Bavarian territorial partitions; for this reason, as the younger son Ludwig was willing even at an early age to asset rigorously his claims to rulership against Rudolf and other competitors.

After the death of his father in 1294, he ascended to co-ruler of his brother as early as 1302. In 1310, Ludwig obtained from Rudolf a partition of the Upper Bavarian duchy on his behalf. The outcome of the Battle of Gammelsdorf in 1313 recommended the young prince as a candidate for election as king. In the battle over the guardianship of the still underage heirs of the Lower Bavarian duchy – a battle that was highly significant in terms of power politics – Ludwig thoroughly defeated the Habsburg army under his cousin Friedrich the Handsome. Subsequently, he was in fact elected as Roman-German King by five electors on 19 October 1314 and shortly thereafter he was crowned by the Archbishop of Mainz in Aachen where coronations traditionally took place. However, he continued to be opposed by his cousin Friedrich of the House of Habsburg, who received four votes in a simultaneous kingly election in Bonn – it was controversially debatet, though, to whom the bohemian and saxon votes were rightfully due – and was crowned and endowed with the Imperial Regalia by the Archbishop of Cologne, who had been authorised to do this from time immemorial. Eight years later, Ludwig came off victorious in the battle for royal dignity against Friedrich as well and defeated the Habsburg army again in the Battle of Mühldorf.

Ludwig's military successes ultimately paved his way to being crowned Emperor in Rome, but also embroiled him in far-reaching political conflicts at European level, primarily with Pope Johannes XXII in Avignon, who claimed the right to decide on the awarding of the crown in case of a ambiguous kingly election for himself. In 1324, he proclaimed excommunication on Ludwig. However, he soon achieved a reconciliation with his old rival Friedrich the Handsome: the Wittelsbacher made the anti-king his co-ruler at Empire level and was now anointed and crowned as Emperor in Rome by anti-papal bishops despite his ongoing conflict with Johannes XXII. Ten years later, Ludwig's conflict with the Pope was to culminate in the issue of several radical imperial laws that made the election of the Roman-German King independent of approval by the Pope.

As the ruler of Bavaria, Emperor Ludwig IV founded Ettal Abbey and rendered outstanding services to the expansion of the Alter Hof in Munich. However, for the house of Wittelsbach and the history of Bavaria, one of Ludwig's achievements in particular is to be emphasised: in 1329, when coming home from Italy, he agreed the "Treaty of Pavia" with the sons of his brother, who had already died in 1319. The treaty awarded the Palatinate and the Upper Palatinate to the descendents of Rudolf as hereditary lands. If one of the two lines died out, its territory was to be awarded to the other. Even 450 years later, this mutual inheritance regulation was to have far-reaching consequences for the fate of the House of Wittelsbach as a Bavarian ruling family.

Ludwig der Bayer

Der junge Herzogssohn Ludwig, geboren 1282 als achtes Kind Ludwigs II. des Strengen von Oberbayern, war zunächst nicht vorgesehen für die „Karriere", die ihn als bedeutendsten Wittelsbacher des Mittelalters in die Geschichte eingehen ließ. Ludwig und sein älterer Bruder Rudolf wurden mitten hineingeboren in die verwirrenden Herrschaftsverhältnisse der Zeit der bayerischen Landesteilungen; Ludwig war als jüngerer Sohn daher schon früh dazu bereit, seine Herrschaftsansprüche gegenüber Rudolf und anderen Konkurrenten rigoros durchzusetzen.

Nach dem Tod des Vaters 1294 stieg er bereits 1302 zum Mitregenten seines Bruders auf, 1310 erwirkte Ludwig bei Rudolf eine Teilung des oberbayerischen Herzogtums zu seinen Gunsten. Der Ausgang der Schlacht bei Gammelsdorf 1313 empfahl den jungen Fürsten als Kandidat für die Königswahl: In der machtpolitisch höchst bedeutsamen Auseinandersetzung um die Vormundschaft der noch unmündigen Erben des niederbayerischen Herzogtums schlug Ludwig das habsburgische Heer unter seinem Vetter Friedrich dem Schönen vernichtend. Daraufhin wurde er tatsächlich am 19. Oktober 1314 von fünf Kurfürsten zum römisch-deutschen König gewählt und kurz darauf im traditionellen Krönungsort Aachen durch den Erzbischof von Mainz gekrönt. Ihm gegenüber stand jedoch weiter sein habsburgischer Vetter Friedrich, der in einer zeitgleichen Königswahl in Bonn vier Kurstimmen – wem die böhmische und die sächsische Stimme rechtmäßig zustund, war allerdings strittig – erhielt und durch den von alters her dazu befugten Erzbischof von Köln gekrönt und mit den Reichskleinodien ausgestattet wurde. Acht Jahre später setzte sich Ludwig auch im Kampf um die Königswürde gegen Friedrich durch und besiegte das habsburgische Heer abermals in der Schlacht bei Mühldorf.

Seine militärischen Erfolge ebneten Ludwig schließlich den Weg zur Kaiserkrönung in Rom, verwickelten ihn aber auch in weitreichende politische Konflikte auf europäischer Ebene, vornehmlich mit Papst Johannes XXII. in Avignon, der bei zwiespältiger Königswahl das Entscheidungsrecht über die Vergabe der Kaiserkrone für sich beanspruchte. Er belegte Ludwig 1324 mit dem Kirchenbann. Mit seinem alten Rivalen Friedrich dem Schönen gelang jedoch eine baldige Aussöhnung: Der Wittelsbacher machte den Gegenkönig zum Mitregenten auf Reichsebene und ließ sich nun trotz des andauernden Konflikts mit Johannes XXII. 1328 in Rom von anti-päpstlichen Bischöfen salben und zum Kaiser krönen. Ludwigs Auseinandersetzung mit dem Papst sollte zehn Jahre später im Erlass mehrerer einschneidender Reichsgesetze gipfeln, die die römisch-deutsche Königswahl von einer Zustimmung durch den Papst unabhängig machte.

Als bayerischer Landesfürst stiftete Kaiser Ludwig IV. unter anderem das Kloster Ettal und machte sich um den Ausbau des Alten Hofs in München verdient. Für das Haus Wittelsbach und die Geschichte Bayerns ist jedoch besonders ein Verdienst Ludwigs hervorzuheben: Auf dem Heimweg von Italien einigte er sich 1329 mit den Söhnen seines bereits 1319 verstorbenen Bruders auf den „Hausvertrag von Pavia", der den rudolfinischen Nachkommen die Pfalz und die Oberpfalz als Erblande zusprach. Beim Aussterben einer der beiden Linien sollte der anderen deren Territorium zugesprochen werden. Noch knapp 450 Jahre später sollte diese einvernehmliche Erbregelung für das Schicksal der Wittelsbacher als bayerische Herrscherfamilie weitreichende Konsequenzen haben.

VON 1180 BIS ZUR ZEIT DER LANDESTEILUNGEN
Kaiser Ludwig der Bayer

Der Pfalzgraf bei Rhein und Herzog von Bayern.
Die Reliefdarstellung gehört zum sogenannten Kurfürstenzyklus am ehemaligen Kaufhaus „am Brand" in Mainz. Die Reliefs der sieben Kurfürsten sowie des Deutschen Königs waren als Zinnen an der Fassade des Hauses angebracht. Das Wappenschild des fürstlichen Ritters zeigt in den diagonal gegenüberliegenden Feldern jeweils den pfälzischen Löwen und die mit der Einheirat Elisabeths von Bogen 1242 erworbenen Rauten. Das Mainzer Relief ist einer der frühesten Hinweise auf das wittelsbachische Wappen in dieser Form.
Sandsteinrelief, um 1330.

Count Palatine of the Rhine and Duke of Bavaria.
The relief representation is part of the so-called Elector Cycle at the former mall "am Brand" in Mainz. The reliefs of the seven electors as well as the German King were attached to the facade of the building as crenellations. The princely knight's shield shows the Palatine lion and the lozenges acquired with the marriage of Elisabeth of Bogen into the family in 1242 in the diagonally opposite fields. The relief in Mainz is one of the earliest indications of the Wittelsbach coat of arms in this form.
Sandstone relief, c. 1330.

Der Deutsche König aus dem Mainzer Kurfürstenzyklus.
Gewandung und Ausrüstung der Figuren des Kurfürstenzyklus lassen auf eine Entstehung in den 30er bis 40er Jahren des 14. Jahrhunderts schließen. Als Deutscher König, der einen Schild mit dem Reichsadler hält, ist hier demnach Ludwig der Bayer dargestellt.
Sandsteinrelief, um 1340.

The German King from the Mainz Elector Cycle.
The garb and equipment of the figures of the Elector Cycle lead to the conclusion that they were created in the 30s to 40s of the 14th century. Accordingly, Ludwig the Bavarian is depicted here as the German King holding a shield with the imperial eagle.
Sandstone relief, c. 1340.

VON 1180 BIS ZUR ZEIT DER LANDESTEILUNGEN
Kaiser Ludwig der Bayer

Die Schlacht bei Gammelsdorf 1313.
In der Schlacht bei Gammelsdorf schlug Herzog Ludwig IV. am 9. November 1313 ein habsburgisches Ritterheer. Zum Krieg war es gekommen, als die Witwen der beiden niederbayerischen Herzöge Otto III. und Stephan I. die Vormundschaft über ihre Kinder an Herzog Friedrich von Österreich übertragen wollten. Dem widersetzten sich die Vettern aus der oberbayerischen Linie, Ludwig und sein älterer Bruder Rudolf I., im Bündnis mit den Städten Niederbayerns. Der Sieg machte Ludwig im ganzen Reich bekannt und trug wesentlich zu seiner Wahl zum deutschen König durch die antihabsburgische Partei im folgenden Jahr bei.
Farblithografie nach Ludwig Behringer, 19. Jahrhundert.

The Battle of Gammelsdorf 1313.
In the Battle of Gammelsdorf on 9 November 1313, Duke Ludwig IV defeated a Habsburg army of knights. War had resulted when the widows of the two Lower Bavarian dukes Otto III and Stephan I wanted to transfer the guardianship of their children to Duke Friedrich of Austria. This was opposed by the cousins from the Upper Bavarian line, Ludwig and his older brother Rudolf I, in alliance with the cities of Lower Bavaria. The victory made Ludwig known throughout the entire empire and contributed significantly to his election as German King by the anti-Habsburg party in the following year.
Colour lithograph based on the original by Ludwig Behringer, 19th century.

Schlacht bei Gammelsdorf,
den 9ten November 1313.

VON 1180 BIS ZUR ZEIT DER LANDESTEILUNGEN
Kaiser Ludwig der Bayer

Ludwig der Bayer (1282–1347) in der Ahnengalerie der Münchner Residenz.
Kurfürst Karl Albrecht (1697–1745) ließ ab 1726 in der Münchner Residenz eine Ahnengalerie errichten, die den dynastischen Herrschaftsanspruch des Hauses Wittelsbach von Karl dem Großen („Carolus Magnus") bis Karl Albrecht („Carolus Albertus") sinnfällig zu legitimieren suchte. Ein zentrales Bildnis dieser ruhmreichen Genealogie ist das Kaiser Ludwigs des Bayern.
Gemälde aus der Werkstatt Jacopo Amigonis, 1728.

Ludwig the Bavarian (1282–1347) in the Ancestral Gallery of the Munich Residenz.
From 1726, Prince-Elector Karl Albrecht (1697–1745) had an ancestral gallery constructed in the Munich Residenz that aimed to legitimise the right to dynastic rulership of the House of Wittelsbach from Charlemagne ("Carolus Magnus") to Karl Albrecht ("Carolus Albertus") in an evident manner. A central image of this glorious genealogy is that of Emperor Ludwig the Bavarian.
Painting from the Workshop of Jacopo Amigonis, 1728.

Die Reichskrone der Könige und Kaiser des Heiligen Römischen Reiches.
Neben Reichskreuz, Reichsschwert und der Heiligen Lanze zählte die Reichskrone zu den zentralen Reichskleinodien. Gemeinsam mit Reichsapfel und Zepter kam sie auch bei der Krönung Ludwigs des Bayern zum Einsatz.
Aus der Werkstatt eines wahrscheinlich niederrheinischen Meisters, 2. Hälfte des 10. Jahrhunderts.

The Imperial Crown of the kings and emperors of the Holy Roman Empire.
In addition to the Imperial Cross, the Imperial Sword and the Holy Lance, the Imperial Crown was a central component of the Imperial Regalia. Along with the Imperial Orb and the Cepter, it was also used in the coronation of Ludwig the Bavarian.
From the workshop of a likely Lower-Rhenish master, 2nd half of the 10th century.

Kaiserwahl Ludwigs des Bayern aus der Wirkteppichfolge „Geschichte der bayerischen Herzöge" von 1735.
Der Bildteppich thematisiert die Königswahl Ludwigs des Bayern.
Gobelinmanufaktur München unter Louis-Arnould d'Arondeau, Residenz München, St.-Georgs-Rittersaal.

Election of Emperor Ludwig the Bavarian from the tapestry sequence "History of the Bavarian Dukes" from 1735.
The tapestry thematises the election as king of Ludwig the Bavarian.
Tapestrymanufactur Munich under Louis-Arnould d'Arondeau, Munich Residenz, St. Georg's Hall of Knights.

VON 1180 BIS ZUR ZEIT DER LANDESTEILUNGEN
Kaiser Ludwig der Bayer

Kaiser Ludwig der Bayer auf Adlerschwingen thronend.
Diese Darstellung des Kaisers wurde seit seiner Krönung 1328 auf goldenen Siegeln im ganzen Reich verbreitet. Das Originalrelief im Nürnberger Rathaussaal wurde 1945 stark beschädigt, ein Abdruck hat sich im Bayerischen Nationalmuseum erhalten.
Reliefabdruck, Original um 1340.

Emperor Ludwig the Bavarian enthroned on eagle wings.
This representation of the Emperor was spread throughout the entire empire since his coronation on golden seals in 1328. The original relief in the Nuremberg Council Chamber was heavily damaged in 1945. A replica has been preserved in the Bavarian National Museum.
Relief replica, original c. 1340.

Kaiser Ludwig der Bayer (1282–1347) und seine zweite Gemahlin Margarete von Holland (1292–1356).
Das Herrscherpaar präsentiert der Muttergottes das Modell der St.-Lorenz-Kapelle. Die alte Hofkirche zum Hl. Lorenz in München gehörte zu einem Ensemble von Palastbauten, das Kaiser Ludwig der Bayer errichten ließ. Erstmals wählte er damit München als feste Residenzstadt. Die Lorenzkapelle bestimmte er zum Aufbewahrungsort der Reichskleinodien.
Stifterrelief für die Burgkapelle St. Lorenz im Alten Hof, München, von Antonius Berthold, um 1324.

Emperor Ludwig the Bavarian (1282–1347) and his second consort Margarete of Holland (1292–1356).
The ruling couple presents the model of St. Lorenz Chapel to the Virgin Mother. The old Hofkirche zum Hl. Lorenz (church) in Munich was part of an ensemble of palace buildings that Emperor Ludwig the Bavarian had constructed. He thus chose Munich as a permanent city of residence for the first time. He elected the Lorenz Chapel as the place where the Imperial Regalia were to be kept.
Founder relief for the castle chapel St. Lorenz in the Alter Hof, Munich, by Antonius Berthold, c. 1324.

VON 1180 BIS ZUR ZEIT DER LANDESTEILUNGEN
Kaiser Ludwig der Bayer

Innenansicht der Alten Hofkirche zum Hl. Lorenz, München.
Aquarellierte Tuschezeichnung von Wilhelm Rehlen, um 1815.

Interior view of the Alte Hofkirche zum Hl. Lorenz, Munich.
Watercoloured ink drawing by Wilhelm Rehlen, c. 1815.

Die St.-Lorenz-Kapelle in München.
Kolorierte Federzeichnung von Carl August Lebschée, 1870.

The St Lorenz Chapel in Munich.
Coloured pen and ink drawing by Carl August Lebschée, 1870.

VON 1180 BIS ZUR ZEIT DER LANDESTEILUNGEN
Der Hausvertrag von Pavia

Der Hausvertrag von Pavia.
Ausfertigung der Pfalzgrafen Rudolf II. und Ruprecht I. für Kaiser Ludwig den Bayern und dessen Söhne. Der Hausvertrag von Pavia ist eine der bedeutendsten Urkunden für die politische und territoriale Entwicklung Bayerns. Er legte die versöhnliche Trennung der pfälzischen Gebiete Oberbayerns (Rheinpfalz und Oberpfalz) fest. Fortan regierte in der Pfalz die rudolfinische Linie der Wittelsbacher, im Rest des bayerischen Herrschaftsgebiets die ludovizische Linie (nach Kaiser Ludwig dem Bayern). Nach dem Aussterben der ludovizischen Linie vereinigte Kurfürst Karl Theodor das Land 1777 wieder zu „Churpfalzbaiern".
Handschrift auf Pergament, Siegel an Seidenschnur, Pavia, 4. August 1329.

The Treaty of Pavia.
Copy of Counts Palatine Rudolf II and Ruprecht I for Emperor Ludwig the Bavarian and his sons. The Treaty of Pavia is one of the most important documents for the political and territorial development of Bavaria. It established the peaceable partition of the Palatine regions of Upper Bavaria (Rhenish Palatinate and Upper Palatinate). From then on, the Rudolfic line of the House of Wittelsbach reigned in the Palatinate, while the line of Emperor Ludwig the Bavarian ruled in the rest of the Bavarian dominion. In 1777, after the line of Ludwig the Bavarian had died out, Prince-Elector Karl Theodor reunited the land as "Electoral Palatinate-Bavaria".
Handwriting on parchment, seals on silk string, Pavia, 4 August 1329.

Der Hausvertrag von Pavia.
Ausfertigung Ludwigs des Bayern für seine Neffen, die Pfalzgrafen.
Handschrift auf Pergament, Siegel an Seidenschnur, Pavia, 4. August 1329.

The Treaty of Pavia.
Copy of Ludwig the Bavarian for his nephews, the counts palatine.
Handwriting on parchment, seals on silk string, Pavia, 4 August 1329.

VON 1180 BIS ZUR ZEIT DER LANDESTEILUNGEN
Herzog Stephan III. von Bayern-Ingolstadt

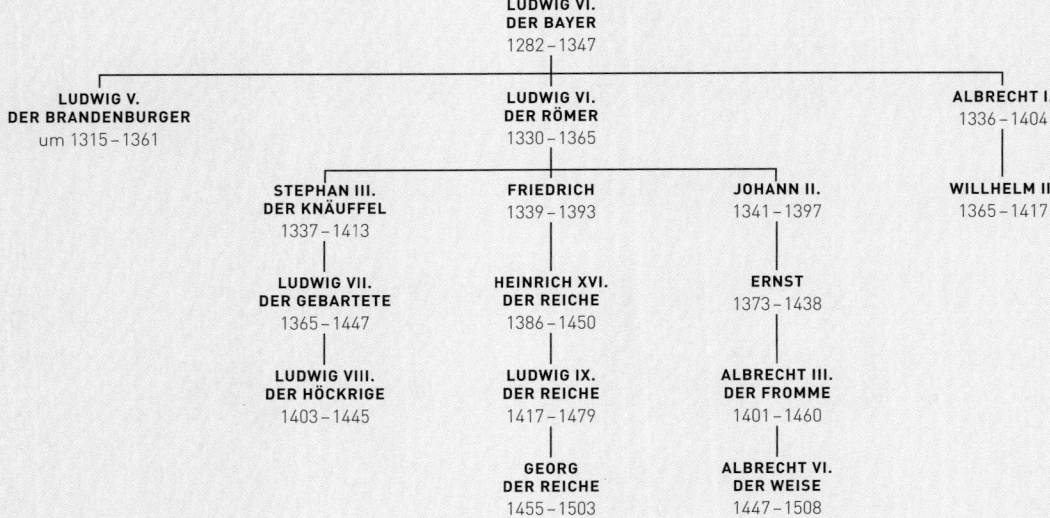

Stephan III. „der Knäuffel" von Bayern-Ingolstadt (um 1337–1413).
Stephan III. regierte bis 1392 gemeinsam mit seinen jüngeren Brüdern Friedrich I. und Johann II. das vereinigte Herzogtum von Oberbayern und Niederbayern-Landshut. Nach einer von Johann II. geforderten weiteren Landesteilung erhielt der Älteste der drei das Herzogtum Oberbayern-Ingolstadt, Johann II. Oberbayern-München und deren Bruder Friedrich Niederbayern-Landshut.
Zeichnung eines unbekannten Künstlers, o. J.

Stephan III "the Knäuffel" of Bavaria-Ingolstadt (c. 1337–1413).
Stephan III ruled the united duchy of Upper Bavaria and Lower Bavaria-Landshut together with his younger brothers Friedrich I and Johann II until 1392. After a further territorial partition demanded by Johann II, the eldest of the three received the duchy of Upper Bavaria-Ingolstadt, Johann II received Upper Bavaria-Munich and their brother Friedrich received Lower Bavaria-Landshut.
Drawing of an artist unknown, undated.

VON 1180 BIS ZUR ZEIT DER LANDESTEILUNGEN
Herzog Ludwig VII. von Bayern-Ingolstadt

Die Initialen Ludwigs „des Gebarteten" im Kopialbuch der Schatzurkunde der Kirche „Zur Schönen Lieben Frau" in Ingolstadt.
Handschrift und Buchmalerei auf Pergament, um 1440.

The initials of Ludwig "the Bearded" in the cartulary of the church "Zur Schönen Lieben Frau" in Ingolstadt.
Handwriting and illumination on parchment, c. 1440.

Einzug der Königin Isabeau von Frankreich in Paris am 22. August 1389.
Elisabeth von Bayern (oder Isabeau de Bavière) war eine Schwester Ludwigs VII. „des Gebarteten" von Bayern-Ingolstadt. Sie heiratete 1385 den französischen König Karl VI., im Sommer 1389 wurde sie in Paris zur Königin gekrönt. Die mehrere Tage andauernden Feierlichkeiten wurden noch Jahre später als das prächtigste Fest beschrieben, welches das Frankenreich je gesehen hatte.
Miniatur aus der Chronik Frankreichs von Jean Froissart, um 1400.

Entry of Queen Isabeau of France into Paris on 22 August 1389.
Elisabeth of Bavaria (or Isabeau de Bavière) was a sister of Ludwig VII "the Bearded" of Bavaria-Ingolstadt. In 1385, she married the French King Karl VI and in the summer of 1389 she was crowned as Queen in Paris. The celebrations, which lasted for several days, were still described years later as the most magnificent the Frankish Empire had ever seen.
Miniature from the Chronicle of France by Jean Froissart, c. 1400.

La requeste con-
templation z plai-
sance de tres hault
et noble prince
mon tres chier seigneur z maistre
Guy de chastillon conte de bloiz
seigneur daursnes de chymay
et de beaumont de conne chone
et de la gode. Je iehan froi-
sart prebstre et chappelain a mon

tres chier seigneur dessus nōme
Et pour le tampz de loze tresorier
et chanonne de chymay et de lille
en flandres ille fus de nouuiel
resueillie et entre dedens ma fo-
rte pour ouurer et fortier en la
haulte et noble matiere de la
quelle du tampz passe ie me
suis ensonne. Laquelle traitte
et propose les fais et aduenues

VON 1180 BIS ZUR ZEIT DER LANDESTEILUNGEN
Herzog Ludwig VII. von Bayern-Ingolstadt

Entwurf für das Grabmal Herzog Ludwigs VII. „des Gebarteten" in Ingolstadt.
In der Liebfrauenkirche zu Ingolstadt sollte ab 1429 das herzogliche Grabmal entstehen, das Ludwig VII. für sich und seine Familie in Auftrag gab. Es wurde jedoch nie ausgeführt, der dem Herzog selbst zugeschriebene bildgewaltige Entwurf wurde nur in einem Musterstein Realität.
Relief aus Solnhofer Stein, wahrscheinlich ausgeführt von Hans Multscher, 1435.

Design for the tomb of Duke Ludwig VIII "the Bearded" in Ingolstadt.
From 1429, the ducal tomb that Ludwig VII mandated for himself and his family was to be created in the Liebfrauenkirche (church) in Ingolstadt. However, it was never carried out, with the visually stunning design attributed to the duke himself becoming reality only in a model stone.
Relief made of Solnhofen stone, likely carried out by Hans Multscher, 1435.

Wappenstein und Inschriftentafel Herzog Ludwigs VII. von Bayern-Ingolstadt in Lauingen.
Ludwig VII. ließ an den Toren der Städte seines Territoriums Wappensteine und Inschriftentafeln anbringen, die an die unter ihm ausgeführte Neubefestigung der Städte erinnern. Der Lauinger Wappenstein zeigt neben dem Wappen auch die persönlichen Devisen (Wahlsprüche) des Herzogs in Form einer strahlenumkränzten, bekrönten Sonne und Motiven der St.-Oswald-Legende.
Wappenstein mit Inschriftentafel, um 1413.

Coat of arms chiselled in stone and inscription tablet of Duke Ludwig VII of Bavaria-Ingolstadt in Lauingen.
Ludwig VII had coats of arms chiselled in stone and inscription tablets attached to the gates of the cities of his territory that remind one of the refortification of the cities carried out under his rule. In addition to the coat of arms, the stone also shows the duke's personal mottos in the form of a rays-surrounded, crowned sun and motifs of the St. Oswald legend.
Coat of arms chiselled in stone with inscription tablet, c. 1413.

The dukes of Bavaria-Munich and the Rich Dukes of Bavaria-Landshut

After the death of Emperor Ludwig in 1347, the Bavarian principalities entered another period of radical change. This approximately 100-year phase until the reconsolidation of rulership conditions temporarily produced four Bavarian sub-duchies; personnel and opposing parties changed almost constantly, so it seems. After the Bavaria-Ingolstadt line – whose most prominent representatives, Stefan III and Ludwig VII "the Bearded" are presented here – died out, a crucial reunification was achieved: from 1450, only two sub-dukes governed in Bavaria, Albrecht III of Bavaria-Munich and Ludwig IX the Rich of Bavaria-Landshut.

Albrecht III is known to most as the Bavarian son of a duke who crossed all social boundaries to fall in love with barber's daughter Agnes Bernauer from Augsburg and presumedly to marry her in secret. In 1435, his father Duke Ernst allowed his son's beloved to drown in the Danube – a marriage outside their social class would have endangered the preservation of power of the Munich line too greatly. Albrecht openly feuded with his father. However, one year later he married a woman of noble status, who gave him ten legitimate heirs. The dramatic events of his youth likely had a permanent impact on Albrecht. From a political perspective, his reign was rather insignificant; however, it earned him the byname "the Pious". In contrast, the reign of his son Albrecht IV was more turbulent, since he assumed rulership from his brother Sigmund and was able to defend it doggedly against his younger brothers Wolfgang and Christoph der Starke.

Meanwhile, the so-called "Rich Dukes" governed in Lower Bavaria. With Heinrich XVI (1393–1450), particular prosperity had come upon the duchy. This was due in part to high-yield agriculture and in part to the income from the salt trade as well as from 1445 from the Rattenberg silver mines in Tyrol. For three generations, the fame of the ducal treasury on Burghausen Castle endured; Heinrich's successor, Ludwig IX, in particular, had a knack for continuing to fill the treasury. Under his rulership, Lower Bavaria experienced a period of cultural prosperity and achieved hegemony among the Southern German principalities. In 1475, Ludwig the Rich arranged the "Landshut Wedding" with Jadwiga (Hedwig), the daughter of the King of Poland, for his son Georg, which is legendary due to its ostentatious outlay.

When Georg der Reiche died without a male descendent in 1503, a war of succession broke out across both sub-duchies of the Landshut line. Georg had married his daughter Elisabeth to the Palatine Ruprecht and appointed the couple as his successors by will. Albrecht IV of Bavaria-Munich saw the applicable law of succession as violated and considered it time to reunite the duchies. He ultimately emerged victorious from the three-year, bitter conflict with the Palatine cousins. With the enactment of the Bavarian Primogeniture Ordinance in 1506, Albrecht, named "the Wise", established the sole right of succession for the firstborn son and thus the indivisibility of the new Bavarian duchy. However, his sons Ludwig and Wilhelm still shared the rulership rights for Lower and Upper Bavaria, since both were born before 1506. It was not until 1545 that Lower Bavaria passed completely to Wilhelm IV of Bavaria-Munich and his descendents.

Die Herzöge von Bayern-München und die Reichen Herzöge von Bayern-Landshut

Nach dem Tod Kaiser Ludwigs 1347 gerieten die bayerischen Fürstentümer erneut in eine Zeit des Umbruchs. Diese knapp 100 Jahre andauernde Phase bis zur Neukonsolidierung der Herrschaftsverhältnisse brachte zwischenzeitlich vier bayerische Teilherzogtümer hervor; Personen und Konfliktparteien wechselten, so scheint es, beinahe stetig. Nach dem Aussterben der Linie Bayern-Ingolstadt, als deren prominenteste Vertreter hier Stefan III. „der Kneißel" und Ludwig VII. „der Gebartete" vorgestellt werden, gelang eine entscheidende Wiedervereinigung: Ab 1450 regierten nur mehr zwei Teilherzöge in Bayern, Albrecht III. von Bayern-München und Ludwig IX. der Reiche von Bayern-Landshut.

Albrecht III. ist den meisten als jener bayerische Herzogssohn bekannt, der sich über alle Standesgrenzen hinweg in die Augsburger Baderstochter Agnes Bernauer verliebte und diese vermutlich sogar heimlich heiratete. Sein Vater Herzog Ernst ließ die Geliebte seines Sohnes 1435 in der Donau ertränken – eine nicht standesgemäße Ehe hätte den Machterhalt der Münchner Linie zu sehr gefährdet. Albrecht befehdete seinen Vater offen, nahm jedoch ein Jahr später eine Adelige zur Frau, die ihm zehn legitime Erben schenkte. Die dramatischen Erlebnisse seiner Jugend prägten Albrecht wohl für immer. Seine Regentschaft verlief aus politischer Sicht eher unbedeutend, brachte ihm jedoch den Beinamen „der Fromme" ein. Die Regierungszeit seines Sohnes Albrecht IV. gestaltete sich dagegen turbulenter, da er von seinem älteren Bruder Sigmund die Herrschaft übernahm und diese gegenüber seinen jüngeren Brüdern Wolfgang und Christoph dem Starken beharrlich zu verteidigen wusste.

In Niederbayern regierten derweil die sogenannten „Reichen Herzöge" von Bayern-Landshut. Mit Heinrich XVI. (1393–1450) war besonderer Wohlstand über das Herzogtum gekommen, der zum einen in der ertragreichen Landwirtschaft, zum anderen in den Einkünften aus dem Salzhandel und ab 1445 aus den Rattenberger Silberbergwerken in Tirol begründet lag. Über drei Generationen lang währte der Ruhm der herzoglichen Schatzkammer auf der Burg zu Burghausen, die vor allem Heinrichs Nachfolger Ludwig IX. weiter zu füllen verstand. Unter ihm erlebte Niederbayern eine kulturelle Blütezeit und erreichte die politische Vormachtstellung unter den süddeutschen Fürstentümern. Für seinen Sohn Georg richtete Ludwig der Reiche im Jahr 1475 die ob ihres prunkvollen Aufwands legendäre „Landshuter Hochzeit" mit der polnischen Königstochter Jadwiga (Hedwig) aus.

Als Georg der Reiche 1503 ohne männliche Nachkommen starb, brach über die beiden Teilherzogtümer der Landshuter Erbfolgekrieg herein: Georg hatte seine Tochter Elisabeth mit dem Pfälzer Ruprecht verheiratet und das Paar testamentarisch als seine Nachfolger eingesetzt. Albrecht IV. von Bayern-München sah das geltende Erbrecht verletzt und die Stunde zur Wiedervereinigung der Herzogtümer gekommen: Aus dem drei Jahre währenden erbitterten Konflikt mit den Pfälzer Vettern ging er am Ende siegreich hervor. Mit Inkraftsetzung der bayerischen Primogeniturordnung im Jahr 1506 legte Albrecht, „der Weise" genannt, das alleinige Erbrecht für den erstgeborenen Sohn und somit die Unteilbarkeit des neuen bayerischen Herzogtums fest. Seine Söhne Ludwig und Wilhelm teilten sich allerdings noch die Herrschaftsrechte für Nieder- und Oberbayern, da beide vor 1506 geboren waren. Erst 1545 fiel Niederbayern restlos an Wilhelm IV. von Bayern-München und seine Nachkommen.

VON 1180 BIS ZUR ZEIT DER LANDESTEILUNGEN
Herzog Albrecht III. von Bayern-München

Kloster Andechs, hoch über dem Ammersee liegend, 1455 von Herzog Albrecht III. von Bayern-München gestiftet.
Der Herzog wählte, wie auch viele seiner Nachfolger, Andechs als letzte Ruhestätte. Auch das gegenwärtige Haus Wittelsbach hat auf einem 1980 neu angelegten Friedhof im Schatten der Kirche seine Grabstätte.
Stich von Jakob Custos (?), 1. Hälfte des 17. Jahrhunderts.

Andechs Abbey, located high above the Ammersee, founded by Duke Albrecht III of Bavaria-Munich in 1455.
Like many of his descendents, the duke chose Andechs as his final resting place. The modern-day House of Wittelsbach also has its burial site on a graveyard created in the shadow of the church in 1980.
Engraving by Jakob Custos (?), 1st half of the 17th century.

Herzog Albrecht III. von Bayern-München schlägt die böhmische Krone aus.
Dieses Gemälde gehört zum Historienzyklus des Alten Herkulessaals in der Münchner Residenz, der ab 1601 von Hans Werl im Auftrag Maximilians I. geschaffen wurde. Albrecht III. lehnte 1440 die ihm angetragene böhmische Königskrone ab.
Ölgemälde von Hans Werl, um 1601 bis 1608.

Duke Albrecht III of Bavaria-Munich rejects the Bohemian crown.
This painting is part of the History Cycle of the Alter Herkulesaal hall in the Munich Residenz, which was created starting in 1601 by Hans Werl on behalf of Maximilian I. In 1440, Albrecht III rejected the Bohemian royal crown, which was offered to him.
Oil painting by Hans Werl, c. 1601 to 1608.

VON 1180 BIS ZUR ZEIT DER LANDESTEILUNGEN
Herzog Albrecht III. von Bayern-München

54 | 55

Predella des Hochaltars des Kastulus-Münsters, Moosburg.
Das Gemälde von Hans Wertinger zeigt betend einen der Söhne Herzog Albrechts III., vermutlich Wolfgang, welcher nie aus eigenem Recht regierte, wohl aber als Vormund für seine Neffen Wilhelm IV. und Ludwig X. Hinter den Türflügeln befindet sich der Reliquienschrein des Hl. Sigismund.
Altarschrein aus Lindenholz mit Malerei von Hans Wertinger, um 1518.

Predella of the high altar of the Kastulus-Münster church, Moosburg.
The painting by Hans Wertinger shows one of the sons of Duke Albrecht III praying, probably Wolfgang, who never governed in his own right, but did do so as the guardian of his nephews Wilhelm IV and Ludwig X. Behind the valves is the reliquary shrine of St. Sigismund.
Altar shrine made of lime wood with painting by Hans Wertinger, c. 1518.

Geschlossener Flügelaltar der Blutenburger Schlosskapelle.
Die Abbildung zeigt auf der rechten Seite Herzog Sigmund von Bayern-München, den Stifter der Kapelle, vom Hl. Bartholomäus empfohlen, kniend vor dem Hl. Sigismund (links).
Blutenburger Hochaltar von Jan Pollack, um 1492.

Winged altar of the chapel of Blutenburg Castle.
On the right hand side of the painting is Duke Sigmund of Bavaria-Munich, the founder of the chapel, recommended by St. Bartholomew, kneeling before St. Sigismund (left).
Blutenburg high altar by Jan Pollack, c. 1492.

VON 1180 BIS ZUR ZEIT DER LANDESTEILUNGEN
Herzog Christoph „der Starke" von Bayern-München

Statuette Christophs „des Starken" von Bayern-München (1449–1493).
Die Figur zeigt den Bayern in der Rolle des drachentötenden St. Georg. Christoph „der Starke" war einer der jüngeren Brüder Herzog Albrechts IV. von Bayern-München. In der rechten Hand hält er ein Schwert, das ca. 300 Jahre später das Ordensschwert des St.-Georg-Ritterordens werden sollte. Mit ihm schlug der Großmeister des Ordens die Kandidaten zum Ritter. Es befindet sich heute in der Schatzkammer der Münchner Residenz.
Aus Silber getriebene Statuette, Künstler unbekannt, um 1470 bis 1490.

Figurine of Christoph "the Strong" of Bavaria-Munich (1449–1493).
The figure shows the Bavarian in the role of the dragon-slaying St. Georg. Christoph "the Strong" was one of the younger brothers of Duke Albrecht IV of Bavaria-Munich. In his right hand he holds a sword that was to become the order sword of the Knightly Order of St. Georg approximately 300 years later. With it, the Grand Master of the Order knighted the candidates. Today, it is found in the treasury of the Munich Residenz.
Figurine embossed of silver, artist unknown, c. 1470 to 1490.

Prunkschwert Herzog Christophs von Bayern-München.
Christoph der Starke tat unter König Matthias Corvinus in Ungarn Dienst und lebte mehrere Jahre als Ritter am ungarischen Königshof.
Werk eines unbekannten Meisters, 15. Jahrhundert.

Elaborately decorated sword of Duke Christoph of Bavaria-Munich.
Christoph der Starke served under King Matthias Corvinus in Hungary and lived as a knight at the Hungarian royal court for several years.
Work of an unknown master, 15th century.

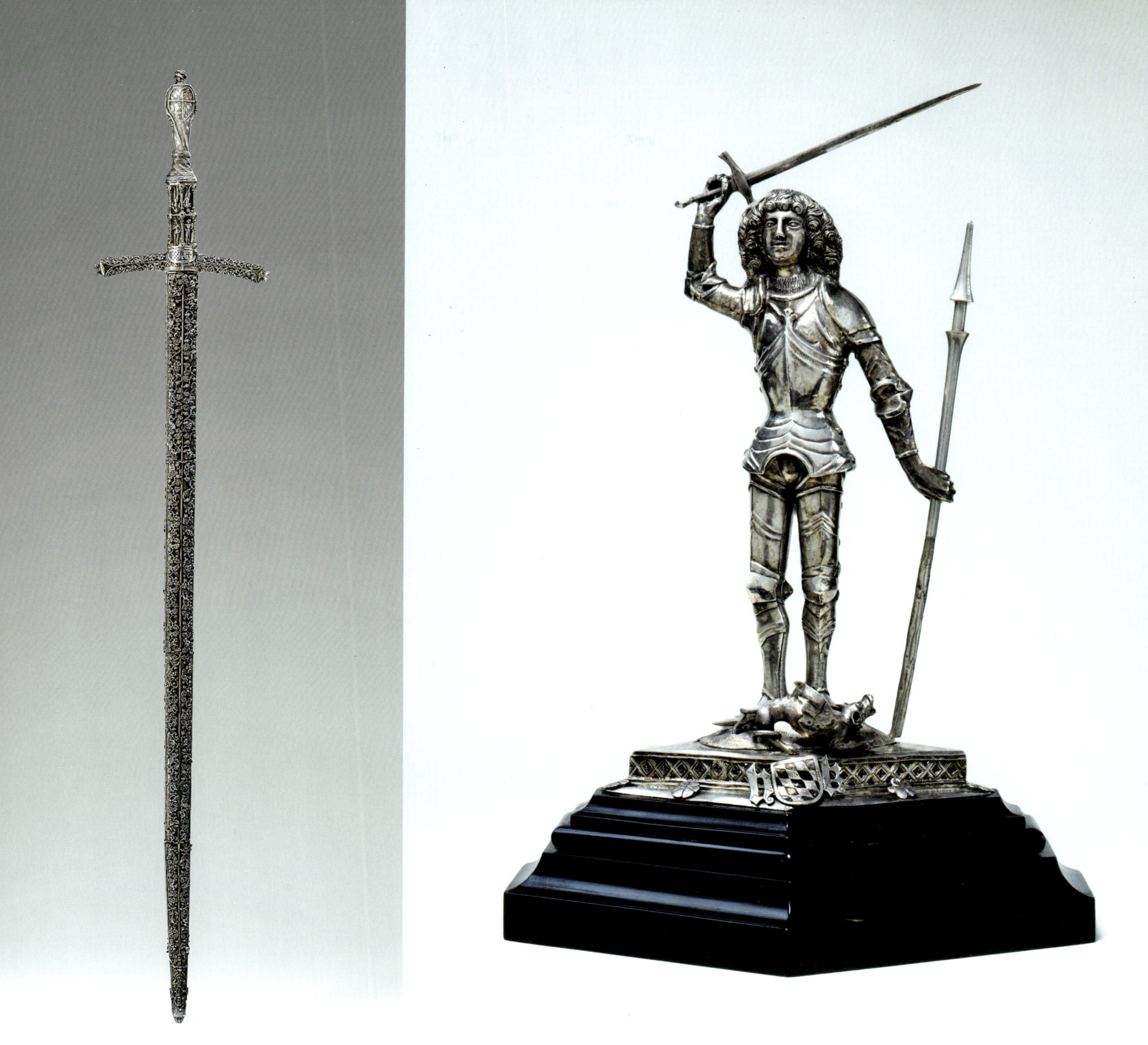

VON 1180 BIS ZUR ZEIT DER LANDESTEILUNGEN
Herzog Christoph „der Starke" von Bayern-München

Triumphzug Kaiser Maximilians I.
Die kolorierte Federzeichnung zeigt u. a. die Herzöge „Ott von Payren", „Cristof von Payren" und „Albrecht von Payren" in Prunkrüstung und mit ihren prächtigen Wittelsbacher Bannern.
Federzeichnung mit Aquarell- und Deckfarbenmalerei auf Pergament von Albrecht Altdorfer (Werkstatt), um 1512/1515.

Triumphal procession of Emperor Maximilian I.
The coloured pen and ink drawing shows dukes "Ott of Payren", "Cristof of Payren" and "Albrecht of Payren", among others, in splendid attire and with their magnificent Wittelsbach banners.
Pen and ink drawing with watercolour and body colour painting on parchment by Albrecht Altdorfer (atelier), c. 1512/1515.

VON 1180 BIS ZUR ZEIT DER LANDESTEILUNGEN
Herzog Albrecht IV. von Bayern-München

Herzog Albrecht IV. von Bayern-München (1447–1508).
Albrecht IV. erhielt von den Geschichtsschreibern den Beinamen „der Weise", wohl da er 1506 das Primogeniturgesetz schuf – das Alleinregierungsrecht für den Erstgeborenen.
Gemälde von Barthel Beham, 1535.

Duke Albrecht IV of Bavaria-Munich (1447–1508).
Historians gave Albrecht IV the byname "the Wise", probably because he created the Primogeniture Act in 1506 – the sole right to government for the firstborn.
Painting by Barthel Beham, 1535.

Herzogin Kunigunde von Bayern-München mit geviertem Wappen Bayern/Österreich.
Kunigunde war eine Tochter Kaiser Friedrichs III. und Gemahlin Herzog Albrechts IV. Sie widersprach der Primogeniturordnung, da ihre Söhne vor dem Erlass derselben bereits geboren waren. So kam es, dass sich Wilhelm IV. und Ludwig X. Ober- und Niederbayern noch teilten.
Kolorierte Federzeichnung aus dem Wappenbuch des Hauses Habsburg, Wien, um 1556 bis 1566.

Duchess Kunigunde of Bavaria-Munich with the four-part coat of arms of Bavaria/Austria.
Kunigunde was a daughter of Emperor Friedrich III and consort of Duke Albrecht IV. She contradicted the Primogeniture Ordinance, since her sons had already been born before it was issued. It thus ensued that Wilhelm IV and Ludwig X still shared Upper and Lower Bavaria.
Coloured pen and ink drawing from the armorial of the House of Habsburg, Vienna, c. 1556 to 1566.

Kunigund Herzogin zu Bayrn.

VON 1180 BIS ZUR ZEIT DER LANDESTEILUNGEN
Die Primogeniturordnung

Die Bayerische Primogeniturordnung.
Die Urkunde vom 8. Juli 1506 legte die Unteilbarkeit des Herzogtums und seine Vererbung an den jeweiligen Erstgeborenen in der männlichen Linie fest. Nach dem Bayerischen Erbfolgekrieg (1504/05) regelte die Primogeniturordnung den Verzicht Herzog Wolfgangs gegenüber Herzog Albrecht IV. (altbayerische Linie), dessen männliche erstgeborene Nachkommen nun de facto allein erbberechtigt waren.
Handschriftliche Urkunde, besiegelt durch die bayerische Landschaft, 8. Juli 1506.

The Bavarian Primogeniture Ordinance.
The document of 8 July 1506 established the indivisibility of the duchy and its inheritance by the respective firstborns in the male line. After the War of the Bavarian Succession (1504/05), the Primogeniture Ordinance regulated the abdication of Duke Wolfgang in favour of Duke Albrecht IV (old Bavarian line), whose male firstborn descendents now had de facto sole right of succession.
Handwritten document, sealed by the Bavarian Landstände, 8 July 1506.

VON 1180 BIS ZUR ZEIT DER LANDESTEILUNGEN
Herzog Ludwig IX. von Bayern-Landshut

Stiftungsbrief der Universität Ingolstadt von 1472.
Herzog Ludwig IX. „der Reiche" von Bayern-Landshut gründete 1472 die erste Universität Bayerns in Ingolstadt. Die Originalurkunde verbrannte im Zweiten Weltkrieg.
Reproduktion nach Götz Freiherr von Pölnitz, o. J.

Charter of the University of Ingolstadt of 1472.
In 1472, Duke Ludwig IX "the Rich" of Bavaria-Landshut founded Bavaria's first university in Ingolstadt. The original document burned in the Second World War.
Reproduction based on the Original by Götz baron of Pölnitz, undated.

Stifterblatt aus dem Matrikelbuch der Universität Ingolstadt von 1472.
Der Jesusknabe reicht dem Stifter Herzog Ludwig IX. von Bayern-Landshut den Arm. Rechts Gründungsrektor Christoph Mendel von Steinfels.
Handschrift und Buchmalerei auf Pergament, 1472.

Founder page from the matriculation register of the University of Ingolstadt of 1472.
The boy Jesus extends his arm towards founder Duke Ludwig IX of Bavaria-Landshut. On the right is founding rector Christoph Mendel of Steinfels.
Handwriting and illumination on parchment, 1472.

Dux ludwicus fundator · Callixtus meradel doctor pm⁹ Rector

Decima octaua die mensis Marcii 1472

Dns Theodericus azan ppus in Munster ic

Dns Iohannes azan Cansing a⁹ retor Bar

Dns Georg azan Kern edie S azanuny Ingolst

Dns Jangman Lin hof Kern edie Pfaffenhofen

Dns Andreas Keder medicinax dortor ordinax

VON 1180 BIS ZUR ZEIT DER LANDESTEILUNGEN
Herzog Georg der Reiche von Bayern-Landshut

Ansicht der Fassade des Landschaftshauses in Landshut gegenüber von St. Martin, einst Sitz der niederbayerischen Landstände.
Zur Straßenseite hin zieren 30 lebensgroße Bildnisse von Wittelsbachern die Fassade des Landschaftshauses. Sie stammen von Hans Pachmayr (Entwurf) und Hans Gnauf (Ausführung) und datieren auf das Jahr 1598. Max Kröz hielt diese Ansicht im 18. Jahrhundert auf Leinwand fest.
Links oben Fotografien der Original-Fassade, rechts Ölgemälde von Max Kröz, 18. Jahrhundert.

View of the facade of the Landschaftshaus in Landshut opposite St. Martin, once the seat of the Lower Bavarian Landstände.
Towards the side of the street, 30 life-size portraits of members of the House of Wittelsbach decorate the facade of the Landschaftshaus. They were designed by Hans Pachmayr and carried out by Hans Gnauf and date from 1598. In the 18th century, Max Kröz captured this view on canvas.
Top left photographs of the original facade, on the right oil painting by Max Kröz, 18th century.

VON 1180 BIS ZUR ZEIT DER LANDESTEILUNGEN
Herzog Georg der Reiche von Bayern-Landshut

Prinzessin Hedwig (Jadwiga) von Polen (1457–1502), später Herzogin von Bayern-Landshut.
Hedwigs Vermählung mit Herzog Georg dem Reichen wurde 1475 mit der Landshuter Hochzeit prächtig gefeiert. Trotz des glanzvollen Beginns verlief ihre Ehe weniger glücklich: Meist lebte die Herzogin getrennt von ihrem Gemahl in der Nebenresidenz Burghausen, wohl auch deshalb, weil sie ihrem Gatten nicht den erhofften männlichen Erben gebar. Seit 1903 wird die Landshuter Hochzeit von 1475 von den Bürgern der Stadt Landshut nachgestellt. Heutzutage findet das historische Fest alle vier Jahre statt.
Mischtechnik auf Pergament, übertragen auf Leinwand, Künstler unbekannt, um 1530.

Princess Hedwig (Jadwiga) of Poland (1457–1502), later Duchess of Bavaria-Landshut.
Hedwig's marriage to Duke Georg der Reiche was celebrated in magnificent fashion with the Landshut Wedding in 1475. Despite its glamorous beginning, their marriage itself was less happy. Most of the time, the Duchess lived separately from her consort in the secondary residence in Burghausen, likely also because she did not bear her husband the hoped-for male heir. Since 1903, the Landshut Wedding has been re-enacted by the citizens of the city of Landshut. Today, the historical celebration takes place every four years.
Mixed technique on parchment, transferred to canvas, artist unknown, c. 1530.

Herzog Georg der Reiche von Bayern-Landshut (1455–1503).
Da aus der Ehe mit der Tochter König Kasimirs IV. von Polen, Hedwig, nur zwei Töchter hervorgingen, sah sich Herzog Georg der Reiche ohne erbberechtigten männlichen Nachfolger. Sein Tod löste 1503 den Bayerischen Erbfolgekrieg aus.
Ölgemälde von Peter Gertner nach einer älteren Abbildung des Herzogs, um 1531/32.

Duke Georg der Reiche of Bavaria-Landshut (1455–1503).
Since his marriage to Hedwig, the daughter of King Kasimir IV of Poland, produced only two daughters, Duke Georg found himself without male successors with right of succession. His death in 1503 triggered the War of the Bavarian Succession.
Oil painting by Peter Gertner based on an older picture of the Duke, c. 1531/32.

VON 1180 BIS ZUR ZEIT DER LANDESTEILUNGEN
Herzog Georg der Reiche von Bayern-Landshut

Stifterrelief an der Empore der Hedwigskapelle, Burghausen.
Herzog Georg der Reiche von Bayern-Landshut und seine Gemahlin Herzogin Hedwig von Polen als Stifter der äußeren Burgkapelle (Hedwigskapelle) zu Burghausen. Im Mittelpunkt der auferstandene Christus, auf seine Wundmale zeigend.
Schnitzerei in Lindenholz eines unbekannten Künstlers, um 1489.

Founder relief at the gallery of the Chapel of St. Hedwig, Burghausen.
Duke Georg der Reiche of Bavaria-Landshut and his consort Duchess Hedwig of Poland as founders of the outer Burgkapelle (Chapel of St. Hedwig) zu Burghausen. In the centre is the resurrected Christ showing his stigmata.
Carving in lime wood of an unknown artist, c. 1489.

Stiftungsgedenkblatt zum Birgittenkloster zu Altomünster mit dem Stifter Herzog Georg dem Reichen von Bayern-Landshut und seiner Gemahlin Hedwig von Polen und deren Wappen.
Im 8. Jahrhundert gründete der Legende nach die Hl. Alto ein Kloster im heutigen Altomünster. Nach wechselvollen Jahrhunderten übertrug man das Kloster 1488 an die Birgitten, 1496 stiftete Georg der Reiche das bis 1803 bestehende Doppelkloster.
Buchmalerei eines unbekannten Künstlers, um 1496.

Foundation memorial sheet of the Birgitten Kloster zu Altomünster abbey with the founder, Duke Georg der Reiche of Bavaria-Landshut, and his consort Hedwig of Poland and their coats of arms.
According to legend, St. Alto founded a monastery in what is today the town of Altomünster in the 8th century. After changeful centuries, the monastery was transferred to the Brigidine Sisters in 1488. In 1496, Georg der Reiche founded the double monastery, which existed until 1803.
Illumination of an unknown artist, c. 1496.

The Confessional Era

It has nothing to do with a reversion à la Treitschke and his saying "Men make history" if, when looking at the era of schism, one concentrates on the succession of Bavarian dukes from Wilhelm IV (1493–1550) to Albrecht V (1528–1579) and Wilhelm V (1548–1626) up to Maximilian I (1573–1651). One receives the impression that, in the context of the Bavarian decision against the new teaching, against the Reformation and for loyalty to the old teaching and the papacy, the individual characteristics of the respective ruling monarchs had a stronger effect than has been supposed to have been the case since the middle of the 17th century.

If one wishes to answer the question of why Bavaria took such a forceful stance against Luther's teaching so early on, why it regarded itself as the spearhead of counter-reformation and Catholic reform, then there is a whole bundle of circumstances and considerations to take into account: perhaps the persevering nature of the Bavarian people; certainly the fact that the state already had sovereignty over the Church, which other princes first had to achieve by alignment with Luther's teaching; importantly, the staving off of the threat of the Peasants' War and the disciplining of the nobility; and then of course the simple discovery that the dukes assumed the dogmatic correctness of the old teaching and regarded Luther's teaching as heresy – right up to Wilhelm V's staunch practice of piety and the Marian enthusiasm of Maximilian I.

The decision against Luther established Bavarian confessional and church policy for the next few centuries; one could say that it paved the way for a Bavarian "Sonderweg" within German history. The behaviour of Bavaria can be regarded as decisive in ensuring that the Catholic cause was not entirely lost in the South and West of the empire and that the traditional imperial system was retained. In the opposite view, however, the decision to stay with the old belief also meant that Germany then became main battleground for the controversial ideas and political-denominational forces. What some regarded as a culturally fertile orientation of Bavaria toward Italy and Spain and a strong will for renewal, others – such as the Protestant historians of the 19th century – saw as the origin of the splitting of the nation and the voluntary withdrawal of Bavaria from the further course of German cultural development.

If one is to understand the whole drama of the period, and especially that of the Wittelsbach family history, it is necessary to take a look at the situation in the Palatine. The abundance of filiations in the Palatine branch of the Wittelsbach family will not be outlined here, but Elector Friedrich V (1596–1632) is particularly noteworthy in this connection: he became the head of the Protestant Union, the exponent of the Protestant Movement Party. The conflict of the age sees the two Wittelsbach cousins Friedrich V and Maximilian I at the top of the two sharply antagonistic denominational parties.

Das Konfessionelle Zeitalter

Es hat nichts mit einem Rückfall à la Treitschke und seinem Motto „Männer machen Geschichte" zu tun, wenn man sich, im Blick auf das Zeitalter der Glaubensspaltung, auf die Abfolge der bayerischen Herzöge von Wilhelm IV. (1493–1550) über Albrecht V. (1528–1579) und Wilhelm V. (1548–1626) bis zu Maximilian I. (1573–1651) konzentriert. Man gewinnt den Eindruck, dass sich im Umfeld der bayerischen Entscheidung gegen die neue Lehre, gegen die Reformation und für die Treue gegenüber der alten Lehre und dem Papsttum in intensiverer Weise die individuellen Charakteristika der jeweils regierenden Monarchen auswirkten, als das dann seit der Mitte des 17. Jahrhunderts der Fall sein sollte.

Wenn man die Frage beantworten will, warum Bayern so früh und so entschieden gegen die Lehre Luthers Stellung bezog, warum es sich als Speerspitze von Gegenreformation und Katholischer Reform verstand, dann hat man ein ganzes Bündel von Umständen und Überlegungen zu berücksichtigen: vielleicht das beharrende Wesen des Bayernvolkes; sicherlich die ohnehin schon vorhandene staatliche Hoheit über die Kirche, die sich andere Fürsten erst durch ihren Anschluss an die Lehre Luthers verschaffen mussten; bedeutend die Abwehr der Bauernkriegsbedrohung und die Disziplinierung des Adels; und dann doch auch der schlichte Befund, dass die Herzöge von der dogmatischen Richtigkeit der alten Lehre ausgingen und die Lehre Luthers für eine Häresie hielten – bis hin zur dezidierten Frömmigkeitspraxis Wilhelms V. und zum marianischen Enthusiasmus Maximilians I.

Mit der Entscheidung gegen Luther wurde die bayerische Konfessions- und Kirchenpolitik für die nächsten Jahrhunderte festgeschrieben; wenn man so will, wurde mit ihr ein bayerischer Sonderweg innerhalb der deutschen Geschichte grundgelegt. Die Haltung Bayerns kann als maßgeblich angesehen werden dafür, dass die katholische Sache im Süden und Westen des Reiches nicht gänzlich verlorenging und dass das tradierte Reichssystem erhalten werden konnte. In der gegenteiligen Sehweise bedeutete die Entscheidung, beim alten Glauben zu bleiben, dann allerdings auch, dass Deutschland zum Hauptkampfplatz der kontroversen Ideen und der politisch-konfessionellen Kräfte wurde. Was den einen als kulturell befruchtende Orientierung Bayerns nach Italien und Spanien hin und als kraftvoller Erneuerungswille gilt, ist den anderen – wie etwa den protestantischen Historikern des 19. Jahrhunderts – Ursprung der Spaltung der Nation und die selbstgewollte Ausschaltung Bayerns vom weiteren Gang der deutschen kulturellen Entwicklung.

Will man die ganze Dramatik des Zeitalters und vor allem auch jene der wittelsbachischen Familiengeschichte ermessen, dann muss man den Blick auf die pfälzischen Verhältnisse lenken. Die Fülle der Filiationen im pfälzischen Zweig der Wittelsbacher ist hier nicht nachzuzeichnen, herauszuheben ist indes Kurfürst Friedrich V. (1596–1632): Er wurde das Haupt der protestantischen Union, der Exponent der evangelischen Bewegungspartei. Der Konflikt des Zeitalters sieht die Wittelsbacher Vettern, Friedrich V. und Maximilian I., an der Spitze der beiden einander scharf bekämpfenden Konfessionsparteien.

DAS KONFESSIONELLE ZEITALTER
Herzog Wilhelm IV. von Bayern

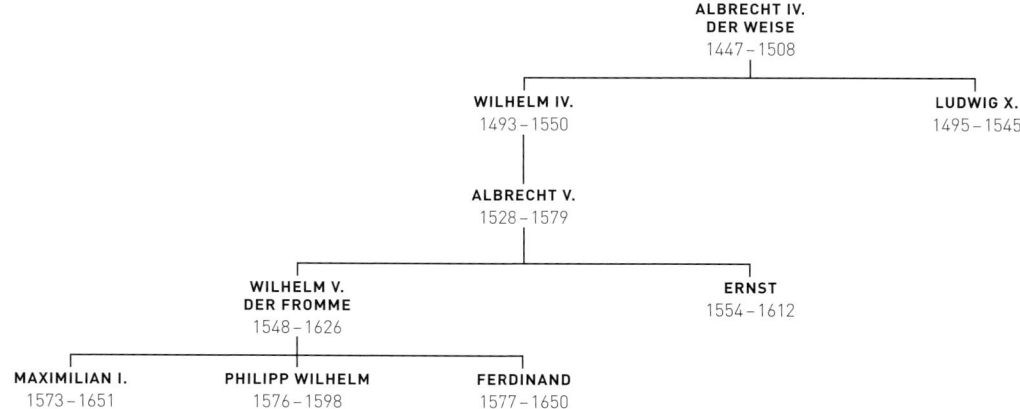

Herzog Wilhelm IV. von Bayern (1493–1550) und seine Gemahlin Maria Jakobäa von Baden (1507–1580).
Das sogenannte Wittelsbachische Familienalbum umfasst elf in Holztafeln gerahmte Miniaturbildnisse der bayerischen Wittelsbacher des 16. Jahrhunderts (diese und folgende Doppelseite). Erwähnt wird es erstmals in der Münchner Kammergalerie Maximilians I. in den Jahren 1627/30.
Miniaturmalerei auf Kupferblech, Christoph Schwarz zugeschrieben, um 1580.

Duke Wilhelm IV of Bavaria (1493–1550) and his consort Maria Jakobäa of Baden (1507–1580).
The so-called Wittelsbach Family Album contains eleven miniature portraits of the Bavarian members of the House of Wittelsbach of the 16th century framed in wooden tablets (this and the following double page). It was mentioned for the first time in the Munich Chamber Gallery of Maximilian I in the years 1627/30.
Miniature painting on copper sheet, attributed to Christoph Schwarz, c. 1580.

Herzog Albrecht V. von Bayern (1528–1579) und seine Gemahlin Anna von Österreich (1528–1590).
Das Wittelsbachische Familienalbum zeigt das berühmte Paar in hohem Alter.
Miniaturmalerei auf Kupferblech, Christoph Schwarz zugeschrieben, um 1580.

Duke Albrecht V of Bavaria (1528–1579) and his consort Anna of Austria (1528–1590).
The Wittelsbach Family Album shows the famous couple in their old age.
Miniature painting on copper sheet, attributed to Christoph Schwarz, c. 1580.

GVILIELM[us] IV: COM: PAL: RHE[ni] VTRIVSQVAE B[a]VARIAE DVX ÆTAT: LVII. ANNO M.D.L.

IACOBE PHILIPPI MARCH: BADEN: FILIA GVILIELMI IV VX[or] ÆTĀ: LXX. AN: M.D.LXXVIII

ALBERTVS V. COM: PALAT: RHENI VTRI: BAVARIÆ DVX ÆTA: L. AN: M.D.LXXVIII.

ANNA NATA ARCHIDVCISSA AVSTRIÆ ALBERTI V. CONIVNX ÆTA: XLIII. AN: M.D.LXXVIII

DAS KONFESSIONELLE ZEITALTER
Herzog Wilhelm IV. von Bayern

Herzog Wilhelm V. von Bayern (1548–1626) und seine Gemahlin Renata von Lothringen (1544–1602).
Miniaturmalerei auf Kupferblech, Christoph Schwarz zugeschrieben, um 1580.

Duke Wilhelm V of Bavaria (1548–1626) and his consort Renata of Lothringen (1544–1602).
Miniature painting on copper sheet, attributed to Christoph Schwarz, c. 1580.

Herzog Ferdinand I. von Bayern (1550–1608) und Kurfürst Ernst von Köln (1554–1612).
Miniaturmalerei auf Kupferblech, Christoph Schwarz zugeschrieben, um 1580.

Duke Ferdinand I of Bavaria (1550–1608) and Prince-Elector Ernst of Cologne (1554–1612).
Miniature painting on copper sheet, attributed to Christoph Schwarz, c. 1580.

GVILIELM⁹ V.COM:PAL:RHEN
VTRIVSQVÆ BAVARIÆ DVX
ÆTA:XXX AN:M.D.LXXVIII

RENATA FRANCISCI LOTHA[R]
DVCIS FILIA, GVILIELMI V.CONI:
ÆTA:XXXIV. AN:M.D.LXXVIII

FERDINANDVS COMES
PALA: RHENI BAVARIÆ DVX
ÆTA:XXVIII. AN:M.D.LXXVIII

ERNESTVS ARCHIEPS:COLON:
S.R.I. ELECTOR.VTR:BAV: DVX
ÆTA: XXIV. AN: M.D.LXXVIII

DAS KONFESSIONELLE ZEITALTER
Herzog Wilhelm IV. von Bayern

Das herzoglich bayerische Wappen an der Holzkassettendecke des Festsaals im Schloss zu Dachau.
Die Herzöge Wilhelm IV. und Albrecht V. ließen das Dachauer Schloss als erste „Zweitresidenz" der Wittelsbacher von 1546 bis 1577 neu ausbauen. Die prachtvolle Holzdecke des Festsaals wurde mit sechs Wappen der Bayernherzöge und deren Gemahlinnen ausgestattet. Zum ersten Mal wurde auch das kaiserliche Wappen Ludwigs des Bayern repräsentiert.
Detail der Holzkassettendecke, ausgeführt von Hans Wisreutter, 1564/65.

The Bavarian ducal coat of arms on the wooden coffered ceiling of the ballroom in Dachau Palace.
From 1546 to 1577, the dukes Wilhelm IV and Albrecht V had Dachau Palace expanded as the first "secondary residence" of the House of Wittelsbach. The magnificent wooden ceiling of the ballroom was furnished with six coats of arms of the Bavarian dukes and their consorts. The imperial coat of arms of Ludwig the Bavarian was also represented for the first time.
Detail of the wooden coffered ceiling, carried out by Hans Wisreutter, 1564/65.

Herzog Wilhelm IV. von Bayern und seine Familie.
Neben dem Herzog sind seine Gemahlin Maria Jakobäa von Baden sowie die Kinder Theodor, Albrecht (der nachmalige Herzog Albrecht V.), Wilhelm und Mechthild (später vermählt mit Markgraf Philibert von Baden) zu sehen.
Gemälde nach Peter Gertner von Ludwig Refinger, nach 1534.

Duke Wilhelm IV of Bavaria and his family.
Beside the duke, his consort Maria Jakobäa of Baden as well as their children Theodor, Albrecht (the future Duke Albrecht V), Wilhelm and Mechthild (later married to Margrave Philibert of Baden) can be seen.
Painting based on Peter Gertner by Ludwig Refinger, after 1534.

DAS KONFESSIONELLE ZEITALTER
Herzog Wilhelm IV. von Bayern

Der handschriftliche Text auf dem oberen Blatt lautet:
Anno 1515 ist ain thunier zu Wienn geschehen unnd gehalten wordenn an sannd Jacobs tag, als Kay[serliche] May[estät] mit den drey khinigen zusamen khomen unnd sind auf der peeden thail 31 thunirer, darunter unnd auf Khay[serlicher] Ma[jestät] seitenn sind mein genediger furst unnd herr hertzog Wilhelm in Bairnn f[ü]r[stliche] Gnaden] unnd der von Mechlburg haubtleut gewesenn, inmassen wie hieniden gemalt ist. Auf der kinigs von Unngern seiten sind margraff Georg unnd margraf Casimir von Pranndenburg bed gebrueder haubtleut gewesen in gestalt wie hieniden stet.

The handwritten text on the above sheet says:
In 1515, a tournament took place and was held in Vienna on St. Jacob's Day, when his Imperial Majesty met with the three kings and there are 31 participants of the tounament, on the side of our Imperial Majesty, my gracious Prince and Lord Duke Wilhelm, princely grace in Bavaria, and the one from Mechlburg were captains, painted down here.
On the side of the king of Hungary, Margrave Georg and Margrave Casimir of Brandenburg, the two brothers, were captains, in form as written below.

Seiten aus einem Turnierbuch des 16. Jahrhunderts.
Fürstliche Turnierbücher dienten vorrangig dazu, die Turniertätigkeit eines Ritters über einen längeren Zeitraum zu dokumentieren. Zugleich waren sie repräsentatives Darstellungsmittel der eigenen Tugenden als ritterlicher Herr und gaben mit den darin kunstvoll ausgestalteten Wappen von Gegnern und Kampfgefährten Aufschluss über die jeweils teilnehmenden Adelsgeschlechter. Die vorliegenden Abbildungen stammen vermutlich aus einem Turnierbuch Herzog Wilhelms IV. von Bayern.
Reproduktionen nach einem Original des 16. Jahrhunderts.

Pages from a tournament book from the 16th century.
Princely tournament books served primarily to document the knight's tournament activity for a longer period of time. At the same time, they were a representative means of presenting one's own values as a knightly lord and with the artfully decorated coats of arms of opponents and fellow soldiers contained therein, they provided information about the participating noble families. The pictures presented here are probably from a tournament book of Duke Wilhelm IV of Bavaria.
Reproductions based on an original from the 16th century.

DAS KONFESSIONELLE ZEITALTER
Herzog Wilhelm IV. von Bayern

Der Erlass des Bayerischen Reinheitsgebots für Bier aus dem Jahre 1516 durch Herzog Wilhelm IV.
Artikel im Gesetzbuch der Bayerischen Landesordnung von 1516.

The issuance of the Bavarian Purity Law for beer from 1516 by Duke Wilhelm IV.
Article in the Statute Book of the Bavarian Law Code of 1516.

Der Vierd tail

das sölhs den pfarrern in vnserm lannde nit gestatt werden sol/ausgenomen was die pfarrer vnd geystlichen von aigen weinwachssen habn/vnd für sich/jr pfarrgesellen/priesterschafft vnnd hausgesynd/auch in der not den kindlpetterin/ vnd krancken leüten/vnärtlich geben/das mag jne gestatt werden. Doch genärlicher weis/von schennckhens vnd gewins wegen/söllen sy khainen wein einlegen.

Wie das Pier summer vnd winter auffm lannd sol geschennckt gepzawen werden.

Item Wir ordnen/setzen/vnnd wöllen/mit Rathe vnnser Lanndtschafft/das füran allennthalben in dem Fürstennthumb Bayrn/auf dem lannde/auch in vnsern Stettn vnd Märckhten/da deshalb hieuor kain sonndere ordnung ist/ von Michaelis bis auf Georij/ain mass oder ain kopf piers über ainen pfenning müncher werung/Vnd von sant Jörgen tag/bis auff Michaelis/die mass über zwen pfenning derselben werung/vnnd derennden der kopf ist/über drey haller/bey nachgesetzter Pene/nicht gegeben noch aufgeschennckht sol werden. Wo auch ainer nit Mertzn/sonnder annder Pier prawen/oder sonnst habn würde/sol Er doch das/kains wegs höher/dan die mass vmb ainen pfenning schennckhen/vnd verkauffen. Wir wöllen auch sonnderlichen/das füran allennthalbn in vnsern Stettn/Märckten/vnnd auf dem Lannde/zu kainem Pier/merer stuckh/ dann allain Gerstn/hopffen/vnd wasser/genomen vnnd geprauncht sölle werden. Welher aber dise vnnsere ordnung wissenntlich überfarn vnd nit hallten würde/dem sol von seiner gerichtzöbrigkait/dasselbig vas pier/zu straff vnnachläslich/so offt es geschicht/genomen werden. Jedoch wo ain Geüwirt von ainem Pierprewen in vnsern Stetten/ Märckten/oder aufm lande/yetzuzeytn ainen Emer piers/

Das xxxvij blat

zwen oder drey/kauffen/vnd wider vnntter dem gemainen Pawrsuolckh ausschennckhen würde/demselbenn allain/ aber sonnst nyemandts/sol die mass/oder der kopff piers/ vmb ainen haller höher dann oben gesetzt ist/zegeben/vnnd auszeschennckhen erlaubt vnd vnuerpotten sein.

Von Newen vnd vngewöndlichen Prewheüsern vnd Tafernen.

Wir wöllen auch/das die Neüwen Prewheüser/vnd Tafern/so vor allter nit Prewheüser/noch Eetafern gewest sein/vnd den Stetten/Märckhten/vnd anndern Lanndsässen/zu nachtail vnnd schmelerung/von Neüwen aufgericht sind/gar vnd gantz abgethan/vnd füran kains wegs gestatt werden/söllen.

Es wäre dann/das ain Prewhauss/von dem Prelaten/ Edlman/oder Hofmarchherrn/zu notturfft seins closters/ oder gesäs/neüwes aufgericht würde/das sol jnen zu jm geprauch zugelassen sein.

Wo auch nit Edlmans gesäss/vnd doch Eetafern daselbs wärn/die vor allter die Prewheüser nit gehabt/vnd dieselben Prewheüser innerhalb zehen jarn aufgericht wärn/die selben söllen auch abgethan/vnd hinfüran auszürichten/nit mer gestatt werden.

G

DAS KONFESSIONELLE ZEITALTER
Herzog Wilhelm IV. von Bayern

Die betenden Stifter des Heilig-Geist-Spitals zu Landshut.
Die Geschwister Herzog Wilhelm IV. von Bayern-München mit Kopfbedeckung und Herzog Ludwig X. von Bayern-Landshut in Harnisch und mit Fahne.
Lindenholzschnitzerei eines unbekannten Künstlers, 1532.

The praying founder of the Heilig-Geist-Spital zu Landshut.
Siblings Duke Wilhelm IV of Bavaria-Munich with a head covering and Duke Ludwig X of Bavaria-Landshut in a suit of armour and with a flag.
Lime wood carving of an unknown artist, 1532.

DAS KONFESSIONELLE ZEITALTER
Herzog Ludwig X. von Bayern-Landshut

Herzog Ludwig X. von Bayern-Landshut (1495–1545).
Ludwig X. regierte als zweitgeborener Sohn Herzog Albrechts IV. von Bayern-München neben seinem Bruder Herzog Wilhelm IV., da er noch vor Erlass der Primogeniturordnung geboren worden war. Er ist der Erbauer der Stadtresidenz zu Landshut, des ersten Renaissancebaus nach italienischem Vorbild nördlich der Alpen.
Gemälde von Barthel Beham, um 1530.

Duke Ludwig X of Bavaria-Landshut (1495–1545).
As the second-born son of Duke Albrecht IV of Bavaria-Munich, Ludwig X ruled alongside his brother Duke Wilhelm IV, since he had been born before the issue of the Primogeniture Ordinance. He is the builder of the Landshut Residence, the first Italian-style Renaissance building north of the Alps.
Painting by Barthel Beham, c. 1530.

DAS KONFESSIONELLE ZEITALTER
Herzog Ludwig X. von Bayern-Landshut

Herzog Ludwig X. von Bayern-Landshut.
Ludwig X. blieb unverheiratet, wodurch sein Bruder Wilhelm IV. Ober- und Niederbayern endgültig vereinigen konnte. Prächtig ist sein Grabmal zu Landshut-Seligenthal.
Gemälde von Hans Wertinger, 1516.

Duke Ludwig X of Bavaria-Landshut.
Ludwig X remained unmarried, which allowed his brother Wilhelm IV ultimately to unify Upper and Lower Bavaria. His Landshut-Seligenthal tomb is magnificent.
Painting by Hans Wertinger, 1516.

Herzog Ludwig X. von Bayern-Landshut als Stifter.
Ludwig X. erscheint hier in voller Rüstung, schwer umgürtet und das Banner des Hauses tragend. Er präsentiert sich mit einem Löwen und den beiden Aposteln Simon und Judas Thaddäus.
Glasgemälde eines unbekannten Meisters, um 1530.

Duke Ludwig X of Bavaria-Landshut as founder.
Ludwig X is shown in full suit of armour, heavily girded and carrying the banner of the house. He is presented with a lion and the Apostles Simon and Jude Thaddaeus.
Stained glass picture of an unknown master, c. 1530.

DAS KONFESSIONELLE ZEITALTER
Herzog Albrecht V. von Bayern-München

Herzog Albrecht V. von Bayern (1528–1579) als Erbprinz.
Der Sohn Herzog Wilhelms VI. heiratete 1546 Anna von Österreich, Tochter Kaiser Ferdinands I. Seine umfangreiche Hofbibliothek begründete die heutige Bayerische Staatsbibliothek. Auch das Münzkabinett und die Schatzkammer in der Residenz gehen auf ihn zurück. Dort schuf er auch das Antiquarium, den gewaltigsten Profanraum der Renaissance nördlich der Alpen.
Gemälde von Hans Mielich, 1545.

Duke Albrecht V of Bavaria (1528–1579) as heir to the throne.
The son of Duke Wilhelm VI married Anna of Austria, the daughter of Emperor Ferdinand I, in 1546. His extensive court library formed the basis for today's Bavarian State Library. The coin cabinet and the treasury in the residence can also be traced back to him. He also created the antiquarium there, the largest secular room of the Renaissance north of the Alps.
Painting by Hans Mielich, 1545.

DAS KONFESSIONELLE ZEITALTER
Herzog Albrecht V. von Bayern-München

Herzog Albrecht V. und seine Gemahlin Anna von Österreich (1528–1590) beim Schachspiel.
Im Hintergrund ihre Söhne Wilhelm (später Wilhelm V.), Ferdinand (Stammvater der Grafen von Wartenberg) und Ernst, später Kurfürst und Erzbischof von Köln, sowie Ratsmitglieder.
Miniatur von Hans Mielich, 1552.

Duke Albrecht V and his consort Anna of Austria (1528–1590) playing chess.
In the background their sons Wilhelm (later Wilhelm V), Ferdinand (progenitor of the counts of Wartenberg) and Ernst, later Prince-Elector and Archbishop of Cologne, as well as council members.
Miniature by Hans Mielich, 1552.

DAS KONFESSIONELLE ZEITALTER
Herzog Albrecht V. von Bayern-München

Turnierharnisch (Helm, Brust, Rücken und Beinzeug) für Herzog Albrecht V. von Bayern.
Angefertigt vom Plattner Anton Peffenhauser in Augsburg 1579, heute im Schlossmuseum zu Berchtesgaden.

Tournament suit of armour (helmet, breastpiece, back and leg defence) for Duke Albrecht V of Bavaria.
Produced by armourer Anton Peffenhauser in Augsburg in 1579, today in the Berchtesgaden Castle Museum.

Konzert in der St. Georgskapelle der Residenz (Neuveste) unter der Leitung von Orlando di Lasso.
Gemälde von Hans Mielich im Auftrag Herzog Albrechts V. von Bayern, um 1565.

Concert in the St. Georg's Chapel of the Residenz (Neuveste) conducted by Orlando di Lasso.
Painting by Hans Mielich on behalf of Duke Albrecht V of Bavaria, c. 1565.

DAS KONFESSIONELLE ZEITALTER
Herzog Albrecht V. von Bayern-München

Antiquarium in der Münchner Residenz mit den Ansichten Straubings, Landshuts, Ingolstadts und Weilheims.

Die künstlerische Ausgestaltung des Antiquariums mit altbayerischen Stadtansichten, das Herzog Albrecht V. 1568 zur Aufbewahrung seiner umfangreichen Sammlungen in Auftrag gab, übernahmen u. a. die Künstler Peter Candid, Hans Donauer d. Ä., Alessandro Scalzi und Antonio Maria Viviani. Dieser größte Renassaincesaal Mitteleuropas wurde erst im Jahr 1600 fertiggestellt.
Residenz München, Antiquarium, 2. Hälfte des 16. Jahrhunderts.

Antiquarium in the Munich Residenz with the views of Straubing, Landshut, Ingolstadt and Weilheim.

The artistic decoration of the Antiquarium – which Duke Albrecht V mandated in 1568 for storing his extensive collections – with views of cities of Altbayern was assumed by artists including Peter Candid, Hans Donauer the Elder, Alessandro Scalzi and Antonio Maria Viviani. This, the largest Renaissance hall in Central Europe, was not completed until 1600.
Munich Residenz, Antiquarium, 2nd half of the 16th century.

DAS KONFESSIONELLE ZEITALTER
Herzog Wilhelm V. von Bayern

Die Hochzeit Herzog Wilhelms V. (1548–1626) mit Renata von Lothringen (1544–1602) am 22. Februar 1568 in der Frauenkirche zu München.
Die Hochzeitsfeierlichkeiten dauerten 18 Tage an. Orlando di Lasso, Hofkapellmeister Wilhelms V., komponierte die Festmusik. Das Herzogspaar hatte zehn Kinder, von denen jedoch nur sechs überlebten, darunter der spätere Kurfürst Maximilian I.
Kolorierter Kupferstich von Nikolaus Solie, 1568.

The wedding of Duke Wilhelm V (1548–1626) and Renata of Lothringen (1544–1602) in the Frauenkirche in Munich on 22 February 1568.
The wedding festivities lasted for 18 days. Orlando di Lasso, Wilhelm V's court music director, composed the music for the festivities. The Duke and Duchess had ten children. However, only six of them survived, including the later Prince-Elector Maximilian I.
Coloured copper engraving by Nikolaus Solie, 1568.

DAS KONFESSIONELLE ZEITALTER
Herzog Wilhelm V. von Bayern

Skizze der Narrentreppe auf Burg Trausnitz mit Motiven aus der Commedia dell'Arte.
Am linken Rand Herzog Wilhelm V. von Bayern. Am St. Michaelstag in Landshut auf Burg Trausnitz geboren, hatte er zu dieser Burg eine besondere Beziehung. Er verbrachte dort zusammen mit seiner 1568 angetrauten Gemahlin Renata von Lothringen viele Jahre. Das berühmteste Kunstwerk der Burg dürfte die sogenannte Narrentreppe mit Motiven der Commedia dell'Arte sein, wo der Herzog sich und seine Gemahlin als Mitspieler verewigen ließ.
Skizze von Max Hailer nach Friedrich Sustris, 1841.

Sketch of the Jester's Staircase in Trausnitz Castle with motifs from commedia dell'arte.
On the left edge, Duke Wilhelm V of Bavaria. Born on St. Michael's Day in Trausnitz Castle in Landshut, he had a special relationship with this castle. He spent many years there with his consort Renata of Lothringen, whom he married in 1568. The castle's most famous artwork is probably the so-called Jester's Staircase with motifs from commedia dell'arte, where the Duke had himself and his consort immortalised as fellow players.
Study by Max Hailer in the style of Friedrich Sustris, 1841.

Prince-Elector Maximilian I

The period of government of Maximilian I, first Duke and from 1623 Prince-Elector of Bavaria, was during one of the most dramatic epochs of European history: the Thirty Years' War. Maximilian's predecessors Wilhelm IV, Albrecht V and Wilhelm V had responded to the confessional conflicts of the Reformation at the start of the 16th century with decided devotion to the Catholic cause. In accordance with the princely upbringing of the time, Maximilian experienced a youth dominated by strong religiosity, self-discipline and military-pragmatic sobriety that was to characterise his later political actions.

With the Landtage of 1605 and 1612 as well as with the reformation of the Bavarian State Law in 1616, Maximilian set the milestones of a policy whose objective was to stabilise the duchy internally and externally. In 1609, he succeeded in bundling the Catholic powers in the empire under his leadership in the amalgamation of the "League". He thus confronted the Protestant princes in the increasingly escalating confessional conflict of the "union" – this also meant military partisanship for Emperor Ferdinand II of the House of Habsburg in the approaching war years from 1618. After Maximilian's victory over the Palatine prince-elector and Bohemian "Winter King" Friedrich V in the Battle of White Mountain, he received electoral dignity back again as a reward from the Emperor in 1623, which the Bavarian line of the House of Wittelsbach had lost in the 14th century.

Maximilian's political and military achievements made him the undisputed most powerful prince in the empire. This was contributed to significantly by the fact that he maintained his own Bavarian army for several decades and thus could operate flexibly in the struggle between the confessional parties. However, when the conflicts with the Emperor increased and the Swedes, led by their King Gustavus Adolphus, came to the support of the Protestant princes, the page turned for Bavaria. In 1632, Swedish troops annihilated the Bavarian army and brought devastation over the land. It was not until two years later that the prince-elector was able to drive back the Swedes and their allied Protestant imperial princes.

In the final phase of the Thirty Years' War, in which France now formed the opposing party of the Imperial forces to an increased degree, Maximilian I made several attempts towards reconciliation and negotiations for peace. The "Great War" ended with the Peace of Westphalia of 1648. Despite the stresses and strains the war exerted for three decades, Maximilian left behind a tightly unitarily organised, confessionally and politically united principality when he died three years later. However, Maximilian is not known only as a great strategist and warlord; his exemplary piety, with which he anchored the worship of Mary into the faith of the Bavarian people, and his promotion of the fine arts, which found expression in the reconstruction of the Munich Residenz and his adoration for Dürer and Rubens, also characterise Bavaria to this day.

Kurfürst Maximilian I.

Die Regierungszeit Maximilians I., zunächst Herzog und ab dem Jahr 1623 Kurfürst von Bayern, fiel in eine der einschneidendsten Epochen der europäischen Geschichte: in die des Dreißigjährigen Krieges. Auf die konfessionellen Auseinandersetzungen der Reformation zu Beginn des 16. Jahrhunderts hatten Maximilians Vorgänger Wilhelm IV., Albrecht V. und Wilhelm V. mit einer entschiedenen Hinwendung zur katholischen Sache geantwortet. Der zeitgemäßen Prinzenerziehung folgend erlebte Maximilian eine von starker Religiosität, Selbstdisziplin und militärisch-pragmatischer Nüchternheit bestimmte Jugend, die sein späteres politisches Handeln prägen sollte.

Mit den Landtagen von 1605 und 1612 sowie mit der Erneuerung des bayerischen Landrechts 1616 setzte Maximilian die Marksteine einer Politik, die die Stabilisierung des Herzogtums nach innen und außen zum Ziel hatte. 1609 gelang es ihm, die katholischen Mächte im Reich unter seiner Führung im Zusammenschluss der „Liga" zu bündeln. Damit trat er im sich immer weiter zuspitzenden Konfessionskonflikt der „Union" der protestantischen Fürsten entgegen – das bedeutete in den aufziehenden Kriegsjahren ab 1618 auch die militärische Parteinahme für den habsburgischen Kaiser Ferdinand II. Nach Maximilians Sieg über den pfälzischen Kurfürst und böhmischen „Winterkönig" Friedrich V. in der Schlacht am Weißen Berg erhielt er zum Dank 1623 die Kurwürde vom Kaiser zurück, die den bayerischen Wittelsbachern im 14. Jahrhundert verloren gegangen war.

Maximilians politische und militärische Erfolge machten ihn unbestritten zum mächtigsten Fürsten des Reiches. Dazu trug wesentlich bei, dass er über mehrere Jahrzehnte eine eigene bayerische Armee unterhalten und damit flexibel im Ringen der Konfessionsparteien agieren konnte. Als sich jedoch die Konflikte mit dem Kaiser mehrten und die Schweden unter ihrem König Gustav Adolf den protestantischen Fürsten beisprangen, wendete sich das Blatt für Bayern: 1632 schlugen schwedische Truppen die bayerische Armee vernichtend und brachten verheerende Verwüstungen über das Land. Erst zwei Jahre später konnte der Kurfürst die Schweden und die mit ihnen verbündeten protestantischen Reichsfürsten zurückdrängen.

In der letzten Phase des Dreißigjährigen Krieges, in der nun verstärkt Frankreich die Gegenpartei zu den Kaiserlichen bildete, bemühte sich Maximilian I. mehrmals um Ausgleich und Friedensverhandlungen. Mit dem Westfälischen Frieden von 1648 endete der „Große Krieg" – trotz seiner über drei Jahrzehnte währenden Belastungen hinterließ Maximilian I. bei seinem Tod drei Jahre später ein straff zentralistisch organisiertes, konfessionell und politisch geeintes Fürstentum. Doch nicht nur als großer Stratege und Kriegsherr ist Maximilian I. bekannt; auch seine vorbildhafte Frömmigkeit, mit der er die Marienverehrung im bayerischen Volksglauben verankerte, und die Förderung der Schönen Künste, die sich u.a. im Neubau der Münchner Residenz und seiner Verehrung für Dürer und Rubens niederschlug, prägen Bayern bis heute.

Eintragung des Kurfürsten Maximilian I. im Bruderschaftsbuch der Corpus-Christi-Bruderschaft bei St. Peter in München.
Die Corpus-Christi-Erzbruderschaft wurde 1609 auf Betreiben von Herzog Wilhelm V. in der ersten Pfarrkirche Münchens – St. Peter – mit dem Ziel gegründet, das allerheiligste Sakrament des Altars, den Leib Christi, auf würdigste Weise öffentlich zu ehren. Im Präsidium der Bruderschaft, der über 50 weitere Bruderschaften aus Altbayern und Schwaben inkorporiert waren, saßen stets Adelige aus Stadt und Land. Über längere Zeit hinweg kam der Bruderschaftspräfekt sogar aus dem Haus Wittelsbach selbst.

Entry of Prince-Elector Maximilian I in the Book of the Brotherhood of the Corpus Christi Brotherhood at St. Peter's Church in Munich.
The Corpus Christi Archbrotherhood was founded at the instigation of Duke Wilhelm V in Munich's first parish church – St. Peter's – in 1609 with the objective of publicly honouring the holiest of sacraments of the altar, the body of the Christ, in the most dignified way possible. The Presidency of the Brotherhood – in which more than 50 other brotherhoods from Old Bavaria and Swabia were incorporated – was always occupied by nobles from the city and the state. For a long time, the brotherhood's prefect even came

Kurfürst Maximilian I. von Bayern (1573 – 1651) im schwarzen Feldharnisch.
Gemälde Joachim von Sandrart zugeschrieben, nach 1641.

Prince-Elector Maximilian I of Bavaria (1573 – 1651) in a black suit of field armour.
Painting attributed to Joachim von Sandrart, after 1641.

DAS KONFESSIONELLE ZEITALTER
Kurfürst Maximilian I. von Bayern

Erbprinz Maximilian mit seinen Schwestern Christina (1571–1580) und Maria Anna (1574–1616).
Maria Anna wurde mit dem späteren Kaiser Ferdinand II. vermählt, der Maximilian im Jahr 1623 zum Kurfürsten von Bayern machen sollte.
Miniaturmalerei auf Kupferblech, Christoph Schwarz zugeschrieben, um 1580.

Heir to the throne Maximilian with his sisters Christina (1571–1580) and Maria Anna (1574–1616).
Maria Anna was wedded to the later Emperor Ferdinand II, who was to make Maximilian Prince-Elector of Bavaria in 1623.
Miniature painting on copper sheet, attributed to Christoph Schwarz, c. 1580.

MAXIMILIANVS ÆT: V. CHRIS:
TIERNA, ÆT: VII. ET MARIA ANNA
III. AN: VTRIVSQVÆ BAVARIÆ DVCES
ANNO M.D.LXXVIII.

DAS KONFESSIONELLE ZEITALTER
Kurfürst Maximilian I. von Bayern

Kurfürstin Elisabeth Renata von Bayern, geb. Herzogin von Lothringen (1574–1635).
Das Bildnis zeigt die erste Gemahlin Maximilians I. in ihren letzten Lebensjahren. Nach fast vierzigjähriger Ehe starb Elisabeth Renata 1635 während der schwedischen Besatzung im Kloster Ranshofen bei Braunau. Der Kurfürst, laut seines Biografen untröstlich über den Verlust, ließ das Bild in seiner Kammergalerie aufstellen. Der Maler stellt die Fürstin als tugendsame und fromme Ehefrau dar.
Ölgemälde eines Münchner Hofmalers, um 1632.

Electress Elisabeth Renata of Bavaria, born Duchess of Lothringen (1574–1635).
The portrait shows the first consort of Maximilian I in the final years of her life. After nearly forty years of marriage, Elisabeth Renata died in 1635 during the Swedish occupation of Ranshofen Abbey, near Braunau. The prince-elector – who, according to his biographer, was inconsolable over the loss – had the picture mounted in his chamber gallery. The painter presents the princess as a virtuous and pious wife.
Oil painting of a Munich court painter, c. 1632.

DAS KONFESSIONELLE ZEITALTER
Kurfürst Maximilian I. von Bayern

Prunktisch aus den Steinzimmern der Münchner Residenz.
Die Platte des großartigen Prunktisches aus der maximilianischen Residenz wurde aus Lapislazuli, Jaspis und Bergkristallen sowie verschiedenen Marmorsorten gefertigt. In der Mitte ziert diese sogenannte „Pietra-Dura-Platte" das kurbayerische Wappen mit dem Monogramm ME für Maximilian und dessen erste Gemahlin Elisabeth Renata von Lothringen, die 1595 in Nancy heirateten. Getragen wird die Tischplatte von einem Scagliola-Gestell.
Ausgeführt von Wilhelm Fistulator, nach 1623.

Ornamental table from the stone rooms of the Munich Residenz.
The top of the splendid ornamental table from Maximilian's residence was made from lapis lazuli, jasper, mountain crystals as well as various types of marble. In the centre, this so-called "pietra dura table top" is decorated by the coat of arms of the Electorate of Bavaria with the monogram ME for Maximilian and his first consort Elisabeth Renata of Lothringen, who wed in Nancy in 1595. The table top is borne by a scagliola frame.
Carried out by Wilhelm Fistulator, after 1623.

Bronzebüste Kurfürst Maximilians I. von Bayern.
Die Büste Maximilians wurde 1897 in der Münchner Michaelskirche gefunden, ihr ursprünglicher Aufstellungsort ist bis heute unbekannt. Der Kurfürst ist hier im Alter von etwa 67 Jahren dargestellt; über dem simplen Feldharnisch trägt er den Orden des Goldenen Vlieses auf der Brust, ein stilisierter Lorbeerkranz ziert sein Haupt. Neben dieser Bronzebüste existiert nur noch eine einzige weitere zeitgenössische plastische Darstellung Maximilians I.
Bronzeguss von Balthasar Ableithner oder Alessandro Abondio, um 1640.

Bronze bust of Prince-Elector Maximilian I of Bavaria.
The bust of Maximilian was found in St. Michael's Church in Munich in 1897. Its original site is unknown to this day. Here, the Prince-Elector is presented at the age of approximately 67; over the simple suit of field armour, he wears the Order of the Golden Fleece on his chest, a stylised bay wreath adorns his head. Apart from this bronze bust, there is only one other contemporary plastic representation of Maximilian I.
Bronze casting by Balthasar Ableithner or Alessandro Abondio, c. 1640.

DAS KONFESSIONELLE ZEITALTER
Kurfürst Maximilian I. von Bayern

Herzog Maximilian I. von Bayern bei der Gründung der Katholischen Liga 1609 in München.
Im Vorfeld des Dreißigjährigen Krieges gründete sich als Reaktion auf den Zusammenschluss der Protestantischen Union die Katholische Liga als Bündnis fast aller katholischen Reichsstände. Maximilian I. gelang es, die widerstrebenden katholischen Kräfte zu einen und sich selbst als Oberbefehlshaber des Ligaheeres zu behaupten.
Historiengemälde von Karl Theodor von Piloty, 1854.

Duke Maximilian I of Bavaria at the foundation of the Catholic League in Munich in 1609.
Prior to the Thirty Years' War, the Catholic League was founded as an alliance of almost all Catholic imperial estates as a reaction to the Protestant Union coalition. Maximilian I successfully united the reluctant Catholic forces and asserted himself as the supreme commander-in-chief of the League's army.
History painting by Karl Theodor von Piloty, 1854.

DAS KONFESSIONELLE ZEITALTER
Kurfürst Maximilian I. von Bayern

Die Schlacht am Weißen Berg bei Prag am 8. November 1620.
Am Weißen Berg standen sich im November 1620 die Katholische Liga und das protestantische Böhmen in einer entscheidenden Schlacht der ersten Phase des Dreißigjährigen Krieges (Böhmisch-Pfälzischer Krieg 1618–1623) gegenüber. Das Gemälde vereint verschiedene Zeitabschnitte des Schlachtgeschehens: Die angreifenden katholischen Truppen unter Graf von Tilly (Vordergrund) treffen im Bildmittelgrund auf die protestantischen Böhmen unter dem „Winterkönig" Friedrich V. von der Pfalz, im Hintergrund fliehen diese bereits. Ihre vernichtende Niederlage besiegelte in der Folge vorerst die Auflösung der Protestantischen Union.
Gemälde von Pieter Snayers (Figuren) und Jan Brueghel (Landschaft), um 1620.

The Battle of White Mountain near Prague on 8 November 1620.
In November 1620, the Catholic League and Protestant Bohemia faced each other at White Mountain in a decisive battle of the first phase of the Thirty Years' War (Bohemian-Palatine War 1618–1623). The painting brings together various time periods of the battle: in the middle ground, the attacking Catholic troops led by the Count of Tilly (foreground) meet the Protestant Bohemians led by the "Winter King" Friedrich V of the Palatinate, with the Bohemians already fleeing in the background. Their crushing defeat sealed the dissolution of the Protestant Union for the time being.
Painting by Pieter Snayers (figures) and Jan Brueghel (landscape), c. 1620.

DAS KONFESSIONELLE ZEITALTER
Kurfürst Maximilian I. von Bayern

Verleihung der Kurwürde an Maximilian I. durch Kaiser Ferdinand II. am 25. Februar 1623 auf dem Reichstag von Regensburg.
Nach 250 Jahren ging mit dieser bedeutenden Zeremonie die Kurwürde wieder an Bayern. Rechts auf dem Thron der Habsburger Ferdinand II., der in erster Ehe mit einer Schwester Maximilians verbunden war, vor ihm kniend Maximilian, dahinter die übrigen deutschen Kurfürsten im Hermelin sowie der Bruder des neuen Kurfürsten, Albrecht, mit dem bayerischen Wappen. Im Hintergrund beobachten unter anderem die Gemahlinnen Ferdinands und Maximilians durch ein Fenster die Szene.
Tafelbild des Scheyerner Fürstenzyklus (Zyklusbild 20), Künstler unbekannt, 1625.

Award of electoral dignity to Maximilian I by Emperor Ferdinand II at the Imperial Diet of Regensburg on 25 February 1623.
With this significant ceremony, electoral dignity was returned to Bavaria after 250 years. On the right on the throne is Ferdinand II of the House of Habsburg, who was bound in his first marriage to a sister of Maximilian; in front of him is the kneeling Maximilian, behind are the rest of the German prince-electors in ermine as well as the brother of the new prince-elector, Albrecht, with the Bavarian coat of arms. In the background, individuals including the consorts of Ferdinand and Maximilian observe the scene through a window.
Panel painting of the Scheyern Prince Cycle (cycle painting 20), artist unknown, 1625.

DAS KONFESSIONELLE ZEITALTER
Kurfürst Maximilian I. von Bayern

Die Schlacht bei Rain am Lech 1632.
Die bayerische Armee unter Johann t'Serclaes Graf von Tilly versuchte bei Rain am Lech vergeblich, den Einmarsch der Schweden unter König Gustav Adolf in bayerisches Territorium zu verhindern. Nach einer Reihe von Siegen musste Tilly sich geschlagen nach Ingolstadt zurückziehen, wo er infolge einer Schussverletzung starb. Der Sieg der Schweden brachte Leid und Zerstörung über das ganze Land, bis es Maximilian I. gelang, seine Kräfte mit denen Wallensteins zu vereinen.
Kolorierter Kupferstich nach Matthäus Merian, 1633.

The Battle near Rain am Lech 1632.
At Rain am Lech, the Bavarian army under Johann t'Serclaes, Count of Tilly, tried in vain to prevent the invasion of Bavarian territory by the Swedes under King Gustavus Adolphus. After a series of victories, the Count of Tilly had to retreat defeated to Ingolstadt, where he died as a consequence of a gunshot wound. The Swedes' victory brought suffering and destruction across the whole land until Maximilian succeeded in uniting his forces with those of Wallenstein.
Coloured copper engraving based on Matthäus Merian, 1633.

DAS KONFESSIONELLE ZEITALTER
Kurfürst Maximilian I. von Bayern

Votivbild der Münchner Schwedengeiseln von 1632.
Da die Stadt die verlangten Kontributionszahlungen nicht an den Schwedenkönig Gustav Adolf leisten konnte, folgten dem Besatzungsheer schließlich 42 Münchner Bürger als Geiseln. Sie erhielten erst während der Verhandlungen zum Prager Frieden 1635 ihre Freiheit zurück. Schon zuvor hatten sie gelobt, nach ihrer Rückkehr eine Wallfahrt zu unternehmen. Das Votivbild, am 19. April 1635 in Maria Ramersdorf aufgestellt, drückt ihre tiefe Dankbarkeit gegenüber der Gottesmutter für die Rettung und wohlbehaltene Rückkehr aus.
Votivgemälde von Matthias Kager, 1632 bis 35.

Votive painting of the Munich hostages of the Swedes of 1632.
Since the city could not afford the demanded contribution payments to Swedish King Gustavus Adolphus, 42 citizens of Munich ultimately followed the occupying army as hostages. They only regained their freedom during the negotiations for the Peace of Prague in 1635. Previously, they had already vowed to undertake a pilgrimage after their return. The votive painting, mounted in St. Mary's Church Ramersdorf on 19 April 1635, expresses their deep gratitude to the Mother of God for their rescue and safe return.
Votive painting by Matthias Kager, 1632 to 35.

DAS KONFESSIONELLE ZEITALTER
Kurfürst Maximilian I. von Bayern

Erzherzogin Maria Anna (1610–1665), Kurfürstin von Bayern. Maximilian I. ehelichte nach dem Tod seiner ersten Frau seine Nichte, Maria Anna von Österreich. Die junge Kurfürstin trägt auf dem Porträt den berühmten großen Diamantanhänger mit drei Hängeperlen an einer schweren Goldkette, der schon im Besitz der ersten Gemahlin Maximilians I. war, die sich ebenfalls mit diesem Anhänger darstellen ließ.
Ölgemälde von Joachim von Sandrart, 1643.

Archduchess Maria Anna (1610–1665), Electress of Bavaria. After the death of his first wife, Maximilian I espoused his niece, Maria Anna of Austria. In the portrait, the young electress wears the famous large diamond pendant with three hanging pearls on a gold chain, which was already owned by Maximilian I's first consort, who was also painted with this pendant.
Oil painting by Joachim von Sandrart, 1643.

DAS KONFESSIONELLE ZEITALTER
Kurfürst Maximilian I. von Bayern

Kurfürst Maximilian I. von Bayern und sein Sohn Ferdinand Maria.
Das Gemälde zeigt den etwa zehnjährigen Erbprinzen an der Seite seines mittlerweile betagten Vaters. Die Darstellung der Gesichtszüge weicht jedoch zeitlich voneinander ab – für den Kurfürsten dürfte wohl ein Gemälde Joachim von Sandrarts von 1641 Vorbild gewesen sein, für Ferdinand Maria ein Stich Johann Sadelers d. J. von 1646.
Ölgemälde von Nikolaus Prugger oder Kaspar Amort, zwischen 1646 und 1674.

Prince-Elector Maximilian I of Bavaria and his son Ferdinand Maria.
The painting shows the approximately ten-year-old heir to the throne beside his now aged father. However, the depiction of the features deviates in terms of time – a painting by Joachim von Sandrarts of 1641 was likely to have been used as the basis for the prince-elector, for Ferdinand Maria an engraving by Johann Sadeler the Younger of 1646.
Oil painting by Nikolaus Prugger or Kaspar Amort, between 1646 and 1674.

DAS KONFESSIONELLE ZEITALTER
Kurfürst Maximilian I. von Bayern

Kurfürst Maximilian I. von Bayern auf kurbettierendem Pferd.
Die während des Dreißigjährigen Krieges aufkommende Darstellungsweise des Feldherrn auf kurbettierendem Pferd versinnbildlicht in monumentaler Weise seinen militärischen Ruhm.
Gemälde Nikolaus Prugger zugeschrieben, nach 1640.

Prince-Elector Maximilian I of Bavaria on a horse about to undertake a curvet.
The manner of representation of a commander on a horse about to undertake a curvet that arose during the Thirty Years' War symbolises his military fame in monumental fashion.
Painting attributed to Nikolaus Prugger, after 1640.

DAS KONFESSIONELLE ZEITALTER
Kurfürst Maximilian I. von Bayern

Die Affäre bei München, 5. Oktober 1648.
Der Überfall der bayerischen und kaiserlichen Kavallerie auf die schwedische Reiterei im Dachauer Moos war das letzte größere Gefecht des Dreißigjährigen Krieges. Ausgelöst wurde der überraschende Angriff durch einen Jagdausflug des schwedischen Feldherrn Wrangel, der sich im Moorgebiet südöstlich von Dachau sicher wähnte. Den Bayern gelang es infolge ihres Blitzangriffs, die Schweden bis hinter den Lech zurückzudrängen.
Ölgemälde von Pieter Snayers, um 1649.

The affair near Munich, 5 October 1648.
The attack of the Bavarian and imperial cavalry on the Swedish cavalry in the Dachau Marsh was the last major battle of the Thirty Years' War. The surprise attack was triggered by a hunting trip of Swedish commander Wrangel, who wrongly believed himself to be safe in the moorland southeast of Dachau. As a consequence of their lightning attack, the Bavarians managed to force the Swedes back behind the Lech.
Oil painting by Pieter Snayers, c. 1649.

Absolutism, Baroque and Enlightenment

No other cultural period has had such a decisive and lasting influence upon the "image" of Bavaria as that of the Baroque. Such an assertion can still be based upon the argumentation of current tourism advertising, into which the topos of supposed exuberant joie de vivre appears to be incorporated into a proverbially Bavarian-Baroque way of life including absolutely everything from the Oktoberfest and beer gardens to the Wieskirche and the Oberammergau Passion Play.

For centuries, this image of a baroque Bavaria has had negative connotations. The talk was of lack of culture, lethargy and intellectual poverty, of the moral neglect of the people, and by the same token the prevalence of the major vices. This was all said to be attributable to "monastic madness", the unhealthy influence of priests, the Jesuit education system and Roman superstition. – It was not until the middle of the 20th century that judgement became fairer in this respect, when it was recognised that church, ecclesiasticism, piety and religiosity were not spiritual ingredients of an otherwise secular reality of life but were instead the core of this reality, as the history of the Baroque period in Bavaria was, to put it another way, understood and classified as history of piety.

The series of electors that followed Maximilian I is impressive: Ferdinand Maria (1636–1679) with the Theatinerkirche and the construction of Schloss Nymphenburg; Max Emanuel (1662–1726) and his role in the Turkish Wars and the War of the Spanish Succession and the construction of Schloß Schleißheim; Karl Albrecht (1697–1745) and the second (after Ludwig the Bavarian) albeit brief Wittelsbach kaisership; Max III Joseph (1727–1777) with the founding of the Academy of Sciences, the construction of the Cuvilliés Theatre and the additional name "the Much-Loved", whose death in 1777 also marked the end of the series of Wittelsbach princes from the house's old-Bavarian line.

Absolutismus, Barock und Aufklärung

Keine andere Kulturepoche hat das „Image" Bayerns so entscheidend und nachhaltig bestimmt wie die des Barock. Eine solche Feststellung kann sich gründen auf die Argumentation der Fremdenverkehrswerbung unserer Tage, in der der Topos einer angeblich überbordenden Lebensfreude integriert erscheint in eine sprichwörtlich bayerisch-barocke Lebensart, zu der dann schier alles gehört, vom Oktoberfest bis zum Biergarten, von der Wieskirche bis zum Oberammergauer Passionsspiel.

Über Jahrhunderte hinweg war dieses Bild des barocken Bayern indes negativ besetzt. Von Unkultur, Trägheit und geistiger Verkümmerung war dabei die Rede, von sittlicher Verwahrlosung des Volkes, vom Überhandnehmen der großen Laster ebenso; und alles sei zurückzuführen auf Mönchswahn und Mönchssinn, auf Priesterdruck und Priesterdünkel, auf das jesuitische Erziehungssystem und den römischen Aberglauben. – Erst seit der Mitte des 20. Jahrhunderts urteilte man hier gerechter, als man nämlich erkannte, dass Kirche, Kirchlichkeit, Frömmigkeit und Religiosität nicht spirituelle Zutaten zu einer ansonsten säkularen Lebenswirklichkeit waren, sondern den Kern dieser Wirklichkeit ausmachten, man also, anders formuliert, die Geschichte des Barockzeitalters in Bayern als Frömmigkeitsgeschichte verstand und einordnete.

Die Reihe der Kurfürsten, die auf Maximilian I. folgten, ist beeindruckend: Ferdinand Maria (1636–1679) mit der Theatinerkirche und dem Bau von Schloss Nymphenburg; Max Emanuel (1662–1726) und seine Rolle in den Türkenkriegen und im Spanischen Erbfolgekrieg sowie beim Bau von Schloß Schleißheim; Karl Albrecht (1697–1745) und das – nach Ludwig dem Bayern – wenn auch nur kurze zweite wittelsbachische Kaisertum; Max III. Joseph (1727–1777) mit der Gründung der Akademie der Wissenschaften, dem Bau des Cuvilliés-Theaters und dem Beinamen „der Vielgeliebte", mit dem 1777 gleichzeitig die Reihe der wittelsbachischen Fürsten aus der altbayerischen Linie des Hauses zu Ende ging.

ABSOLUTISMUS, BAROCK UND AUFKLÄRUNG
Kurfürst Ferdinand Maria von Bayern

Eintrag des Kurfürsten Ferdinand Maria von Bayern im Bruderschaftsbuch der Corpus-Christi-Bruderschaft bei St. Peter in München.

Entry of Prince-Elector Ferdinand Maria of Bavaria in the Book of the Brotherhood of the Corpus Christi Brotherhood at St. Peter's Church in Munich.

Kurfürst Ferdinand Maria von Bayern (1636–1679) im Hermelin.
Ferdinand Marias Urenkel Kurfürst Maximilian III. Joseph ließ dieses Porträt im Speisesaal des Neuen Schlosses Schleißheim anbringen.
Gemälde von George Desmarées, um 1750.

Prince-Elector Ferdinand Maria of Bavaria (1636–1679) in ermine.
Ferdinand Maria's great grandson Prince-Elector Maximilian III Joseph had this portrait mounted in the dining hall of the New Schleissheim Palace.
Painting by George Desmarées, c. 1750.

ABSOLUTISMUS, BAROCK UND AUFKLÄRUNG
Kurfürst Ferdinand Maria von Bayern

Kurprinz Ferdinand Maria (1636–1679), vierjährig, und sein Bruder Maximilian Philipp (1638–1705), fünfjährig, 1644.
Wachs-Votivfiguren der beiden Söhne des Kurfürsten Maximilians I. in der St.-Benno-Kapelle des Doms „Zu Unserer Lieben Frau" in München.
Wahrscheinlich von Alessandro Abondio modelliert, 1640 bis 44.

Electoral Prince Ferdinand Maria (1636–1679), four years old, and his brother Maximilian Philipp (1638–1705), five years old, 1644.
Wax votive figures of the two sons of Prince-Elector Maximilian I in the St. Benno Chapel of the Cathedral "Zu Unserer Lieben Frau" in Munich.
Likely moulded by Alessandro Abondio, 1640 to 44.

Kurfürst Ferdinand Maria von Bayern.
Die Darstellung des 22-jährigen Kurfürsten entstand im Zuge der „Beschreibung und Abbildung aller Königl. und Churfürstl. Ein-Züge / Wahl und Crönungs Acta", eines Gedenkbuchs zur Wahl- und Krönungszeremonie des habsburgischen Kaisers Leopold I. 1658 in Frankfurt am Main.
Kupferstich von Caspar Merian, 1658.

Prince-Elector Ferdinand Maria of Bavaria.
The image of the 22-year-old prince-elector was produced as part of the "Description and depiction of all royal and electoral entries / election and coronation act", a memorial book for the election and coronation ceremony of Emperor Leopold I of the House of Habsburg in Frankfurt am Main in 1658.
Copper engraving by Caspar Merian, 1658.

FERDINANDVS MARIA DVX BAVAR ET PALAT SVP. S. ROM. IMP. ARCHIDAPIFER. PRINC. ELECT. COM PALAT. AD RHEN. etc.

Der DurchLeüchtigste Fürst vnd Herr, Herr
Ferdinand Maria, inn Ober: vndt Nieder
Bayern, auch der Ober Pfaltz Hertzog, Pfaltzgrav
bey Rhein, deß Heyl: Röm: Reichs Ertz Truchses
vnd Churfurst, Landgrav zu Leüchtenberg

Cum Privileg: S.C.M.   Casp: Merian Excudit

ABSOLUTISMUS, BAROCK UND AUFKLÄRUNG
Kurfürst Ferdinand Maria von Bayern

Kurfürstin Henriette Adelaide von Savoyen (1636 – 1676).
Henriette Adelaide war eine Cousine Ludwigs XIV., des französischen Sonnenkönigs. Die Ehe mit ihr rückte Ferdinand Maria und Bayern politisch näher an Frankreich und schwächte den Einfluss der Habsburger auf das Kurfürstentum.
Gemälde von Paul Mignard im Kurfürstensaal des ehemaligen Zisterzienserklosters zu Fürstenfeld, um 1640.

Electress Henriette Adelaide of Savoy (1636 – 1676).
Henriette Adelaide was a cousin of Ludwig XIV, the French Sun King. Ferdinand Maria's marriage to her moved him and Bavaria politically closer to France and weakened the influence of the House of Habsburg on the electorate.
Painting by Paul Mignard in the Elector Hall of the former Fürstenfeld Cistercian Abbey, c. 1640.

Kurfürst Ferdinand Maria von Bayern (1636 – 1679).
Die Ehe zwischen Henriette Adelaide und Ferdinand Maria wurde noch auf Wunsch seines Vaters, des alten Kurfürsten Maximilian, geschlossen. Unter dem neuen Kurfürstenpaar avancierte der Münchner Hof bald zu einem Zentrum des mitteleuropäischen Hochbarock.
Gemälde von Paul Mignard, o. J.

Prince-Elector Ferdinand Maria of Bavaria (1636 – 1679).
The marriage between Henriette Adelaide and Ferdinand Maria took place at the request of his father, the old Prince-Elector Maximilian. Under the new elector couple, the Munich court soon developed into a centre of Central European high baroque.
Painting by Paul Mignard, undated.

ABSOLUTISMUS, BAROCK UND AUFKLÄRUNG
Kurfürst Ferdinand Maria von Bayern

Feierlicher Einzug der Prinzessin Violante von Bayern auf der illuminierten Piazza del Campo in Siena am 12. April 1717.
Violante Beatrix, die jüngste Tochter Ferdinand Marias, heiratete 1688 Ferdinand III. de Medici, Erbprinz von Toskana. Nach dessen Tod 1713 ernannte sie ihr Schwiegervater Cosimo III. 1717 zur Gouverneurin von Siena, wo sie maßgeblich zur wirtschaftlichen und kulturellen Blüte der Stadt beitrug. Sie erneuerte u.a. das Regelwerk für den „Palio", das berühmte Pferderennen von Siena. Noch heute wird der Palio nach diesen Regeln abgehalten.
Kolorierter Kupferstich eines unbekannten Künstlers, um 1717.

Ceremonial entry of Princess Violante of Bavaria onto the illuminated Piazza del Campo in Siena on 12 April 1717.
Violante Beatrix, the youngest daughter of Ferdinand Maria, married Ferdinand III de Medici, heir to the throne of Tuscany, in 1688. After his death in 1713, her father-in-law, Cosimo III, appointed her Governor of Siena, where she made a key contribution to the city's economic and cultural prosperity. She renewed the rules of the "Palio", Siena's famous horse race. Today, the Palio is still held according to these rules.
Coloured copper engraving of an unknown artist, c. 1717.

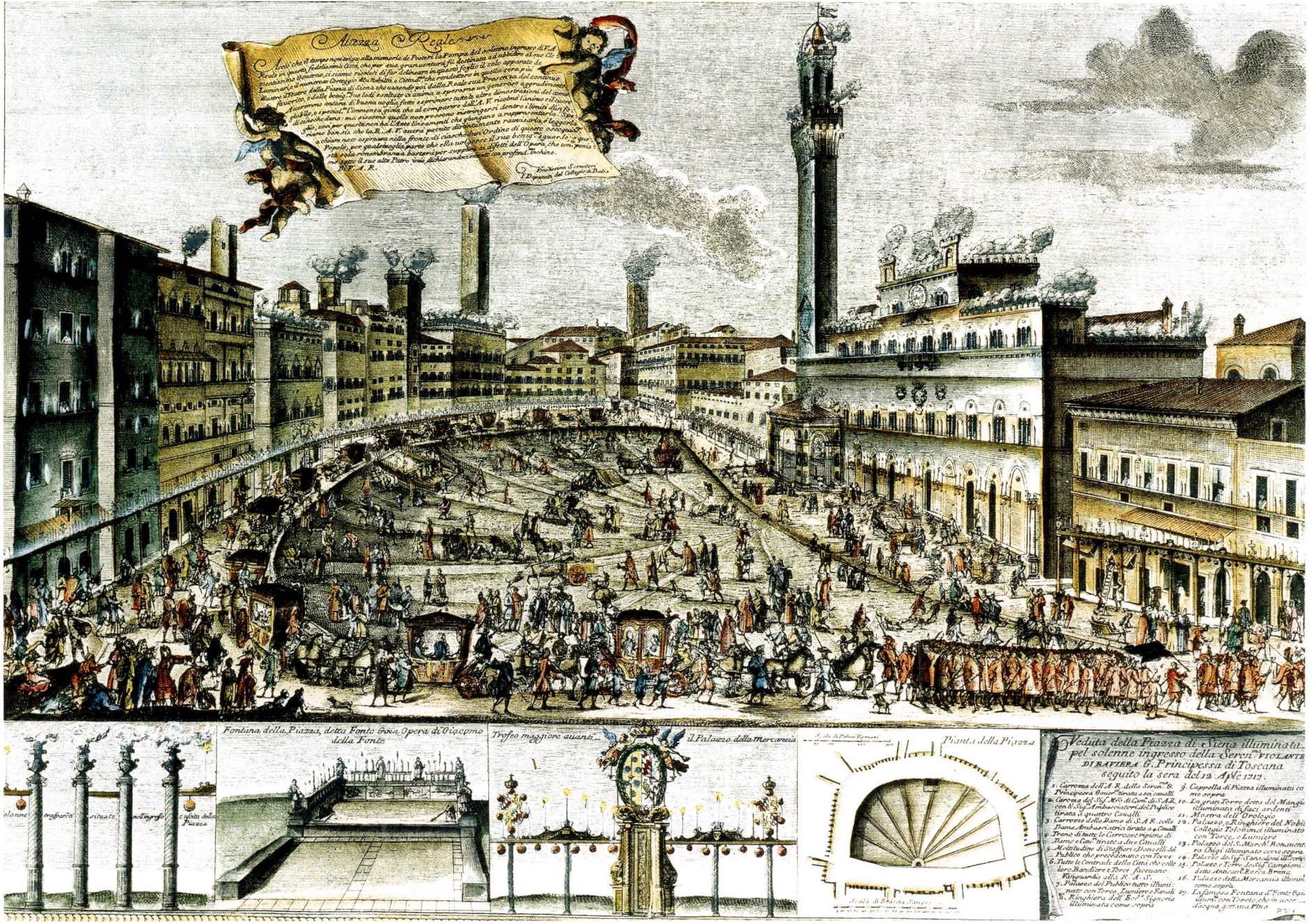

ABSOLUTISMUS, BAROCK UND AUFKLÄRUNG
Kurfürst Ferdinand Maria von Bayern

Entwurf zum Hochaltarblatt der Theatinerkirche in München.
Als im Juli 1662 der ersehnte Erbprinz Max Emanuel das Licht der Welt erblickte, veranlasste der Kurfürst zum Dank den Bau der Theatinerkirche in München. Das kurfürstliche Stifterpaar Ferdinand Maria und Henriette Adelaide wurde auf dem Hochaltarblatt zusammen mit seinen vier Kindern im unteren Bildbereich verewigt.
Gemälde von Antonio Zanchi, 1672 (Original im Zweiten Weltkrieg zerstört).

Design for the high altarpiece of the Theatine Church in Munich.
When the longed-for heir to the throne Max Emanuel was born in July 1662, the prince-elector instigated the construction of the Theatine Church in Munich to express his gratitude. The founding elector couple Ferdinand Maria and Henriette Adelaide were immortalised together with their four children on the high altarpiece in the lower part of the image.
Painting by Antonio Zanchi, 1672 (original destroyed in the Second World War).

ABSOLUTISMUS, BAROCK UND AUFKLÄRUNG
Kurfürst Ferdinand Maria von Bayern

Die von Kurfürst Maximilian I. erbaute kurfürstliche Residenz in München von der Hofgartenseite aus gesehen.
Zeichnung von Mathias Disel nach einem Kupferstich von J. A. Corvinus, Kurfürst Maximilian II. Emanuel gewidmet, um 1720.

The electoral residence in Munich built by Prince-Elector Maximilian I, seen from the court garden side.
Drawing by Mathias Disel based on a copper engraving by J. A. Corninus, dedicated to Prince-Elector Maximilian II Emanuel, c. 1720.

Das „Lusthaus Nymphenburg".
Anlässlich der Geburt des Kurprinzen Max Emanuel schenkte Kurfürst Ferdinand Maria seiner Gemahlin einen „borgo delle ninfe" – Nymphenburg. Das vor der Residenzstadt gelegene Gut wurde nach italienischen und savoyischen Vorbildern in Auftrag gegeben. Zunächst umfasste die Anlage einen mächtigen Pavillon, umgeben von der Hofmarkkirche und einem ummauerten kleinen Park. In den folgenden Jahrzehnten wurden das „Lusthaus" und sein Garten beständig erweitert.
Kupferstich von Michael Wening, 1701.

The "Nymphenburg fun house".
To mark the birth of heir to the throne Max Emanuel, Prince-Elector Ferdinand Maria gave his consort a "borgo delle ninfe" – Nymphenburg (nymph's castle). The property located by the city of residence was mandated according to Italian and Savoyard models. Initially, the complex included a huge pavilion, surrounded by the Hofmarkkirche church and a small, walled park. In the following decades, the "fun house" and its garden were continuously expanded.
Copper engraving by Michael Wening, 1701.

ABSOLUTISMUS, BAROCK UND AUFKLÄRUNG
Kurfürst Ferdinand Maria von Bayern

Das Prunkschiff „Bucentaur" auf dem Starnberger See.
Von Kurfürst Ferdinand Maria 1663 in Auftrag gegeben, war das große Prunkschiff mit dem seltsam anmutenden Namen bevorzugter Ort von Hoffesten vor imposanter Naturkulisse und bis 1758 unter Max III. Joseph in Betrieb. Italienische Künstler und Handwerker, die unter dem Einfluss Henriette Adelaides das Münchner Hofleben „italienisierten", schufen die barocke Prunkgaleere nach seinem venezianischen Vorbild „Bucintoro", dem Prunkschiff des Dogen von Venedig.
Gemälde von Ignaz oder Ferdinand Bidermann, 1738.

The splendorous ship "Bucentaur" on Lake Starnberg.
Commissioned by Prince-Elector Ferdinand Maria in 1663, the large glamour ship with the strange-seeming name was the preferred location for court festivals before an imposing natural backdrop and was operated under Max III Joseph until 1758. Italian artists and craftsmen, who "italianised" Munich court life under the influence of Henriette Adelaide, created the baroque glamour galley based on its Venetian model "Bucintoro", the glamour ship of the Doge of Venice.
Painting by Ignaz or Ferdinand Bidermann, 1738.

ABSOLUTISMUS, BAROCK UND AUFKLÄRUNG
Kurfürst Ferdinand Maria von Bayern

Turnierhaus am Hofgarten zu München.
Das einst weltberühmte Turnierhaus wurde 1660/61 von Kurfürst Ferdinand Maria in Auftrag gegeben und von Max Schinnagl erbaut. Es diente der höfischen Reitschule als Turnier- und Übungsplatz und der Hofgesellschaft als Vergnügungsort: Bis zu seinem Abriss im Jahr 1822 veranstaltete der Hof in diesem langgezogenen Bau auch große Redouten und Bälle.
Kupferstich nach Mathias Disel, um 1722.

Tournament house at the Munich Court Garden.
The once world-famous tournament house was commissioned by Prince-Elector Ferdinand Maria in 1660/61 and constructed by Max Schinnagl. It served the court riding school as a place for tournaments and training and the court society as a place of entertainment. Until its demolition in 1822, the court also held large masquerade balls and other dance events in this elongated building.
Copper engraving based on Mathias Disel, c. 1722.

ABSOLUTISMUS, BAROCK UND AUFKLÄRUNG
Kurfürst Ferdinand Maria von Bayern

Decke des Herzkabinetts der Münchner Residenz.
Nach Plänen von Agostini Barelli und Antonio Francesco Pistorini ließ Kurfürstin Henriette Adelaide im Zuge des Ausbaus der Residenz eine private Zimmerfolge für sich einrichten, die jedoch schon im Jahr 1674 durch ein Feuer teilweise zerstört wurde. Nur Teile des kleinen Kabinetts dieser Raumfolge überstanden den Brand wie auch die Wirren des Zweiten Weltkriegs. Die allegorischen Gemälde an der vergoldeten Kassettendecke stellen, angelehnt an die Handlung eines französischen Romans, alle Phasen eines fühlenden Herzens dar.
Caspar Amort d. Ä. zugeschrieben, um 1666.

Ceiling of the heart cabinet of the Munich Residenz.
In accordance with the plans of Agostini Barelli and Antonio Francesco Pistorini, Electress Henriette Adelaide had a private suite installed for herself as part of the expansion of the Residenz, although this suite was partially destroyed due to a fire in 1674. Only parts of this small cabinet survived the fire as well as the turmoil of the Second World War. The allegoric paintings on the gold-plated coffered ceiling represent – based on the plot of a French novel – all the phases of a sentient heart.
Attributed to Caspar Amort the Elder, c. 1666.

Max Emanuel, the "Blue King"

The birth of heir to the throne Max Emanuel on 11 July 1662 was celebrated in true baroque pomp by his parents, the electoral couple Ferdinand Maria and Henriette Adelaide: a grand celebration lasting several days with theatre and fireworks was held to mark the little prince's baptism and to express their gratitude for their son the couple founded the Theatine Church in Munich.

Max II Emanuel, who ascended to the position of Prince-Elector at the age of just 18 after the early death of his parents, lived up to this pompous start to his life in every respect. In accordance with the spirit of the times, he ruled Bavaria true to an absolutistic interpretation of rulership that caused him to strive after greater things throughout his life. In French style, he constructed the New Schleissheim Palace, expanded Nymphenburg Palace to a veritable size and occupied himself as a patron of the arts. In the power play of the competing houses of Bourbon and Habsburg over European hegemony, he tried to position himself favourably by changing sides several times. His marriage to the Emperor's daughter Maria Antonia in 1685 initially brought him closer to Leopold I of the House of Habsburg. Previously, he had already supported the Emperor in the war against the Ottomans; he thus made a crucial contribution to the liberation of Vienna with his Bavarian contingent in the Battle of Vienna in 1683. The bold conquest of Belgrade under his leadership in 1688 earned him the honourable byname "Blue King" among his enemies – the Turks who weren't familiar with the term "Elector" named him "Mavi Kral" which was borrowed from the South Slav words for "Blue King". In 1692, the King of Spain, Karl II, rewarded his military achievements by intercession of the Emperor with the governorship of the Spanish Netherlands, whereupon Max Emanuel relocated his court to Brussels.

Max Emanuel saw himself near to the objective of his political ambitions when the Spanish royal throne beckoned for his son Joseph Ferdinand due to his mother's heritage. Her uncle, the childless Karl II of Spain, appointed the heir to the Bavarian throne as his sole heir. However, the boy died suddenly and unexpectedly in 1699. In hopes of saving part of his son's hereditary right for himself, Max Emanuel sided with France in the subsequent War of the Spanish Succession. However, this brought him into political isolation within the empire. On the side of France, he was defeated by the imperial troops at the Battle of Blenheim in 1704 – Bavaria was conquered by the Austrian army and the Prince-Elector saw himself forced to withdraw into exile in France. It was not until 1715 that Max Emanuel was able to return to Munich and effect a rapprochement with the Emperor.

After his return, Max Emanuel also reconciled with Prince-Elector Johann Wilhelm of the Palatinate – who was a bitter enemy of Bavaria during the war – and with his brother and successor Karl III Philipp. In 1718, he met the Palatine in Scheyern in order to negotiate the rapprochement of the two Wittelsbach lines, which was sealed in a series of agreements in 1722 and 1724. Other princely family members joined this new house union, including Prince-Elector and Archbishop Clemens August of Cologne. It formed the basis for the sovereign state of Bavaria of the 19th century.

Max Emanuel, der „Blaue König"

Die Geburt des Erbprinzen Max Emanuel am 11. Juli 1662 feierten seine Eltern, das Kurfürstenpaar Ferdinand Maria und Henriette Adelaide, in wahrlich barockem Prunk: Ein mehrtägiges, prachtvolles Fest mit Theater und Feuerwerk wurde zur Taufe des kleinen Prinzen abgehalten, und zum Dank für ihren Sohn stiftete das Paar die Theatinerkirche in München.

Max II. Emanuel, der nach dem frühen Tod seiner Eltern schon mit 18 Jahren zum Kurfürsten aufstieg, machte diesem prunkvollen Beginn seines Lebens in jeder Hinsicht Ehre. Dem Zeitgeist entsprechend regierte er Bayern getreu einer absolutistischen Herrschaftsauffassung, die ihn sein Leben lang nach Höherem streben ließ. Nach französischem Vorbild errichtete er das Neue Schloss Schleißheim, baute Schloss Nymphenburg zu veritabler Größe aus und betätigte sich als Kunstmäzen. Im Mächtespiel der konkurrierenden Häuser der Bourbonen und Habsburger um die europäische Vorherrschaft versuchte er, sich durch mehrere Seitenwechsel günstig zu positionieren. Die Heirat mit der Kaisertochter Maria Antonia 1685 brachte ihn zunächst dem Habsburger Leopold I. näher. Schon zuvor hatte er den Kaiser im Krieg gegen die Osmanen unterstützt; so trug er in der Schlacht am Kahlenberg 1683 mit seinem bayerischen Kontingent entscheidend zur Befreiung Wiens bei. Die wagemutige Eroberung von Belgrad unter seiner Führung im Jahr 1688 brachte ihm unter den Gegnern den ehrenvollen Beinamen „Blauer König" ein – die Türken, denen der Begriff „Kurfürst" unbekannt war, nannten ihn „Mavi Kral", was aus dem Südslawischen entlehnt „Blauer König" bedeutet. Seine militärischen Erfolge belohnte der König von Spanien, Karl II., auf Fürsprache des Kaisers 1692 mit der Statthalterschaft über die Spanischen Niederlande, woraufhin Max Emanuel seinen Hof nach Brüssel verlegte.

Kurz vor dem Ziel seiner politischen Ambitionen sah sich Max Emanuel, als seinem Sohn Joseph Ferdinand durch das Erbe seiner Mutter die spanische Königskrone winkte: Ihr Onkel, der kinderlose Karl II. von Spanien, setzte den bayerischen Erbprinzen zu seinem Universalerben ein, doch der Junge starb jäh und unvermittelt bereits 1699. In der Hoffnung, durch die Ansprüche seines Sohnes noch einen Teil des Erbrechts für sich selbst retten zu können, schlug sich Max Emanuel im folgenden Spanischen Erbfolgekrieg auf die Seite Frankreichs, geriet dadurch aber innerhalb des Reiches in politische Isolation. An der Seite Frankreichs unterlag er den Reichstruppen 1704 in der Schlacht bei Höchstädt – Bayern wurde von der österreichischen Armee besetzt und der Kurfürst sah sich gezwungen, in das französische Exil auszuweichen. Erst 1715 konnte Max Emanuel nach München zurückkehren und eine Wiederannäherung an den Kaiser erwirken.

Auch mit Kurfürst Johann Wilhelm von der Pfalz, der während des Krieges ein erbitterter Gegner des Bayern war, und mit dessen Bruder und Nachfolger Karl III. Philipp söhnte sich Max Emanuel nach seiner Rückkehr aus. 1718 traf er sich mit dem Pfälzer in Scheyern, um die Annäherung der beiden Wittelsbacher Linien auszuhandeln, die in einer Reihe von Verträgen 1722 und 1724 besiegelt wurde. Dieser neuen Hausunion traten weitere fürstliche Familienangehörige bei, so u.a. der Kurfürst und Erzbischof Clemens August von Köln. Sie legte den Grundstein für den souveränen Staat Bayern des 19. Jahrhunderts.

ABSOLUTISMUS, BAROCK UND AUFKLÄRUNG
Kurfürst Max II. Emanuel von Bayern

Eintrag des Kurfürsten Max II. Emanuel im Bruderschaftsbuch der Corpus-Christi-Bruderschaft bei St. Peter in München.

Entry of Prince-Elector Max II Emanuel in the Book of the Brotherhood of the Corpus Christi Brotherhood at St. Peter's Church in Munich.

Kurfürst Max II. Emanuel (1662–1726) als Feldherr vor Mons. Als Verbündeter Frankreichs nahm Max II. Emanuel im Zuge des Spanischen Erbfolgekriegs auch an den militärischen Auseinandersetzungen vor der Stadt Mons, damals in den Spanischen Niederlanden, heute in Belgien gelegen, teil.
Gemälde in Pastelltechnik von Joseph Vivien, 1706.

Prince-Elector Max II Emanuel (1662–1726) as commander by Mons. As an ally of France, Max II Emanuel also participated in the conflicts by the city of Mons – then in the Spanish Netherlands and now part of Belgium – during the War of the Spanish Succession.
Painting in pastel technique by Joseph Vivien, 1706.

ABSOLUTISMUS, BAROCK UND AUFKLÄRUNG
Kurfürst Max II. Emanuel von Bayern

Kurprinz Max Emanuel mit seiner älteren Schwester Maria Anna Christina, nachmalige Dauphine von Frankreich.
Der Erbprinz ist hier im Alter von vier Jahren abgebildet, seine ältere Schwester als Sechsjährige. Das Bildnis veranschaulicht die repräsentative Rolle, die den Kindern des Kurfürstenpaars von Beginn an auferlegt wurde. Vor allem Max Emanuel scheint sich in Bombellis Darstellung seiner Bestimmung als künftiger Herrscher bewusst zu sein.
Gemälde von Sebastiano Bombelli, 1666.

Prince-Elector Max Emanuel with his older sister Maria Anna Christina, later Dauphine of France.
Here, the heir to the throne is depicted at the age of four, his older sister as a six-year-old. The portrait illustrates the representative role that was imposed upon the children of the electoral couple from the beginning. Max Emanuel, in particular, seems aware of his destiny as a future ruler in Bombelli's painting.
Painting by Sebastiano Bombelli, 1666.

ABSOLUTISMUS, BAROCK UND AUFKLÄRUNG
Kurfürst Max II. Emanuel von Bayern

Die Eroberung der Festung Neuhäusel 1685.
Während des Rückzugs der Türken nach Osten nahm Kurfürst Max Emanuel mit seinem Heer die ungarische Festung Neuhäusel an der Neutra im Sturm. Kurz darauf folgte der bedeutende Sieg der kaiserlichen Truppen bei Gran (heute Esztergom).
Gemälde von Franz Joachim Beich im Viktoriensaal des Neuen Schlosses Schleißheim, um 1685.

The conquest of the fortress of Neuhäusel 1685.
During the retreat of the Turks towards the east, Prince-Elector Max Emanuel and his army took the Hungarian fortress of Neuhäusel an der Neutra by assault. This was followed soon after by the significant victory of the imperial troops at Gran (Esztergom).
Painting by Franz Joachim Beich in the Victoria Hall of the New Schleissheim Palace, c. 1685.

ABSOLUTISMUS, BAROCK UND AUFKLÄRUNG
Kurfürst Max II. Emanuel von Bayern

Kurfürst Max Emanuel mit seiner Gemahlin Maria Antonia von Österreich und Kurprinz Joseph Ferdinand. Da die Mutter des kleinen Kurprinzen, Maria Antonia, schon wenige Wochen nach der Geburt des Sohnes starb, ist fraglich, ob das Miniaturbildnis nicht eher Max Emanuels zweite Gemahlin Therese Kunigunde darstellt. Wäre jedoch Maria Antonia gemeint, könnte das Bildnis den Anspruch des Prinzen auf die spanische Krone versinnbildlichen, der sich auf seine österreichische Mutter und deren Erbe gründete.
Gouachemalerei Karl Ferdinand Bruni zugeschrieben, 1695.

Prince-Elector Max Emanuel with his consort Maria Antonia of Austria and heir to the throne Joseph Ferdinand. Since the mother of the little heir to the throne, Maria Antonia, died just a few weeks after the birth of her son, it is questionable whether the miniature portrait does not rather depict Max Emanuel's second consort, Therese Kunigunde. However, if Maria Antonia were meant, the portrait could symbolise the prince's claim to the Spanish crown, which was based on his Austrian mother and her heritage.
Gouache painting attributed to Karl Ferdinand Bruni, 1695.

ABSOLUTISMUS, BAROCK UND AUFKLÄRUNG
Kurfürst Max II. Emanuel von Bayern

König Ludwig XIV. von Frankreich und Kurfürst Max II. Emanuel von Bayern auf dem großen Kanal von Versailles. Im Spanischen Erbfolgekrieg schlug sich Max Emanuel auf die Seite Frankreichs. Damit stellte er sich gegen seinen langjährigen Bündnispartner, den Kaiser in Wien.
Tellerentwurf zu einer Serie für König Ludwig II., Carl Grünwedel zugeschrieben, o. J.

King Ludwig XIV of France and Prince-Elector Max II Emanuel of Bavaria on the Grand Canal of Versailles. In the War of the Spanish Succession, Max Emanuel sided with France. He thus took up a position against his long-term ally, the Emperor in Vienna.
Plate design for a series for King Ludwig II, attributed to Carl Grünwedel, undated.

Kurprinz Joseph Ferdinand (1692–1699) als Fürst von Asturien. Durch den frühen Tod seiner habsburgischen Mutter erbte Joseph Ferdinand ihren Anspruch auf den spanischen Thron. Der Prinz starb jedoch 1699 im Alter von nur sieben Jahren. Sein unerwarteter Tod sowie der des spanischen Königs ein Jahr später, der Joseph Ferdinand zum Alleinerben eingesetzt hatte, lösten den Spanischen Erbfolgekrieg aus. Auf dem Bild weist der Prinz auf eine im Hafen liegende Flotte, einen großen Globus im Rücken: Beides kann als Hinweis auf das spanische Weltreich und die damit verbundene Machtposition gedeutet werden, die ihm in Aussicht stehen.
Pastellgemälde von Joseph Vivien, 1698.

Heir to the throne Joseph Ferdinand (1692–1699) as Prince of Asturias. Due to the early death of his mother, of the House of Habsburg, Joseph Ferdinand inherited her claim to the Spanish throne. However, the prince died in 1699 at the age of just seven. His unexpected death as well as that of the Spanish King a year later, who had appointed Joseph Ferdinand as his sole heir, triggered the War of the Spanish Succession. In the painting, the prince is pointing to a fleet in the port, with a large globe behind him. Both can be interpreted as an indication of the Spanish global empire and the associated position of power that he has in prospect.
Pastel painting by Joseph Vivien, 1698.

ABSOLUTISMUS, BAROCK UND AUFKLÄRUNG
Kurfürst Max II. Emanuel von Bayern

Kurfürst Max II. Emanuel befehligt eine marschierende Armee („La Marche").
Das Bild ist ein Ausschnitt einer 1696 in Brüssel für das Neue Schloss Schleißheim gewirkten Wandteppichserie, die verschiedene Szenen des Kriegslebens wiedergibt.
Tapisserie von Jerôme Le Clerck und Gaspar van der Borcht aus Wolle, Seide und Metallfäden, 1696.

Prince-Elector Max II Emanuel commands a marching army ("La marche").
The image is an extract from a tapestry series woven in Brussels for the New Schleissheim Palace in 1696 that conveys various scenes of war life.
Tapestry by Jerôme Le Clerck and Gaspar van der Borcht from wool, silk and metal threads, 1696.

Kurfürst Max II. Emanuel von Bayern im Großen Türkenkrieg 1683–1688.
Max Emanuel schlug in der Schlacht am Kahlenberg 1683 an der Seite der kaiserlichen und polnischen Truppen die türkische Bedrohung vor Wien erfolgreich zurück. Seine Siege im Türkenkrieg, besonders die Erstürmung Belgrads im Jahr 1688, trugen ihm bei den Osmanen nach seiner blauen Uniform den Beinamen „Mavi Kral", Blauer König, ein.
Miniatur auf Pergament, Karl Ferdinand Bruni zugeschrieben, um 1690.

Prince-Elector Max II Emanuel of Bavaria in the Great Turkish War 1683–1688.
On the side of the imperial and Polish troops, Max Emanuel successfully repulsed the Turkish threat by Vienna in the Battle of Vienna in 1683. His victories in the Turkish War, especially the storming of Belgrade in 1688, earned him the byname "Mavi Kral", Blue King, among the Ottomans after his blue uniform.
Miniature on parchment attributed to Karl Ferdinand Bruni, c. 1690.

ABSOLUTISMUS, BAROCK UND AUFKLÄRUNG
Kurfürst Max II. Emanuel von Bayern

Herzogin Maria Anna Karolina von Bayern (1696 – 1750), nachmalig Emanuela Theresa de Corde Jesu.
Max II. Emanuels Tochter trat 1719 in den Münchner Klarissenorden ein. Sie ist die einzige Wittelsbacherin, die während der österreichischen Besatzung (1704 – 1715) in der Residenz verblieb. Vier ihrer Brüder wurden 1706 von den Besatzern nach Klagenfurt und Graz verschleppt.
Gemälde von Jakob Amigone, um 1720.

Duchess Maria Anna Karolina of Bavaria (1696 – 1750), later Emanuela Theresa de Corde Jesu.
In 1719, Max II Emanuel's daughter joined the Munich Order of St. Clare. She is the only member of the House of Wittelsbach who remained in the residence during the Austrian occupation (1704 – 1715). In 1706, four of her brothers were deported to Klagenfurt and Graz by the occupying forces.
Painting by Jakob Amigone, c. 1720.

Prinzessin Therese Kunigunde von Polen, zweite Gemahlin des Kurfürsten Max II. Emanuel, mit einem Porträtmedaillon ihres Sohns Karl Albrecht.
Aus Max Emanuels zweiter Ehe mit der Tochter des polnischen Königs Johann Sobieski gingen zehn Kinder hervor, wovon sechs das Erwachsenenalter erreichten, darunter der Erbprinz Karl Albrecht, späterer Kurfürst von Bayern.
Gemälde von Johann Andreas Wolff, 1704.

Princess Therese Kunigunde of Poland, second consort of Prince-Elector Max II Emanuel, with a portrait medallion of her son Karl Albrecht.
Max Emanuel's second marriage to the daughter of the Polish King Johann Sobieski produced ten children, six of whom reached adult age, including heir to the throne Karl Albrecht, later Prince-Elector of Bavaria.
Painting by Johann Andreas Wolff, 1704.

ABSOLUTISMUS, BAROCK UND AUFKLÄRUNG
Kurfürst Max II. Emanuel von Bayern

Die „Sendlinger Mordweihnacht" von 1705.
Als Reaktion auf die Strenge der österreichischen Besatzer erhoben sich im Winter 1705/06 Bauern in ganz Bayern gegen die Fremdherrschaft, in der Hoffnung, der ins Exil verbannte Kurfürst möge zu Hilfe eilen. Der Aufstand der „Oberländer" Bauern gipfelte in einem Marsch auf München, der in der Nacht vom 24. auf den 25. Dezember 1705 von den kaiserlichen Truppen bei Sendling blutig niedergeschlagen wurde. Rund 1.100 Bayern ließen dort ihr Leben, während auf der Gegenseite nur etwa 40 Soldaten umkamen. Bis heute gilt die Sendlinger Mordweihnacht als eines der traumatischsten Ereignisse der bayerischen Geschichte.
Kreidelithografie von Peter Elmer, um 1831.

"Sendling's Night of Murder" of 1705.
In reaction to the strictness of the Austrian occupying forces, farmers throughout Bavaria rose up against the foreign domination in the winter of 1705/06 in the hope that the exiled prince-elector might rush to their aid. The uprising of the "uplander" farmers climaxed in a march on Munich, which was bloodily defeated by the imperial troops at Sendling in the night of 24/25 December 1705. Approximately 1,100 Bavarians lost their lives there, while on the opposing side only approximately 40 soldiers died. To this day, Sendling's Night of Murder is considered one of the most traumatic events in Bavarian history.
Chalk lithograph by Peter Elmer, c. 1831.

ABSOLUTISMUS, BAROCK UND AUFKLÄRUNG
Kurfürst Max II. Emanuel von Bayern

Allegorie auf die Wiedervereinigung Max II. Emanuels mit seiner Familie nach dem französischen Exil im Jahr 1715.
Nach knapp elfjähriger Abwesenheit kehrte Max II. Emanuel im April 1715 nach München zurück. Die meisten Familienmitglieder hatte er seit über neun Jahren nicht gesehen. In der Darstellung Viviens begleiten mehrere Figuren der griechischen Mythologie das Wiedersehen der kurfürstlichen Familie.
Gemälde von Joseph Vivien, 1715.

Allegory of Max II Emanuel's reunion with his family after his French exile in 1715.
After an absence of approximately eleven years, Max II Emanuel returned to Munich in April 1715. He had not seen most of his family members for more than nine years. In Vivien's depiction, several figures from Greek mythology accompany the electoral family's reunion.
Painting by Joseph Vivien, 1715.

ABSOLUTISMUS, BAROCK UND AUFKLÄRUNG
Kurfürst Max II. Emanuel von Bayern

Kurfürst Max II. Emanuel von Bayern (1662–1726).
Eine Supraporte im großen Treppenhaus des Klosters Ettal zeigt Kurfürst Max II. Emanuel, sein plastisches Porträt in ovalem Rahmen wird von zwei Löwen und einem Engel flankiert.
Relief eines unbekannten Künstlers, o. J.

Prince-Elector Max II Emanuel of Bavaria (1662–1726).
An overdoor in the large staircase of Ettal Abbey shows Prince-Elector Max II Emanuel; his plastic portrait in an oval frame is flanked by two lions and an angel.
Relief of an unknown artist, undated.

Neues Schloss Schleißheim von der Ostseite.
In der Tradition der großen barocken Schlossbauten des 17. Jahrhunderts gab Max II. Emanuel das Neue Schloss Schleißheim als prachtvolle Residenz in Auftrag. Bei seinem Tod 1726 war es noch nicht vollendet, doch führte sein Sohn Karl Albrecht den Ausbau gemäß seinen Planungen fort. Im Hintergrund Schloss Dachau.
Aquarellminiatur im Miniaturenkabinett in den Reichen Zimmern der Münchner Residenz von Michael Geer, um 1730.

New Schleissheim Palace from the east side.
In the tradition of the large baroque palace buildings of the 17th century, Max II Emanuel commissioned the New Schleissheim Palace as a grand residence. When he died in 1726, it was not yet complete. However, his son Karl Albrecht continued the expansion according to his plannings. Dachau Palace can be seen in the background.
Miniature watercolour in the miniatures cabinet in the Rich Rooms of the Munich Residenz by Michael Geer, c. 1730.

ABSOLUTISMUS, BAROCK UND AUFKLÄRUNG
Kaiser Karl VII. Albrecht, Kurfürst von Bayern

Eintrag des Kurfürsten Karl Albrecht im Bruderschaftsbuch der Corpus-Christi-Bruderschaft bei St. Peter in München.

Entry of Prince-Elector Karl Albrecht in the Book of the Brotherhood of the Corpus Christi Brotherhood at St. Peter's Church in Munich.

Kaiser Karl VII. Albrecht, Kurfürst von Bayern (1697–1745).
Der Sohn und Erbe Max II. Emanuels wurde nach dem Tod des habsburgischen Kaisers Karl VI. und damit dem Aussterben der habsburgischen Linie im Mannesstamm im Jahr 1742 zum römisch-deutschen Kaiser gekrönt. Im österreichischen Erbfolgekrieg konnte er sich zunächst mit Hilfe Verbündeter bei der Kaiserwahl gegen die Habsburgerin Maria Theresia durchsetzen. Doch blieb er militärisch und politisch machtlos, sodass er als zweiter „bayerischer Kaiser" bis kurz vor seinem Tod im Exil leben musste.
Gemälde aus dem Atelier von George Desmarées, nach 1742.

Emperor Karl VII Albrecht, Prince-Elector of Bavaria (1697–1745).
The son and heir to Max II Emanuel was crowned the German Holy Roman Emperor in 1742 following the death of Emperor Karl VI of the House of Habsburg resulting in the male Habsburg line dying out. During the War of the Austrian Succession he was initially able to win the imperial election against Maria Theresia of the House of Habsburg with the help of his allies. However, he remained powerless in political and military terms resulting in him being the second "Bavarian Emperor" to have to live in exile just before his death.
Painting from the atelier of George Desmarées, after 1742.

ABSOLUTISMUS, BAROCK UND AUFKLÄRUNG
Kaiser Karl VII. Albrecht, Kurfürst von Bayern

Kurprinz Karl Albrecht um 1703 (1697–1745).
Das Bildnis des kurfürstlichen Erbprinzen gehört zu einer Porträtserie der Kinder Max Emanuels und seiner zweiten Gemahlin Therese Kunigunde, die der Hofmaler Maingaud anfertigte. Karl Albrecht wurde noch während der Statthalterschaft des Kurfürsten in Brüssel geboren. Während des Exils ihres Vaters und des Onkels, Kur-Erzbischof Joseph Clemens von Köln, in Frankreich kamen Karl Albrecht und seine Brüder als Faustpfand Österreichs nach Klagenfurt in Gefangenschaft.
Gemälde von Martin Maingaud, um 1703.

Electoral Prince Karl Albrecht c. 1703 (1697–1745).
This portrait of the electoral heir is part of a portrait series of the children of Max Emanuel and his second wife Therese Kunigunde, which was painted by the court painter Maingaud. Karl Albrecht was born in Brussels during the Prince-Elector's governorship. During the exile of his father and uncle, Joseph Clemens Archbishop-Elector of Cologne, in France Karl Albrecht and his brothers were imprisoned in Klagenfurt as Austria's bargaining chip.
Painting by Martin Maingaud, c. 1703.

ABSOLUTISMUS, BAROCK UND AUFKLÄRUNG
Kaiser Karl VII. Albrecht, Kurfürst von Bayern

Kurfürst Karl Albrecht wechselt nach einem Jagdunfall seine Stiefel am Blauen Haus im Forstenrieder Park. Seit ca. 1715 pflegte die Hofgesellschaft im kurfürstlichen Hirschjagdpark zu jagen, der von Nymphenburg bis nach Krailling und Solln reichte. Im umzäunten Jagdpark standen den Adeligen vier Lusthäuser, das Rote, das Gelbe, das Grüne und das Blaue Haus, für Rast und Verpflegung zur Verfügung. Horemans verewigte sie in mehreren Bildnissen in der Amalienburg im Nymphenburger Schlosspark.
Gemälde von Peter Jakob Horemans, um 1739.

Prince-Elector Karl Albrecht changing his boots after a hunting accident at the Blue House in Forstenrieder Park. Court society used to hunt in the electoral stag hunting park that extended from Nymphenburg to Krailling and Solln from approximately 1715. In the fenced off hunting park four hunting houses were available for the nobility to rest and dine in: the Red, Yellow, Green and Blue House. Horemans immortalised them in several paintings in the Amalienburg hunting lodge in the grounds of Nymphenburg Palace.
Painting by Peter Jakob Horemans, c. 1739.

Kurprinz Karl Albrecht auf der Jagd. Der Kurprinz (sitzend) wird begleitet von Johann Maximilian Graf von Preysing-Hohenaschau, Joseph Hannibal Freiherr von Mayrhofen und Kammerdiener und Wachtelhundeführer Charles Balustrier. Das Bild stellt eines der Hauptwerke Viviens aus seiner Münchner Schaffensperiode dar.
Gemälde von Joseph Vivien, 1723/24.

Electoral Prince Karl Albrecht out hunting. The Electoral Prince (seated) is accompanied by Johann Maximilian Count of Preysing-Hohenaschau, Joseph Hannibal Baron of Mayrhofen and the valet and spaniel handler Charles Balustrier. The painting is considered to be one of Vivien's major works from his creative period in Munich.
Painting by Joseph Vivien, 1723/24.

ABSOLUTISMUS, BAROCK UND AUFKLÄRUNG
Kaiser Karl VII. Albrecht, Kurfürst von Bayern

Kurfürst Karl Albrecht bei der schweren Jagd am Roten Haus im Forstenrieder Park.
Das Rote Haus im kurfürstlichen Hirschjagdpark lag zwischen den im Park eingeschlossenen Orten Pasing und Lochham. Auch andere Siedlungen, wie Allach, Hadern oder Planegg, waren Teil der als Gesamtkunstwerk zu verstehenden, riesigen barocken Parkanlage: Eine waldreiche „Insel der Vergnügungen" für Karl Albrecht und seine Entourage.
Gemälde von Peter Jakob Horemans, 1739.

Prince-Elector Karl Albrecht during a serious hunt at the Red House in Forstenrieder Park.
The Red House in the electoral stag hunting park was situated between the towns of Pasing and Lochham that were enclosed within the park. Other settlements such as Allach, Hadern and Planegg were also part of the huge Baroque park, which is to be seen as an all-encompassing work of art: a densely wooded "island of pleasures" for Karl Albrecht and his entourage.
Painting by Peter Jakob Horemans, 1739.

ABSOLUTISMUS, BAROCK UND AUFKLÄRUNG
Kaiser Karl VII. Albrecht, Kurfürst von Bayern

Einzug Kurfürst Karl Albrechts in Frankfurt am Main zur Kaiserkrönung, Februar 1742.
Der Kupferstich zeigt in großem Format den prachtvollen Festzug anlässlich der Krönung Karl Albrechts zum Kaiser des Heiligen Römischen Reiches Deutscher Nation. Die Krönungsstadt ist am oberen Bildrand in Panoramaansicht dargestellt. Der Zug umfasst gleichermaßen Fußvolk, Reiterei sowie zahlreiche prachtvolle Kutschen.
Kolorierter Kupferstich von Michael Rößler, um 1742.

The arrival of Prince-Elector Karl Albrecht in Frankfurt am Main for his coronation as Emperor, February 1742.
The copperplate shows the magnificent procession on the occasion of Karl Albrecht's coronation as Holy Roman Emperor of the German Nation in a large-scale format. The coronation town is depicted in panorama view at the top of the painting. The procession includes the infantry, cavalry and numerous resplendent coaches.
Coloured copperplate by Michael Rößler, c. 1742.

ABSOLUTISMUS, BAROCK UND AUFKLÄRUNG
Kaiser Karl VII. Albrecht, Kurfürst von Bayern

Zug der Kaiserin Maria Amalia vom Dom zum Römer in Frankfurt am 8. März 1742.
Karl Albrechts Gemahlin wurde nur wenige Tage nach der Krönung ihres Mannes ebenfalls in Frankfurt am Main zur Kaiserin gekrönt.
Kolorierter Kupferstich von Michael Rößler, um 1742.

Procession of Empress Maria Amalia from the cathedral to the Römer in Frankfurt on 8 March 1742.
Karl Albrecht's consort was also crowned Empress in Frankfurt am Main, just a few days after her husband's coronation.
Coloured copperplate by Michael Rößler, c. 1742.

ABSOLUTISMUS, BAROCK UND AUFKLÄRUNG
Kurfürst Maximilian III. Joseph von Bayern

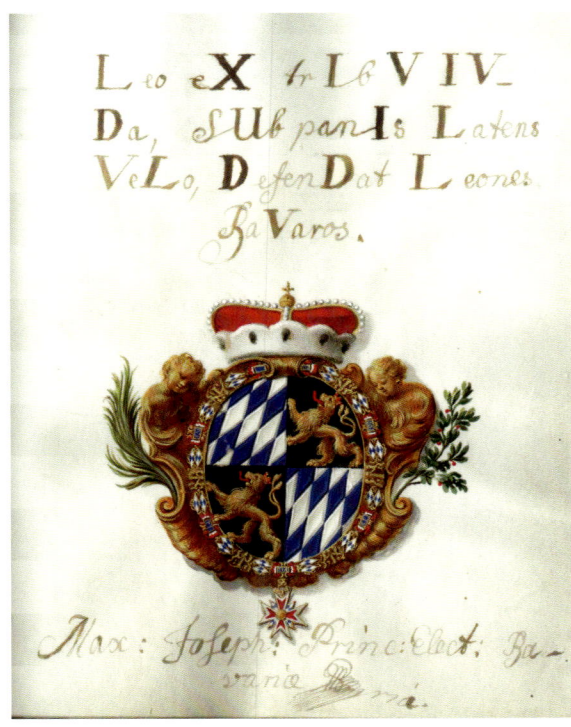

Eintrag des Kurfürsten Maximilian III. Joseph (1727–1777) im Bruderschaftsbuch der Corpus-Christi-Bruderschaft bei St. Peter in München.

Entry of Prince-Elector Maximilian III Joseph in the Book of the Brotherhood of the Corpus Christi Brotherhood at St. Peter's Church in Munich.

Kurfürst Maximilian III. Joseph von Bayern (1727–1777) in Rüstung und Hermelin mit Feldherrnstab.
Im Alter von nur 18 Jahren folgte Maximilian Joseph seinem Vater als Kurfürst von Bayern nach; die politische Situation im europäischen Mächtespiel zwang ihn jedoch dazu, auf den Anspruch auf das habsburgische Erbe und somit auf die Kaiserkrone zu verzichten.
Porträt George Desmarées zugeschrieben, um 1750.

Prince-Elector Maximilian III Joseph of Bavaria (1727–1777) in armour and ermine with general's baton.
Maximilian Joseph succeeded his father as Prince-Elector of Bavaria at the age of just 18; however, the political situation within the European power games forced him to waive his claim to the Habsburg inheritance and therefore the imperial crown too.
Portrait attributed to George Desmarées, c. 1750.

ABSOLUTISMUS, BAROCK UND AUFKLÄRUNG
Kurfürst Maximilian III. Joseph von Bayern

Damenkarussell vor Schloss Fürstenried um 1727.
Im Geburstjahr Maximilian III. Josephs wurde am 14. Mai ein Damenkarussell veranstaltet. Die Menschen strömten zu den eigens für dieses Reiter- und Turnierspektakel errichteten Gelegenheitsbauten vor den Toren von Schloss Fürstenried.
Ölgemälde von Heinrich van Waterschoot, um 1727.

Ladies' Carousel in front of Fürstenried Palace c. 1727.
During Maximilian III Joseph's year of birth, a Ladies' Carousel was organised on 14 May. People flocked to the buildings erected especially for this riding and tournament spectacle in front of Fürstenried Palace's gates.
Oil painting by Heinrich van Waterschoot, c. 1727.

ABSOLUTISMUS, BAROCK UND AUFKLÄRUNG
Kurfürst Maximilian III. Joseph von Bayern

Kurprinz Maximilian Joseph mit seinem Bruder Joseph Ludwig (1728–1733).
Maximilian Joseph wurde als viertes Kind des Kurfürstenpaares Karl Albrecht und Maria Amalia 1727 geboren. Sein Bruder Joseph Ludwig (hier rechts) kam nur ein Jahr später zur Welt, verstarb jedoch schon im Alter von fünf Jahren.
Doppelporträt aus der Werkstatt von George Desmarées, um 1740.

Electoral Prince Maximilian III Joseph of Bavaria with his brother Joseph Ludwig (1728–1733).
Maximilian Joseph was the fourth child born to the electoral couple Karl Albrecht and Maria Amalia in 1727. His brother Joseph Ludwig (on the right) came into the world just a year later but died at the tender age of five.
Double portrait from the atelier of George Desmarées, c. 1740.

ABSOLUTISMUS, BAROCK UND AUFKLÄRUNG
Kurfürst Maximilian III. Joseph von Bayern

Kurprinz Maximilian Joseph als Knabe auf einem prächtigen Schimmel reitend.
Der junge Kurprinz wird hier mit Rüstung, Degen und Marschallstab auf kurbettierendem Pferd im Stil eines fürstlichen Feldherrn inszeniert. Im Hintergrund ist die Residenzstadt München zu sehen.
Gemälde eines unbekannten Künstlers, vor 1704.

Electoral Prince Maximilian Joseph as a boy riding a magnificent grey horse.
The young Electoral Prince is staged here in the style of a princely general on a curvetting horse with armour, sword and marshal's baton. The royal seat of Munich can be seen in the background.
Painting by an unknown artist, before 1704.

ABSOLUTISMUS, BAROCK UND AUFKLÄRUNG
Kurfürst Maximilian III. Joseph von Bayern

Schloss Nymphenburg von der Parkseite aus gesehen.
Maximilian III. Joseph führte die Bautätigkeit seines Vaters und Großvaters in Nymphenburg fort. In seine Regierungszeit fällt u. a. die Ausgestaltung des großen Rokokofestsaals sowie die Ansiedelung der noch heute bestehenden Porzellanmanufaktur im Schloss.
Gemälde von Bernado Bellotto, genannt Canaletto, 1761.

Nymphenburg Palace seen from the park side.
Maximilian III Joseph continued his father and grandfather's building work at Nymphenburg. Among other things, the large Rococo ballroom was embellished and the porcelain factory that still exists at the palace today was located there during his reign.
Painting by Bernado Bellotto, named Canaletto, 1761.

ABSOLUTISMUS, BAROCK UND AUFKLÄRUNG
Kurfürst Maximilian III. Joseph von Bayern

Hochzeit im Neudecker Garten in der Münchner Au.
Die dargestellte Hochzeitsgesellschaft entstammt nach Kleidung und Habitus dem gehobenen Bürgertum oder dem niederen Adel. Die Erhebung links ist der Nockherberg, rechts neben den Feiernden fließt der Auer Mühlbach. Die Kirche St. Borromäus (Hintergrund) existiert heute nicht mehr, ebensowenig wie das Jagdschloss Neudeck ob der Au, wo bis 1761 die kurfürstliche Porzellanmanufaktur untergebracht war, bevor sie nach Nymphenburg umzog.
Gemälde von Peter Jakob Horemans, 1747.

Wedding in Neudecker garden in the Munich Au district.
Judging by the clothing and habitus, the wedding party portrayed are either upper bourgeoisie or lower nobility. The elevation on the left is the Nockherberg and the Auer Mühlbach is flowing on the right next to the people celebrating. The St. Borromäus church (background) no longer exists today, nor does the Neudeck ob der Au hunting lodge where the imperial porcelain factory was housed until 1761 when it moved to Nymphenburg.
Painting by Peter Jakob Horemans, 1747.

ABSOLUTISMUS, BAROCK UND AUFKLÄRUNG
Kurfürst Maximilian III. Joseph von Bayern

Kurfürst Maximilian III. Joseph am Ende einer Parforcejagd.
Die Szene zeigt das Ende einer „Hohen Jagd" des kurfürstlichen Hofes; die Jäger scheinen nach der vorangegangenen Anstrengung ins Gespräch vertieft, der Kurfürst auf weißem Pferd überblickt das Geschehen. Jagdhelfer zerlegen das Wild und halten mit Mühe die Hundemeute zurück, die auf ihren Anteil der Beute hofft.
Gemälde eines unbekannten Künstlers, um 1750.

Prince-Elector Maximilian III Joseph at the end of a Parforce hunt.
The scene shows the end of a "big hunt" at the imperial court; the hunters appear to be in deep conversation following the efforts they have just made, while the Prince-Elector is surveying what is happening on a grey horse. Hunting assistants are cutting up the game and holding back with great difficulty the pack of hounds who are hoping for their share of the prey.
Painting by an unknown artist, c. 1750.

Kurfürst Maximilian III. Joseph (1727–1777) zu Pferd.
Gemälde aus der Werkstatt von George Desmarées, um 1755.

Prince-Elector Maximilian III Joseph (1727–1777) on a horse.
Painting from the atelier of George Desmarées, c. 1755.

ABSOLUTISMUS, BAROCK UND AUFKLÄRUNG
Kurfürst Maximilian III. Joseph von Bayern

Kurfürst Maximilian III. Joseph von Bayern (1727–1777) und seine Gemahlin Maria Anna Sophie von Sachsen (1728–1797) im Jagdkostüm. Die beiden Porträts aus gleicher Hand zeigen das Kurfürstenpaar im Kostüm und mit Attributen der Jagd. Auch für fürstliche Damen war es nicht unüblich, am höfischen Jagdvergnügen teilzunehmen. Die Ehe der beiden blieb kinderlos, sodass die altbayerische Linie der Wittelsbacher mit Maximilian III. Joseph schließlich ausstarb.
Porträts Franz Joseph Winter zugeschrieben, um 1750.

Prince-Elector Maximilian III Joseph of Bavaria (1727–1777) and his consort Maria Anna Sophie of Saxony (1728–1797) in hunting attire. Both the portraits painted by the same hand show the electoral couple in hunting attire with hunting accoutrements. It was not uncommon for princely ladies to take part in courtly hunts as well. The couple's marriage remained childless so the old Bavarian line of the House of Wittelsbach ultimately died out with Maximilian III Joseph.
Portraits attributed to Franz Josef Winter, c. 1750.

ABSOLUTISMUS, BAROCK UND AUFKLÄRUNG
Kurfürst Maximilian III. Joseph von Bayern

Kurfürst Maximilian III. Joseph von Bayern (1727 – 1777) mit Hoftheaterintendant Graf Joseph Ferdinand von Salern beim Lever.
Als Lever bezeichnete man den Morgenempfang in den Privaträumen, meist Schlafzimmern, des Hochadels. Nur ausgewählten Personen wurde das Privileg dieser ersten, intimen Audienz gewährt.
Gemälde von George Desmarées, 1755.

Prince-Elector Maximilian III Joseph of Bavaria (1727 – 1777) with Court Theatre Director Count Joseph Ferdinand of Salern at the levee.
The morning receptions in private rooms, mostly bedrooms, of the high nobility were called levees. The privilege of this first, intimate audience was granted only to selected persons.
Painting by George Desmarées, 1755.

Kurfürst Maximilian III. Joseph an der Drechselbank mit Graf Joseph Ferdinand von Salern (Seeau).
Seit Kurfürst Maximilian I. von Bayern nahmen sich alle Kurfürsten dem Kunsthandwerk des Drechselns an, dem schon die Bayernherzöge Wilhelm IV. und Albrecht V. als Zeitvertreib folgten.
Gemälde von Johann Jakob Dorner, 1765.

Prince-Elector Maximilian III Joseph at the woodturning lathe with Count Joseph Ferdinand of Salern (Seeau).
Since Prince-Elector Maximilian I of Bavaria, all the prince-electors took up the craft of woodturning, which even the Bavarian Dukes Wilhelm IV and Albrecht V pursued as a pastime.
Painting by Johann Jakob Dorner, 1765.

ABSOLUTISMUS, BAROCK UND AUFKLÄRUNG
Kurfürst Maximilian III. Joseph von Bayern

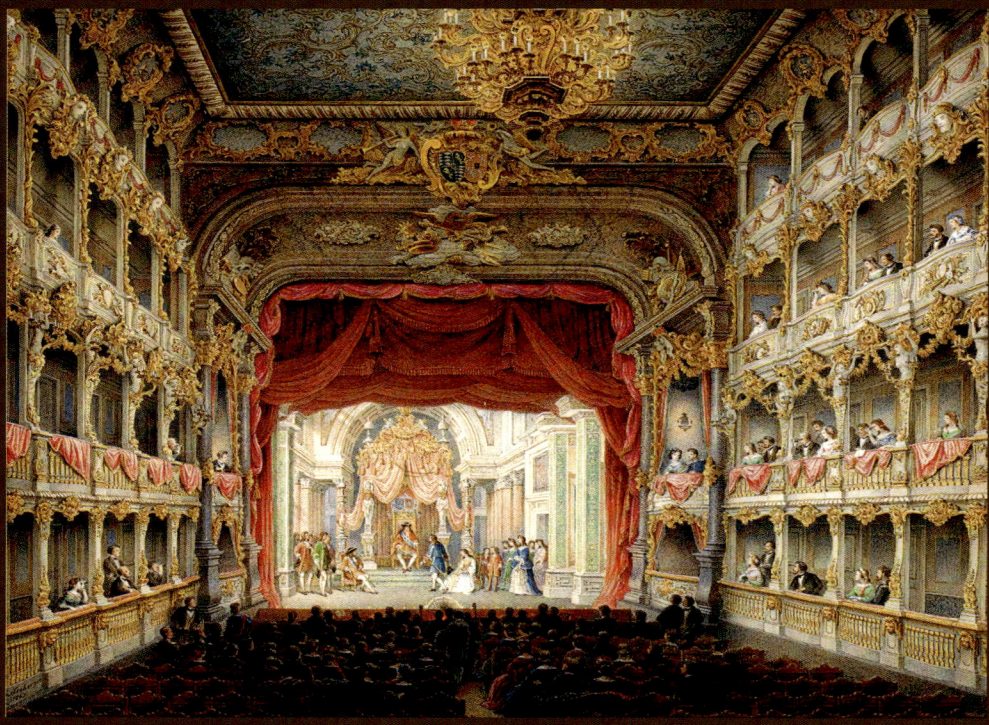

Das im Auftrag Kurfürst Maximilian III. Josephs von François de Cuvilliés 1751–53 erbaute Residenztheater. Als Förderer der Künste ließ Maximilian III. Josef in der Residenz ein prachtvolles Rokoko-Theater erbauen. Die im Zweiten Weltkrieg ausgelagerte Inneneinrichtung überstand die fast vollständige Zerstörung der Münchner Residenz, sodass das Cuvilliés-Theater heute wieder in seiner ursprünglichen Schönheit zugänglich ist.
Gemälde von Gustav Seeberger im Auftrag Ludwigs II. geschaffen, 1867.

The Residence Theatre built by François de Cuvilliés in 1751–53 by order of Prince-Elector Maximilian III Joseph. As a promoter of the arts Maximilian III Joseph had a magnificent Rococo theatre built in the Residenz. The interior design, which was moved out during the Second World War, survived the almost total destruction of the Munich Residenz, so the Cuvilliés Theatre can be enjoyed again today in its original beauty.
Painting created by Gustav Seeberger by order of Ludwig II, 1867.

Kurfürst Maximilian III. Joseph mit seiner Gemahlin Maria Anna Sophie und seiner Schwester Maria Antonia Walpurga. Ein weiteres Vergnügen am Hof Maximilians III. Joseph stellte das Musizieren dar. Der Kurfürst selbst spielte begeistert die Gambe. Auf diesem Bild begleitet ihn seine Gemahlin am Cembalo. Dass eine Reihe bayerischer Kurfürsten große Musiker waren, ist weitgehend unbekannt. Maximilian III. Joseph reichte einst ein von ihm komponiertes „Stabat Mater" bei einem anonymen Wettbewerb in Italien ein und gewann. Dennoch sind seine musikalischen Werke, im Gegensatz zu denen Friedrichs des Großen, heute in Vergessenheit geraten.
Gemälde von Johann Nikolaus de Grooth, 1758.

Prince-Elector Maximilian III Joseph with his wife Maria Anna Sophie and his sister Maria Antonia Walpurga. Another pleasure at the court of Maximilian III Joseph was music. The Prince-Elector himself was a keen viola player. In this painting his wife is accompanying him on the harpsichord. It is largely unknown that a number of Bavarian prince-electors were great musicians. Maximilian III Joseph once submitted one of his own compositions "Stabat Mater" into an anonymous competition in Italy and won. Despite this his musical works, in contrast to those of Friedrich der Große, have been forgotten today.
Painting by Johann Nikolaus de Grooth, 1758.

ABSOLUTISMUS, BAROCK UND AUFKLÄRUNG
Kurfürst Maximilian III. Joseph von Bayern

Ruhmesgenien präsentieren das kurbayerische Wappen. Ausschnitt des Deckengemäldes im Fürstensaal des Klosters Andechs aus der Zeit Kurfürst Maximilian III. Josephs. Das zentrale rechteckige Gemälde mit dem kurbayerischen Wappen wird dort von vier großen, ovalen Medaillons mit Reliefdarstellungen der vier Tugenden umrahmt: Gerechtigkeit, Klugheit, Tapferkeit und – anstelle der vierten Kardinaltugend Mäßigung – Glaube.
Ölgemälde aus dem Umfeld des Münchner Hofmalers Antonio Triva, um 1680/85.

Angels of glory present the electoral Bavarian coat of arms. Extract of ceiling fresco in the Fürstensaal of Andechs Monastery from the era of Prince-Elector Maximilian III Joseph. The central rectangular painting with the electoral Bavarian coat of arms is framed by four large oval medallions with reliefs: justice, wisdom, bravery and instead of temperance, the fourth cardinal virtue, faith.
Oil painting associated with the Munich court painter Antonia Triva, c. 1680/85.

ABSOLUTISMUS, BAROCK UND AUFKLÄRUNG
Die Wittelsbacher als Kirchenfürsten – Fürstbischof Albrecht Sigismund

Wittelsbacher als geistliche Reichsfürsten
Wittelsbacher as clerical Imperial Princes

- **Albrecht (1440–1506),** Pfalzgraf, 1478 Bischof von Straßburg
- **Albrecht Sigismund (1663–1685),** Herzog in Bayern, 1652 Bischof von Freising, 1668 Bischof von Regensburg
- **Alexander Sigmund (1663–1737),** Pfalzgraf, 1690 Bischof von Augsburg
- **Clemens August (1700–1761),** Herzog in Bayern, 1716–1719 Bischof von Regensburg, 1719 Bischof von Münster und Paderborn, 1723 Erzbischof und Kurfürst von Köln, 1724 Bischof von Hildesheim, 1728 Bischof von Osnabrück, 1732 Hoch- und Deutschmeister
- **Ernst (1500–1560),** Herzog in Bayern, 1540–1554 Erzbischof von Salzburg
- **Ernst (1554–1612),** Herzog in Bayern, 1566 Bischof von Freising, 1573 Bischof von Hildesheim, 1581 Bischof von Lüttich, 1583 Erzbischof und Kurfürst von Köln, 1585 Bischof von Münster
- **Ferdinand (1577–1650),** Herzog in Bayern, 1612 Bischof von Hildesheim, Lüttich und Münster, 1612 Erzbischof und Kurfürst von Köln, 1618 Bischof von Paderborn
- **Franz Ludwig (1664–1732),** Pfalzgraf, 1683 Bischof von Breslau, 1694 Fürstpropst von Ellwangen, 1694 Bischof von Worms, 1694 Hoch- und Deutschmeister, 1716–1729 Kurfürst von Trier, 1729 Kurfürst von Mainz
- **Georg (1486–1529),** Pfalzgraf, 1513 Bischof von Speyer
- **Heinrich (1487–1552),** Pfalzgraf, 1521 Fürstpropst von Ellwangen, 1523 Bischof von Worms, 1524/28 Bischof von Utrecht, 1541 Bischof von Freising
- **Johann (um 1429–1475),** Pfalzgraf, 1457–1465 Bischof von Münster, 1464 Erzbischof von Magdeburg
- **Johann III. (1374–1425),** Herzog in Bayern, Graf von Holland, 1390–1418 (resigniert) Bischof von Lüttich
- **Johann III. (1488–1538),** Pfalzgraf, 1507 Bischof von Regensburg
- **Joseph Clemens (1671–1723),** Herzog in Bayern, 1685 Bischof von Freising, 1688 Erzbischof und Kurfürst von Köln, 1694 Bischof von Lüttich, 1714 Bischof von Hildesheim
- **Johann Theodor (1703–1763),** Herzog in Bayern, 1719 Bischof von Regensburg, 1727 Bischof von Freising, 1744 Bischof von Lüttich, 1746 Kardinal
- **Konrad († 1200),** Graf von Wittelsbach, 1161–1165 und wieder ab 1183 Erzbischof von Mainz, 1165 Kardinal, 1177–1183 Bischof von Salzburg
- **Ludwig Anton (1660–1694),** Pfalzgraf, 1681 Hoch- und Deutschmeister, 1689 Fürstpropst von Ellwangen, 1691 Bischof von Worms
- **Maximilian Heinrich (1621–1688),** Herzog in Bayern, 1650 Erzbischof und Kurfürst von Köln, 1650 Bischof von Hildesheim und Lüttich, 1683 Bischof von Münster
- **Philipp (1480–1541),** Pfalzgraf, 1499 Bischof von Freising
- **Philipp Moritz Maria (1698–1719),** Herzog in Bayern, 1719 Bischof von Münster und Paderborn
- **Philipp Wilhelm (1576–1598),** Herzog in Bayern, 1595 Bischof von Regensburg, 1597 Kardinal
- **Rupprecht (1420–1478),** Pfalzgraf, 1440 Bischof von Straßburg
- **Rupprecht (1461–1507),** Pfalzgraf, 1492 Bischof von Regensburg
- **Rupprecht (1481–1504),** Pfalzgraf, 1495–98 Bischof von Freising (resigniert)

Albrecht Sigismund von Bayern, Fürstbischof von Freising.
Obwohl Albrecht Sigismund, ein Sohn Herzog Albrechts VI., niemals die Priesterweihe empfing, wurde er 1652 Bischof von Freising und 1668 Bischof von Regensburg. Er nahm außerdem weitere kirchliche Ämter als Stiftspropst von Altötting, als Domherr zu Salzburg und Augsburg sowie als Dompropst von Konstanz an.
Gemälde von Benjamin v. Block, um 1675.

Albrecht Sigismund of Bavaria, Prince-Bishop of Freising.
Although Albrecht Sigismund, a son of Duke Albrecht VI, was never ordained as a priest, he became Bishop of Freising in 1652 and Bishop of Regensburg in 1668. He also held other ecclesiastical offices as Provost of Altötting, Canon of Salzburg and Cathedral Provost of Constance.
Painting by Benjamin von Block, c. 1675.

ABSOLUTISMUS, BAROCK UND AUFKLÄRUNG
Die Wittelsbacher als Kirchenfürsten – Fürstbischof Joseph Clemens

Einzug des Fürstbischofs Joseph Clemens in den Dom zu Freising am 19. Juni 1690.
Prinz Joseph Clemens war schon 1688 zum Erzbischof von Köln gewählt worden und hatte somit wie sein Bruder Max Emanuel die Kurwürde inne. Zwei Jahre später nahm er mit dem feierlichen Einzug in Freising das dortige Bistum an. Michael Wening hielt die genaue Anordnung des Zugs sowie die Feierlichkeiten in mehreren Kupferstichen fest.
Kolorierter Kupferstich von Michael Wening, 1691.

Procession of Prince-Bishop Joseph Clemens to the cathedral in Freising on 19 June 1690.
Prince Joseph Clemens had already been elected as Archbishop of Cologne in 1688 and therefore already held the position of elector like his brother Max Emanuel. Two years later he took on the diocese of Freising with his ceremonial entrance procession there. Michael Wening recorded the exact order of the procession as well as the ceremonies in several copperplates.
Coloured copperplate by Michael Wening, 1691.

ABSOLUTISMUS, BAROCK UND AUFKLÄRUNG
Die Wittelsbacher als Kirchenfürsten – Kur-Erzbischof Clemens August

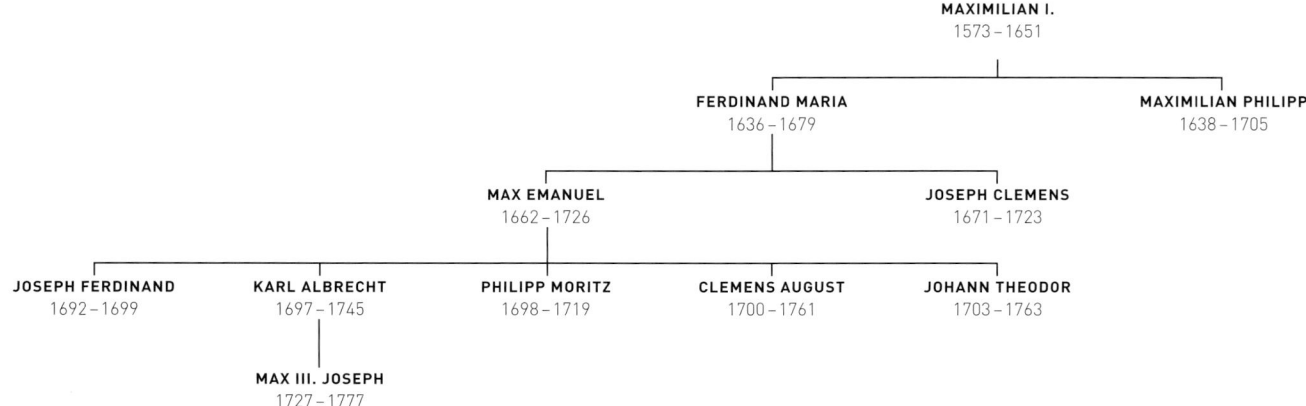

„Konversationsstück": die kurbayerische und kursächsische Familie beim Musizieren und Kartenspiel.
Während des Siebenjährigen Krieges weilte ein Teil der polnischen Königsfamilie sowie des kurfürstlich-sächsischen Hofes in München. Das Bild zeigt u. a. Kurprinz Friedrich Christian von Sachsen (im Rollstuhl), Erzbischof Clemens August von Köln (Cello spielend) sowie Kurfürst Maximilian III. Joseph (am Tisch, vor ihm ein Jagdhund).
Gemälde von Peter Jakob Horemans, 1761.

"Conversation piece": the electoral Bavarian and Saxon family making music and playing cards.
During the Seven Years' War some of the Polish royal family and electoral Saxon court spent time in Munich. The picture shows among other things the Electoral Prince Friedrich Christian of Saxony (in a wheelchair), Archbishop Clemens August of Cologne (playing the piano) and Elector Maximilian III Joseph (at the table with a hunting hound in front of him).
Painting by Peter Jakob Horemans, 1761.

ABSOLUTISMUS, BAROCK UND AUFKLÄRUNG
Die Wittelsbacher als Kirchenfürsten – Kur-Erzbischof Clemens August

Prinz Clemens August von Bayern als Fürstbischof von Münster und Paderborn 1719.
Der vierte Sohn Kurfürst Max II. Emanuels aus zweiter Ehe erlangte früh hohe geistliche Würden: Bereits im Alter von 19 Jahren war er Fürstbischof von Münster und Paderborn. Als Clemens August I. regierte er ab 1723 als Erzbischof und Kurfürst zu Köln. Er sollte der letzte Wittelsbacher sein, der diesen Titel trug.
Gemälde von Joseph Vivien, 1717/19.

Prince Clemens August of Bavaria as Prince-Bishop of Münster and Paderborn 1719.
The fourth son of Elector Max II Emanuel from his second marriage gained high priestly office early on: at the age of 19 he was already Prince-Bishop of Münster and Paderborn. As Clemens August I he reigned as Archbishop and Elector of Cologne from 1723. He was to be the last member of the House of Wittelsbach to hold this title.
Painting by Joseph Vivien, 1717/19.

ABSOLUTISMUS, BAROCK UND AUFKLÄRUNG
Die Wittelsbacher als Kirchenfürsten – Kur-Erzbischof Clemens August

Clemens August erteilt seinen ersten bischöflichen Segen in der Kirche Santa Maria della Quercia bei Viterbo. Obwohl Clemens August schon 1723 die Kölner Kurwürde erhalten hatte, wurde er erst 1725 zum Priester und 1727 durch den Papst zum Bischof geweiht.
Gemälde von Francesco Fernandi, genannt Imperiali, 1727.

Clemens August issues his first blessing as a bishop in the Santa Maria della Quercia church near Viterbo. Although Clemens August had already received the Cologne electorship in 1723, he only became a priest in 1725 and was ordained as a bishop by the Pope in 1727.
Painting by Francesco Fernandi, named Imperiali, 1727.

Kurfürst Clemens August auf der Falkenjagd bei Schloss Falkenlust, Brühl.
Zwischen 1729 und 1737 ließ Clemens August im Augustusburger Schlosspark durch den kurbayerischen Hofbaumeister Cuvilliés ein kleines, jedoch kostbar ausgestattetes Jagdschloss erbauen. Nach der Jagd pflegte die Hofgesellschaft in den intimen Räumlichkeiten von Schloss Falkenlust zu soupieren.
Gemälde von François Rousseau,

Elector Clemens August on a falcon hunt at Falkenlust Palace, Brühl.
Between 1729 and 1737 Clemens August had a small but elaborately furnished hunting lodge built at the Augustusburg palace park by the electoral Bavarian court architect Cuvilliés. After the hunt, court society dined in the intimate rooms of Falkenlust palace.
Painting by François Rousseau, 1763/64.

Kur-Erzbischof Clemens August mit Maximilian Graf von Preysing und Graf von Seinsheim als Falkenjäger.
Die Falkenjagd gehörte als hochadeliges Privileg zur prächtigen Hofhaltung Clemens Augusts am Rhein und galt als seine besondere Leidenschaft.
Gemälde nach Peter Jakob Horemans, Künstler unbekannt, um 1735.

Archbishop-Elector Clemens August with Maximilian Count of Preysing and Court of Seinsheim as falconer.
The falcon hunt was a privilege of the upper nobility that was part of Clemens August's magnificent household on the Rhine and it was considered to be a great passion of his.
Painting based on Peter Jakob Horemans, unknown artist, c. 1735.

ABSOLUTISMUS, BAROCK UND AUFKLÄRUNG
Die Wittelsbacher als Kirchenfürsten – Kur-Erzbischof Clemens August

Einzug Clemens Augusts in Frankfurt am Main anlässlich der Krönung seines Bruders Karl VII. Albrecht zum Kaiser, 1742.
Als Bruder des designierten Kaisers und Kurfürst von Köln zog Clemens August mit großem Prunk zur Krönung nach Frankfurt. Sein Hofstaat soll den Karl Albrechts an Zahl noch übertroffen haben.
Kolorierter Kupferstich von Michael Rößler, um 1742.

The arrival of Clemens August in Frankfurt am Main on the occasion of his brother Karl VII Albrecht's coronation as Emperor, 1742.
As the brother of the designated Emperor and Elector of Cologne, Clemens August arrived for the coronation in Frankfurt with a grand procession and great pomp. His court household supposedly exceeded Karl Albrecht's in number.
Coloured copperplate by Michael Rößler, c. 1742.

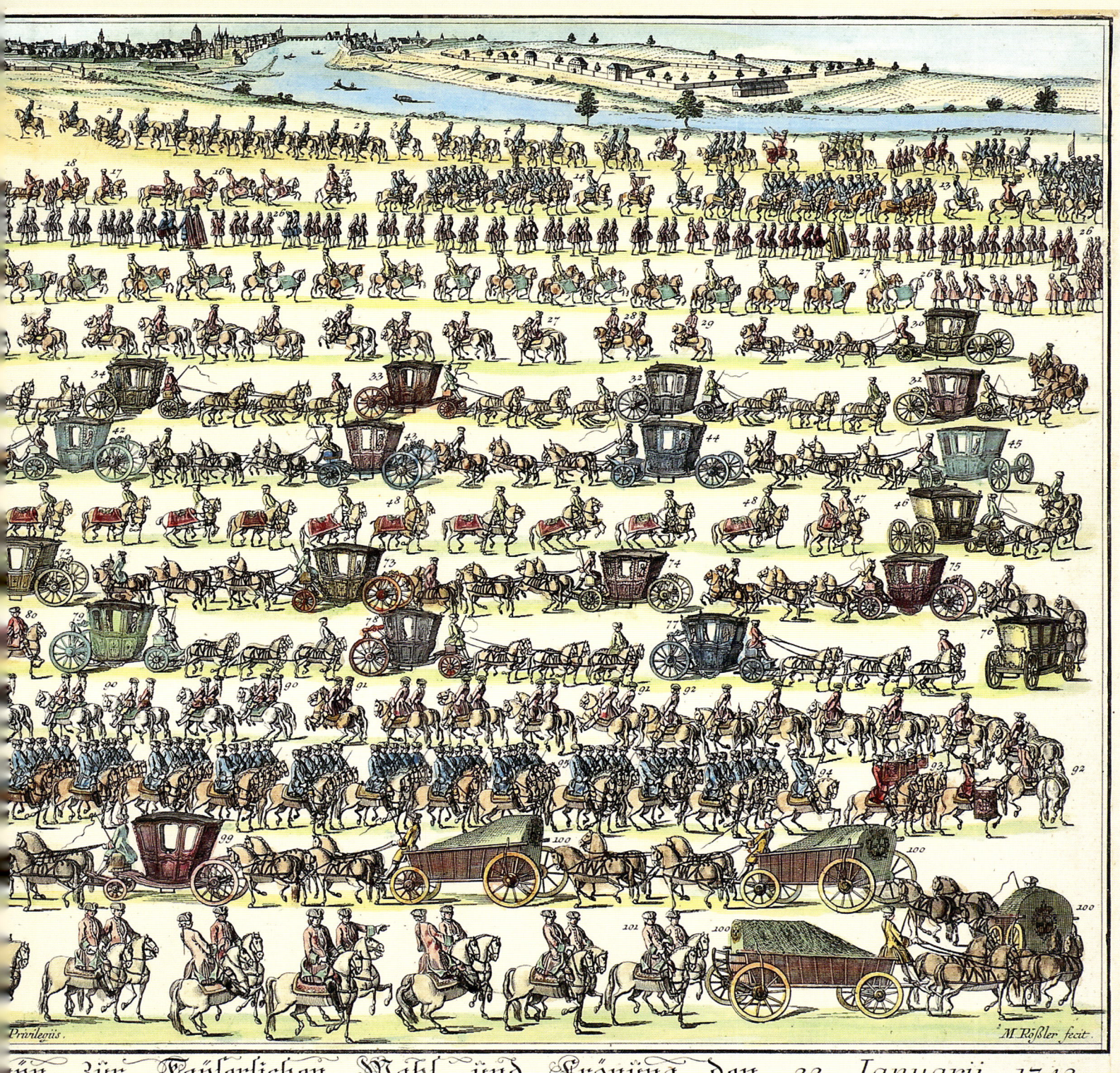

...yn zür Kayserlichen Wahl und Crönüng den 22. Ianuarij 1742.

ABSOLUTISMUS, BAROCK UND AUFKLÄRUNG
Die Wittelsbacher als Kirchenfürsten – Kur-Erzbischof Clemens August

Maskentreiben im Hoftheater zu Bonn unter Kur-Erzbischof Clemens August.
Clemens August herrschte nicht nur als geistliches Oberhaupt über das Erzbistum Köln, sondern ganz im Stil seiner Zeit auch als prunkliebender weltlicher Landesfürst. Das Bildnis eines Maskentreibens der kurbischöflichen Hofgesellschaft gilt als älteste Darstellung eines rheinischen Maskenballs.
Gemälde von François Rousseau, 1754.

Masquerade ball at the Court Theatre in Bonn under Archbishop-Elector Clemens August.
Clemens August ruled over the archdiocese of Cologne not only as an ecclesiastical leader but also – completely in keeping with the style of that time – as a pomp-loving, secular Prince of the Land. This painting of an electoral court society masked ball is considered to be the oldest representation of a masked ball on the Rhine.
Painting by François Rousseau, 1754.

ABSOLUTISMUS, BAROCK UND AUFKLÄRUNG
Die Wittelsbacher als Kirchenfürsten – Kur-Erzbischof Clemens August

Kurfürst Clemens August mit der Teetasse.
Gemälde von Joseph Vivien im Lackkabinett des Schlosses Falkenlust in Brühl, vor 1723.

Elector Clemens August with tea cup.
Painting by Joseph Vivien in a lacquer cabinet at Falkenlust Palace in Brühl, before 1723.

Festbankett in der Casa Nani, Venedig, zu Ehren Clemens Augusts, 1755.
Miniatur von Pietro Longhi, 1755.

Banquet at Casa Nani, Venice, in honour of Clemens August, 1755.
Miniature by Pietro Longhi, 1755.

ABSOLUTISMUS, BAROCK UND AUFKLÄRUNG
Die Wittelsbacher als Kirchenfürsten – Fürstbischof Johann Theodor

Fürstbischof Johann Theodor von Bayern (1703–1763).
Johann Theodor folgte seinem älteren Bruder Clemens August auf die Bischofssitze von Regensburg und Freising nach. Rechts das Wappen des Herzogs von Bayern und links das Wappen des Bistums Freising mit dem Mohrenhaupt.
Kupferstich aus dem Hochstiftskalender Freising, unbekannter Künstler, 1728.

Prince-Bishop Johann Theodor of Bavaria (1703–1763).
Johann Theodor succeeded his older brother Clemens August in the episcopal sees of Regensburg and Freising. On the right is the Duke of Bavaria's coat of arms and on the left the diocese of Freising's coat of arms with the Maure.
Copperplate from Freising cathedral chapter's calendar, artist unknown, 1728.

The Palatine Lines

As well as the old-Bavarian line, the various Palatine lines with their thoroughly striking personalities flourished until late in the 18th century: Elector Ottheinrich (1502–1559), who built the Ottheinrich Building of Heidelberg Castle and extended the old castle complex in Neuburg; Wolfgang Wilhelm (1578–1653), who assumed his Jülich inheritance in Düsseldorf and commissioned large altar paintings from Peter Paul Rubens for Neuburg; the three kings of Sweden – Karl X Gustav (1622–1660), Karl XI (1655–1697) and Karl XII (1682–1718) – from the branch line of Zweibrücken-Kleeburg; Princess Elisabeth Charlotte (1652–1722), granddaughter of Elector Friedrich V, wife of Duke Philippe of Orléans, brother of Ludwig XIV of France, known as "Liselotte von der Pfalz".

And another special feature of the house of Wittelsbach's status in the empire should be pointed out: the rulers of the ecclesiastical principalities, who take on a hybrid role in that, as bishops and territorial princes, they were religious and worldly leaders at the same time. 25 male members of the house of Wittelsbach – from both the Bavarian and the Palatine line – managed to gain the dignity of such an ecclesiastical imperial principality before the end of the old empire: later-born sons were maintained in a manner befitting their rank, and the house's imperial political position was thereby enhanced.

In 1724, the Wittelsbacher Hausunion was agreed, which envisaged an alternation of succession between the old-Bavarian and Palatine lines. The whole panorama of Wittelsbach rule in the empire around this year appears impressive enough: in the Electorate of Bavaria, which also included the Upper Palatinate, Elector Max Emanuel had had his rights reinstated; the electoral dignity of the Palatinate was held by Elector Karl III Philipp (1661–1742), who was at the same time Elector of Jülich and Berg and the Duke of Palatinate-Neuburg; Elector Clemens August (1700–1761) reigned in Cologne, the son of Max Emanuel, Elector Franz Ludwig (1664–1732), a brother of Karl III Philipp, ruled Trier; the episcopal thrones of Breslau, Worms, Munster, Osnabruck, Hildesheim and Regensburg were also occupied by members of the house. Four of nine electoral hats were worn by members of the house of Wittelsbach; it was no longer possible to choose a king or emperor against the will of the Wittelsbach family; in the West and South of the empire no other dynasty could still compete with the house of Wittelsbach.

Die Pfälzer Linien

Neben der altbayerischen Linie blühten bis ins ausgehende 18. Jahrhundert die diversen pfälzischen Linien mit ihren durchaus markanten Persönlichkeiten: Kurfürst Ottheinrich (1502–1559), der den Ottheinrichsbau des Heidelberger Schlosses errichtete und die alte Schloßanlage in Neuburg erweiterte; Wolfgang Wilhelm (1578–1653), der sein Jülicher Erbe in Düsseldorf antrat und für Neuburg große Altarbilder bei Peter Paul Rubens bestellte; die drei schwedischen Könige – Karl X. Gustav (1622–1660), Karl XI. (1655–1697) und Karl XII. (1682–1718) – aus der Nebenlinie Zweibrücken-Kleeburg; Prinzessin Elisabeth Charlotte (1652–1722), Enkelin von Kurfürst Friedrich V., Gemahlin des Herzogs Philippe von Orléans, des Bruders Ludwigs XIV. von Frankreich, bekannt als „Liselotte von der Pfalz".

Und auf ein weiteres Spezifikum der wittelsbachischen Stellung im Reich ist hinzuweisen; es geht dabei um die Inhaber der geistlichen Fürstentümer, die eine Zwitterstellung einnahmen insofern, als sie Bischöfe und Territorialfürsten, geistliche und weltliche Herren in einem waren. 25 männlichen Mitgliedern des Hauses Wittelsbach – der bayerischen wie der pfälzischen Linie – gelang es bis zum Ende des Alten Reiches, die Würde eines solchen geistlichen Reichsfürsten zu erringen: Nachgeborenen Söhnen konnte eine standesgemäße Versorgung verschafft, die reichspolitische Stellung des Hauses dadurch erhöht werden.

1724 wurde die Wittelsbacher Hausunion vereinbart, die die wechselseitige Sukzession der altbayerischen und der pfälzischen Linie vorsah. Wie sich um dieses Jahr das ganze Panorama wittelsbachischer Herrschaft im Reich darstellte, erscheint imposant genug: Im Kurfürstentum Bayern, wozu auch die Oberpfalz zählte, war Kurfürst Max Emanuel wieder in seine Rechte eingesetzt worden; die pfälzische Kurwürde lag bei Kurfürst Karl III. Philipp (1661–1742), der gleichzeitig Jülich und Berg innehatte und Herzog von Pfalz-Neuburg war; in Köln regierte Kurfürst Clemens August (1700–1761), der Sohn von Max Emanuel, in Trier Kurfürst Franz Ludwig (1664–1732), ein Bruder von Karl III. Philipp; die Bischofsstühle von Breslau, Worms, Münster, Osnabrück, Hildesheim und Regensburg waren gleichfalls in wittelsbachischer Hand. Vier von neun Kurhüten wurden von Mitgliedern des Hauses Wittelsbach getragen; gegen den Willen der Wittelsbacher konnte man keinen König, keinen Kaiser mehr wählen; im Westen und Süden des Reichs konnte keine andere Dynastie mit dem Haus Wittelsbach mehr konkurrieren.

DIE PFÄLZER LINIEN
Alte Pfälzische Kurlinie

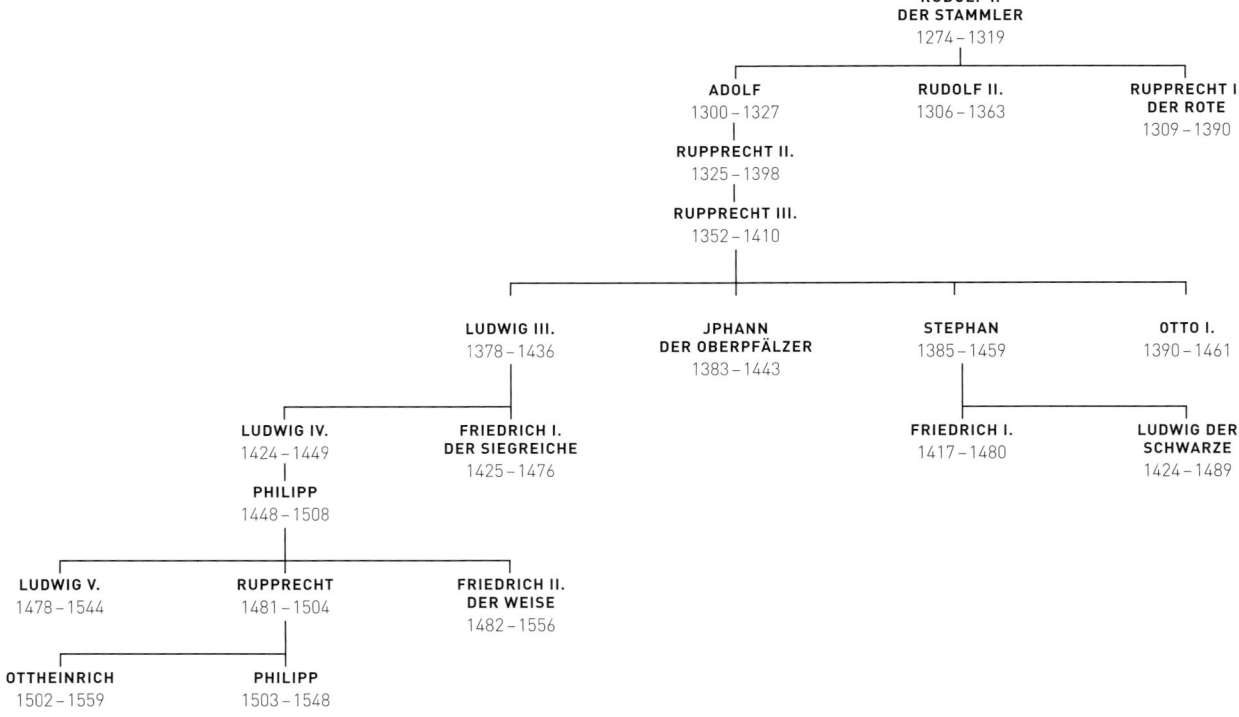

Herzog Rudolf I. von Bayern (gen. der Stammler, 1294–1317), Pfalzgraf bei Rhein, mit seiner Gemahlin Mechthild von Nassau sowie sein Sohn Adolf (gen. der Redliche, 1300–1327) mit seiner Gemahlin Irmengard von Oettingen. Dieser und die Bildteile auf der folgenden Doppelseite entstammen einer der berühmtesten Ahnenreihen aus gotischer Zeit, die sich in der Heidelberger Residenz sowie seit dem 17. Jahrhundert als Kopie im Amberger Schloss befand. Zur Verdeutlichung ihres Herrschaftsanspruchs zogen in elf monumentalen Wandgemälden die Regenten der Pfälzer Linie des Hauses Wittelsbach samt ihren Ehefrauen vorüber. Der Zyklus hat sich lediglich in einer farbigen Miniaturkopie auf Pergament erhalten.
Gouachemalerei auf Pergament von Anna Maria Johanna Wisger und Eva Margretha Wisger, 1772/73.

Duke Rudolf I of Bavaria (named the Stutterer, 1294–1317), Count Palatine of the Rhine, with his consort Mechthild of Nassau, as well as his son Adolf (named the Upright, 1300–1327) with his consort Irmengard of Oettingen. This picture part and those on the following double page come from one of the most famous ancestral lines from Gothic times, which was found in the Heidelberg Residence, with a copy of it also being kept in the Amberg Palace since the 17th century. To make clear their claim to rulership, the rulers of the Palatine line of the House of Wittelsbach along with their wives passed by in eleven monumental wall paintings. Only a miniature colour copy of the cycle on parchment has survived.
Gouache painting on parchment by Anna Maria Johanna Wisger and Eva Margretha Wisger, 1772/73.

Rudolf sein Sohn die Chur besaß
Der Keyser Ludwigs bruder was
Sein Weib von Nassaw Königs Kindt
Der Pfaltz vil weißheit daher dient.

Adolff zu Kurfürst was geborn
Mit Dorheit hat er die verlorn
Sein bruder Ruprecht war der wert
Von Oting eins Weibs er begert.

ist nach dem Original welches 6. Schue lang, 3. Schue hoch: accurat Copiret worden, von A: Maria Johanna Wisgerin. 1773.

Irmengard

DIE PFÄLZER LINIEN
Alte Pfälzische Kurlinie

Ruprecht I. (gen. der Rote, 1309–1390), Pfalzgraf und Kurfürst von der Pfalz, mit Elisabeth von Namur und Beatrix von Berg. Daneben Ruprecht II. (gen. der Harte, 1325–1398), Pfalzgraf und Kurfürst von der Pfalz, mit seiner Gemahlin Beatrix von Aragon-Sizilien.
Teil der Heidelberger bzw. Amberger Ahnenreihe.
Gouachemalerei auf Pergament von Anna Maria Johanna Wisger und Eva Margretha Wisger, 1772/73.

Ruprecht I (named the Red, 1309–1390), Count Palatine and Prince-Elector of the Palatinate, with Elisabeth of Namur and Beatrix of Berg. Beside them is Ruprecht II (named the Severe, 1325–1398), Count Palatine and Prince-Elector of the Palatinate, with his consort Beatrix of Aragon-Sicily.
Part of the Heidelberg respectively Amberg ancestral lines.
Gouache painting on parchment by Anna Maria Johanna Wisger and Eva Margretha Wisger, 1772/73.

Ruprecht III., Pfalzgraf und Kurfürst von der Pfalz (1352–1410, von 1400 bis 1410 als römisch-deutscher König Ruprecht I.), und seine Gemahlin Elisabeth von Nürnberg. Daneben Ludwig III. (gen. der Bärtige, 1378–1436) mit seinen Gemahlinnen Blanka von England und Mechthild von Savoyen.
Teil der Heidelberger bzw. Amberger Ahnenreihe.
Gouachemalerei auf Pergament von Anna Maria Johanna Wisger und Eva Margretha Wisger, 1772/73.

Ruprecht III, Count Palatine and Prince-Elector of the Palatinate (1352–1410, from 1400 to 1410 as Roman-German King Ruprecht I) and his consort Elisabeth of Nuremberg. Beside them is Ludwig III (named the Bearded, 1378–1436) with his consorts Blanka of England and Mechthild of Savoy.
Part of the Heidelberg respectively Amberg ancestral lines.
Gouache painting on parchment by Anna Maria Johanna Wisger and Eva Margretha Wisger, 1772/73.

Ruprecht den man den Roten nandt
Die Pfaltz bracht er in gulen standt
Zwo furstin waren im auserkorn
Von Namur und Berg geboren.

Ruprecht von hert was Klein genandt
Drey freidt sich eins tag vnterwandt
Zwen waren gewin vnd einer verlust
Von Sicilien der Künigen gelüst.

ist accurat nach dem Original, welches 5. Schu: 5. Zoll Lang, und 3. Schu hoch ist, Copiret worden von A: Maria Johanna Wisgerin.
x nach bayrischer Maas.

Ruprecht König des Römischen Reich
An Würden hoch was hart sein gleich
Von Nürnberg ein Burckgrewin
Was sein vermelte Königin.

Ludwig der Bärtig genant Gottesfreint
Hat in die Pfaltz vil nütz gezeünt
Er vermehlt ein Englisch Königin Vnd vo Sophoy ei Princessin.

ist nach dem Original welches 5. Schu 1. Zoll Lang und 3. Schu hoch: accurat Copiret worden von Anna Maria Johanna Wisgerin 1772.

DIE PFÄLZER LINIEN
Alte Pfälzische Kurlinie

Wappen von Kurfürst Ruprecht III. (nachmals König Ruprecht I.) von der Pfalz.
Daneben (rechts) das Wappen von Johann Kämmerer von Worms, genannt Dalberg, darunter jene der oberpfälzischen Orte Parsberg und Lichteneck.
Seite aus dem Bruderschaftsbuch von St. Christoph am Arlberg, o. J.

Coat of arms of Prince-Elector Ruprecht III (later King Ruprecht I) of the Palatinate.
Next to it (to the right) is the coat of arms of Johann Kämmerer of Worms, named Dalberg, while underneath are those of Parsberg and Lichteneck (Upper Palatinate).
Page from the Book of the Brotherhood of St. Christoph am Arlberg, undated.

König Ruprecht I. als geharnischter Ritter (1352–1410).
Das Bildnis König Ruprechts I. leitet den reich verzierten Stammbaum Philipps des Aufrichtigen (Kurfürst von der Pfalz, 1448–1508) und seiner Gemahlin Margarethe von Bayern-Landshut ein. Die mit zahlreichen Wappenbildern geschmückte Ahnenreihe diente der dynastischen Selbstlegitimation und repräsentativen Darstellung des Fürsten nach außen.
Kolorierte Schablonenzeichnung von Herold Hermann von Bruninghaus, um 1520.

King Ruprecht I as a knight in armour (1352–1410).
The portrait of King Ruprecht I introduces the richly decorated genealogy of Philipp the Upright (Prince-Elector of the Palatinate, 1448–1508) and his consort Margarethe of Bavaria-Landshut. The ancestral line decorated with numerous heraldic figures was conducive to dynastic self-legitimisation and external representative presentation of the prince.
Coloured stencil drawing by harbinger Hermann of Bruninghaus, c. 1520.

DIE PFÄLZER LINIEN
Alte Pfälzische Kurlinie

Doppelgrabdenkmal von König Ruprecht I., vormalig als Kurfürst von der Pfalz Ruprecht III. (1352–1410), und seiner Gemahlin Elisabeth (1358–1411) in der Hl.-Geist-Kirche in Heidelberg.

Das Doppelgrabmal ist das einzige, das in der Kirche noch erhalten ist. Der Fürst wurde im Kölner Dom am 6. Januar 1401 gekrönt, nachdem er dem in Jahre 1400 abgesetzten König Wenzel, einem Sohn Karls IV., auf den Thron gefolgt war. Er wurde nicht mit der tatsächlichen Kaiserkrone gekrönt, die heute in Wien aufbewahrt wird. Stattdessen lieh man sich in Frankreich zu diesem Akt eine Krone aus. König Ruprecht I. war am 21. August 1400 nach der Wahl durch die geistlichen Fürsten zum König proklamiert worden.
Holzstich um 1880 nach dem Original einer Grabplatte aus Sandstein einer unbekannten Werkstatt, vor 1419.

Double gravestone of King Ruprecht I, formerly as Prince-Elector of the Palatinate Ruprecht III (1352–1410) and his consort Elisabeth (1358–1411) in the Church of the Holy Spirit in Heidelberg.

The double gravestone is the only thing still intact in the church. The prince was crowned King in Cologne Cathedral on 6 January 1401 after he had followed King Wenzel, a son of Karl IV who was dethroned in 1400, onto the throne. He was not crowned with the actual Emperor's crown, which is kept in Vienna today. Instead, a crown was borrowed in France for this act. King Ruprecht I had been proclaimed King on 21 August 1400 after he was elected by the clerical princes.
Wood engraving c. 1880 based on the original: grave slab made of sandstone by an unknown atelier, before 1419.

DIE PFÄLZER LINIEN
Alte Pfälzische Kurlinie

Kurfürst Ludwig III. von der Pfalz bei der Hinrichtung von Jan Hus.
Während des Konzils von Konstanz vertrat Ludwig III. von der Pfalz, der Sohn des alten Königs Ruprecht I., als Protektor des Konzils König Sigismund. Er überwachte somit den Vollzug der durch das Konzil getroffenen Verurteilungen, so auch die Verbrennung des böhmischen Reformators Jan Hus. Zu erkennen ist der Kurfürst an der Fahne mit dem gevierten Wappenschild der pfälzischen Wittelsbacher.
Buchmalerei aus einer Miniaturen-Handschrift des Klosters St. Gallen bei Villingen, 1465.

Prince-Elector Ludwig III of the Palatinate at the execution of Jan Hus.
During the Council of Constance, Ludwig III of the Palatinate, the son of the former king Ruprecht I, represented King Sigismund as protector of the Council. He thus supervised the execution of the judgments of the Council, including the burning of Bohemian reformer Jan Hus. The Prince-Elector can be recognised by the flag with the quarterly parted coat of arms of the Palatine line of the House of Wittelsbach.
Illumination from a miniature manuscript of the Abbey of St. Gall near Villingen, 1465.

DIE PFÄLZER LINIEN
Alte Pfälzische Kurlinie

Votivbild im Lehenbuch des Kurfürsten Friedrich I. des „Siegreichen".
Das Lehnsbuch verzeichnet alle aktiven Lehen, die Friedrich I. (1425–1476) an seine Vasallen vergab, sowie die passiven Lehen, die er selbst inne hatte. Zugleich dokumentiert die prächtige Ausführung des Buches den fast königglichen Machtanspruch des Pfalzgrafen. Das hier wiedergegebene Blatt zeigt ihn, beschützt von den Aposteln Petrus und Philippus, in Anbetung Marias und des Jesuskindes.
Buchmalerei eines unbekannten Künstlers, 1471.

Votive painting in the fief book of Prince-Elector Friedrich I the "Victorious".
The fief book recorded all the active fees that Friedrich I (1425–1476) issued to his vassals, as well as the passive fees that he held himself. At the same time, the magnificent design of the book documents the almost royal claim to power of the Count Palatine. The page reproduced here shows him, protected by the Apostles Peter and Philippus, worshipping Mary and baby Jesus.
Illumination of an unknown artist, 1471.

Das „Heidelberger Mahl".
Kurfürst Friedrich I. feiert seinen Sieg in der Schlacht bei Seckenheim am 30. Juni 1462. Da er sich die Pfalzgrafen- und Kurwürde durch Arrogation (Adoption eines Neffen) angeeignet und somit gegen das Reichsrecht verstoßen hatte, führte er ständige Fehden gegen die angrenzenden Fürstentümer. In Seckenheim schlug er Bischof Georg von Metz, Graf Ulrich von Württemberg und Markgraf Karl von Baden. Sein Sieg sicherte der Pfalz die politische Vormachtstellung im Reich.
Holzschnitt von Christoph Schwitzer, Mitte des 16. Jahrhunderts.

The "Heidelberg Meal".
Prince-Elector Friedrich I celebrates his victory in the Battle of Seckenheim on 30 June 1462. Since he had acquired count palatine and electoral dignity by means of arrogation (adoption of a nephew) and had thus infringed upon imperial law, he led constant feuds against the neighbouring principalities. In Seckenheim, he defeated Bishop Georg of Metz, Count Ulrich of Württemberg and Margrave Karl of Baden. His victory secured the Palatinate political hegemony in the empire.
Woodcarving by Christoph Schwitzer, mid-16th century.

DIE PFÄLZER LINIEN
Alte Pfälzische Kurlinie

Unbekannter geharnischter Ritter (Pfalzgraf bei Rhein) mit geviertem wittelsbachischen Wappenschild.
Die Darstellung des namenlosen Ritters im Stammbaum Philipps des Aufrichtigen und seiner Gemahlin Margarethe zeigt auf der Pferdedecke das gevierte Wappen der Wittelsbacher mit dem goldenen Pfälzischen Löwen auf schwarzem Grund, den weiß-blauen Rauten (vormals Grafen von Bogen) und dem roten Kurschild in der Mitte.
Kolorierte Schablonenzeichnung von Herold Hermann von Bruninghaus, um 1520.

Unknown knight in armour (Count Palatine of the Rhine) with a quarterly parted Wittelsbach coat of arms.
The presentation of the nameless knight in the genealogy of Philipp the Upright and his consort Margarethe shows on the horse blanket the quarterly parted coat of arms of the House of Wittelsbach with the golden Palatine Lion on a black background, the white-blue lozenges (formerly Counts of Bogen) and the red electoral shield in the middle.
Coloured stencil drawing by harbinger Hermann von Bruninghaus, c. 1520.

Pfalzgraf Ruprecht (1481 – 1504) mit seiner Gemahlin Elisabeth von Bayern-Landshut (1478 – 1504).
Im Hintergrund des Bildes sind ein brennendes Dorf, eine Burgruine und kämpfende Truppen zu sehen. Das Kriegsgeschehen verweist auf den Landshuter Erbfolgekrieg. Georg der Reiche hatte seine Tochter Elisabeth und seinen Schwiegersohn Ruprecht entgegen den Wittelsbacher Hausverträgen als Erben eingesetzt, sodass Herzog Albrecht IV. von Bayern-München gegen sie ins Feld zog.
Radierung von Jost Amman, um 1581/1583.

Count Palatine Ruprecht (1481 – 1504) with his consort Elisabeth of Bavaria-Landshut (1478 – 1504).
In the background of the image, a burning village, the ruins of a castle and fighting troops can be seen. The warfare refers to the War of the Succession of Landshut. Georg der Reiche had appointed his daughter Elisabeth and his son-in-law Ruprecht as his heirs contrary to the treaties of the House of Wittelsbach, causing Duke Albrecht IV of Bavaria-Munich to launch warfare against them.
Etching by Jost Amman, c. 1581/1583.

DIE PFÄLZER LINIEN
Alte Pfälzische Kurlinie

Reiterbildnis des Kurfürsten Friedrich II. (1482–1556).
Der Kurfürst ist hier als Kriegsherr dargestellt. Er nahm zwischen 1529 und 1532 an den Türkenkriegen teil – das Reiterbildnis entstammt einer Sammlung von Drucken zu den Schlachten bei Wien. Über dem Ritter prangen das Wappen des Pfalzgrafen bei Rhein (links) und das des Herzogs von Bayern (rechts), verbunden durch die Collane des Ordens vom Goldenen Vlies.
Kolorierter Holzschnitt von Michael Ostendorfer, 1534.

Knight portrait of Prince-Elector Friedrich II (1482–1556).
The Prince-Elector is here presented as a warlord. He participated in the Ottoman Wars between 1529 and 1532 – the knight portrait comes from a collection of prints related to the battles at Vienna. The coat of arms of the Count Palatine of the Rhine (left) and that of the Duke of Bavaria (right) are displayed above the knight, linked by the collar of the Order of the Golden Fleece.
Coloured woodcarving by Michael Ostendorfer, 1534.

Kurfürst Friedrich II. von der Pfalz (1482–1556).
Friedrich war der vierte Sohn von Kurfürst Philipp und seiner Gemahlin Margarethe von Bayern-Landshut. Nach dem Tod seines Bruders Ludwig V. übernahm er 1544 das Kurfürstentum. Da er selbst ebenfalls kinderlos blieb, folgte ihm sein Neffe Ottheinrich nach. Bessers Gemälde zeigt Friedrich im Alter von etwa 60 Jahren.
Ölgemälde von Hans Besser, 1545.

Prince-Elector Friedrich II of the Palatinate (1482–1556).
Friedrich was the fourth son of Prince-Elector Philipp and his consort Margarethe of Bavaria-Landshut. After the death of his brother Ludwig V, he assumed rulership of the electorate in 1544. Since he remained childless himself, he was succeeded by his nephew Ottheinrich. Besser's painting shows Friedrich at the age of approximately 60.
Oil painting by Hans Besser, 1545.

DIE PFÄLZER LINIEN
Linie Zweibrücken-Veldenz

Pfalzgraf Ludwig II. zu Zweibrücken-Veldenz (1502–1532) mit seiner Familie und seinem Bruder Ruprecht. Ludwig II. starb bereits mit 30 Jahren. Sein Sohn Wolfgang aus der Ehe mit Elisabeth von Hessen begründete durch seine Nachkommen u. a. die pfälzischen Linien Neuburg-Hilpoltstein und Zweibrücken.
Kopie nach einem Gemälde von Peter Gertner, nach 1532.

Count Palatine Ludwig II of Zweibrücken-Veldenz (1502–1532) with his family and his brother Ruprecht. Ludwig II already died at the age of 30. Through his descendents, his son Wolfgang from his marriage with Elisabeth of Hesse established lines including the Palatine lines of Neuburg-Hilpoltstein and Zweibrücken.
Copy based on a painting by Peter Gertner, after 1532.

DIE PFÄLZER LINIEN
Linie Pfalz-Neuburg (I)

**Pfalzgräfin Susanna
von Neuburg (1502–1543).**
Die Tochter Herzog Albrechts IV.
von Bayern heiratete nach dem Tod
ihres ersten Gemahls Kasimir von
Brandenburg-Kulmbach 1529
Pfalzgraf Ottheinrich.
Gemälde von Bartel Beham, 1533.

**Countess Palatine Susanna
of Neuburg (1502–1543).**
The daughter of Duke Albrecht IV
of Bavaria married Count Palatine
Ottheinrich in 1529 after the death
of her first consort Kasimir of
Brandenburg-Kulmbach.
Painting by Bartel Beham, 1533.

Pfalzgraf Ottheinrich von Neuburg (1502–1559), ab 1556 auch Kurfürst von der Pfalz.
Ottheinrich war ein Enkel Herzog Georgs von Bayern-Landshut. Das Bildnis Behams zeigt ihn im Alter von 31 Jahren. Es ist Teil einer bedeutenden Porträtserie, die Herzog Wilhelm IV. von Bayern von seinen nächsten Verwandten in Auftrag gab. Das Bild des Pfalzgrafen ist in direktem Bezug zu dem seiner Gemahlin zu setzen, das die bayerische Linie der Familie betont, während das Ottheinrichs die pfälzische Linie repräsentiert.
Gemälde von Barthel Beham, 1533.

Count Palatine Ottheinrich of Neuburg (1502–1559), from 1556 also Prince-Elector of the Palatinate.
Ottheinrich was a grandson of Duke Georg of Bavaria-Landshut. Beham's portrait shows him at the age of 31 years. It is part of an important series of portraits that Duke Wilhelm IV of Bavaria commissioned of his closest relatives. The picture of the Count Palatine can be directly related to that of his consort, which emphasises the Bavarian line of the family, while that of Ottheinrich represents the Palatine line.
Painting by Barthel Beham, 1533.

DIE PFÄLZER LINIEN
Linie Pfalz-Neuburg (I)

Wappen der Pfalzgrafen Ottheinrich und Philipp.
Im gevierten Wappenschild sind im vornehmeren linken oberen sowie im rechten unteren Feld der rot bewehrte, rot gekrönte goldene pfälzische Löwe auf schwarzem Grund und im rechten oberen und linken unteren Feld die weiß-blauen Rauten zu sehen. Die Helmzier zeigt in Wiederholung und Abwandlung des Wappens zwei rot bewehrte, rot gekrönte goldene Pfälzer Löwen zwischen Krummhörnern bzw. mit gefiederten Flügeln im weiß-blauen Rautenmuster der Wittelsbacher.
Kolorierter Holzschnitt von Hans Burgkmair d. A., 1525.

Coat of arms of Counts Palatine Ottheinrich and Philipp.
In the quarterly parted coat of arms, the red armoured, red crowned golden Palatine lion on a black background can be seen in the more elegant top-left field as well as in the bottom-right field and in the top-right and bottom-left fields the white-blue lozenges can be seen. In repetition and variation of the coat of arms, the crest shows two red armoured, red crowned golden Palatine Lions between cromornes and with feathered wings respectively in the white-blue lozenge pattern of the House of Wittelsbach.
Coloured woodcarving by Hans Burgkmair the Elder, 1525.

Ottheinrich von der Pfalz (1502–1559).
Das reich verzierte Brustbildnis zeigt Ottheinrich mit den Insignien des Kurfürsten, dem Mantel mit Hermelinbesatz, dem Kurhut und dem Kurschwert in der linken Hand. Der Reichsapfel in seiner Rechten versinnbildlicht das Erztruchsessamt, das traditionell mit der Pfälzer Kurwürde verbunden war.
Kolorierter Holzschnitt aus der Bibelausgabe von Kurfürst Ludwig VI. (1539–1583), wohl von Virgil Solis, 1560.

Ottheinrich of the Palatinate (1502–1559).
The richly decorated half-length portrait shows Ottheinrich with the insignia of the Prince-Elector, the coat with ermine, the electoral hat and the electoral sword in his left hand. The globus cruciger in his right hand symbolises the office of Arch-Steward, which was traditionally associated with Palatine electoral dignity.
Coloured woodcarving from the Bible edition by Prince-Elector Ludwig VI (1539–1583), likely by Virgil Solis, 1560.

DIE PFÄLZER LINIEN
Linie Pfalz-Neuburg (I)

Pfalzgraf Wolfgang von Zweibrücken und Neuburg (1526–1569).
Durch seinen jüngsten Sohn Karl, der die Linie Zweibrücken-Birkenfeld begründete, ist Pfalzgraf Wolfgang der Stammvater aller heutigen Wittelsbacher. Nach dem Tod Ottheinrichs von der Pfalz erbte er das protestantische Fürstentum Neuburg.
Gemälde vermutlich von Hans Sebald Lautensack, 1559/1569.

Count Palatine Wolfgang of Zweibrücken and Neuburg (1526–1569).
Through his youngest son Karl, who established the Zweibrücken-Birkenfeld line, Count Palatine Wolfgang is the progenitor of all members of the House of Wittelsbach today. After the death of Ottheinrich of the Palatinate, he inherited the protestant principality of Neuburg.
Painting likely by Hans Sebald Lautensack, 1559/1569.

DIE PFÄLZER LINIEN
Linie Pfalz-Neuburg (I)

Auszug des Pfalzgrafen Johann Casimir (1543–1592) am 19. Juni 1578 zum Feldzug nach Flandern.
Um die politische und konfessionelle Position der Kurpfalz im europäischen Mächtespiel zu stärken, unterstützte Johann Casimir reformierte Glaubensbrüder in anderen Ländern. Im Juni 1578 brach er daher mit ca. 15.000 Soldaten nach Flandern auf.
Aquarellmalerei im „Thesaurus Picturarum" des Kirchrates Dr. Marcus zum Lamm, um 1600.

Departure of Count Palatine Johann Casimir (1543–1592) on the expedition to Flanders on 19 June 1578.
In order to strengthen the political and confessional position of the Electoral Palatinate in the European power plays, Johann Casimir supported reformed fellow brethren in other countries. Therefore, in June 1578 he set off for Flanders with approximately 15,000 soldiers.
Watercolour in the "Thesaurus Picturarum" of Consistory Dr. Marcus zum Lamm, c. 1600.

Kuradministrator Johann Casimir (1543–1592).
Als Kufürst Ludwig VI. von der Pfalz 1583 starb, gelang es seinem jüngeren Bruder Johann Casimir, die Vormundschaft über dessen minderjährigen Sohn an sich zu bringen und das Land in seinem Sinne zu regieren. Rigoros setzte er die Wiedereinsetzung des Calvinismus in der durch Ludwig VI. lutherisch geprägten Kurpfalz durch.
Aquarellmalerei („Johann Casimir in Festtagskleidung") im „Thesaurus Picturarum" des Kirchrates Dr. Marcus zum Lamm, um 1600.

Electoral Administrator Johann Casimir (1543–1592).
When Prince-Elector Ludwig VI of the Palatinate died in 1583, his younger brother Johann Casimir succeeded in acquiring guardianship of his minor son and in governing the land in his interests. He rigorously implemented the re-establishment of Calvinism in the Electoral Palatinate, which had been influenced by the Lutheran impact of Ludwig VI.
Watercolour ("Johann Casimir in festive clothing") in the "Thesaurus Picturarum" of Consistory Dr. Marcus zum Lamm, c. 1600.

IOANNES CASIMIRVS PALATI:
NVS RHENI, DVX BAVARIÆ. Etc.

DIE PFÄLZER LINIEN
Linie Pfalz-Neuburg (I)

Kurfürst Friedrich IV. (1574–1610) schützt die Handelsschiffe der Straßburger gegen Übergriffe der Speyrer.
Zu Ende des 16. Jahrhunderts kam es zu Grenzstreitigkeiten des protestantischen Pfälzer Kurfürstentums mit der katholischen Domstadt Speyer. Das Bild zeigt die vom Kurfürsten Friedrich IV. entsandten Truppen zur Verteidigung der Zollhoheit am Rhein.
Aquarell eines unbekannten Künstlers, 1601.

Prince-Elector Friedrich IV (1574–1610) protects the Strasbourg trading ships against attacks by forces from Speyer.
At the end of the 16th century, border conflicts occurred between the Protestant Palatine principality and the Catholic cathedral town of Speyer. The picture shows the troops dispatched by Prince-Elector Friedrich IV to defend the customs regime on the Rhine.
Watercolour of an unknown artist, 1601.

DER UMBRUCH VOM 18. AUF DAS 19. JAHRHUNDERT
Linie Pfalz-Neuburg (I)

258 | 259

Der „Hortus Palatinus" in Heidelberg. Der weitläufige Renaissancegarten des Heidelberger Schlosses galt einst als achtes Weltwunder. „Magische" Wasserspiele und fantastische Gestaltungselemente wie Irrgärten und Lustgrotten bezauberten die zeitgenössichen Besucher. Salomon de Caus legte den terrassierten Garten von 1616 bis 1619 für Kurfürst und „Winterkönig" von Böhmen Friedrich V. an.
Gemälde von Jacques Fouquières, um 1620.

The "Hortus Palatinus" in Heidelberg. The extensive Renaissance garden of Heidelberg Castle was once considered the eighth Wonder of the World. "Magic" fountains and fantastic design elements such as mazes and pleasure grottos enchanted the contemporary visitors. Salomon de Caus laid out the terraced garden from 1616 to 1619 for Prince-Elector and "Winter King" of Bohemia Friedrich V.
Painting by Jacques Fouquières, c. 1620.

DIE PFÄLZER LINIEN
Linie Pfalz-Simmern-Sponheim

Kurfürst Karl I. Ludwig von der Pfalz (1617–1680).
Nach den Wirren des Dreißigjährigen Krieges, die seinen Vater Friedrich V. ins Exil getrieben hatten, regierte Karl Ludwig ab 1649 in der wiedererlangten, jedoch verkleinerten Kurpfalz.
Ölgemälde von Johann Baptist de Ruell, um 1676.

Prince-Elector Karl I Ludwig of the Palatinate (1617–1680).
After the turmoil of the Thirty Years' War, which had driven his father Friedrich V into exile, Karl Ludwig governed in the regained but reduced-in-size Electoral Palatinate.
Oil painting by Johann Baptist de Ruell, c. 1676.

DIE PFÄLZER LINIEN
Linie Pfalz-Simmern-Sponheim

Elisabeth Charlotte von der Pfalz (1652–1721), spätere Herzogin von Orléans.
„Liselotte", wie die Tochter Kurfürst Karl I. Ludwigs schon zu Lebzeiten gerufen wurde, genoss einen Großteil ihrer Erziehung am Hof ihrer Tante Sophie von Hannover. 1671 heiratete sie den Bruder des Königs von Frankreich, fühlte sich jedoch zeitlebens als Pfälzerin. Ihre bis heute erhaltenen zahlreichen Briefe in die deutsche Heimat geben tiefe Einblicke in das Leben am Hof zu Versailles unter Ludwig XIV.
Ölgemälde eines unbekannten Künstlers, um 1670.

Elisabeth Charlotte of the Palatinate (1652–1721), later Duchess of Orléans.
"Liselotte", as the daughter of Prince-Elector Karl I Ludwig was called during her life, received most of her upbringing at the court of her aunt Sophie of Hanover. In 1671, she married the brother of the King of France. However, she considered herself a Palatine throughout her life. Her numerous letters to her German home – which have been preserved until this day – provide deep insight into life at the court of Versailles under Ludwig XIV.
Oil painting of an unknown artist, c. 1670.

Kurfürst Karl I. Ludwig von der Pfalz (1617–1680).
Während der Regierungszeit Karl I. Ludwigs, der die geschwächte Pfalz wieder zu stärken versuchte, erfolgte durch die Verheiratung seiner Tochter Elisabeth Charlotte mit Philippe von Orléans eine außenpolitische Annäherung an Frankreich. Kurz nach dem Tod Karl Ludwigs verwüstete das französische Heer im Pfälzischen Erbfolgekrieg das Fürstentum mehrmals.
Ölgemälde von Johann Baptist de Ruell, um 1670.

Prince-Elector Karl I Ludwig of the Palatinate (1617–1680).
During the period of government of Karl I Ludwig, who tried to restrengthen the weakened Palatinate, the marriage of his daughter Elisabeth Charlotte to Philippe of Orléans resulted in a foreign-policy approximation towards France. Shortly after the death of Karl Ludwig, the French army devastated the principality several times in the Nine Years' War.
Oil painting by Johann Baptist de Ruell, c. 1670.

DIE PFÄLZER LINIEN
Linie Pfalz-Simmern-Sponheim

König Ludwig XIV. empfängt Kurprinz Friedrich August von Sachsen in Fontainebleau am 27.9.1714.
In der Mitte ist die Schwägerin des Königs, Elisabeth Charlotte („Liselotte") von der Pfalz, Gemahlin des Herzogs von Orléans, prominent dargestellt. Durch die Ehe seines Bruders mit Elisabeth Charlotte begründete Ludwig XIV. seinen Anspruch auf die Pfalz, die er im Pfälzischen Erbfolgekrieg (1688–1697) einzunehmen versuchte. Liselotte stammte in direkter Linie von Friedrich V., dem böhmischen „Winterkönig", ab.
Ölgemälde von Louis de Silvestre, um 1715.

King Ludwig XIV receives Electoral Prince Friedrich Augustus of Saxony in Fontainebleau on 27 September 1714.
In the middle, the sister-in-law of the King, Elisabeth Charlotte ("Liselotte") of the Palatinate, consort of the Duke of Orléans, is prominently presented. Ludwig XIV based his claim to the Palatinate on the marriage of his brother to Elisabeth Charlotte and he tried to conquer it in the Nine Years' War (1688–1697). Liselotte descended directly from Friedrich V, the Bohemian "Winter King".
Oil painting by Louis de Silvestre, c. 1715.

DIE PFÄLZER LINIEN
Linie Pfalz-Neuburg (II)

Herzog Wolfgang Wilhelm von Pfalz-Neuburg (1578–1653). Wolfgang Wilhelm ist der älteste Sohn von Philipp Ludwig von Pfalz-Neuburg. Gegen den Willen seines protestantischen Vaters konvertierte er 1614 zum Katholizismus und schlug sich damit politisch auf die Seite der Katholischen Liga. Im gleichen Jahr trat Wolfgang Wilhelm die Herrschaft im Herzogtum Jülich-Berg an, der ein langer Erbfolgestreit vorausgegangen war. Eine private Leidenschaft des streitbaren Reichsfürsten war die Zucht von Doggen, die sich in diesem Bildnis van Dycks widerspiegelt. *Gemälde von Anton van Dyck, um 1629.*

Duke Wolfgang Wilhelm of Palatinate-Neuburg (1578–1653). Wolfgang Wilhelm is the oldest son of Philipp Ludwig of Palatinate-Neuburg. Against the will of his Protestant father, he converted to Catholicism in 1614 and thus sided politically with the Catholic League. In the same year, Wolfgang Wilhelm began to rule in the Duchy of Jülich-Berg after a long dispute over succession. A private passion of the disputatious imperial prince was breeding mastiffs, which is reflected in this portrait by van Dyck. *Painting by Anton van Dyck, c. 1629.*

DIE PFÄLZER LINIEN
Linie Pfalz-Neuburg (II)

Herzog Philipp Wilhelm von Pfalz-Neuburg und seine zweite Gemahlin Elisabeth Amalie Magdalena von Hessen-Darmstadt. Philipp Wilhelm war der einzige Sohn Wolfgang Wilhelms von Pfalz-Neuburg. 1653 ehelichte er nach dem Tod seiner ersten Frau die Landgräfin Elisabeth Amalie Magdalena von Hessen-Darmstadt. Aus der Ehe gingen 17 Kinder hervor, darunter die späteren Kurfürsten von der Pfalz Johann Wilhelm („Jan Wellem" genannt) und Karl III. Philipp. *Gemälde Johann Spilberg d. J. zugeschrieben, 1660/1670.*

Duke Philipp Wilhelm of Palatinate-Neuburg and his second consort Elisabeth Amalie Magdalena of Hesse-Darmstadt. Philipp Wilhelm was the only son of Wolfgang Wilhelm of Palatinate-Neuburg. After the death of his first wife, he married Landgravine Elisabeth Amalie Magdalena of Hesse-Darmstadt in 1653. Their marriage produced 17 children, including the later Prince-Electors of the Palatinate Johann Wilhelm (named "Jan Wellem") and Karl III Philipp. *Painting attributed to Johann Spilberg the Younger, 1660/1670.*

Der Ruhm des Hauses Pfalz-Neuburg. Allegorie auf den Ruhm- und Machtanspruch der Jungen Pfalz. *Gemälde eines unbekannten Künstlers, 1708/1716.*

The fame of the House of Palatinate-Neuburg. Allegory of the claim to fame and power of the Young Palatinate. *Painting by an unknown artist, 1708/1716.*

DIE PFÄLZER LINIEN
Linie Pfalz-Neuburg (II)

Kurfürst Johann Wilhelm von der Pfalz (1658–1716) und Anna Maria Luisa von der Pfalz (1691–1743), geborene de' Medici.
Johann Wilhelm übernahm im Jahr 1690 von seinem Vater Philipp Wilhelm die Kurwürde der Pfalz und machte nun Düsseldorf zu seiner Residenzstadt. 1691 heiratete er in zweiter Ehe Anna Maria Luisa de' Medici. Die hochgebildete Prinzessin der Toskana gilt als besondere Förderin der Schönen Künste und machte den Düsseldorfer Hof zu einer wahren Kunstmetropole.
Beide Ölgemälde von Jan Frans van Douven, vor 1708.

Prince-Elector Johann Wilhelm of the Palatinate (1658–1716) and Anna Maria Luisa of the Palatine (1691–1743), born de' Medici.
Johann Wilhelm assumed the electoral dignity of the Palatinate from his father Philipp Wilhelm in 1690 and now made Düsseldorf his seat of power. In 1691, he married his second wife, Anna Maria Luisa de' Medici. The highly educated Princess of Tuscany is considered a particular promoter of the fine arts and made the court of Düsseldorf a genuine art centre.
Both oil paintings by Jan Frans van Douven, before 1708.

DIE PFÄLZER LINIEN
Linie Pfalz-Neuburg (II)

„Markt am Jan Wellem",
Alter Markt von Düsseldorf.
Die Szene zeigt einen Markttag auf dem Düsseldorfer Alten Markt mit dem Reiterdenkmal des Kurfürsten Johann Wilhelm von der Pfalz (gen. „Jan Wellem", 1658–1716) und dem Alten Rathaus.
Gemälde von Heinrich Hermanns (1862–1942), o. J.

"Markt am Jan Wellem",
Old Market of Düsseldorf.
The scene shows a market day at Düsseldorf's Old Market with the equestrian monument of Prince-Elector Johann Wilhelm of the Palatinate (named "Jan Wellem", 1658–1716) and the Old Town Hall.
Painting by Heinrich Hermanns (1862–1942), undated.

DIE PFÄLZER LINIEN
Linie Pfalz-Neuburg (II)

Kurfürst Karl III. Philipp von der Pfalz (1661–1742).
1716 folgte Karl Philipp seinem älteren Bruder Johann Wilhelm als Kurfürst von der Pfalz nach, nachdem dieser kinderlos gestorben war. Zuvor durchlief er eine militärische Karriere im Heer des habsburgischen Kaisers und regierte ab 1705 als kaiserlicher Statthalter von Tirol in Innsbruck. Als pfälzischer Kurfürst ließ er in Mannheim die repräsentative barocke Schlossanlage errichten, eine der größten und modernsten ihrer Zeit.
Gemälde von Jan Philipps von der Schlichten, 1729.

Prince-Elector Karl III Philipp of the Palatinate (1661–1742).
In 1716, Karl Philipp succeeded his older brother Johann Wilhelm as Prince-Elector of the Palatinate after the latter had died childless. Previously, he pursued a military career in the army of the Emperor – of the House of Habsburg – and was Imperial Governor of Tyrol in Innsbruck from 1705. As Prince-Elector of the Palatinate, he had the representative baroque palace complex constructed in Mannheim, one of the biggest and most modern of its time.
Painting by Jan Philipps von der Schlichten, 1729.

Prince-Elector Karl Theodor of the Palatinate and Bavaria

In 1777, the case arose for which provision had existed in the treaties of the House of Wittelsbach since 1329: the Bavarian Prince-Elector Maximilian III Joseph, "the Much-loved", died without a male heir. After 448 years, the two Wittelsbach lands, the Palatinate and Bavaria, were reunited into one dominion. The title of the new Prince-Elector of the Palatinate and Bavaria was now held by Karl Theodor from the Neuburg-Sulzbach line, who had already become Duke of Palatinate-Sulzbach in 1733 and Prince-Elector of the Palatinate nine years later. Originally only a descendent of a Wittelsbach branch line, Karl Theodor received his education at the court of the Palatine Prince-Elector Karl III Philipp, who – also without an heir – had already chosen him as his successor and prepared him for this objective. The young prince studied public economy, law and history in Leiden and Leuven and developed a personal passion for music.

When on New Year's Eve 1777 the news reached Karl Theodor of the death of his Bavarian relative Maximilian III Joseph, he left for Munich on the same evening to take up his position as successor – with a threat coming from the east of a takeover of Bavaria by the House of Habsburg. Karl Theodor, who probably would have preferred to keep his seat of power in his Palatine home, entered into negotiations with Emperor Joseph II, who offered him territories of the Spanish Netherlands in exchange if the Prince-Elector were to cede extensive parts of the Bavarian territory to him. He thus held out to Karl Theodor the prospect of the establishment of a kingdom around the seat of power of Mannheim, Düsseldorf and Brussels. Karl Theodor's new Bavarian subjects were furious about such exchange negotiations, with the Bavarian Landstände announcing their opposition. Prussia, which feared strengthening on the part of Austria, and duke Karl August of Palatinate-Zweibrücken, the next contender for the heritage, spoke out against the exchange. The Prince-Elector ultimately rejected the offer, leading to the outbreak of the War of the Bavarian Succession with Austria in 1778, a war that was called only "Potato War" or "Plum Fuss" due to its barely noteworthy battles.

Although Karl Theodor, of his own volition, did not defer to later exchange offers of Joseph II, did not release the Bavarian territories and was a devoted sovereign for the Bavarians from that time on, the mistrust of the Bavarian people towards the Palatine and his advisers never vanished completely. He maintained a sophisticated, progressive governmental style, modernised the administrative machinery and initiated reforms of the military and the social system. At the same time, however, he also combated revolutionary trends towards the monarchical principle. Both for the Palatinate and for Bavaria, he did great things as a promoter of the sciences and arts. He initiated, for example, the Academy of Sciences and the National Theatre in Mannheim as well as the English Garden in Munich and the opening of the grounds of Nymphenburg Palace, the Court Painting Gallery (now Graphic Collections) and the Court Library for the People.

Kurfürst Karl Theodor von der Pfalz und Bayern

1777 trat der Fall ein, für den in den Wittelsbacher Hausverträgen seit 1329 Vorsorge betrieben worden war: Der bayerische Kurfürst Maximilian III. Joseph, „der Vielgeliebte", starb ohne männlichen Erben. Nach 448 Jahren wurden die beiden wittelsbachischen Länder, die Pfalz und Bayern, zu einem Herrschaftsgebiet wiedervereinigt. Den Titel des neuen Kurfürsten von der Pfalz und Bayern hatte nun Karl Theodor aus der Linie Neuburg-Sulzbach inne, der schon 1733 Herzog von Pfalz-Sulzbach und neun Jahre später Kurfürst von der Pfalz geworden war. Ursprünglich nur Nachkomme einer wittelsbachischen Nebenlinie, erhielt Karl Theodor seine Erziehung am Hofe des pfälzischen Kurfürsten Karls III. Philipp, der – ebenfalls ohne Erben geblieben – ihn bereits zu seinem Nachfolger auserkoren hatte und ihn auf dieses Ziel vorbereitete. Der junge Prinz studierte in Leiden und Löwen Staatswirtschaft, Recht und Geschichte und entwickelte eine persönliche Leidenschaft für die Musik.

Als Karl Theodor am Silvestertag des Jahres 1777 die Nachricht vom Tod seines bayerischen Verwandten Maximilian III. Joseph erreichte, brach er noch am selben Abend nach München auf, um sein Erbe anzutreten – von Osten drohte eine Übernahme Bayerns durch die Habsburger. Karl Theodor, der seine Residenz wohl lieber in seiner pfälzischen Heimat belassen hätte, trat mit Kaiser Joseph II. in Verhandlungen, der ihm Gebiete der Spanischen Niederlande zum Tausch anbot, sollte ihm der Kurfürst weite Teile des bayerischen Territoriums überlassen. Damit stellte er Karl Theodor die Errichtung eines Königreichs um die Residenzstädte Mannheim, Düsseldorf und Brüssel in Aussicht. Karl Theodors neue bayerische Untertanen waren empört über solcherlei Tauschverhandlungen, die bayerischen Landstände kündigten ihren Widerstand an. Auch Preußen, das eine Stärkung Österreichs befürchtete, und Herzog Karl August von Pfalz-Zweibrücken als nächster Erbanwärter sprachen sich gegen den Tausch aus. Der Kurfürst lehnte schließlich ab, und so kam es 1778 zum Bayerischen Erbfolgekrieg mit Österreich, der ob seiner kaum nennenswerten Gefechte schon von Zeitgenossen nur als „Kartoffelkrieg" oder „Zwetschgenrummel" bezeichnet wurde.

Obwohl Karl Theodor auf spätere Tauschangebote Josephs II. nicht mehr einging, die bayerischen Gebiete aus eigenem Entschluss nicht freigab und den Bayern fortan ein treusorgender Landesfürst war, wich das Misstrauen des bayerischen Volks gegenüber dem Pfälzer und seinen Beratern nie ganz. Er pflegte einen aufgeklärt-fortschrittlichen Regierungsstil, modernisierte den Verwaltungsapparat und regte Reformen des Militär- und Sozialwesens an, bekämpfte gleichermaßen aber auch revolutionäre Tendenzen gegenüber dem monarchischen Prinzip. Für die Pfalz wie für Bayern tat er Großes als Förderer der Wissenschaften und Künste: Auf seine Initiative gehen u. a. die Akademie der Wissenschaften und das Nationaltheater in Mannheim sowie der Englische Garten in München und die Öffnung des Nymphenburger Schlossparks, der Hofgemäldegalerie (heute: Graphische Sammlungen) und der Hofbibliothek für das Volk zurück.

DIE PFÄLZER LINIEN
Linie Pfalz-Bayern

Eintrag des Kurfürsten Karl Theodor von der Pfalz, ab 1777 von Pfalz-Bayern, im Bruderschaftsbuch der Corpus-Christi-Bruderschaft bei St. Peter in München.

Entry of Prince-Elector Karl Theodor of the Palatinate, from 1777 of Palatinate-Bavaria, in the Book of the Brotherhood of the Corpus Christi Brotherhood at St. Peter's Church in Munich.

Staatsporträt des Kurfürsten Karl Theodor von der Pfalz und Bayern (1724–1799).
Karl Theodor entstammte der pfälzischen Linie Neuburg-Sulzbach. Durch Erbfall und Heirat folgte er Kurfürst Karl III. Philipp 1742 als pfälzischer Landesherr nach. 1777 beerbte er Maximilian III. Joseph als Kurfürst von Bayern; mit ihm war die bayerische Linie Wittelsbach faktisch ausgestorben.
Gemälde von Pompeo Girolamo Batoni, Rom, 1775.

State Portrait of Prince-Elector Karl Theodor of the Palatinate and Bavaria (1724–1799).
Karl Theodor came from the Neuburg-Sulzbach Palatine line. Through accrual of the inheritance and marriage, he succeeded Prince-Elector Karl III Philipp as Palatine sovereign in 1742. In 1777, he succeeded Maximilian III Joseph as Prince-Elector of Bavaria; with him, the Bavarian line of the House of Wittelsbach had effectively died out.
Painting by Pompeo Girolamo Batoni, Rome, 1775.

DIE PFÄLZER LINIEN
Linie Pfalz-Bayern

Kurfürstin Elisabeth Auguste (1721–1794) mit ihren beiden Schwestern Maria Anna (1722–1790) und Maria Franziska Dorothea (1724–1794) beim Musizieren.
Die Kurfürstin begleitet den Gesang Maria Franziskas von Pfalz-Sulzbach (rechts) am Clavichord, Maria Anna von Bayern spielt die Laute. Jedoch ist die Kammermusik nur das vordergründige Thema des Gemäldes; tatsächlich steht mit den Bildnissen der bedeutenden Ehemänner der drei Damen im Hintergrund der herrschaftliche Machtanspruch der Familie im Mittelpunkt.
Gemälde von Jan Philips van der Schlichten, um 1745.

Electress Elisabeth Auguste (1721–1794) with her two sisters Maria Anna (1722–1790) and Maria Franziska Dorothea (1724–1794) playing music.
The Electress accompanies Maria Franziska of Palatinate-Sulzbach's (right) singing on the clavichord, while Maria Anna of Bavaria plays the lute. However, the chamber music is only the superficial theme of the painting; with the portraits of the important husbands of the three ladies in the background, the focus is actually on the family's claim to ruling power.
Painting by Jan Philips van der Schlichten, c. 1745.

DIE PFÄLZER LINIEN
Linie Pfalz-Bayern

Das jungvermählte Kurfürstenpaar Elisabeth Auguste und Karl Theodor.
Der alte pfälzische Kurfürst Karl III. Philipp hatte seine Lieblingsenkelin Elisabeth Auguste und Karl Theodor schon im Kindesalter verlobt. Obwohl sich die beiden in den späteren Jahren ihrer Ehe entzweiten, führten sie den Mannheimer Hof gemeinsam zu einer neuen kulturellen Blüte.
Gemälde von Felix Anton Besoldt, um 1743.

The newlywed electoral couple Elisabeth Auguste and Karl Theodor.
The old Palatine Prince-Elector Karl III Philipp had already betrothed his favourite granddaughter Elisabeth Auguste and Karl Theodor when they were children. Together they led the Mannheim court to new cultural prosperity, although the two fell out with each other in the later years of their marriage.
Painting by Felix Anton Besoldt, c. 1743.

DIE PFÄLZER LINIEN
Linie Pfalz-Bayern

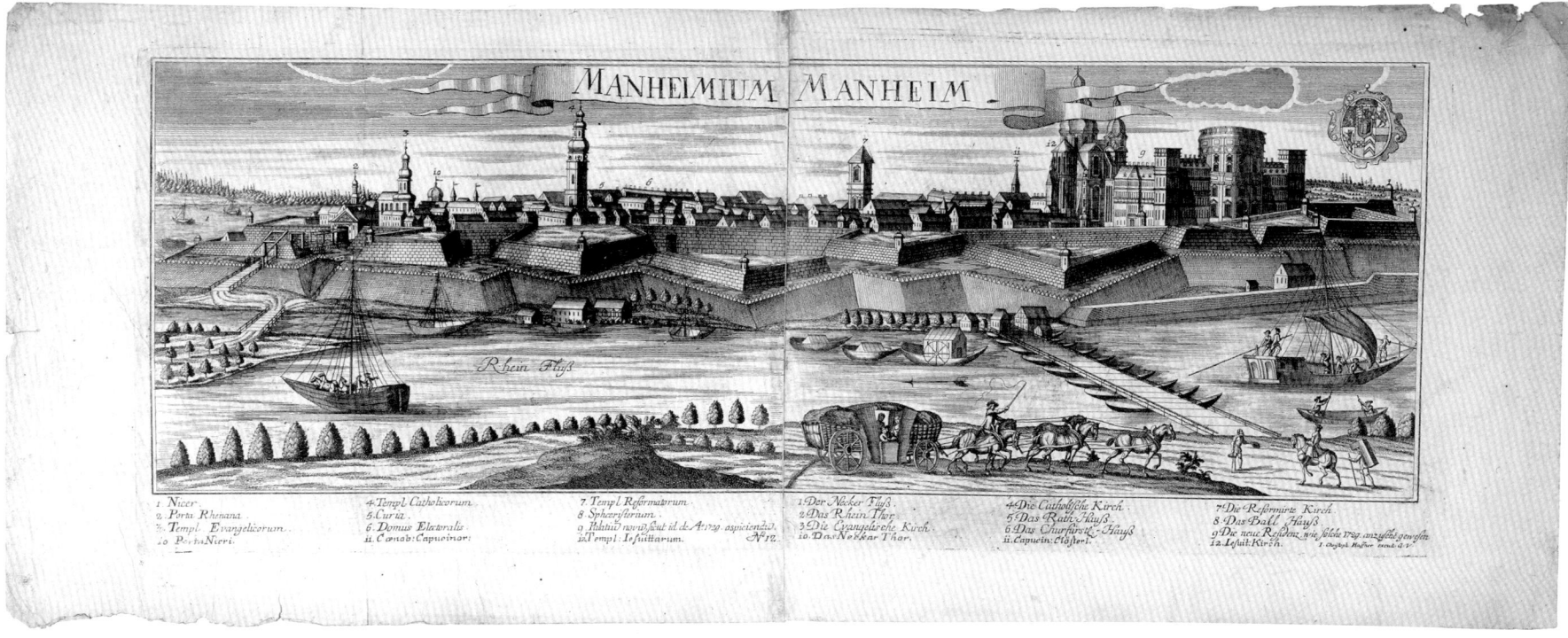

Gesamtansicht der Stadt Mannheim vom linken Rheinufer aus.
Im Jahr 1720 verlegte Karl III. Philipp den Kurfürstenhof von Heidelberg nach Mannheim. Die Residenz (im Bild Nr. 9), die er dort neu erbaute, dominiert neben der neuen Jesuitenkirche (Nr. 12) den rechten Bildteil. Im Vordergrund die bastionäre Stadtbefestigung und der Rhein als Verkehrsader der Hauptstadt.
Kupferstich/Radierung (zwei Platten) von Johann Christoph Haffner, 2. Drittel des 18. Jahrhunderts.

Overall view of the city of Mannheim from the left bank of the Rhine.
In 1720, Karl III Philipp relocated the electoral court from Heidelberg to Mannheim. The new residence (in picture no. 9) that he constructed there dominates the right-hand side of the picture alongside the new Jesuit Church (no. 12). In the foreground are the bastion-like city wall and the Rhine as the capital's artery.
Copper engraving/etching (two slabs) by Johann Christoph Haffner, 2nd third of the 18th century.

Festung Mannheim mit Rheinschanze.
Die Rheinschanze vor Mannheim entstand zu Beginn des 17. Jahrhunderts als befestigter Vorposten bzw. Brückenkopf am linken Rheinufer. Nach wiederholten Zerstörungen und mehrmaligem Wiederaufbau fiel die mittlerweile stark befestigte bastionäre Verteidigungsanlage in den französischen Revolutionskriegen 1795 an Frankreich. Im Bild verweist der auf der Schanze errichtete Freiheitsbaum auf diesen militärischen Erfolg der Revolutionäre. Mannheim selbst ist vereinfacht und z. T. stark verzeichnet wiedergegeben, um verschiedene Betrachterperspektiven auf einem Blatt zu vereinen.
Kolorierter Kupferstich von Dominicus Tessaro (Zeichner) und J. G. F. Knoell (?) (Stecher), 1795.

Mannheim fortress with Rhine entrenchment.
The Rhine entrenchment beside Mannheim came into existence at the start of the 17th century as a fortified outpost and bridgehead at the left bank of the Rhine. After repeated destructions and several reconstructions, the now heavily reinforced bastion-like defensive fortification fell into the hands of France in the French Revolutionary Wars in 1795. In the picture, the liberty tree set up on the entrenchment references this military success of the revolutionaries. Mannheim itself is presented in a simplified and in part distorted manner in order to unite various observer perspectives onto one sheet.
Coloured copper engraving by Dominicus Tessaro (drawer) and J.G.F. Knoell (?) (engraver), 1795.

1 tens. Mannheim auf der Erd Zunge des Rhein und Nekers 2 tens. Rheinschantze und Fleschen 3 tens. Das Schloß 4 tens. Jesuiter Kirch 5 tens. Opservations Thurn 6 tens. Kaufhaus 7 tens. Stadthaus 8 tens. Reformirte Kirch 9 tens. Evangelische Kirch 10 tens. Capuciner 11 tens. Rheinthor 12 tens. Zeughaus 13 tens. Mühlau 14 tens. Schanze auf den Pestilenz Bukel 15 tens. Nekerschanz 16 tens. Nekerfluß 17 tens. Rhein Fluß 18 tens. Rhein Schiffbruk 19 tens. Holzhof 20 tens. Aereste.

DIE PFÄLZER LINIEN
Linie Pfalz-Bayern

Karl Theodor von der Pfalz im Kurfürstenornat, auf seine Residenzstadt Mannheim weisend.
Gemälde von Johann Georg Ziesenis, um 1750.

Karl Theodor of the Palatinate in the electoral regalia, pointing to his seat of power, Mannheim.
Painting by Johann Georg Ziesenis, c. 1750.

DIE PFÄLZER LINIEN
Linie Pfalz-Bayern

Die „Moschee" (Festsaal im Stil einer solchen) im Schlosspark von Schwetzingen.
Karl Theodor folgte mit der Errichtung einer Moschee im Schlossgarten von Schwetzingen ganz der europäischen Mode. Geplant von Nicolas de Pigage, versinnbildlicht der orientalische Bau in Verbindung mit okzidentalen Architekturelementen die aufgeklärte, weltoffene Haltung des Kurfürsten. Der Verweis auf den Islam und andere Religionen sollte den Besucher zum Nachdenken anregen.
Aquarell von Karl Kuntz, 1793.

The "mosque" (ballroom in the style of suchlike) in the grounds of Schwetzingen Palace.
With the construction of a mosque in the garden of Schwetzingen Palace, Karl Theodor followed the European fashion completely. Planned by Nicolas de Pigage, the oriental structure combined with occidental architectural elements symbolises the Prince-Elector's enlightened, liberal-minded attitude. The reference to Islam and other religions is supposed to stimulate thinking on the part of the visitor.
Watercolour by Karl Kuntz, 1793.

Ansicht von Schloss Benrath.
Das Schloss wurde im Auftrag des Kurfürsten Karl Theodor durch seinen Bau- und Gartendirektor Nicolas de Pigage von 1756 bis 1770 als Lust- und Jagdschloss vor den Toren der Residenzstadt Düsseldorf erbaut.
Gemälde von Pierre Paulet (Kopie nach einem Gemälde von Antoine Charles Vernet, 1806), o. J.

View of Benrath Palace.
The palace was constructed by order of Prince-Elector Karl Theodor by his building and garden director Nicolas de Pigage from 1756 to 1770 as a maison de plaisance and hunting house at the doors of the seat of power of Düsseldorf.
Painting by Pierre Paulet (copy based on a painting by Antoine Charles Vernet, 1806), undated.

DIE PFÄLZER LINIEN
Linie Pfalz-Bayern

Entwurf des Heidelberger Fasses.
1751 wurde von Kurfürst Karl Theodor das vierte Große Fass des Heidelberger Schlosses in Auftrag gegeben. Noch heute zieht dieses überdimensionale Weinfass (es fasst nach Eintrocknung des Holzes derzeit noch ca. 219.000 Liter) Touristenscharen in das Schloss.
Entwurf des Bildhauers Augustin (?) Egell, 1752.

Design of the Heidelberg Tun.
In 1751, the fourth Great Tun of Heidelberg Castle was commissioned by Prince-Elector Karl Theodor. Today, this huge wine barrel (which, after the wood has dried, currently still holds approximately 219,000 litres) still attracts hoards of tourists to the castle.
Design by sculptor Augustin (?) Egell, 1752.

Die Jesuitenkirche in Mannheim.
Mit der Verlegung des kurfürstlichen Hofes von Heidelberg nach Mannheim im Jahr 1720 förderte Karl Philipp den Bau einer großen Hofkirche. 1733 konnte mit der Errichtung der dem Jesuitenkolleg zugehörigen Basilika begonnen werden. Unter Kurfürst Karl Theodor wurde die Jesuitenkirche 1756 schließlich vollendet und am 18. Mai 1760 feierlich eingeweiht.
Titelkupferstich aus „Basilica Carolina", 1760.

The Jesuit Church in Mannheim.
With the relocation of the electoral court from Heidelberg to Mannheim in 1720, Karl Philipp encouraged the construction of a large chapel royal. In 1733, the construction of the basilica belonging to the Jesuit college was started. Under Prince-Elector Karl Theodor, the Jesuit Church was finally completed in 1756 and was formally inaugurated on 18 May 1760.
Title copper engraving from "Basilica Carolina", 1760.

Aspectus
A. Collegii, B. Templi, et C. Gymnasii,
Societatis JESU Manhemii ab Oriente.

DIE PFÄLZER LINIEN
Linie Pfalz-Bayern

Kammerherrenschlüssel um 1785 unter Kurfürst Karl Theodor mit dessen Monogramm.
Kammerherrenschlüssel mit den kurfürstlichen Initialen „CT" für „Carl Theodor", darüber der Kurhut. Nur enge Vertraute des Kurfürsten und der Kurfürstin trugen diesen Schlüssel. Der Inhaber dieses Schlüssels hatte Zutritt zu den herrschaftlichen Gemächern.
Messing, feuervergoldet, wahrscheinl. aus der Werkstatt von Franz Xaver Grubener, um 1785.

Chamberlain's key c. 1785 under Prince-Elector Karl Theodor with his monogram.
Chamberlain's key with the electoral initials "CT" for "Carl Theodor", with the electoral hat overhead. Only close confidants of the Prince-Elector and the Electress carried this key. The owner of this key had access to the lordly apartments.
Brass, fire-gilded, likely by the atelier of Franz Xaver Grubener, c. 1785.

Kurfürst Karl Theodor mit Traversflöte und Hund.
Nach Aussagen von Zeitgenossen brachte es der Kurfürst auf seinem Lieblingsinstrument zu bemerkenswerter Fertigkeit. Karl Theodor ist hier im privaten Rahmen, mit heruntergerutschten Strümpfen und legerem Seidenmantel dargestellt. Die etwas nachlässig erscheinende Haltung des Kurfürsten soll jedoch nicht darüber hinwegtäuschen, dass es sich auch bei diesem Porträt um eine politische Aussage des kunstfördernden, absolutistischen Fürsten handelt.
Gemälde von Johann Georg Ziesenis, 1757.

Prince-Elector Karl Theodor with German flute and dog.
According to contemporaries, the Prince-Elector achieved remarkable proficiency with his favourite instrument. Here, Karl Theodor is presented in a private setting, with worked-down stockings and a casual silk coat. However, the somewhat lax-seeming attitude of the Prince-Elector should not belie the fact that this portrait too is a political statement on the part of the art-promoting, absolutistic prince.
Painting by Johann Georg Ziesenis, 1757.

DIE PFÄLZER LINIEN
Linie Pfalz-Bayern

Kurfürst Karl Theodor empfängt Papst Pius VI. im April 1782 in der Loretokapelle des Klosters Ramsau bei Haag.
Papst Pius VI. wurde auf seiner Reise nach München vom Kurfürsten bei Haag vorzeitig in Empfang genommen, um dann gemeinsam in die Residenzstadt München weiterzureisen. Dort verweilte Papst Pius einige Tage für die Besichtigung der Kirchen. Das Georgi-Ritter-Ordensfest von 1782 wurde um einige Tage verschoben, damit der Papst diesem beiwohnen konnte.
Wandgemälde in der Pfarrkirche St. Maria in Ramsau bei Haag, Künstler unbekannt, nach 1782.

Prince-Elector Karl Theodor receives Pope Pius VI at the loretto chapel of Ramsau bei Haag Abbey in April 1782.
On his journey to Munich, Pope Pius VI was received ahead of schedule by the Prince-Elector near Haag so that they could continue the journey to the seat of power, Munich, together. Pope Pius spent a few days there to visit the churches. The Festival of the Royal Order of Saint George of 1782 was postponed for a few days so that the Pope could attend it.
Mural painting in St. Mary's Parish Church in Ramsau bei Haag, artist unknown, after 1782.

DIE PFÄLZER LINIEN
Linie Pfalz-Bayern

Zusammenkunft des Kurfürsten Karl Theodor mit Kaiser Franz II. bei dessen Durchreise nach Frankfurt zur Krönung, 1792.
An der Seite des Kurfürsten schreitet im Vordergrund Kaiserin Maria Theresia, geborene Prinzessin von Neapel und Sizilien. An der Seite des Kaisers sind Maria Anna Sophie, Witwe des Kurfürsten Max III. Joseph, und Erzherzog Joseph zu sehen. Münchner Bürger betrachten die Szene.
Gemälde von Johann Baptist Hoechle, 1792.

Meeting of Prince-Elector Karl Theodor with Emperor Franz II on his journey to Frankfurt to be coronated, 1792.
Walking beside the Prince-Elector in the foreground is Empress Maria Theresia, born Princess of Naples and Sicily. Maria Anna Sophie, widow of Prince-Elector Max III Joseph, and Archduke Joseph can be seen beside the Emperor. Citizens of Munich observe the scene.
Painting by Johann Baptist Hoechle, 1792.

DIE PFÄLZER LINIEN
Linie Pfalz-Bayern

298 | 299

Chinesischer Turm im Englischen Garten zu München um 1795.
Ab 1789 ließ Karl Theodor in den herrschaftlichen Isarauen „zur allgemeinen Ergötzung" für das Volk den Englischen Garten anlegen. Der Chinesische Turm wurde nach dem Vorbild der „Great Pagode" im Schlossgarten von Kew (England) als Aussichtsturm schon 1789/90 errichtet.
(Wahrschl. Aquarell-) Malerei von Johann Michael Mettenleiter, um 1795.

Chinese Tower in the English Garden, Munich, c. 1795.
From 1789, Karl Theodor had the English Garden laid out in the grand Isar meadows "for the general delight" of the people. The Chinese Tower was constructed as early as 1789/90 as a viewpoint tower modelled on the "Great Pagoda" in the garden of Kew Palace (England).
Painting (likely watercolour) by Johann Michael Mettenleiter, c. 1795.

DIE PFÄLZER LINIEN
Linie Pfalz-Zweibrücken

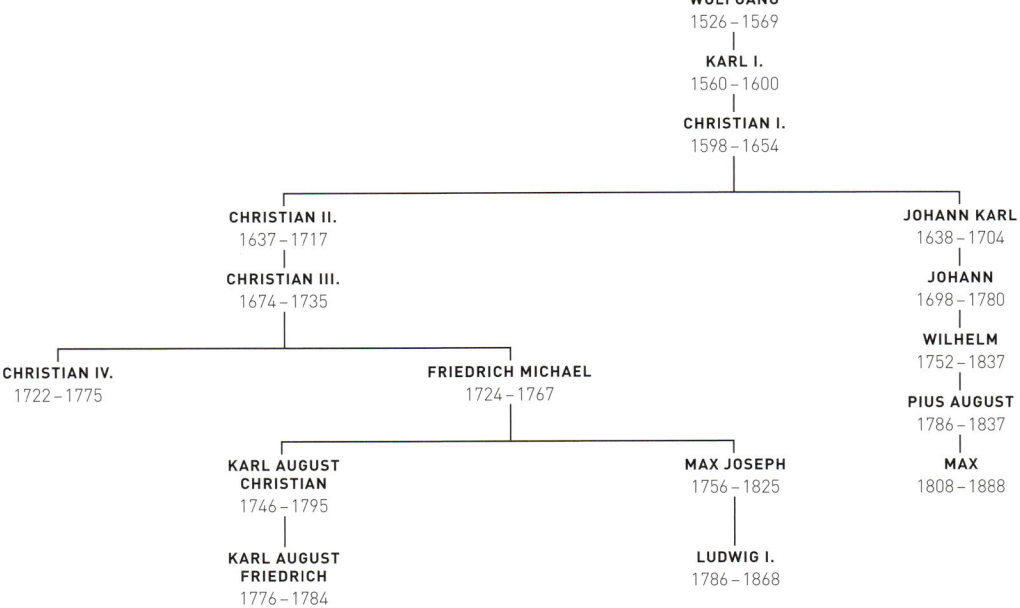

300 | 301

Christian III., Pfalzgraf von Birkenfeld, Herzog von Zweibrücken (1674–1735).
Herzog Christian zeichnete sich mit seinem Regiment „Royal Alsace" besonders bei militärischen Erfolgen unter Ludwig XIV. von Frankreich aus.
Gemälde eines unbekannten Künstlers, o. J.

Christian III, Count Palatine of Birkenfeld, Duke of Zweibrücken (1674–1735).
Duke Christian's most notable achievements were his military successes with his "Royal Alsace" regiment under Ludwig XIV of France.
Painting by an unknown artist, undated.

Herzog Christian IV. (1722–1775).
Der ältere Sohn Herzog Christians III. erhielt seine Erziehung u. a. am französischen Hof zu Versailles. Er schloss 1751 mit der bürgerlichen Marianne Camasse eine morganatische Ehe. Später wurde sie zu einer Gräfin von Forbach erhoben, weshalb ihre Söhne den Titel „Grafen von Zweibrücken-Forbach" trugen.
Gemälde eines unbekannten Künstlers des 18. Jahrhunderts.

Duke Christian IV (1722–1775).
The older son of Duke Christian III received part of his education at the court of Versailles, France. In 1751, he wed the untitled Marianne Camasse in a morganatic marriage. Later, she was elevated to the position of Countess of Forbach, for which reason her sons bore the title "Counts of Zweibrücken-Forbach".
Painting of an unknown artist of the 18th century.

DIE PFÄLZER LINIEN
Linie Pfalz-Zweibrücken

Pfalzgraf Friedrich Michael von Zweibrücken-Birkenfeld (1724–1767).
Friedrich Michael war der jüngere Bruder Herzog Christians IV. von Zweibrücken. Er galt als Riese und war wohl an die zwei Meter groß. Er diente ebenfalls im Regiment „Royal Alsace" und begann schon in jungen Jahren eine bedeutende militärische Karriere, die ihm schließlich u. a. den Rang des kaiserlichen Feldmarschalls des Oberrheinischen Kreises einbrachte.
Gemälde von Louis Tocqué, um 1745.

Count Palatine Friedrich Michael of Zweibrücken-Birkenfeld (1724–1767).
Friedrich Michael was the younger brother of Duke Christian IV of Zweibrücken. He was considered a giant and was likely about two metres tall. He also served in the Royal Alsace regiment and began a significant military career at a young age, a career that ultimately earned him the rank of Imperial Field Marshal of the Upper Rhine district.
Painting by Louis Tocqué, c. 1745.

Pfalzgraf Friedrich Michael von Zweibrücken-Birkenfeld.
Der Pfalzgraf ist hier in der Uniform des kaiserlichen Generalfeldmarschalls abgebildet. Am Coulant trägt er den Orden des Goldenen Vlieses, außerdem ein rot-weiß-rot gestreiftes Ordensband mit dem Bruststern des Maria-Theresia-Ordens, den ihm die österreichische Kaiserin im Jahr 1760 verliehen hatte.
Ölgemälde von Heinrich Carl Brandt, um 1760.

Count Palatine Friedrich Michael of Zweibrücken-Birkenfeld.
The Count Palatine is here depicted in the uniform of the imperial General Field Marshal. On his loop he wears the Order of the Golden Fleece as well as a red-white-red-striped cordon with the breast star of the Order of Maria Theresia, which the Austrian Empress had granted him in 1760.
Oil painting by Heinrich Carl Brandt, c. 1760.

DIE PFÄLZER LINIEN
Linie Pfalz-Zweibrücken

Herzog Karl August von Pfalz-Zweibrücken im Alter von fünf Jahren.
Karl August war der erstgeborene Sohn des „Soldatenpfalzgrafen" Friedrich Michael und seiner Gemahlin Maria Franziska von Pfalz-Sulzbach.
Ölgemälde von Johann Georg Ziesenis, 1751.

Duke Karl August of Palatinate-Zweibrücken at the age of five.
Karl August was the firstborn son of "Soldier Count Palatine" Friedrich Michael and his consort Maria Franziska of Palatinate-Sulzbach.
Oil painting by Johann Georg Ziesenis, 1751.

Brustbild des Herzogs Karl II. August von Pfalz-Zweibrücken (1756–1795).
Da Kurfürst Karl Theodor keine erbberechtigten Nachkommen besaß, war Karl August präsumptiver Erbe des Kurfürstentums Pfalz-Bayern. Unter Karl Augusts Onkel Christian IV. wurde das Regiment „Royal Deux-Ponts" als deutsches Infanterieregiment der französischen Armee aufgestellt. Karl Augusts Cousins Christian und Wilhelm führten das Regiment im Amerikanischen Unabhängigkeitskrieg an. Das Bildnis des Zweibrücker Hofmalers Pitz zeigt ihn im Alter von 37 Jahren.
Gemälde von Karl Kaspar Pitz, 1783.

Half-length portrait of Duke Karl II August of Palatinate-Zweibrücken (1756–1795).
Since Prince-Elector Karl Theodor did not have any descendents with the right to succeed him as heir, Karl August was the presumptive heir of the principality of Palatinate-Bavaria. The "Royal Deux-Ponts" regiment was set up as the German infantry regiment of the French army under Karl August's uncle Christian IV. Karl August's cousins Christian and Wilhelm led the regiment in the American War of Independence. Zweibrücken court painter Pitz's portrait shows him at the age of 37.
Painting by Karl Kaspar Pitz, 1783.

DIE PFÄLZER LINIEN
Linie Pfalz-Zweibrücken

Schloss Karlsberg, erbaut unter Herzog Karl II. August von Pfalz-Zweibrücken von 1776–1784.
Schloss Karlsberg galt zu seiner Entstehungszeit als die größte und modernste Schlossanlage Mitteleuropas. Schon kurze Zeit nach seiner Fertigstellung wurde es jedoch von französischen Revolutionstruppen niedergebrannt. Die Inneneinrichtung konnte z. T. evakuiert werden und befindet sich heute in Museen in ganz Süddeutschland.
Kopie eines Aquarells der herzoglichen Kadetten F. und G. de Luder (1791) von Heinrich Lau, 1978.

Karlsberg Castle, constructed under Duke Karl II August of Palatinate-Zweibrücken from 1776–1784.
At the time of its creation, Karlsberg Castle was considered the largest and most modern castle complex in Central Europe. However, it was burned down by French revolutionary troops only a short time after its completion. Some of the interior furnishings were evacuated and can be found in museums throughout Southern Germany today.
Copy of a watercolour of the ducal cadets F. and G. de Luder (1791) by Heinrich Lau, 1978.

DIE PFÄLZER LINIEN
Linie Pfalz-Zweibrücken

Kapitulation von Lord Cornwallis bei Yorktown, 1781.
Die Szene beschreibt die Niederlage der Britischen Armee bei Yorktown, Virginia. Christian Freiherr von Zweibrücken-Forbach und sein Bruder Wilhelm, beide Söhne Herzog Christians IV. aus morganatischer Ehe, führten in Yorktown während der entscheidenden Phase des Amerikanischen Unabhängigkeitskriegs ihr Regiment „Royal Deux-Ponts" im Oktober 1781 zum Erfolg. In der Mitte nimmt General Benjamin Lincoln auf einem Schimmel die Niederlage der britischen Offiziere entgegen, rechts im Hintergrund auf einem braunen Pferd George Washington an der Seite der Amerikanischen Revolutionstruppen, links die Franzosen unter Christian von Zweibrücken („Deux Ponts").
Gemälde von John Trumbull, 1819/20, nach einer Vorlage von 1789.

Surrender of Lord Cornwallis at Yorktown, 1781.
The scene describes the defeat of the British army at Yorktown, Virginia. Christian Baron of Zweibrücken-Forbach and his brother Wilhelm, both sons of Duke Christian IV of a morganatic marriage, led their "Royal Deux-Ponts" regiment to victory in Yorktown in October 1781 during the decisive phase of the American War of Independence. In the centre, General Benjamin Lincoln accepts the defeat of the British officers on a white horse; on the right in the foreground on a brown horse is George Washington on the side of the American revolutionary troops; on the left are the French under Christian of Zweibrücken ("Deux Ponts").
Painting by John Trumbull, 1819/20, based on a template from 1789.

DIE PFÄLZER LINIEN
Linie Pfalz-Zweibrücken

Errichtung eines Freiheitsbaumes in Zweibrücken am 11.2.1793 durch französische Revolutionstruppen.
Die Errichtung der Freiheitsbäume entsprang vielfach nicht einem spontanen Entschluss der heimischen Bürger, sondern geschah auf Anordnung der französischen Besatzung. Auf diesem Kupferstich wendet sich der Zweibrücker Hofmaler Johann Kaspar Pitz, der sich im Vordergrund rechts selbst dargestellt hat, voller Abscheu vom derben Treiben um den Freiheitsbaum ab, der gerade vor dem Zweibrücker Schloss errichtet wird. Pitz hatte durch die Revolution seinen Arbeitgeber, den ins Exil geflüchteten Zweibrücker Herzog Karl II. August, verloren und musste das Land auf der Suche nach neuen Aufträgen verlassen.
Aquarellierter Kupferstich von Hieronymus Löschenkohl nach Johann Kaspar Pitz (1756–1795), um 1793.

Set-up of a liberty tree in Zweibrücken by French revolutionary troops on 11 February 1793.
On many occasions, the set-up of liberty trees did not arise from a spontaneous decision by the local citizens, but happened by order of the French occupying forces. In this copper engraving, Zweibrücken court painter Johann Kaspar Pitz, who has represented himself in the foreground on the right, turns away full of abhorrence from the gross goings-on related to the liberty tree that is being set-up in front of Zweibrücken Palace. Due to the Revolution, Pitz had lost his employer, Duke Karl II August of Zweibrücken, who had fled into exile, and had to leave the country in search of new assignments.
Watercoloured copper engraving by Hieronymus Löschenkohl based on Johann Kaspar Pitz (1756–1795), c. 1793.

DIE PFÄLZER LINIEN
Linie Zweibrücken-Birkenfeld-Gelnhausen – Herzog Wilhelm in Bayern

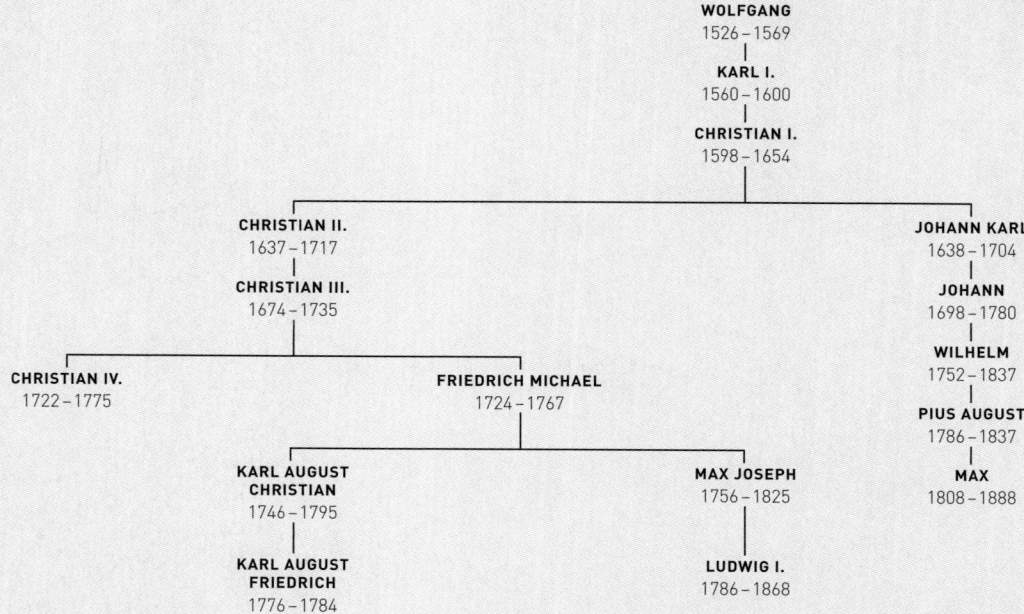

Herzog Wilhelm in Bayern (1752–1837) aus der nicht regierenden Nebenlinie Zweibrücken-Birkenfeld-Gelnhausen.
Durch Wilhelm wurde die Linie der „Herzöge in Bayern" 1799 begründet, da ihm sein Vetter und Schwager, Kurfürst Maximilian IV. Joseph, diesen Titel verlieh. Er regierte als Statthalter des Kurfürsten von 1803 bis 1805 das Herzogtum Berg bei Düsseldorf.
Öl auf Porzellan, signiert P. K., 19. Jahrundert.

Duke Wilhelm in Bavaria (1752–1837) from the non-ruling Zweibrücken-Birkenfeld-Gelnhausen branch line.
Wilhelm established the line of "Dukes in Bavaria" in 1799, since his cousin and brother-in-law Prince-Elector Maximilian IV Joseph gave him this title. He ruled over the Duchy of Berg, near Düsseldorf, as the Prince-Elector's governor from 1803 to 1805.
Oil on porcelain, signed P. K., 19th century.

DIE PFÄLZER LINIEN
Linie Zweibrücken-Birkenfeld-Gelnhausen – Herzog Wilhelm in Bayern

Herzog Wilhelm in Bayern beim Ausritt.
Im Hintergrund ist „Schloss" Banz zu sehen, ein vormaliges Benediktinerkloster, das Wilhelm 1814 erwarb. Er reitet hier in Begleitung seines Stallmeisters und Leibjägers Kegel und Lakaien.
Ölgemälde wahrschl. von Sebastian Scharnagl, nach 1814.

Duke Wilhelm in Bavaria going for a ride.
In the background, Banz "Castle", a former Benedictine monastery acquired by Wilhelm in 1814, can be seen. Here he rides accompanied by his stable master and gamekeeper Kegel and Lakaien.
Oil painting likely by Sebastian Scharnagl, after 1814.

DIE PFÄLZER LINIEN
Linie Zweibrücken-Birkenfeld-Gelnhausen – Herzog Pius in Bayern

Herzog Pius in Bayern (1786–1837) als Kind mit Hubertusorden auf der Terrasse von Schloss Banz.
Pius August war der zweite Sohn und nach dem Tod des Erstgeborenen der Stammhalter von Herzog Wilhelm in Bayern und seiner Gemahlin Maria Anna.
Gouachemalerei eines unbekannten Künstlers, Ende des 18. Jahrhunderts.

Duke Pius in Bavaria (1786–1837) as a child with the Order of St. Hubert on the terrace of Banz Castle.
Pius August was the second son and after the death of the firstborn the son and heir of Duke Wilhelm in Bavaria and his consort Maria Anna.
Gouache painting by an unknown artist, end of the 18th century.

Herzog Pius in Bayern im Englischen Garten in München.
Herzog Pius heiratete 1807 Amalia Luise von Arenberg. Traurige Berühmtheit erlangte er durch seine cholerischen Ausbrüche und psychischen Auffälligkeiten, aufgrund derer er den größten Teil seines Erwachsenenlebens zurückgezogen in Bayreuth oder auf Schloss Seehof bei Bamberg verbrachte.
Ölgemälde von Moritz oder Joseph Kellerhoven, 1815.

Duke Pius in Bavaria in the English Garden in Munich.
In 1807, Duke Pius married Amalia Luise of Arenberg. He gained notoriety due to his choleric outbursts and mental problems, on account of which he spent the majority of his adult life in seclusion in Bayreuth or at Seehof Palace near Bamberg.
Oil painting by Moritz or Joseph Kellerhoven, 1815.

DIE PFÄLZER LINIEN
Linie Zweibrücken-Birkenfeld-Gelnhausen – Herzog Maximilian in Bayern

Herzogin Amalia Luise in Bayern, geborene Prinzessin und Herzogin von Arenberg (1789 – 1823), mit Sohn Maximilian.
Maximilian Joseph war der einzige Sohn Herzog Pius' und seiner Gemahlin Amalia Luise in Bayern. Seine Erziehung übernahm allerdings sein Großvater, Herzog Wilhelm.
Ölgemälde von Louis André Gabriel Bouchet, 1811.

Duchess Amalia Luise in Bavaria, born Princess and Duchess of Arenberg (1789 – 1823), with son Maximilian.
Maximilian Joseph was the only son of Duke Pius and his consort Amalia Luise in Bavaria. However, he was raised by his grandfather, Duke Wilhelm.
Oil painting by Louis André Gabriel Bouchet, 1811.

Herzog Max in Bayern (1808 – 1888).
Der junge Max genoss eine umfassende Schulbildung im „Königlichen Erziehungs-Insitut für Studierende" in München. Seine freie Zeit verbrachte er vor allem im Kreise der königlichen Familie.
Ölgemälde, signiert S. Diez, 1837.

Duke Max in Bavaria (1808 – 1888).
The young Max enjoyed comprehensive schooling at the "Royal Educational Institute for Students" in Munich. He spent most of his free time with the royal family.
Oil painting, signed S. Diez, 1837.

DIE PFÄLZER LINIEN
Linie Zweibrücken-Birkenfeld-Gelnhausen – Herzog Maximilian in Bayern

Hochzeit von Herzog Maximilian in Bayern und Prinzessin Ludovika von Bayern in Tegernsee am 9. September 1828.
Lithografie nach Franz Xaver Nachtmann, um 1828.

Marriage of Duke Maximilian in Bavaria and Princess Ludovika of Bavaria in Tegernsee on 9 September 1828.
Lithography based on Franz Xaver Nachtmann, c. 1828.

Herzog Maximilian in Bayern (1808–1888) und seine Gemahlin Ludovika, geb. Prinzessin von Bayern (1808–1892), als junges Ehepaar am Tegernsee.
Die Hochzeit Maximilians und der gleichaltrigen Ludovika, einer der jüngeren Töchter von König Max I. Joseph, versprach den Fortbestand der herzoglichen Linie. Dem Paar wurden zehn Kinder geboren, von denen acht das Erwachsenenalter erreichten; darunter die spätere Kaiserin von Österreich Elisabeth und die König Ludwig II. anverlobte Sophie.
Ölgemälde von Joseph Karl Stieler, 1830.

Duke Maximilian in Bavaria (1808–1888) and his consort Ludovika, born Princess of Bavaria (1808–1892), as a young married couple by the Tegernsee.
The marriage of Maximilian and the same-aged Ludovika, one of the younger daughters of King Max I Joseph, was to mean the preservation of the ducal line. Ten children were born to the couple, eight of whom reached adult age; these included the later Empress of Austria, Elisabeth, and Sophie, who was affianced to King Ludwig II.
Oil painting by Joseph Karl Stieler, 1830.

DIE PFÄLZER LINIEN
Linie Zweibrücken-Birkenfeld-Gelnhausen – Herzog Maximilian in Bayern

Innere Ansicht des Circus im Hofraum des Herzog-Max-Palais in München.
Herzog Maximilian in Bayern unterhielt einen privaten Circus in seinem von 1828 bis 1831 errichteten Stadtpalais. Er war ein hervorragender Kunstreiter und bildete auch seine Tochter Elisabeth, die spätere Kaiserin von Österreich, zu einer exzellenten Reiterin aus. Hier ist er selbst auf zwei Pferderücken stehend („Ungarische Post") in seinem Circus zu sehen.
Tuschezeichnung von Heinrich von Mayr, um 1830.

Interior view of the circus in the courtyard of the Prince Max Palace in Munich.
Duke Maximilian in Bavaria maintained a private circus in his town house, which was constructed between 1828 and 1831. He was an outstanding circus rider and also trained his daughter Elisabeth, the later Empress of Austria, to be an excellent rider. Here, he himself can be seen in his circus standing on two horsebacks ("Roman riding").
Ink drawing by Heinrich von Mayr, c. 1830.

Herzog Maximilian in Bayern bei seiner Orientreise in Theben, Oberägypten.
Herzog Max unternahm viele ausgedehnte Reisen. Eine seiner bekanntesten ist zweifellos sein Aufenthalt im Vorderen Orient im Jahr 1838. Im Schatten der Pyramiden soll der Kunstsinnige sogar die Zither, sein Lieblingsinstrument, gespielt haben. Wie viele andere Ägytenreisende seiner Zeit verewigte sich Herzog Max auf einer der gigantischen Ramses-Statuen des großen Tempels bei Abu Simbel namentlich mit einer eingemeißelten lateinischen Inschrift und einer stilisierten bayerischen Krone.
Lithographie von Heinrich von Mayr, nach 1839.

Duke Maximilian in Bavaria on his oriental trip in Thebes, Upper Egypt.
Duke Max went on many extensive trips. Undoubtedly one of his best-known is his stay in the Near East in 1838. The art enthusiast is even said to have played the zither, his favourite instrument, in the shadows of the pyramids. Like many other travellers to Egypt of his time, Duke Max immortalised himself on one of the huge Ramesses statues of the large temple near Abu Simbel with a carved Latin inscription of his name and a stylised Bavarian crown.
Lithography by Heinrich von Mayr, after 1839.

DIE PFÄLZER LINIEN
Linie Zweibrücken-Birkenfeld-Gelnhausen – Herzog Maximilian in Bayern

Schloss Possenhofen.
1834 erwarb Herzog Max Possenhofen bei Pöcking am Starnberger See. Es war fortan ein beliebter Aufenthaltsort der herzoglichen Familie.
Ölgemälde von Matthias Wehli, 1866.

Possenhofen Castle.
In 1834, Duke Max acquired Possenhofen in Pöcking by Lake Starnberg. From then on, it was a popular abode of the ducal family.
Oil painting by Matthias Wehli, 1866.

Elisabeth in Bayern (1837–1898), spätere Kaiserin von Österreich und Königin von Ungarn, vor Schloss Possenhofen am Starnberger See.
Elisabeth verbrachte mit ihren zahlreichen Geschwistern in Possenhofen eine meist unbeschwerte Kindheit. Als sie im Alter von 16 Jahren Kaiserin wurde, konnte sie sich nur schwer mit den Zwängen des österreichischen Hoflebens in Wien abfinden.
Ölgemälde von Karl Theodor Piloty, 1853.

Elisabeth in Bavaria (1837–1898), later Empress of Austria and Queen of Hungary, in front of Possenhofen Castle by Lake Starnberg.
Elisabeth spent a mostly carefree childhood with her numerous siblings in Possenhofen. When she became Empress at the age of 16, she found it difficult to come to terms with the constraints of life at the Austrian court in Vienna.
Oil painting by Karl Theodor Piloty, 1853.

DIE PFÄLZER LINIEN
Linie Zweibrücken-Birkenfeld-Gelnhausen – Herzog Maximilian in Bayern

Herzog Maximilian Emanuel in Bayern (1849–1893), der vierte Sohn von Herzog Maximilian und Herzogin Ludovika.
Kreidezeichnung von Joseph Karl Stieler, 1854.

Duke Maximilian Emanuel in Bavaria (1849–1893), the fourth son of Duke Maximilian and Duchess Ludovika.
Chalk drawing by Joseph Karl Stieler, 1854.

Die Kinder Herzog Maximilians und der Herzogin Ludovika in Bayern.
V. l. n. r.: Sophie, die spätere Herzogin von Alençon, Max Emanuel, Karl Theodor, Helene, die spätere Erbprinzessin von Thurn und Taxis, Ludwig Wilhelm in der Uniform des 1. Chevaulegers-Regiments, Mathilde, die spätere Gräfin von Trani, Marie, die spätere Königin beider Sizilien. Es fehlen Elisabeth und ein kurz nach der Geburt verstorbener Sohn Maximilian. König Ludwig I. ließ dieses Gemälde als Geschenk für Elisabeth, die zweite Tochter des Paares, zu ihrer Hochzeit mit Kaiser Franz Joseph von Österreich malen.
Ölgemälde von Joseph Karl Stieler, 1854.

The children of Duke Maximilian and Duchess Ludovika in Bavaria.
From left to right: Sophie, the later Duchess of Alençon, Max Emanuel, Karl Theodor, Helene, the later heir to the throne of the Thurn and Taxis family, Ludwig Wilhelm in the uniform of the 1st Chevau-légers regiment, Mathilde, the later Countess of Trani, Marie, the later Queen of the Two Sicilies. Elisabeth and Maximilian – the latter of whom died shortly after his birth – are missing. King Ludwig I had this painting produced as a gift for Elisabeth, the couple's second daughter, to mark her wedding to Emperor Franz Joseph of Austria.
Oil painting by Joseph Karl Stieler, 1854.

DIE PFÄLZER LINIEN
Linie Zweibrücken-Birkenfeld-Gelnhausen – Herzog Karl Theodor in Bayern

Herzog Karl Theodor in Bayern und seine Familie bei einem Ausritt.
Ölgemälde von Richard B. Adam, 1901.

Duke Karl Theodor in Bavaria and his family going for a ride.
Oil painting by Richard B. Adam, 1901.

Herzog Karl Theodor in Bayern (1839–1909) bei einem Ausritt mit seiner zweiten Gemahlin Herzogin Marie José, Infantin von Portugal (1857–1943).
Karl Theodor, der zweite Sohn Herzog Maximilians, schlug eine „unstandesgemäße", aber äußerst erfolgreiche medizinische Laufbahn ein. 1895/96 gründete er die heute noch bestehende „Augenklinik Herzog Carl Theodor" in München.
Ölgemälde von Julius Blaas, 1896.

Duke Karl Theodor in Bavaria (1839–1909) going for a ride with his second consort Duchess Marie José, Infanta of Portugal (1857–1943).
Karl Theodor, the second son of Duke Maximilian, pursued a medical career that was "out of keeping with his class" but extremely successful. In 1895/96, he founded the "Duke Carl Theodor Eye Clinic" in Munich, which still exists today.
Oil painting by Julius Blaas, 1896.

DIE PFÄLZER LINIEN
Linie Zweibrücken-Birkenfeld-Gelnhausen – Herzog Karl Theodor in Bayern

Herzogin Marie Gabriele in Bayern (1878–1912) und ihre Schwester Herzogin Elisabeth in Bayern (1876–1965).
Marie Gabriele war eine Tochter Karl Theodors und erste Gemahlin von Kronprinz Rupprecht von Bayern. Ihre Schwester Elisabeth heiratete im Jahr 1900 Kronprinz Albert von Belgien und wurde so 1909 Königin von Belgien.
Pastellzeichnung von Albertine „Tini" Rupprecht, vor 1912.

Duchess Marie Gabriele in Bavaria (1878–1912) and her sister Duchess Elisabeth in Bavaria (1876–1965).
Marie Gabriele was a daughter of Karl Theodor and the first consort of Crown Prince Rupprecht of Bavaria. Her sister Elisabeth married Crown Prince Albert of Belgium in 1900, thus becoming Queen of Belgium in 1909.
Pastel drawing by Albertine "Tini" Rupprecht, before 1912.

Herzog Karl Theodor in Bayern mit seiner zweiten Gemahlin Herzogin Marie José, Infantin von Portugal, Prinzessin von Braganza.
Kreidezeichnung von Franz von Lenbach, 1894.

Duke Karl Theodor in Bavaria with his second consort Duchess Marie José, Infanta of Portugal, Princess of Braganza.
Chalk drawing by Franz von Lenbach, 1894.

DIE PFÄLZER LINIEN
Linie Zweibrücken-Birkenfeld-Gelnhausen – Herzog Karl Theodor in Bayern

Im Hörsaal Theodor Billroths.
Der Chirurg Professor Theodor Billroth (1829–1894) während einer Demonstration vor Studenten im Hörsaal des Allgemeinen Krankenhauses zu Wien. Unter den Hörern befand sich auch Herzog Karl Theodor in Bayern (dritter von links in der untersten Sitzreihe). Er praktizierte als Arzt für Allgemeinmedizin und Chirurgie, bevor er sich der Augenheilkunde zuwandte.
Gemälde von Adalbert Franz Seligmann, 1890.

In Theodor Billroth's lecture theatre.
Surgeon Professor Theodor Billroth (1829–1894) during a demonstration in front of students in the lecture theatre of Vienna General Hospital. Among the listeners was Duke Karl Theodor in Bavaria (third from the left in the lowest row of seats). He practised as a doctor of general medicine and surgery before turning his attention to ophthalmology.
Painting by Adalbert Franz Seligmann, 1890.

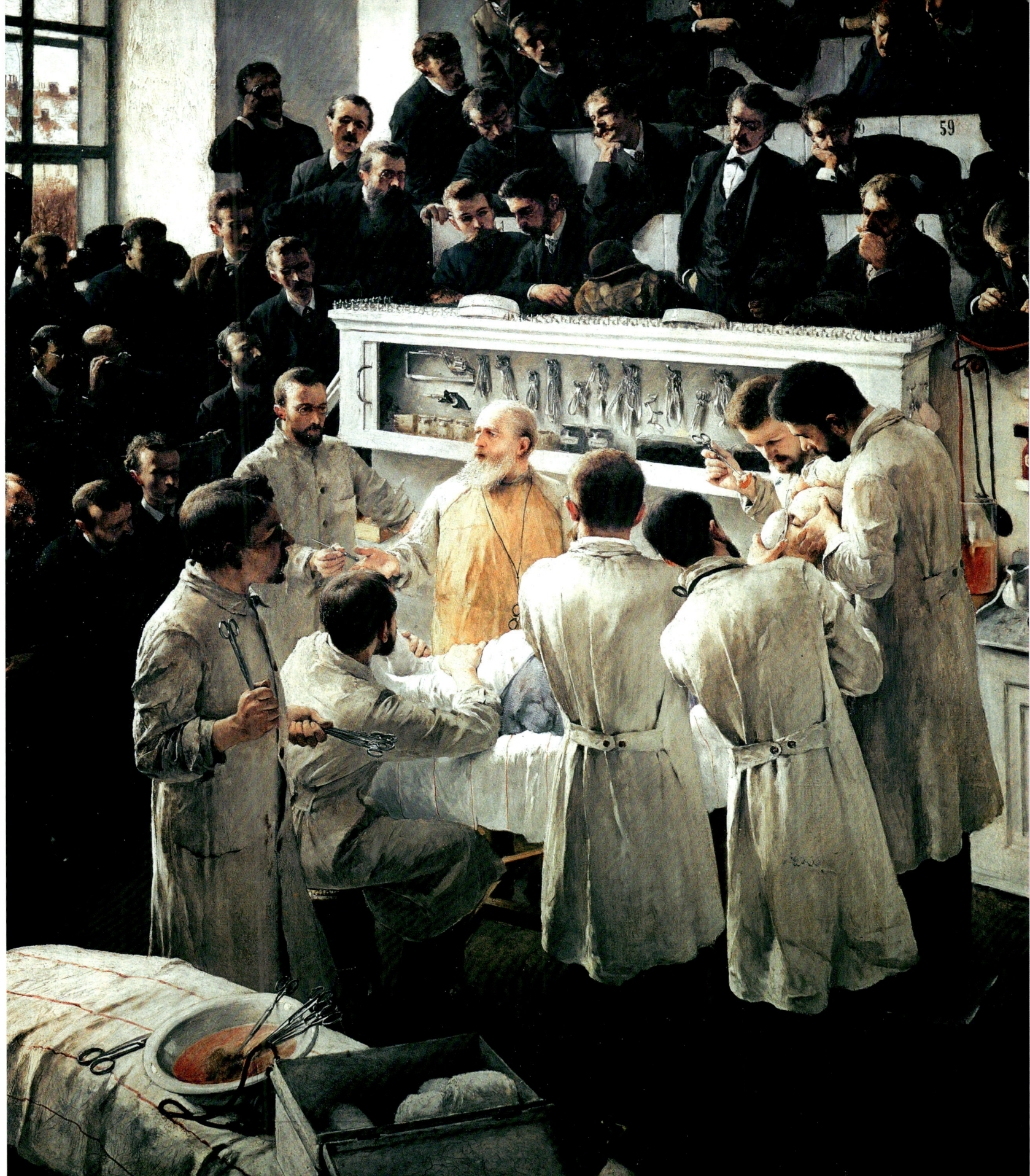

DIE PFÄLZER LINIEN
Linie Zweibrücken-Birkenfeld-Gelnhausen – Herzog Ludwig Wilhelm in Bayern

Herzogin Eleonore in Bayern (1880 – 1965), Gemahlin von Herzog Ludwig Wilhelm, geborene Prinzessin zu Sayn-Wittgenstein-Berleburg.
Ölgemälde von Friedrich Klein-Chevalier, o. J.

Duchess Eleonore in Bavaria (1880 – 1965), consort of Duke Ludwig Wilhelm, born Princess of Sayn-Wittgenstein-Berleburg.
Oil painting by Friedrich Klein-Chevalier, undated.

Herzog Ludwig Wilhelm in Bayern (1884 – 1968).
Ludwig Wilhelm war nach vier Töchtern der erste Sohn Herzog Karl Theodors in Bayern und ein bedeutender Förderer der bayerischen Volksmusik. Von seinem Vater erbte er Schloss Tegernsee. 1917 heiratete er Prinzessin Eleonore zu Sayn-Wittgenstein-Berleburg.
Gouachemalerei von Th. Baumgartner, 1954.

Duke Ludwig Wilhelm in Bavaria (1884 – 1968).
Ludwig Wilhelm was the first son of Duke Karl Theodor in Bavaria, after four daughters, and an important promoter of Bavarian folk music. He inherited Tegernsee Castle from his father. In 1917, he married Princess Eleonore of Sayn-Wittgenstein-Berleburg.
Gouache painting by Th. Baumgartner, 1954.

DIE PFÄLZER LINIEN
Linie Zweibrücken-Birkenfeld-Gelnhausen – Herzog Luitpold in Bayern

Herzog Luitpold in Bayern vor dem Panorama des Kreuther Tals südlich von Schloss Ringberg. Luitpold Emanuel Ludwig Maria war ein Enkel Herzog Maximilians in Bayern. Sein Vater Maximilian Emanuel war der jüngste Sohn des Herzogspaares Ludovika und Max. Als Kunsthistoriker baute Herzog Luitpold über 60 Jahre an seinem Lebensprojekt, dem Schloss Ringberg. Er blieb unverheiratet. *Ölgemälde von Friedrich Attenhuber, 1944.*

Duke Luitpold in Bavaria in front of the panorama of Kreuth Valley, south of Ringberg Castle. Luitpold Emanuel Ludwig Maria was a grandson of Duke Maximilian in Bavaria. His father Maximilian Emanuel was the youngest son of the ducal couple Ludovika and Max. As an art historian, Duke Luitpold spent over 60 years building his life project, Ringberg Castle. He remained unmarried. *Oil painting by Friedrich Attenhuber, 1944.*

Herzog Luitpold in Bayern (1890–1973) bei der Lektüre. *Ölgemälde wahrschl. von Friedrich Attenhuber, um 1920.*

Duke Luitpold in Bavaria (1890–1973), reading. *Oil painting likely by Friedrich Attenhuber, c. 1920.*

The Kingdom of Bavaria

From 1799, for the first time since the days of Ludwig the Bavarian, there was again a solely ruling line of the house of Wittelsbach. Although the family branched out into several lines in the generations following Max Joseph, there was no further division of either territory or rule.

Of course, the monarchs particularly stand out among these branches of the royal house: King Max I Joseph (1756/1806–1825), King Ludwig I (1786/1825–1868), King Maximilian II (1811/1848–1864), King Ludwig II (1845/1864 1886), King Otto (1848/1886–1916), Prince Regent Luitpold (1821/1886–1912) and the last King of Bavaria Ludwig III (1845/1912–1918).

The original royal line died out with the grandsons of Ludwig I (Ludwig II and Otto), while two later-born sons of Ludwig I (Luitpold and Adalbert) became for their part the originators of lines: the Luitpoldine line, which became the royal line after the royal crisis of 1886, and the Adalbertine Line, both of which still flourish.

Two features still need to be added: firstly, the fact that another son of Ludwig I, Otto, was King of Greece from 1832 to 1862, and that in 1799 the later-born Palatine line of Birkenfeld-Gelnhausen became the ducal line in Bavaria, which produced such striking figures as Duke Maximilian (1808–1888), called "Zithermaxl", and his daughter the Austrian Empress Elisabeth (1837–1898), and which exists to the present day.

The members of the royal family, most of all of course the respective reigning monarchs, were confronted with the challenges of the 19th century in an extremely intense way: on the one hand, with the consequences of the upheaval of the 18th to 19th century, and on the other with those new developments and dramatic changes that characterised the 19th century itself. In this context one will recognise the dangers to the sovereignty of the Kingdom of Bavaria in view of the movement for a German nation and the incorporation of Bavaria into the German Empire of 1871, and also the social processes of transformation following industrialisation, which took hold only slowly in Bavaria, and finally the shifts of strength in the triangle of power between monarch, ministers and parliament.

Das Königreich Bayern

Seit 1799 gab es zum ersten Mal seit den Tagen Ludwigs des Bayern wieder eine allein regierende Linie des Hauses Wittelsbach. Zwar verästelte sich die Familie in den auf Max Joseph folgenden Generationen wiederum in verschiedene Linien, aber es kam zu keiner Teilung mehr, weder des Territoriums noch der Herrschaft.

Natürlich ragen aus diesen Verästelungen des Königlichen Hauses die Monarchen in besonderer Weise heraus: König Max I. Joseph (1756/1806–1825), König Ludwig I. (1786/1825–1868), König Maximilian II. (1811/1848–1864), König Ludwig II. (1845/1864–1886), König Otto (1848/1886–1916), Prinzregent Luitpold (1821/1886–1912) und der letzte König Bayerns Ludwig III. (1845/1912–1918).

Die ursprüngliche Königliche Linie starb mit den Enkeln Ludwigs I. (Ludwig II. und Otto) aus, während zwei nachgeborene Söhne Ludwigs I. (Luitpold und Adalbert) ihrerseits zu Linienstiftern wurden: der luitpoldinischen Linie, die nach der Königskatastrophe von 1886 zur Königlichen Linie wurde, und der adalbertinischen Linie, die beide noch heute blühen.

Zwei Besonderheiten wird man noch hinzufügen: zum einen den Umstand, dass ein weiterer Sohn Ludwigs I., Otto, von 1832 bis 1862 König von Griechenland war, und dass 1799 aus der nachgeborenen pfälzischen Linie Birkenfeld-Gelnhausen die Linie der Herzöge in Bayern wurde, aus der so markante Figuren wie der „Zithermaxl" genannte Herzog Maximilian (1808–1888) und seine Tochter, die österreichische Kaiserin Elisabeth (1837–1898), stammten und die bis zum heutigen Tag existiert.

Die Angehörigen des Königlichen Hauses, vornehmlich natürlich die jeweils regierenden Monarchen, waren mit den Herausforderungen des 19. Jahrhunderts auf das Heftigste konfrontiert: einmal mit den Konsequenzen des skizzierten Umbruchs vom 18. auf das 19. Jahrhundert, zum anderen mit jenen neuen Entwicklungen und dramatischen Veränderungen, die das 19. Jahrhundert selbst kennzeichneten. In diesem Zusammenhang wird man die Gefährdungen der Souveränität des Königreichs Bayern angesichts der deutschen Nationalstaatsbewegung und die Eingliederung Bayerns in das deutsche Kaiserreich von 1871 sehen, ferner die gesellschaftlichen und sozialen Wandlungsprozesse im Gefolge der in Bayern nur langsam einsetzenden Industrialisierung und schließlich die Schwergewichtsverlagerungen im Machtdreieck von Monarch, Ministerium und Parlament.

King Max I Joseph

For a long time, it looked as if Maximilian Joseph of Birkenfeld-Zweibrücken would never have to assume a ruling position. A military career seemed predestined for him and the younger son of Count Palatine Friedrich Michael, who received a highly advanced education in the Rousseauian style, received his first position as Colonel in the French Royal Alsace regiment at the age of 20. Even during the life of Prince-Elector Karl Theodor, who remained without a living heir, it became apparent that the electoral dignity would go to Friedrich Michael or his eldest son Karl August.

As a young soldier, Maximilian Joseph spent carefree years in Alsace and Paris – his happy-go-lucky nature being finally ended with his marriage to Auguste Wilhelmine of Hesse-Darmstadt in 1785. During the French Revolution, Max Joseph fled with his family first to Mannheim and later to Ansbach. In 1797, he remarried after the premature death of his beloved first wife; this time he married Princess Karoline of Baden, who was to become Electress at his side in 1799. Since Karl II August had died unexpectedly in 1795, his younger brother was now the one to assume rulership as the successor to Karl Theodor after all.

Even in the difficult years of the Revolution and the Napoleonic wars, Max Joseph assisted Maximilian Count von Montgelas as his primary adviser and became his First Minister in 1799. In 1801, Bavaria lost all its territories west of the Rhine to France in the Treaty of Lunéville.

However, with the German mediatisation of 1803 it received the secularised and mediatised territories of the ecclesiastical principalities and former imperial cities of Franconia and Swabia as compensation. In 1805, Max Joseph ultimately sided with Napoleon, on whose initiative Bavaria was proclaimed as a kingdom in 1806 and the Prince-Elector was proclaimed as King Max I Joseph. His firstborn son Ludwig was thus now Crown Prince.

In this collapse of the structures of the Old Empire, Montgelas successfully reorganised Bavaria according to the French model. With the territorial changes during the Coalition Wars and the constitution of 1808, Max Joseph and Montgelas made Bavaria a largely cohesive middle power in terms of its surface area. Fundamental reforms were implemented in almost all areas of public life and the state was now governed in a strict centralistic fashion. After Napoleon's disastrous Russia expedition in 1812, which also claimed the lives of approximately 30,000 Bavarian soldiers, the King turned his back on the French Emperor; from now on, the Bavarian army fought alongside the allied forces in the campaign against france. Napoleon was defeated in the Battle of Leipzig in 1813. Partly owing to the endeavours of Crown Prince Ludwig, who was an avowed opponent of Montgelas, the young kingdom received a second constitution in 1818 that made Bavaria a constitutional monarchy. The first king of Bavaria died in 1825. However, in his son Ludwig he left an extremely well-prepared successor.

König Max I. Joseph

Lange Zeit sah es nicht danach aus, als ob Maximilian Joseph von Birkenfeld-Zweibrücken je als Regent würde antreten müssen. Eine militärische Karriere schien ihm vorbestimmt und so erhielt der sehr fortschrittlich im Rousseau'schen Stil erzogene jüngere Sohn des Pfalzgrafen Friedrich Michael im Alter von 20 Jahren seine erste Position als Oberst im französischen Regiment Royal Alsace. Schon zu Lebzeiten des Kurfürsten Karl Theodor, der ohne lebenden Erben blieb, zeichnete sich ab, dass die Kurwürde einmal an Friedrich Michael bzw. an seinen ältesten Sohn Karl August gehen würde.

Als junger Soldat verbrachte Maximilian Joseph unbeschwerte Jahre im Elsass und in Paris – seiner Leichtlebigkeit wurde schließlich in der Eheschließung mit Auguste Wilhelmine von Hessen-Darmstadt 1785 ein Ende gesetzt. Während der Französischen Revolution floh Max Joseph mit seiner Familie zuerst nach Mannheim, später nach Ansbach. 1797 heiratete er nach dem frühen Tod seiner geliebten ersten Frau erneut: die badische Prinzessin Karoline, die 1799 an seiner Seite Kurfürstin werden sollte. Da Karl II. August 1795 unerwartet verstorben war, lag es nun doch an seinem jüngeren Bruder, die Herrschaft als Nachfolger Kurfürst Karl Theodors anzutreten.

Bereits in den schwierigen Jahren der Revolution und der napoleonischen Kriege stand Max Joseph als erster Berater Maximilian Graf von Montgelas zur Seite, der 1799 zu seinem Ersten Minister aufstieg. 1801 verlor Bayern im Frieden von Lunéville alle linksrheinischen Gebiete an Frankreich, erhielt jedoch durch den Reichsdeputationshauptschluss von 1803 als Entschädigung u. a. die säkularisierten und mediatisierten Gebiete der kirchlichen Fürstentümer und ehemaligen Reichsstädte Frankens und Schwabens. 1805 schlug sich Max Joseph endgültig auf die Seite Napoleons, auf dessen Initiative Bayern 1806 zum Königreich und der Kurfürst zu König Max I. Joseph proklamiert wurde. Sein erstgeborener Sohn Ludwig war somit nun Kronprinz.

In diesem Zusammenbruch der Strukturen des Alten Reiches gelang Montgelas eine Neuorganisation Bayerns nach französischem Vorbild. Mit den Gebietsveränderungen im Zuge der Koalitionskriege und der Verfassung von 1808 machten Max Joseph und Montgelas Bayern zu einem flächenmäßig weitgehend zusammenhängenden Mittelstaat. Grundlegende Reformen in nahezu allen Bereichen des öffentlichen Lebens wurden durchgesetzt und der Staat nun straff zentralistisch verwaltet. Nach Napoleons desaströsem Russlandfeldzug 1812, dem auch etwa 30.000 bayerische Soldaten zum Opfer fielen, wandte sich der König vom französischen Kaiser ab; die bayerische Armee beteiligte sich nun an der Seite der alliierten Mächte am Feldzug gegen Frankreich. Napoleon wurde 1813 in der Völkerschlacht bei Leipzig besiegt. 1818 erhielt das junge Königreich u. a. auf Bestreben des Kronprinzen Ludwig, der ein erklärter Gegner Montgelas' war, eine zweite Verfassung, die Bayern zu einer konstitutionellen Monarchie machte. 1825 starb der erste König Bayerns, doch hinterließ er mit seinem Sohn Ludwig einen mehr als bestens vorbereiteten Nachfolger.

DAS KÖNIGREICH BAYERN
König Maximilian I. Joseph von Bayern

Eintrag mit Wappen von König Maximilian I. Joseph im Bruderschaftsbuch der Corpus-Christi-Bruderschaft bei St. Peter in München.

Entry with coat of arms of King Maximilian I Joseph in the Book of the Brotherhood of the Corpus Christi Brotherhood at St. Peter's Church in Munich.

König Maximilian I. Joseph von Bayern (1756–1825) im Thronornat mit Krone, Szepter und Schwert.
Am 1. Januar 1806 wurde Kurfürst Maximilian IV. Joseph zum König proklamiert. Er nannte sich fortan Max I. Joseph. Eine tatsächliche Krönung fand jedoch nie statt.
Gemälde von Joseph Karl Stieler, 1822.

King Maximilian I Joseph of Bavaria (1756–1825) in the king's regalia with crown, sceptre and sword.
On 1 January 1806, Prince-Elector Maximilian IV Joseph was proclaimed King. From then on, he called himself Max I Joseph. However, an actual coronation never took place.
Painting by Joseph Karl Stieler, 1822.

DAS KÖNIGREICH BAYERN
König Maximilian I. Joseph von Bayern

Pfalzgraf Maximilian Joseph als vierjähriger Knabe beim Federballspiel.
Dem unbeschwerten, sorglosen Federballspiel des kindlichen Prinzen steht mit den Spielsachen im rechten Bildbereich bereits das Kriegsspiel als Vorbereitung auf den Ernst des Lebens gegenüber. Dem Zweitgeborenen Max Joseph schien, wie seinem Vater, eine militärische Laufbahn vorherbestimmt.
Ölgemälde von Johann Georg Ziesenis, 1760.

Count Palatine Maximilian Joseph as a four-year old boy playing badminton.
With the toys in the right-hand area of the picture opposite the child prince's light-hearted, carefree badminton game is already the war game as preparation for the serious side of life. Like his father, the second-born Max Joseph seemed pre-destined for a military career.
Oil painting by Johann Georg Ziesenis, 1760.

DAS KÖNIGREICH BAYERN
König Maximilian I. Joseph von Bayern

Auguste Wilhelmine Marie Landgräfin von Hessen-Darmstadt (1765–1796).
Auguste Wilhelmine wurde 1785 Max Josephs erste Gemahlin. Ihre Ehe währte nur wenige Jahre: Nach der Geburt ihres fünften Kindes starb die geschwächte Pfalzgräfin schon 1796.
Pastellgemälde von Johann Friedrich Dryander, um 1785.

Auguste Wilhelmine Marie Landgravine of Hesse-Darmstadt (1765–1796).
Auguste Wilhelmine became Max Joseph's first consort in 1785. Their marriage lasted only a few years: after the birth of their fifth child, the weakened Countess Palatine died in 1796.
Pastel painting by Johann Friedrich Dryander, c. 1785.

Pfalzgraf/Prinz Max Joseph als Oberst des Regiments „Royal Alsace".
Als Geschenk zur Geburt seines Erben Ludwig überreichten die Offiziere des von Max Joseph geführten Regiments „Royal Alsace" ihrem Oberst ein Kissen für den kleinen Prinzen, das mit ihren Bärten und Haaren gefüllt war.
Gemälde von Johann Friedrich Dryander, 1785.

Count Palatine/Prince Max Joseph as Colonel of the Royal Alsace regiment.
As a gift to mark the birth of his heir Ludwig, the officers of the "Royal Alsace" regiment, led by Max Joseph, handed their Colonel a pillow for the little prince that was filled with their beards and hair.
Painting by Johann Friedrich Dryander, 1785.

DAS KÖNIGREICH BAYERN
König Maximilian I. Joseph von Bayern

Auguste Wilhelmine von Zweibrücken mit ihren Kindern Ludwig, dem späteren König Ludwig I., und Auguste Amalie.
Die junge Pfalzgräfin ist hier mit ihren beiden ersten Kindern in einer Parklandschaft, möglicherweise bei Schloss Rohrbach, dargestellt. Das Bildnis erinnert an englische Porträttypen der Romantik.
Gemälde von Johann J. F. Langenhöffel, 1791.

Auguste Wilhelmine of Zweibrücken with her children Ludwig, the later King Ludwig I, and Auguste Amalie.
The young Countess Palatine is here represented with her first two children in a parkland, possibly at Rohrbach Palace. The portrait is reminiscent of English portrait types of the Romantic period.
Painting by Johann J. F. Langenhöffel, 1791.

DAS KÖNIGREICH BAYERN
König Maximilian I. Joseph von Bayern

Porträt des Maximilian Joseph Graf von Montgelas (1759–1838).
Der Politiker und Staatsreformer Montgelas war von 1799 bis 1817 Minister unter Kurfürst, später König Maximilian I. Joseph. Die Modernisierung der bayerischen Verwaltung lag ihm besonders am Herzen. Als treibende Kraft stand Montgelas hinter der Säkularisation von 1802/03 und legte durch geschickte Bündniswechsel mit Napoleon Bonaparte den Grundstein für den heutigen Flächenstaat Bayern.
Stich von C. Hess, 1816.

Portrait of Maximilian Joseph Count of Montgelas (1759–1838).
From 1799 to 1817, politician and state reformer Montgelas was a minister under Prince-Elector and later King Maximilian I Joseph. Modernising the Bavarian administration was particularly important to him. Montgelas was the driving force behind the secularisation of 1802/03 and by means of a skilful change of alliance with Napoleon Bonaparte he laid the foundation for today's territorial state of Bavaria.
Engraving by C. Hess, 1816.

DAS KÖNIGREICH BAYERN
König Maximilian I. Joseph von Bayern

Kloster Kaisheim, perspektivische Ansicht von Osten.
Die Säkularisation nahm in Bayern bereits 1802 ihren Anfang: Minister Montgelas setzte die Aufgabe kirchlichen Grundbesitzes, der etwa die Hälfte des landwirtschaftlich nutzbaren bayerischen Bodens betrug, durch. 1803 folgte der Reichsdeputationshauptschluss, der die territorialen Verluste im Heiligen Römischen Reich ausgleichen sollte. Beinahe alle geistlichen Reichsstände wurden aufgelöst und ihr Grund den Landesherren als Entschädigung für die linksrheinischen napoleonischen Eroberungen zugeschlagen. Kloster Kaisheim, ehemals zur Diözese Augsburg gehörig, ist hier noch in voller Pracht abgebildet: im Vordergrund die Prälatur mit dem mittig gelegenen Kaisersaal, dahinter Gästetrakt und Wirtschaftsgebäude.
Ölgemälde eines unbekannten Meisters, 1721/22.

Kaisheim Abbey, perspectival view from the east.
The secularisation began in Bavaria as early as 1802. In that year, minister Montgelas implemented the relinquishment of church property ownership, which amounted to approximately half of the agriculturally usable Bavarian land. This was followed by the Final Recess of the Reichsdeputation in 1803, which was to compensate for the territorial losses in the Holy Roman Empire. Almost all clerical imperial estates were dissolved and their land was allocated to the territorial princes as compensation for the Napoleonic conquests west of the Rhine. Here, Kaisheim Abbey, formerly belonging to the Bishopric of Augsburg, is still depicted in its full splendour: the prelature with the centrally located Emperor's Hall in the foreground; the guesthouse and the farm building are in the background.
Oil painting by an unknown master, 1721/22.

DAS KÖNIGREICH BAYERN
König Maximilian I. Joseph von Bayern

Einzug der Franzosen in München, 8. (12.) Oktober 1805.
Am Morgen des 12. Oktober 1805 zogen die verbündeten französisch-bayerischen Truppen in München ein. Die österreichischen Besatzer hatten die Stadt bereits am vorigen Abend verlassen, als die Nachricht vom Heranrücken der Männer unter Marschall Bernadotte und General Wrede die bayerische Hauptstadt erreichte. Ganz München begrüßte seine Befreier mit einem Freudenfest. Bei der von Pappeln gesäumten Landstraße handelt es sich um die heutige Landsberger Straße, auf der die Truppen durch das Karlstor in die Stadt einzogen.
Aquarell von Jean-Antoine-Siméon Fort, 1835.

Entry of the French into Munich, 8 (12) October 1805.
On the morning of 12 October 1805, the allied French-Bavarian troops entered Munich. The Austrian occupying forces had already left the city the previous evening when the news reached the Bavarian capital that the men under Marshal Bernadotte and General Wrede were advancing towards the Bavarian capital. The whole of Munich welcomed its liberators with a joyful celebration. The poplar-lined road is today's Landsberger Straße, on which the troops entered the city through the Karlstor.
Watercolour by Jean-Antoine-Siméon Fort, 1835.

DAS KÖNIGREICH BAYERN
König Maximilian I. Joseph von Bayern

Die Ziviltrauung Eugène de Beauharnais' und Auguste Amalies von Bayern in der Grünen Galerie der Münchner Residenz am 13. Januar 1806.
Die Hochzeit von Prinzessin Auguste Amalie, der ältesten Tochter König Max' I. Joseph, mit dem Stiefsohn Napoleons war einer der Höhepunkte der Feierlichkeiten zur Erhebung Bayerns zum Königreich. Auf der Estrade im Vordergrund sitzen das französische Kaiserpaar Napoleon und Joséphine, dahinter das bayerische Königspaar. Das Brautpaar tritt in weißem Spitzenkleid und grünem Rock auf die Brauteltern zu. Rings um sie versammelt sich ein Großteil des Hofstaats, darunter Kronprinz Ludwig, vom Betrachter aus rechts der Estrade, sowie der französische Außenminister Fürst Talleyrand als Trauzeuge Eugènes.
Gemälde von François-Guillaume Ménageot, 1806/08.

The civil marriage of Eugène de Beauharnais and Auguste Amalie of Bavaria in the Green Gallery of the Munich Residenz on 13 January 1806.
The wedding of Princess Auguste Amalie, the eldest daughter of King Max I Joseph, to Napoleon's stepson was one of the highlights of the festivities celebrating the elevation of Bavaria to the status of kingdom. On the estrade in the foreground sits the French imperial couple, Napoleon and Joséphine, with the Bavarian royal couple behind them. The bride and groom walk towards the bride's parents in a white lace dress and a green skirt respectively. Most of the court is congregated around them, including Crown Prince Ludwig, right of the estrade from the observer's perspective, as well as the French Foreign Minister Prince Talleyrand as Eugène's best man.
Painting by François-Guillaume Ménageot, 1806/08.

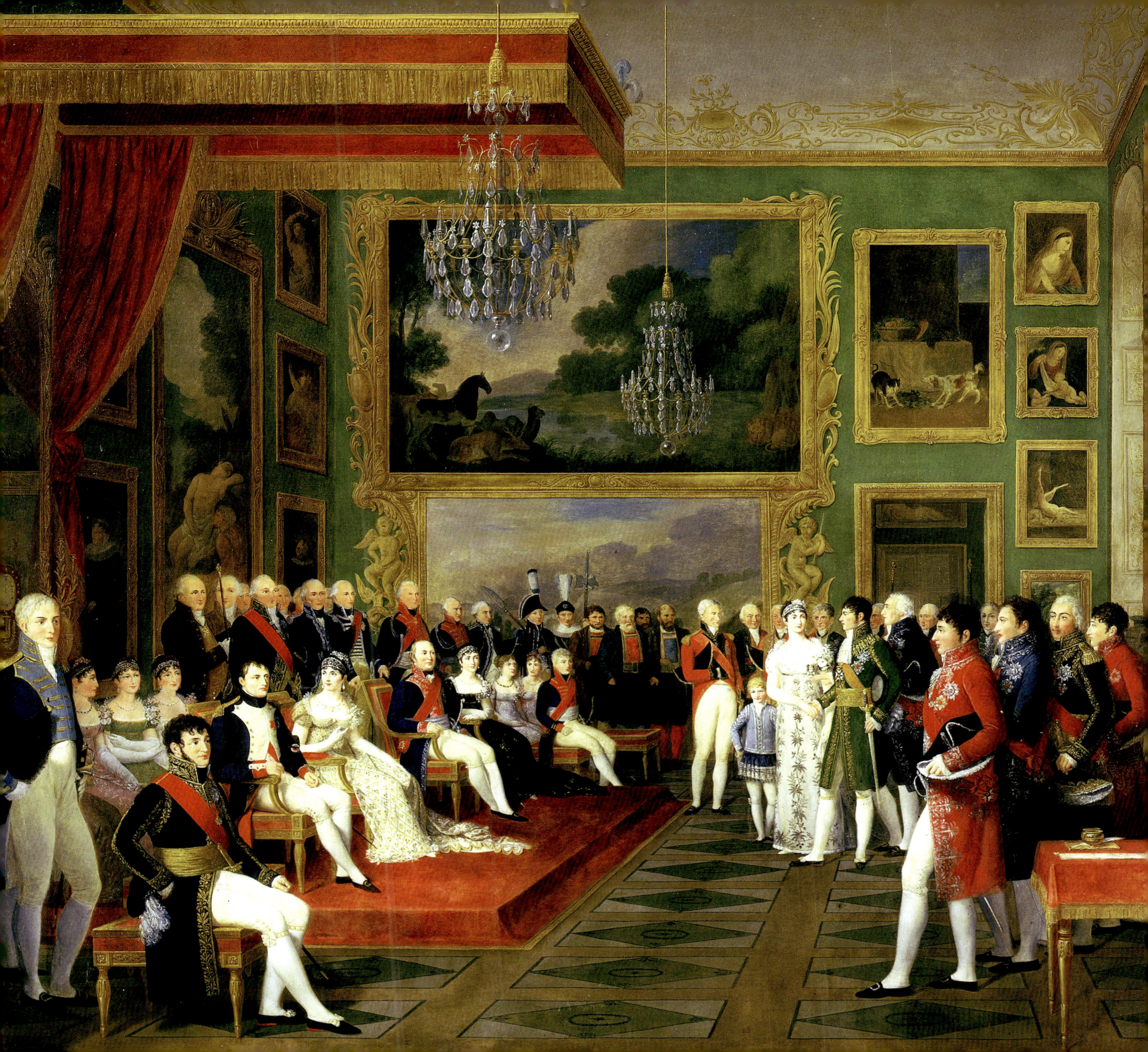

DAS KÖNIGREICH BAYERN
König Maximilian I. Joseph von Bayern

Eugène de Beauharnais (1781–1824), kaiserlicher Prinz von Frankreich, Vizekönig von Italien, nach 1817 Herzog von Leuchtenberg und Fürst von Eichstätt.
Aus der Ehe von Eugène und Auguste Amalie ging eine international weitverzweigte Familie hervor: Tochter Joséphine heiratete König Oskar I. von Schweden, Sohn August heiratete Königin Maria II. von Portugal, Tochter Amélie heiratete Kaiser Don Pedro I. von Brasilien, Sohn Maximilian heiratete Marija Nikolajewna Romanowa, Großfürstin von Russland, Tochter des Zaren Nikolaus I.
Gemälde von Joseph Karl Stieler, 1815.

Eugène de Beauharnais (1781–1824), Imperial Prince of France, Viceroy of Italy, after 1817 Duke of Leuchtenberg and Prince of Eichstätt.
The marriage of Eugène and Auguste Amalie produced an internationally ramified family: daughter Joséphine married King Oscar I of Sweden, son August married Queen Maria II of Portugal, daughter Amélie married Emperor Don Pedro I of Brazil, son Maximilian married Marija Nikolajewna Romanowa, Grand Duchess of Russia, daughter of Tsar Nicholas I.
Painting by Joseph Karl Stieler, 1815.

Auguste Amalie Herzogin von Leuchtenberg (1788–1851).
Nach dem Sturz Napoleons 1814 kehrte die mit dessen Stiefsohn Eugène de Beauharnais verheiratete Prinzessin nach Bayern zurück. Das vormalige Vizekönigspaar von Italien erhielt den Titel Herzog und Herzogin von Leuchtenberg.
Gemälde von Joseph Karl Stieler, um 1824/25.

Auguste Amalie Duchess of Leuchtenberg (1788–1851).
After the fall of Napoleon in 1814, the princess, who was married to Napoleon's stepson Eugène de Beauharnais, returned to Bavaria. The former viceroyal couple of Italy received the title Duke and Duchess of Leuchtenberg.
Painting by Joseph Karl Stieler, c. 1824/25.

DAS KÖNIGREICH BAYERN
König Maximilian I. Joseph von Bayern

Eugène de Beauharnais.
Zeichnung eines unbekannten Künstlers, o. J.

Eugène de Beauharnais.
Drawing by an unknown artist, undated.

König Maximilian I. Joseph von Bayern (1756 – 1825).
Gemälde eines unbekannten Künstlers, um 1808.

King Maximilian I Joseph of Bavaria (1756 – 1825).
Painting by an unknown artist, c. 1808.

DAS KÖNIGREICH BAYERN
König Maximilian I. Joseph von Bayern

Napoleon bei der 1. Bayerischen Division vor der Schlacht bei Abensberg 1809.
Vor der Schlacht bei Abensberg am 20. April 1809 gegen die in Bayern einmarschierenden österreichischen Truppen hielt Napoleon eine flammende Rede vor der bayerischen Division, die an vorderster Front kämpfen sollte. Kronprinz Ludwig (auf braunem Pferd in der Mitte), nach eigener Aussage ein „Todfeind" Napoleons, war gezwungen, die Worte des Kaisers ins Deutsche zu übersetzen.
Gemälde von Jean Baptist Debret, 1810.

Napoleon with the 1st Bavarian Division before the Battle of Abensberg, 1809.
Before the Battle of Abensberg against the Austrian troops marching into Bavaria on 20 April 1809, Napoleon held a fiery speech in front of the Bavarian Division, which was to fight at the front line. Crown Prince Ludwig (on a brown horse in the centre), who described himself as a "deadly enemy" of Napoleon, was forced to translate the Emperor's words into German.
Painting by Jean Baptist Debret, 1810.

Napoleon I. blickt auf das brennende Regensburg.
Nach den Schlachten bei Abensberg und Eggmühl besetzten die geschlagenen Österreicher Regensburg, um ihren Rückzug zu decken. Am 23. April 1809 kam es daher zur Schlacht um Regensburg mit den bayerisch-französischen Truppen unter Napoleon, der die Kämpfe von einer nahegelegenen Anhöhe aus leitete.
Ölgemälde von Albrecht Adam, 1840.

Napoleon I looks at the burning Regensburg.
After the battles of Abensberg and Eggmühl, the defeated Austrians occupied Regensburg in order to cover their retreat. This led to the Battle of Regensburg on 23 April 1809 with the Bavarian-French troops under Napoleon, who led the fighting from a nearby height.
Oil painting by Albrecht Adam, 1840.

DAS KÖNIGREICH BAYERN
König Maximilian I. Joseph von Bayern

Die bevollmächtigten Diplomaten auf dem Wiener Kongress 1815.
Nach dem Sturz Napoleons verhandelten die europäischen Großmächte die Neuaufteilung des Kontinents; Bayern verlor Tirol, Salzburg und Vorarlberg, konnte jedoch Unterfranken und die Pfalz zurückerwerben. Das Bild zeigt eine Konferenzpause der wichtigsten Delegierten im Palais am Ballhausplatz in Wien, darunter Fürst Metternich (stehend), der auf den englischen Vertreter Lord Castlereagh weist (im Vordergrund sitzend). Rechts außen am Tisch sitzend Fürst Talleyrand (Frankreich), links im Vordergrund sitzend Fürst von Hardenberg (Preußen). Der Künstler Isabey war während des Kongresses anwesend; nach seiner Skizze wurden wenige wertvolle Drucke hergestellt, von denen König Max I. Joseph von Bayern allein drei besaß.
Kolorierter Stich von J. Godefroy nach einer Kreidezeichnung von Jean-Baptiste Isabey, 1819.

The authorised diplomats at the Congress of Vienna, 1815.
After the fall of Napoleon, the major European powers negotiated the redistribution of the continent; Bavaria lost Tyrol, Salzburg and Vorarlberg; however, it reacquired Lower Franconia and the Palatinate. The picture shows a conference break of the most important delegates in the palace at the Ballhausplatz in Vienna, including Prince Metternich (standing), who is pointing at the English representative Lord Castlereagh (in the foreground, sitting). Sitting at the table on the far right is Prince Talleyrand (France), sitting on the left in the foreground is Prince von Hardenberg (Prussia). The artist Isabey was present during the congress; a few valuable prints were produced based on his study, of which King Max I Joseph of Bavaria alone owned three.
Coloured print by J. Godefroy based on a chalk drawing by Jean-Baptiste Isabey, 1819.

DAS KÖNIGREICH BAYERN
König Maximilian I. Joseph von Bayern

Kammerherrenschlüssel aus der Zeit von König Max I. Joseph.

Chamberlain's key from the time of King Max I Joseph.

König Max I. Joseph beim Billardspiel in der Münchner Residenz.
Der reich ausgeschmückte Billardsaal war Teil der Steinzimmer in der Münchner Residenz. Max I. Joseph (hier am Tisch ein Schriftstück lesend dargestellt) pflegte das Billardspiel gerne als vornehmen, höfischen Zeitvertreib.
Gemälde von Wilhelm Rehlen, 1821.

King Max I Joseph playing billiards at the Munich Residenz.
The richly decorated billiard hall was part of the Stone Rooms in the Munich Residenz. Max I Joseph (represented here at the table reading a document) enjoyed playing billiards, considering it an elegant courtly pastime.
Painting by Wilhelm Rehlen, 1821.

DAS KÖNIGREICH BAYERN
König Maximilian I. Joseph von Bayern

Brand des königlichen Neuen Hoftheaters in München am 14. Januar 1823.
1811 beschloss König Max I. Joseph den Neubau eines Königlichen Hof- und Nationaltheaters in unmittelbarer Nähe der Residenz. In der Nacht des 14. Januar 1823 brannte das von Carl von Fischer entworfene Haus jedoch vollständig nieder.
Zeitgenössischer kolorierter Stich eines unbekannten Künstlers, o. J.

Burning of the royal New Court Theatre in Munich on 14 January 1823.
In 1811, King Max I Joseph decided to construct a new Royal Court and National Theatre in direct proximity to the Residenz. However, in the night of 14 January 1823, the building, designed by Carl von Fischer, completely burned down.
Contemporary coloured print by an unknown artist, undated.

Das Neue Hof- und Nationaltheater, daneben das Alte Residenztheater (Cuvilliéstheater).
Nach dem Brand des ersten Baus von Carl von Fischer 1823, übernahm Leo von Klenze den Wiederaufbau des Königlichen Theaters, das schon zwei Jahre später seine Pforten öffnete.
Lithografie von Eugen Neureuther, 1825.

The new Royal Court and National Theatre, next to it the Old Residence Theatre (Cuvilliés Theatre).
After Carl von Fischer's first building burned down in 1823, Leo von Klenze assumed the reconstruction of the Royal Theatre, which opened its doors just two years later.
Lithography by Eugen Neureuther, 1825.

DAS KÖNIGREICH BAYERN
König Maximilian I. Joseph von Bayern

Das Königliche Isartor-Theater.
Am 12. Oktober 1811 wurde die feierliche Einweihung des Königlichen Hof-Theaters am Isartor in Anwesenheit der königlichen Familie begangen. Max I. Joseph engagierte dafür die Schauspieltruppe des Münchner Theaterdirektors Johann Weinmüller, dessen Holztheater vor dem Isartor im gleichen Jahr abgebrannt war.
Sepia-Aquarell von Ludwig Huber nach Karl Friedrich Heinzmann, um 1820.

The royal Isartor-Theater.
On 12 October 1811, the Royal Court Theatre at the Isartor was formally inaugurated in the presence of the royal family. For this, Max I Joseph engaged the services of Munich impresario Johann Weinmüller's theatrical company, Weinmüller's wooden theatre in front of the Isartor having burnt down in the same year.
Sepia watercolour by Ludwig Huber based on Karl Friedrich Heinzmann, c. 1820.

Die königliche Schlittenfahrt.
Blick über den Münchner Promenadeplatz auf die Häuser der Südseite. Dahinter links die Frauenkirche, rechts die St. Michaelskirche, davor die ehemalige Karmelitenkirche. Im königlichen Schlittenzug befinden sich u. a. König Max I. Joseph, Herzog Eugen (Eugène) von Leuchtenberg und Kronprinz Ludwig.
Zeichnung von Gustav Kraus, 1824/25.

The royal slay ride.
View across Munich's Promenade Square towards the buildings on the south side. At the back on the left is the Frauenkirche, on the right is St. Michael's Church, in front of it is the former Carmelite Church. Those in the slay include King Max I Joseph, Duke Eugen (Eugène) of Leuchtenberg and Crown Prince Ludwig.
Drawing by Gustav Kraus, 1824/25.

DAS KÖNIGREICH BAYERN
König Maximilian I. Joseph von Bayern

König Max I. Joseph von Bayern und Gemahlin werden von einer Bauernfamilie bewirtet.
Lorenzo Quaglio versetzt Max I. Joseph und Königin Karoline (sitzend) in eine biedermeierliche Szenerie, die im Hintergrund den Tegernsee und den Wallberg zeigt. Das bäuerliche Anwesen ist der Pfliegelhof bei Tegernsee, die Magd am Tisch trägt zeitgenössische Tegernseer Tracht.
Gemälde von Lorenzo II Quaglio, 1824.

King Max I Joseph of Bavaria and his consort are hosted by a family of farmers.
Lorenzo Quaglio places Max I Joseph and Queen Karoline (sitting) in a Biedermeier setting that shows the Tegernsee and the Wallberg in the background. The farming estate is the Pfliegelhof, Tegernsee; the maid at the table is wearing contemporary Tegernsee attire.
Painting by Lorenzo II Quaglio, 1824.

DAS KÖNIGREICH BAYERN
Prinz Karl von Bayern

Vor dem Prinz-Karl-Palais um 1830. Das Bildnis zeigt die Ostseite des von 1804 bis 1806 von Carl von Fischer erbauten ehemaligen Palais Salabert am Eingang zum Englischen Garten. Nach dem Zweiten Weltkrieg war es zeitweise der Sitz des bayerischen Ministerpräsidenten.
Aquarellierte Zeichnung von Friedrich Poppel, 1846.

In front of the Prinz-Carl-Palais, c. 1830. The image shows the east side of the former Salabert House – constructed by Carl von Fischer between 1804 and 1806 – at the entrance to the English Garden. After the Second World War, it was temporarily the seat of the Bavarian Minister-President.
Watercoloured drawing by Friedrich Poppel, 1846.

Prinz Karl von Bayern (1797–1875), Feldmarschall und Generalinspektor der bayerischen Armee. Prinz Karl war das letzte der fünf Kinder Max I. Josephs aus erster Ehe. Während der Befreiungskriege begann er eine äußerst erfolgreiche militärische Laufbahn. 1823 ging Prinz Karl eine morganatische (unstandesgemäße) Ehe ein; seine Nachkommen verloren dadurch alle Ansprüche auf den bayerischen Königsthron.
Gemälde von Joseph Bernhardt, 1855.

Prince Karl of Bavaria (1797–1875), field marshal and general inspector of the Bavarian army. Prince Karl was the last of Max I Joseph's five children from his first marriage. During the German Campaign, he began an extremely successful military career. In 1823, Prince Karl entered into a morganatic marriage (mésalliance); his descendents thus lost all claims to the Bavarian royal throne.
Painting by Joseph Bernhardt, 1855.

DAS KÖNIGREICH BAYERN
Prinz Karl von Bayern

Prinz Karl von Bayern kutschiert einen rassigen Landauer.
Bleistiftzeichnung, Künstler unbekannt, um 1820.

Prince Karl of Bavaria drives a racy landau.
Pencil drawing, artist unknown, c. 1820.

Prinz Karl von Bayern zu Pferd als preußischer Regimentsinhaber.
Neben den zahlreichen Rängen, die Prinz Karl in der Armee des Bayerischen Königreichs während seiner langen militärischen Laufbahn inne hatte, war er seit 1846 auch Bundesinspektor in Preußen. 1848 erhielt er den Oberbefehl über das 7. und 8. Deutsche Bundesarmeekorps.
Ölmalerei auf Metall von Carl Preuss, 19. Jahrhundert.

Prince Karl of Bavaria on horseback as Prussian regimental proprietor.
In addition to the numerous ranks that Prince Karl held in the army of the Bavarian Kingdom during his long military career, he was also Federal Inspector from 1846 on. In 1848, he received supreme command of the 7th and 8th German Federal Army Corps.
Oil painting on metal by Carl Preuss, 19th century.

King Ludwig I

Ludwig, born in 1786, probably experienced a childhood that could not be called easy during the turmoil of the French Revolution and the wars that followed. The loss of his home and his mother Auguste Wilhelmine particularly influenced Ludwig during his era as Crown Prince: his aversion to anything French, particularly Napoleon Bonaparte, whose goodwill the Bavarian Electors and future royal family had to secure, decisively contributed to Ludwig's political stance, which was often enough in complete contrast to that of his Francophile father Max Joseph and his minister Montgelas.

Despite this, Ludwig was a fun-loving prince whose first longer trip to Italy in 1804/05 made a lasting impression on him. There he discovered his lifelong passion for the art of classical antiquity, poetry and the lifestyle of German romanticism with like-minded people. The Crown Prince's wedding to Princess Therese of Saxony-Hildburghausen in 1810 secured the succession to the throne and gave Bavaria the gift of its national festival today: the Munich Oktoberfest.

When Ludwig began to reign in 1825, he already had fixed ideas about the kingdom's future. Whilst early on he appeared rather moderately liberal, from 1830 he took a more conservative course, warned by the events of the July revolution in France. From the late 1830s he developed a totally unprogressive and autocratic style of governance. His top political objective was to consolidate the Kingdom and monarchical order, combined with battling against anything revolutionary. The King mainly saw the key to success for his concept in integrating regions newly acquired from 1803 and later on.

Besides administrative reforms and business promotion, Ludwig used the idea of a cultural policy that should make the whole nation aware of the new values of Bavarian (national) statehood in an emotional way as a means of power politics for these integration efforts. The reference to a shared glorious past that goes back a long way, manifested in monumental buildings like the Walhalla and Befreiungshalle near Kelheim, was one of the basic constants of this policy as well as strengthening popular religious belief by rebuilding and founding monasteries that had been a victim of secularisation. Not least the development of the imperial city of Munich into a glamorous "Athens on the Isar", which is still testament to Ludwig's love of Ancient Greece today, is the result of this educational philosophy and Ludwig's will to drive creativity.

Ludwig I's reign ended abruptly with the affair over dancer Lola Montez from 1846 to 1848. However, the King's "personal transgression", his lifelong penchant for extramarital relationships, was hardly the sole reason for his abdication. It was rather the events with the politically charged climate of the "Vormärz" era and the breakthrough of the liberal public movement in the March Revolution 1848, whose objectives contradicted the self-image of the autocrat Ludwig, that led to tension. He lived until 1868 and saw his grandson Ludwig II ascend to the throne.

König Ludwig I.

Der 1786 geborene Ludwig erlebte in den Wirren der Französischen Revolution und der sich anschließenden Kriege wohl keine leicht zu nennende Kindheit. Der Verlust der Heimat und seiner Mutter Auguste Wilhelmine prägten Ludwig vor allem in seiner Kronprinzenzeit: Seine Abneigung gegen alles Französische, vor allem gegen Napoleon Bonaparte, dessen Wohlwollen sich die bayerische Kurfürsten- und spätere Königsfamilie sichern musste, trug entscheidend zu Ludwigs politischer Haltung bei, die sich oft genug gegen die seines frankophilen Vaters Max Joseph und dessen Ministers Montgelas richtete.

Dennoch war Ludwig ein lebenslustiger Prinz, auf den eine erste längere Italienreise in den Jahren 1804/05 nachhaltigen Eindruck machte. Er entdeckte dort mit Gleichgesinnten seine lebenslang andauernde Leidenschaft für die Kunst der klassischen Antike, die Dichtkunst und das Lebensgefühl der deutschen Romantik. Die Hochzeit des Kronprinzen mit Prinzessin Therese von Sachsen-Hildburghausen 1810 sicherte die Thronfolge und bescherte den Bayern ihr heutiges „Nationalfest": das Münchner Oktoberfest.

Als Ludwig 1825 die Regentschaft übernahm, hatte er bereits feste Vorstellungen von der Zukunft des Königreichs. Hatte er sich früher eher gemäßigt liberal gezeigt, läutete er ab 1830, gewarnt durch die Ereignisse der Julirevolution in Frankreich, einen konservativeren Kurs ein. Ab dem Ende der dreißiger Jahre entwickelte er gänzlich einen reaktionär-autokratischen Regierungsstil. Das oberste politische Ziel war dabei die Konsolidierung des Königreichs und der monarchischen Ordnung, verbunden mit dem Kampf gegen alles Revolutionäre. Vor allem in der Integration der ab 1803 und später neu hinzugewonnenen Landesteile sah der König den Schlüssel zum Erfolg seines Konzepts.

Neben Verwaltungsreformen und Wirtschaftsförderung nutzte Ludwig als machtpolitisches Mittel dieser Integrationsbestrebungen die Idee einer Kulturpolitik, die die neuen Werte der bayerischen (National-)Staatlichkeit in emotionaler Weise dem gesamten Volk nahebringen sollte. Die Berufung auf eine weit zurückreichende, gemeinsame ruhmreiche Vergangenheit, manifestiert in Monumentalbauten wie der Walhalla und der Befreiungshalle bei Kelheim, war eine der Grundkonstanten dieser Politik, aber auch die Stärkung der Volksreligiosität durch die Wiedererrichtung und Neugründung von Klöstern, die der Säkularisation zum Opfer gefallen waren. Nicht zuletzt der Ausbau der Residenzstadt München zum glanzvollen „Isarathen", das bis heute von Ludwigs Liebe zur hellenistischen Antike zeugt, ist das Ergebnis dieses Bildungsgedankens und des besonderen Gestaltungswillens Ludwigs.

Mit der Affäre um die Tänzerin Lola Montez in den Jahren 1846 bis 1848 endete die Regierungszeit Ludwigs I. abrupt. Doch war die „persönliche Verfehlung" des Königs, der zeitlebens außerehelichen Verbindungen nicht abgeneigt war, kaum der alleinige Grund für seinen Rücktritt von der Regentschaft. Vielmehr verspannen sich die Ereignisse mit dem politisch aufgeladenen Klima des Vormärz und dem Durchbruch der liberalen Volksbewegung in der Märzrevolution von 1848, deren Ziele dem Selbstverständnis des Autokraten Ludwig widersprachen. Er lebte bis 1868 und sah noch seinen Enkelsohn Ludwig II. den Thron besteigen.

DAS KÖNIGREICH BAYERN
König Ludwig I. von Bayern

Eintrag mit Wappen König Ludwigs I. im Bruderschaftsbuch der Corpus-Christi-Bruderschaft bei St. Peter in München.

Entry of King Ludwig with coat of arms in the Book of the Brotherhood of the Corpus Christi Brotherhood at St. Peter's Church in Munich.

König Ludwig I. von Bayern (1786–1868) im Thronornat.
Als zweiter König von Bayern trat Ludwig I. im Jahr 1825 die Nachfolge seines Vaters Max I. Joseph an. Stielers Porträt verweist auf das Kunstkönigtum des Monarchen; links im Hintergrund ist die von ihm geschaffene Walhalla, der „Ehrentempel" bedeutender deutscher Persönlichkeiten, zu sehen.
Gemälde von Joseph Karl Stieler, 1828.

King Ludwig I of Bavaria (1786–1868) in coronation regalia
Ludwig I succeeded his father Max I Joseph as the second King of Bavaria in 1825. Stieler's portrait refers to the monarch's artistic kingship; the Walhalla, a "temple of honour" to important German personalities that he created, can be seen on the left in the background.
Painting by Joseph Karl Stieler, 1828.

DAS KÖNIGREICH BAYERN
König Ludwig I. von Bayern

Kronprinz Ludwig von Bayern (1786–1868) mit einem englischen Setter.
Gemälde von Johann Jakob Louver d. Ä., o. J.

Crown Prince Ludwig of Bavaria (1786–1868) with English setter.
Painting by Johann Jakob Louver the Elder, undated.

Kronprinz Ludwig in der Uniform seines I. Chevaulegers-Regiments.
Kobells Porträt zeigt den 21-jährigen Ludwig als Oberst-Inhaber des dritten Chevaulegersregiments „Kronprinz". Für den antinapoleonisch eingestellten Prinzen war es eine schwere Pflicht, an der Seite Frankreichs gegen Preußen und Russland in den Krieg ziehen zu müssen. Trotz des engen politischen Bündnisses des Kaisers mit Bayern verlor er seine Abneigung gegen Napoleon nie.
Gemälde von Wilhelm von Kobell, um 1807.

Crown Prince Ludwig in the uniform of his 1st Chevau-légers regiment.
Kobell's portrait shows the 21-year old Ludwig as the Colonel of the third "Crown Prince" Chevau-légers regiment. For the Prince, who was anti-Napoleon, it was a difficult duty to have to go to war against Prussia and Russia on France's side. Despite the Emperor's close political alliance with Bavaria he never lost his dislike of Napoleon.
Painting by Wilhelm von Kobell, c. 1807.

DAS KÖNIGREICH BAYERN
König Ludwig I. von Bayern

Das Schwabinger Tor und das Gelände des heutigen Odeonsplatzes vor Anlage der Ludwigstraße.
Zur Zeit Ludwigs I. war das Schwabinger Tor eines der vier Hauptstadttore Münchens. Die daraus hervorgehende Straße führte nach Norden in Richtung Freising. 1816 beauftragte Kronprinz Ludwig ihren Ausbau zu einer repräsentativen Prachtstraße, der heutigen Ludwigstraße, im Zuge dessen das Schwabinger Tor verschwand.
Ölgemälde von J. Cogels, 1814.

Schwabinger Tor and the site where Odeonsplatz stands today before Ludwigstraße was built.
During the era of Ludwig I, the Schwabinger Tor was one of four main city gates in Munich. The road that started from there led northwards in the direction of Freising. In 1816 Crown Prince Ludwig ordered it to be developed into an imposing boulevard, today's Ludwigstraße, which led to the disappearance of the Schwabinger Tor.
Oil painting by J. Cogels, 1814.

Feierliche Enthüllung des Denkmals für König Max I. Joseph am 13. Oktober 1835.
Die schon unter Max I. Joseph begonnenen Bauarbeiten für den Platz vor dem neuen Nationaltheater in unmittelbarer Nähe der Residenz führte Ludwig I. mit der Errichtung des „Königsbaus" an seiner Nordseite fort. 1835 wurde das monumentale Denkmal seines Vaters vor dem Nationaltheater eingeweiht.
Farblithografie von Gustav Wilhelm Kraus, um 1835.

The official unveiling of the monument for King Max I Joseph on 13 October 1835.
Ludwig I continued the building work for the square in front of the new National Theatre in the direct vicinity of the Residenz that was already started under Max I Joseph by building the "Königsbau" on the north side. The huge monument to his father in front of the National Theatre was inaugurated in 1835.
Colour lithography by Gustav Wilhelm Kraus, c. 1835.

DAS KÖNIGREICH BAYERN
König Ludwig I. von Bayern

Das Pferderennen „bey der Vermählungs Feyer Seiner Königlichen Hoheit des Kronprinzen von Bayern", dem Münchner Oktoberfest.
Den Zeltbaldachin der Hochzeitsgesellschaft in der Bildmitte zieren zwei Halbmonde. Er wurde während der Türkenkriege im 17. Jahrhundert von den Truppen des „Blauen Königs" Max Emanuel vor den Toren Wiens erbeutet. Die Bildunterschrift spricht im Zusammenhang mit den Feierlichkeiten erstmals von „October-Festen".
Kolorierter Konturenstich von Peter Hess, 1810.

The horse race "bey der Vermählungs Feyer Seiner Königlichen Hoheit des Kronprinzen von Bayern", the Munich Oktoberfest.
Two half moons decorate the wedding party's tent canopy in the middle of the picture. It was captured by "Blue King" Max Emanuel's troops at the gates of Vienna during the Ottoman Wars in the 17th century. The painting caption talks about the "October-Festen" for the first time in connection with the celebrations.
Coloured contour drawing by Peter Hess, 1810.

DAS KÖNIGREICH BAYERN
König Ludwig I. von Bayern

Königin Therese von Bayern (1792–1854), Gemahlin König Ludwigs I.
Im Jahr 1809 warb der bayerische Kronprinz erfolgreich um Therese von Sachsen-Hildburghausen. Die Hochzeit des Kronprinzenpaares feierten die Münchner Bürger im Oktober 1810 mit einem großen Pferderennen, das jährlich wiederholt zu einem großen Volksfest, dem heutigen Münchner Oktoberfest, anwuchs.
Ölgemälde von Julie Gräfin von Egloffstein, 1836.

Queen Therese of Bavaria (1792–1854), consort of King Ludwig I.
The Bavarian Crown Prince successfully courted Therese of Saxony-Hildburghausen in 1809. Munich citizens celebrated the crown princely couple's wedding in October 1810 with a grand horse race, which was repeated every year, growing into a folk festival that is today's Munich Oktoberfest.
Oil painting by Julie Countess of Egloffstein, 1836.

DAS KÖNIGREICH BAYERN
König Ludwig I. von Bayern

Prinz Otto von Bayern (1815–1867), späterer erster König von Griechenland (1832–1867).
Gemälde eines unbekannten Künstlers, o. J.

Prince Otto of Bavaria (1815–1867), later the first King of Greece (1832–1867).
Painting of an unknwon artist, undated.

Prinz Luitpold von Bayern (1821–1912), der spätere Prinzregent (1886–1912).
Gemälde eines unbekannten Künstlers, o. J.

Prince Luitpold of Bavaria (1821–1912), later Prince Regent (1886–1912).
Painting of an unknwon artist, undated.

Prinzessin Mathilde von Bayern (1813–1862), spätere Großherzogin von Hessen-Darmstadt.
Gemälde eines unbekannten Künstlers, o. J.

Princess Mathilde of Bavaria (1813–1862), later Grand Duchess of Hesse-Darmstadt.
Painting of an unknwon artist, undated.

DAS KÖNIGREICH BAYERN
König Ludwig I. von Bayern

Geschichts-Doppeltaler.
Die Idee der sogenannten „Geschichts-Doppeltaler" übernahm Ludwig I. von König Friedrich Wilhelm II. von Preußen, der sie 1790 entwickelt, aber nicht umgesetzt hatte. Anlässlich der Geburt seines jüngsten Sohnes Adalbert ließ Ludwig I. 1828 diesen Geschichts-Konventionaltaler unter dem Leitwort „Segen des Himmels" mit den Porträts der Königin Therese und ihrer acht Kinder gestalten. Der Monarch selbst ziert die andere Seite der Münze.
Silbermünze, 1828.

Historical double Thalers.
Ludwig I adopted the idea of so-called "historical double Thalers" from King Friedrich Wilhelm II of Prussia, who created them in 1790 but had not actually implemented them. To mark the birth of his youngest son, Adalbert, Ludwig I had this historical conventional Thaler designed under the motto "Heaven's blessing" with the portraits of Queen Therese and her eight children. The monarch himself decorates the other side of the coin.
Silver coin, 1828.

Prinzessin Adelgunde von Bayern (1823 – 1914), spätere Herzogin von Modena, Erzherzogin von Österreich-Este.
Gemälde eines unbekannten Künstlers, o. J.

Princess Adelgunde of Bavaria (1823 – 1914), later Duchess of Modena, Archduchess of Austria-Este.
Painting of an unknwon artist, undated.

Prinzessin Hildegard von Bayern (1825 – 1865), spätere Gemahlin des Erzherzogs Albrecht von Österreich.
Gemälde eines unbekannten Künstlers, o. J.

Princess Hildegard of Bavaria (1825 – 1865), later consort of Archduke Albrecht of Austria.
Painting of an unknwon artist, undated.

DAS KÖNIGREICH BAYERN
König Ludwig I. von Bayern

Die von König Ludwig I. als Wohnsitz bei seinen Aufenthalten in Rom angekaufte Villa Malta.
1804/05 reiste Kronprinz Ludwig erstmals nach Rom, das ihm sein ganzes Leben lang eines der beliebtesten Ziele bleiben sollte. Während dieser ersten Italienreise entdeckte er seine Liebe zur antiken Klassik, die fortan sein (politisches) Kunstideal stark beeinflussen sollte.
Gemälde von Domenico Quaglio, 1830.

The Villa Malta purchased by King Ludwig I as his residence when staying in Rome.
In 1804/05, Crown Prince Ludwig travelled to Rome for the first time and it was to remain one of his favourite destinations throughout his whole life. During his first trip to Italy, he discovered his love for classical antiquity, which supposedly heavily influenced his (political) artistic ideal from then on.
Painting by Domenico Quaglio, 1830.

Kronprinz Ludwig in der spanischen Weinschenke Don Raffaele in Rom.
Seine Erlebnisse und Reiseeindrücke ließ Kronprinz Ludwig gerne in sogenannten Erinnerungsbildern verewigen. Der Maler Catel hielt für ihn eine weinselige Zusammenkunft mit deutschen Künstlerfreunden, darunter Klenze und Thorvaldsen, in einer Schenke auf der Ripa Grande in Rom fest.
Ölgemälde von Franz Ludwig Catel, 1824.

Crown Prince Ludwig in the Spanish wine bar Don Raffaele in Rome.
Crown Prince Ludwig liked to have his experiences and impressions from travelling immortalised in so-called souvenir pictures. The painter Catel captured a sociable meeting with German artist friends including Klenze and Thorvaldsen over a glass of fine wine in a wine bar on the Ripa Grande in Rome for him on canvas.
Oil painting by Franz Ludwig Catel, 1824.

DAS KÖNIGREICH BAYERN
König Ludwig I. von Bayern

396 | 397

König Ludwig I. von Bayern.
Gemälde von Joseph Karl Stieler, o. J.

King Ludwig I of Bavaria.
Painting by Joseph Karl Stieler, undated.

Auffahrt König Ludwigs I. zur Eröffnung des Landtages im Jahre 1827 in der Prannerstraße in München, wo er früher sein Domizil hatte.
Der Galawagen befindet sich heute im Marstall-Museum zu Nymphenburg in München.
Lithografie von Gustav Wilhelm Kraus, 1827.

Approach of King Ludwig I for the opening of the Landtag on Prannerstraße in Munich, where he used to reside, in 1827.
The gala carriage can be found in the Marstall Museum in Nymphenburg in Munich today.
Lithography by Gustav Wilhelm Kraus, 1827.

DAS KÖNIGREICH BAYERN
König Ludwig I. von Bayern

König Ludwig I. von Bayern (1786–1868) in der Uniform eines Generalmajors, das Leibregiment grüßend, vor dem Fest- und Thronsaalbau der Münchner Residenz. Gustav Kraus porträtierte zwischen 1837 und 1847 in loser Abfolge verschiedene Mitglieder des bayerischen, badischen, württembergischen und österreichischen Hochadels zu Pferd. So entstanden zwölf Fürstenporträts im Großformat, darunter die acht hier wiedergegebenen Darstellungen der Söhne des Hauses Wittelsbach. *Lithografie von Gustav Wilhelm Kraus, 1839.*

King Ludwig I of Bavaria (1786–1868) in the uniform of a General Major, greeting the Leib regiment in front of the ballroom and throne room building in the Munich Residenz. Gustav Kraus painted portraits of various members of the Bavarian, Baden, Württemberg and Austrian nobility on horseback on an occasional basis between 1837 and 1847. Resulting in twelve large format portraits of princes including the eight paintings of the sons of the House of Wittelsbach shown here. *Lithography by Gustav Wilhelm Kraus, 1839.*

Feldmarschall Prinz Karl von Bayern (1795–1875), der zweite Sohn des König Max' I. Joseph, in Galauniform als Oberst und Inhaber des 1. Kürassierregiments. Im Hintergrund der Obelisk des Karolinenplatzes in München. *Lithografie von Gustav Wilhelm Kraus, 1840.*

Field Marshall Prince Karl of Bavaria (1795–1875), the second son of King Max I Joseph, in gala uniform as a Colonel and bearer of the 1st Kürassier regiment. The obelisk on Karolinenplatz in Munich can be seen in the background. *Lithography by Gustav Wilhelm Kraus, 1840.*

Kronprinz Maximilian von Bayern (1811–1864) in der Uniform eines Generalmajors vor Schloss Hohenschwangau mit Flügeladjutant von Hartmann.
Lithografie von Gustav Wilhelm Kraus, 1840.

Crown Prince Maximilian of Bavaria (1811–1864) in the uniform of a General Major in front of Hohenschwangau Palace with aide-de-camp von Hartmann.
Lithography by Gustav Wilhelm Kraus, 1840.

König Otto I. von Griechenland (1815–1867), früher Prinz Otto von Bayern, im griechischen Nationalkostüm vor der Akropolis in Athen.
Lithografie von Gustav Wilhelm Kraus, um 1839.

King Otto I of Greece (1815–1867), formerly Prince Otto of Bavaria, in Greek national costume in front of the Acropolis in Athens.
Lithography by Gustav Wilhelm Kraus, c. 1839.

DAS KÖNIGREICH BAYERN
König Ludwig I. von Bayern

Prinz Luitpold von Bayern (1821–1912) im Alter von 19 Jahren als Oberstinhaber des 1. Artillerieregiments.
Lithografie von Gustav Wilhelm Kraus, 1840.

Prince Luitpold of Bavaria (1821–1912) at the age of 19 as Colonel of the 1st Artillery regiment.
Lithography by Gustav Wilhelm Kraus, 1840.

Prinz Adalbert von Bayern (1828–1875) als Oberstinhaber des 2. Kürassierregiments in Landshut vor der alten Herzogstadt.
Im Hintergrund die Burg Trausnitz und das Martinsmünster.
Lithografie von Gustav Wilhelm Kraus, 1847.

Prince Adalbert of Bavaria (1828–1875), as Colonel of the 2nd Kürassier regiment in Landshut in front of the old ducal city.
Trausnitz Castle and the St. Martin's church can be seen in the background.
Lithography by Gustav Wilhelm Kraus, 1847.

Herzog Maximilian von Leuchtenberg (1817–1852) als Oberstinhaber des kaiserlich-russischen 11. Husarenregiments vor St. Petersburg.
Maximilians Eltern waren Eugène de Beauharnais, der Stiefsohn Napoleons, und Prinzessin Auguste Amalie von Bayern.
Lithografie von Gustav Wilhelm Kraus, 1839.

Duke Maximilian of Leuchtenberg (1817–1852) as Colonel of the Imperial and Russian 11th Hussars regiment by St. Petersburg.
Maximilian's parents were Eugène de Beauharnais, Napoleon's stepson, and Princess Auguste Amalie of Bavaria.
Lithography by Gustav Wilhelm Kraus, 1839.

Herzog Maximilian in Bayern (1808–1888) in Chevaulegers-Uniform als Kommandant der Landwehrtruppen von Oberbayern.
Im Hintergrund der Dom zu Unserer Lieben Frau in München.
Lithografie von Gustav Wilhelm Kraus, 1839.

Duke Maximilian in Bavaria (1808–1888) in Chevau-légers uniform as Commander of the Landwehr Company of Upper Bavaria.
The Zu Unserer Lieben Frau cathedral in Munich can be seen in the background.
Lithography by Gustav Wilhelm Kraus, 1839.

DAS KÖNIGREICH BAYERN
König Ludwig I. von Bayern

Eröffnung der Eisenbahnlinie München-Augsburg am 1. September 1839.
Vier Jahre nach der Eröffnung der ersten Eisenbahnstrecke Nürnberg – Fürth im Jahre 1835 konnten auch die Münchner ihre erste Eisenbahnfahrt erleben. 1839 konnte bereits ein Teilstück von München nach Maisach befahren werden, ein Jahr später erfolgte die Eröffnung der gesamten Strecke.
Lithografie von Gustav Wilhelm Kraus, um 1840.

Opening of the Munich-Augsburg railway line on 1 September 1839.
Four years after the opening of the first railway from Nuremberg to Fürth in 1835, the people of Munich were also able to experience their first journey by railway. In 1839 a section from Munich to Maisach could already be travelled; one year later the entire route was opened.
Lithography by Gustav Wilhelm Kraus, c. 1840.

Feldherrnhalle und Theatinerkirche am Odeonsplatz in München.

Die Feldherrnhalle wurde von 1841 bis 1844 im Auftrag Ludwigs I. geschaffen, um der königlich-bayerischen Armee am Beginn der neuen Prachtstraße, der Ludwigstraße, ein würdiges Denkmal zu setzen. Das Bildnis zeigt den Originalzustand des Denkmals mit den Standbildern der Feldherren Tilly und von Wrede.
Kolorierter Stahlstich von Johann Gabriel Friedrich Poppel nach einer Zeichnung von Gustav Seeberger, um 1850.

The Feldherrnhalle and Theatine Church at Odeonsplatz in Munich.

The Feldherrnhalle was created from 1841 to 1844 by order of Ludwig I to place a worthy monument to the royal Bavarian army at the start of the new boulevard, Ludwigstraße. The picture shows the original condition of the monument with the statues of the generals Tilly and von Wrede.
Coloured steel engraving by Johann Gabriel Friedrich Poppel based on a drawing by Gustav Seeberger, c. 1850.

Eröffnung des Siegestores am 15. Oktober 1850.

1840 gab Ludwig I. bei Friedrich von Gärtner einen Triumphbogen nach dem Vorbild des Konstantinsbogens in Rom als Abschluss der Ludwigstraße in Auftrag. Das Siegestor ist dem Ende der Befreiungskriege von 1815 gewidmet. Nach dem Zweiten Weltkrieg wurde die Inschrift „Dem Krieg geweiht, im Krieg zerstört, zum Frieden mahnend" hinzugefügt. Auf der Darstellung ist die in Wirklichkeit erst 1852 aufgestellte Quadriga bereits vorhanden.
Lithografie von Matthias Berger, 1851.

Opening of the Siegestor on 15 October 1850.

In 1840, Ludwig I commissioned Friedrich von Gärtner with a triumphal arch based on the Arch of Constantine in Rome for the end of the Ludwigstraße. The Siegestor is dedicated to the end of the Liberation War in 1815. After the Second World War, the inscription "Dedicated to victory, destroyed by war, reminding of peace" was added. The quadriga, which was only erected in 1852 in reality, is included in this picture.
Lithography by Matthias Berger, 1851.

DAS KÖNIGREICH BAYERN
König Ludwig I. von Bayern

Präsentation des in Bronze gegossenen Kopfes der Bavaria.
Die Bautätigkeit Ludwigs I. sah auch die Errichtung der Ruhmeshalle an der Theresienwiese mit einer monumentalen Bronzestatue als Personifikation Bayerns vor. Nach Entwürfen von Leo von Klenze und Ludwig Schwanthaler realisierte der Erzgießer Ferdinand von Miller von 1844 bis 1849 nach vielen Jahren der Planung die riesenhafte Bavaria-Statue in vier Teilgüssen. Zeitgenossen galt sie als Meisterwerk der modernen Technik.
Ölgemälde von Wilhelm Gail, um 1844.

Presentation of the head of Bavaria cast in bronze.
Ludwig I's building work also provided for the erection of the Ruhmeshalle with a monumental bronze statue as personification of Bavaria on the Theresienwiese. After years of planning, brass founder Ferdinand von Miller created the huge Bavaria statue in four cast parts from 1844 to 1849 based on drafts by Leo von Klenze and Ludwig Schwanthaler. Contemporaries considered it to be a masterpiece of modern engineering.
Oil painting by Wilhelm Gail, c. 1844.

DAS KÖNIGREICH BAYERN
König Ludwig I. von Bayern

Das Pompejanum in Aschaffenburg.
Nach einer seiner Italienreisen ließ König Ludwig I., inspiriert von der antiken Stadt Pompeji, deren Ausgrabungen er 1839 besichtigt hatte, ab 1840 ein „pompejanisches Haus" oberhalb des Mains bei Aschaffenburg errichten. Das Pompejanum war von vornherein als Besichtigungsobjekt gedacht: Es sollte die Architektur und künstlerische Ausgestaltung eines römischen Hauses aus dem 1. Jahrhundert n. Chr. darstellen und somit das Studium der antiken Kunst und Kultur am „Original" ermöglichen.
Gemälde eines unbekannten Künstlers, o. J.

The Pompejanum in Aschaffenburg.
King Ludwig I had a "Pompeian house" built above the Main near Aschaffenburg after one of his trips to Italy when he was inspired by the ancient city of Pompeii, whose excavations he had visited in 1839. The Pompejanum was conceived as a sightseeing attraction right from the start: it was to represent the architecture and artistic design of a Roman house from the first century AD and therefore enable ancient art and culture to be studied from the original.
Painting by an unknown artist, undated.

Salvatorkirche zu Donaustauf mit Walhalla.
Die Kirche St. Salvator zu Donaustauf war zu Zeiten Ludwigs I. bereits ein jahrhundertealter Wallfahrtsort. Die im Hintergrund sichtbare, über dem Donautal nach dem Vorbild des Parthenon in Athen neu erbaute Walhalla wirkt in Klenzes Komposition perfekt in die Szenerie eingepasst.
Ölgemälde von Leo von Klenze, 1839.

St. Salvator church in Donaustauf with the Walhalla.
St. Salvator church in Donaustauf had already been a centuries-old place of pilgrimage in the times of Ludwig I. The newly built Walhalla modelled on the Parthenon in Athens, which is visible in the background above the Danube valley, appears to fit perfectly into the scenery in Klenze's painting.
Oil painting by Leo von Klenze, 1839.

DAS KÖNIGREICH BAYERN
König Ludwig I. von Bayern

Ansichten von Kelheim und Nürnberg.
1847 beschrieb der Schriftsteller und Journalist Friedrich Schultheis den Bau des sogenannten Ludwig-Donau-Main-Kanals, den Ludwig I. ab 1830 plante und der von 1836 bis 1846 realisiert wurde. Ergänzt wurden Schultheis' Ausführungen durch 26 Stahlstiche, die in romantisierender Weise die schwierigsten Bauabschnitte und die umgebende Landschaft veranschaulichen.
Beide Stahlstiche von Alexander Marx, 1847.

Views of Kelheim and Nuremberg.
In 1847, author and journalist Friedrich Schultheis described the building of the so-called Ludwig Danube Main Canal, which Ludwig I planned from 1830 and was constructed between 1836 and 1846. Schultheis' statements are complemented by 26 steel engravings that illustrate the most difficult building sections and the surrounding landscape in a romantic way.
Both steel engravings by Alexander Marx, 1847.

Faltdiorama „Canal du Roi Louis. Ludwigs-Kanal. King Lewis' Canal".
Guckkästen wie dieses Diorama führten auf Märkten und öffentlichen Plätzen wie in einem Miniaturtheater sensationelle Neuigkeiten vor. Der Kanalbau als technische Meisterleistung wird hier in seiner Bedeutung überhöht und als Unternehmung zugleich legitimiert. Die Bildsymbolik verbindet Kunst, Religion und Geschichte und entsprach so dem Herrschaftsprogramm König Ludwigs I.

The "Canal du Roi Louis. Ludwigs-Kanal. King Lewis' Canal" folding diorama.
Raree shows like this diorama presented sensational news on markets and public squares like in a miniature theatre. The importance of the canal construction as a technical masterpiece is inflated here and at the same time legitimised as an undertaking. The imagery combines art, religion and history and was therefore totally in keeping with the agenda of King Ludwig I's reign.

DAS KÖNIGREICH BAYERN
König Ludwig I. von Bayern

Prunkvase mit dem Bildnis König Ludwigs I. von Bayern.
Vasenmodell nach Friedrich von Gärtner, Malerei von Matthias Adler nach Vorlagen von Joseph Karl Stieler. Porzellan, bemalt und vergoldet, um 1831.

Ornate vase with portrait of King Ludwig I of Bavaria.
Vase model in the style of Friedrich von Gärtner, painting by Matthias Adler based on templates by Joseph Karl Stieler. Porcelain, painted and gilded, c. 1831.

Prunkvase mit dem Bildnis der Königin Therese von Bayern.
Vasenmodell nach Friedrich von Gärtner, Malerei von Matthias Adler nach Vorlagen von Joseph Karl Stieler. Porzellan, bemalt und vergoldet, 1831.

Ornate vase with portrait of Queen Therese of Bavaria.
Vase model in the style of Friedrich von Gärtner, painting by Matthias Adler based on templates by Joseph Karl Stieler. Porcelain, painted and gilded, 1831.

Die Porzellanmalerei in der Porzellanmanufaktur Nymphenburg.
Zur Entstehungszeit des Gemäldes war Eugen Napoleon Neureuther Leiter der Porzellanmanufaktur Nymphenburg. Hier prüft er eines der Werkstücke, während der Porzellanmaler Ferdinand Lefeubure ein vor ihm aufgestelltes Gemälde auf eine Prunkvase überträgt.
Gemälde von Wilhelm von Kaulbach, 1853.

Porcelain painting at the porcelain factory in Nymphenburg.
At the time this painting originated, Eugen Napoleon Neureuther was head of the Nymphenburg porcelain factory. Here he is checking one of the works of art, while porcelain painter Ferdinand Lefeubure transfers a painting in front of him onto an ornate vase.
Painting by Wilhelm von Kaulbach, 1853.

DAS KÖNIGREICH BAYERN
König Ludwig I. von Bayern

Die neu erbaute Allerheiligen-Hofkirche der Münchner Residenz vom Marstallplatz aus gesehen.
An der Ostseite der Residenz plante Leo von Klenze auf Anweisung König Ludwigs I. die neue Allerheiligen-Hofkirche. Sie entstand zwischen 1826 und 1837 nach dem Vorbild der Capella Palatina in Palermo. Links anschließend das Alte Residenztheater.
Aquarellierte Zeichnung von Heinrich Schönfeld, 1837.

The newly built All Saints' Court Church in the Munich Residenz seen from the Marstallplatz.
Leo von Klenze planned the new All Saints' Court Church on the eastern side of the Residenz at the instruction of King Ludwig I. It was built between 1826 and 1837 modelled on the Capella Palatina in Palermo. To its left is the Old Residence Theatre.
Watercolour drawing by Heinrich Schönfeld, 1837.

Das Innere der Allerheiligen-Hofkirche der Münchner Residenz.
Heinrich von Heß malte nach der Fertigstellung des Kirchenbaus dessen Inneres im byzantinischen Stil aus. Ludwig II. nahm sich den Kirchenraum für seinen Thronsaal auf Schloss Neuschwanstein zum Vorbild. 1944 wurde die Allerheiligen-Hofkirche und damit auch ihr prächtiges Inneres im Bombenkrieg schwer beschädigt.
Aquarell von Franz Xaver Nachtmann, 1839.

Inside the All Saints' Court Church in the Munich Residenz.
After construction of the church was completed, Heinrich von Heß painted the interior in the Byzantine style. Ludwig II modelled his throne room at Neuschwanstein Castle on this church. In 1944, the All Saints' Court Church and its splendid interior was seriously damaged in a bombing campaign.
Watercolour by Franz Xaver Nachtmann, 1839.

DAS KÖNIGREICH BAYERN
König Ludwig I. von Bayern

Die Abteikirche St. Bonifaz zu München.
St. Bonifaz war die erste Pfarrkirche, die in München nach der Säkularisation von 1803 neu erbaut wurde. Mit der neuen Abtei- und Pfarrkirche und dem nahen Königsplatz realisierte Ludwig I. architektonisch den symbolischen Dreiklang von Kunst, Wissenschaft und Religion. Im Zweiten Weltkrieg wurde die Kirche fast völlig zerstört, sodass der Innenraum heute modern ausgestaltet ist. Eine „Kopie" von St. Bonifaz steht in dem von Ludwig I. mitfinanzierten Kloster St. Vincent in Latrobe (Pennsylvania, USA).
Stahlstich von Johann Poppel, 1843.

St. Boniface Abbey in Munich.
St. Boniface was the first new parish church that was built in Munich after secularisation in 1803. With the new abbey and parish church and nearby Königsplatz square, Ludwig I realised the symbolic triad of art, science and religion in terms of architecture. During the Second World War, the church was almost completely destroyed; thus the interior has a modern design today. A copy of St. Boniface stands in the St. Vincent monastery in Latrobe (Pennsylvania, USA), which was co-financed by Ludwig I.
Steel engraving by Johann Poppel, 1843.

Die Propyläen in München.
Die idealisierte Darstellung der Propyläen mit den anderen Bauten des Königsplatzes und dem Obelisken auf dem Karolinenplatz in Sichtweite verdeutlicht in besonderer Weise die Verkörperung der Philhellenismus-Idee, die hinter Klenzes Architekturprogramm für München stand.
Ölgemälde von Leo von Klenze, 1848.

The Propyläen in Munich.
The idealised portrayal of the Propyläen with the other buildings in the Königsplatz and the obelisk on Karolinenplatz within sight makes the embodiment of the Philhellenic idea behind Klenze's architectural agenda for Munich clear in a very special way.
Oil painting by Leo von Klenze, 1848.

DAS KÖNIGREICH BAYERN
König Ludwig I. von Bayern

Prinzessin Alexandra Amalie von Bayern (1826–1875) in der Schönheitengalerie Ludwigs I.
Stieler fertigte von 1827 bis 1850 36 Bildnisse junger Frauen aus allen Gesellschaftsschichten für Ludwig I. an, die in der sog. Schönheitengalerie (heute auf Schloss Nymphenburg) zusammengetragen wurden. Alexandra Amalie war die jüngste Tochter des Königspaares Ludwig I. und Therese von Bayern. Das Porträt zeigt sie im Alter von etwa 19 Jahren. Sie wurde Äbtissin der Damenstifte zur Hl. Anna in München und Würzburg.
Gemälde von Joseph Karl Stieler, 1845.

Princess Alexandra Amalie of Bavaria (1826–1875) in Ludwig I's gallery of beauties.
Stieler produced 36 portraits of young women from all walks of life for Ludwig I between 1827 and 1850, which were displayed together in the so-called Gallery of Beauties (in Nymphenburg Palace today). Alexandra Amalie was the youngest daughter of the royal couple Ludwig I and Therese of Bavaria. This portrait shows her aged roughly 19 years old. She became the Abbess of the Royal Chapter for Ladies of Saint Anne in Munich and Wurzburg.
Painting by Joseph Karl Stieler, 1845.

Prinzessin Sophie Friederike von Bayern (1805–1872), Gemahlin des Erzherzogs Franz Karl von Österreich, Mutter von Kaiser Franz Joseph von Österreich.
Das Porträt der Halbschwester Ludwigs Sophie Friederike entstand nach ihrer Verheiratung mit Erzherzog Franz Karl von Österreich.
Ölgemälde von Joseph Karl Stieler, 1832.

Princess Sophie Friederike of Bavaria (1805–1872), consort of Archduke Franz Karl of Austria, mother of Emperor Franz Joseph of Austria.
The portrait of Ludwig's half-sister Sophie Friederike was painted after her marriage to Archduke Franz Karl of Austria.
Oil painting by Joseph Karl Stieler, 1832.

DAS KÖNIGREICH BAYERN
König Ludwig I. von Bayern

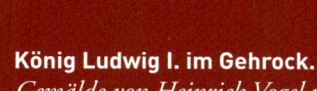

Federkiel König Ludwigs I., mit dem er 1848 seine Abdankung unterzeichnete.
Die Affäre mit der irischen Tänzerin Lola Montez (bürgerl. Elizabeth Susanna Gilbert) stürzte Ludwig I. in politische Verwicklungen. Münchner Bürger und Studenten hatten zunächst gegen ihre Einbürgerung und Erhebung zu einer Gräfin von Landsfeld protestiert und dann – von der Februarrevolution in Frankreich angeregt – liberale Verfassungsreformen gefordert. Der König willigte in Zugeständnisse ein, fühlte sich in seinem Selbstverständnis als Monarch jedoch so erschüttert, dass er die Abdankung vorzog.

King Ludwig I's quill, with which he signed his abdication in 1848.
The affair with the Irish dancer Lola Montez (née Elizabeth Susanna Gilbert) threw Ludwig I into a political mess. Munich's citizens and students had initially protested against her naturalisation and elevation to Countess of Landsfeld and then demanded liberal constitutional reforms, spurred on by the February revolution in France. The King acquiesced to concessions but felt that his self-image as monarch was so undermined that he abdicated.

Gehrock König Ludwigs I.
Frack aus schwarzem Tuch (Wolle und Seide), enger Halsausschnitt, Umlegkragen, vorn doppelte Knopfreihe, lange Ärmel mit Bündchen, im Rücken hoher Schlitz.

King Ludwig I's frock coat.
Tail coat made from black cloth (wool and silk), narrow neckline, turn down collar, double-buttoning on the front, long sleeves with cuffs, high slit in the back.

König Ludwig I. im Gehrock.
Gemälde von Heinrich Vogel nach Joseph Karl Stieler, 1841.

King Ludwig I in frock coat.
Painting by Heinrich Vogel based on Joseph Karl Stieler, 1841.

DAS KÖNIGREICH BAYERN
König Otto I. von Griechenland

Wappen Seiner Königlichen Majestät Otto I., König von Griechenland.

Coat of arms of His Majesty King Otto I of Greece.

Sogenanntes Erstes Staatsporträt König Ottos von Griechenland (1815–1867).
Nach dem von den europäischen Großmächten propagandistisch aufgeladenen Freiheitskampf der Griechen gegen die türkische Herrschaft auf dem Balkan von 1821 bis 1829, trugen die drei „Schutzmächte" des jungen griechischen Staates, Russland, England und Frankreich, zunächst Ottos Onkel Prinz Karl von Bayern, danach ihm selbst die Königskrone an. Otto bzw. sein Vater Ludwig I. akzeptierte nach dem zustimmenden Beschluss der griechischen Nationalversammlung.
Gemälde eines unbekannten Künstlers, 1832.

The so-called first state portrait of King Otto of Greece (1815–1867).
Following the Greeks' struggle for freedom against the Turkish rulers in the Balkans from 1821 to 1829, which was charged for propaganda purposes by the major European powers, the three "protective powers" of the young Greek state, Russia, England and France, first offered Otto's uncle Prince Karl of Bavaria the king's crown and then afterwards Otto himself. Otto respectively his father King Ludwig I accepted after the resolution was passed by the Greek National Assembly.
Painting by an unknown artist, 1832.

DAS KÖNIGREICH BAYERN
König Otto I. von Griechenland

Abschied des Prinzen Otto, des erwählten Königs von Griechenland, vom Münchner Hof im Winter 1832.
Die offizielle Verabschiedung Prinz Ottos von seiner Familie und den Hofangehörigen in der Münchner Residenz hielt Foltz in diesem Gemälde fest. Als reproduzierbare Lithografie verbreitete sich die denkwürdige Abschiedsszene bald darauf im ganzen Land. Ludwig I. begleitete Otto bei seiner Abreise nach Griechenland noch bis zum heutigen Ottobrunn, die Königin sogar bis Aibling – ihr soll die Trennung am schwersten gefallen sein.
Gemälde von Philipp Foltz, 1832.

Parting of Prince Otto, the elected King of Greece, from the Munich court in the winter of 1832.
The official parting of Prince Otto from his family and members of the court in the Munich Residenz was recorded in a painting by Foltz. As a reproducible lithography the memorable farewell scene soon spread throughout the whole country. Ludwig I accompanied Otto on his journey to Greece as far as today's Ottobrunn; the Queen even went as far as Aibling – she is said to have found the parting the most difficult.
Painting by Philipp Foltz, 1832.

DAS KÖNIGREICH BAYERN
König Otto I. von Griechenland

Einzug König Ottos von Griechenland in Nauplia im Jahre 1833.
Im Winter 1832/33 reiste Otto auf einer englischen Fregatte nach Nauplia. Er regierte zunächst, da noch minderjährig, mit Unterstützung eines bayerischen Regentschaftsrats, ab dem 1. Juni 1835 jedoch selbständig. 1862 kehrte er nach einem Militärputsch zurück nach Bayern und residierte fortan in Bamberg.
Gemälde von Peter von Hess, 1835.

The arrival of King Otto of Greece in Nafplio in 1833.
In the winter of 1832/33, Otto travelled on an English frigate to Nafplio. Initially he governed with the support of a Bavarian regency council as he was still a minor, before starting to govern independently from 1 June 1835. In 1862 he returned to Bavaria after a military coup and resided in Bamberg from then on.
Painting by Peter von Hess, 1835.

DAS KÖNIGREICH BAYERN
König Otto I. von Griechenland

Die Residenz König Ottos in Nauplia.
Aquarell von Adalbert Marc, 1833/35.

King Otto's residence in Nafplio.
Watercolour by Adalbert Marc, 1833/35.

Die königliche Residenz zu Athen.
Aquarell von August Löffler, 1854.

The royal residence in Athens.
Watercolour by August Löffler, 1854.

Einzug König Ottos von Griechenland mit seiner Gemahlin Amalie, geb. Herzogin von Oldenburg, in Athen.
1834 verlegte Otto seine Residenz von Nauplia nach Athen. Zwei Jahre später heiratete er Amalie Marie von Oldenburg. Als absehbar wurde, dass die Ehe kinderlos bleiben würde, ging die Thronfolge nominell auf Prinz Adalbert, dem nach Luitpold zweitjüngeren Bruder Ottos, und dessen Nachkommen über.
Lithografie von Franz Wolf, 1837.

Arrival of King Otto of Greece and his wife Amalie, née Duchess of Oldenburg, in Athens.
In 1834, Otto moved his residence from Nafplio to Athens. Two years later he married Amalie Marie of Oldenburg. Once it became foreseeable that the couple would remain childless, the succession to the throne was transferred nominally to Prince Adalbert, Otto's second younger brother after Luitpold, and his children.
Lithography by Franz Wolf, 1837.

DAS KÖNIGREICH BAYERN
König Otto I. von Griechenland

Die Otto-Kapelle bei Kiefersfelden.
An der Stelle, an der Prinz Otto von Bayern das Land verließ, um seine Regentschaft in Griechenland anzutreten, errichtete Daniel Ohlmüller 1834 eine Kapelle.
Aquarell von Philipp Wepperer nach Gustav Wilhelm Kraus, 1837.

The Otto Chapel near Kiefersfelden.
Daniel Ohlmüller built a chapel in 1834 at the spot where Prince Otto of Bavaria left the country to start his reign in Greece.
Watercolour by Philipp Wepperer based on Gustav Wilhelm Kraus, 1837.

Enthüllung der König-Otto-Säule 1834 im Hechenkirchner Forst, jetzt Gemeinde Ottobrunn.
Die König-Otto-Säule bezeichnet noch heute den Ort, an dem sich Ludwig I. 1833 vor den Toren der Stadt von seinem zweitgeborenen Sohn Otto verabschiedete. Eine über die Jahre in unmittelbarer Nähe des Denkmals erstandene Siedlung wurde 1921 zur Gemeinde Ottobrunn.
Lithografie von Gustav Wilhelm Kraus, um 1834.

Unveiling of the King Otto column in Hechenkirchner forest, now the municipality of Ottobrunn, in 1834.
The King Otto column still signifies today the place where Ludwig I bid farewell to his second-born son Otto before the gates to the town in 1833. A settlement that developed over the years near the monument became the municipality of Ottobrunn in 1921.
Lithography by Gustav Wilhelm Kraus, c. 1834.

DAS KÖNIGREICH BAYERN
Prinz Adalbert von Bayern – Adalbertinische Linie

Prinz Adalbert von Bayern (1828–1875).
Adalbert war der jüngste Sohn König Ludwigs I. und Königin Thereses von Bayern. Als nachgeborener Prinz schlug er die klassische Militärlaufbahn ein, war jedoch besonders auch auf musischem Gebiet begabt.
Gemalter Scherenschnitt eines unbekannten Künstlers, nach 1851.

Prince Adalbert of Bavaria (1828–1875).
Adalbert was the youngest son of King Ludwig I and Queen Therese of Bavaria. As later-born prince in line, he pursued a classic military career but had a particular talent for music too.
Painted paper cut by an unknown artist, after 1851.

Prinz Adalbert von Bayern.
Prinz Adalbert hegte eine besondere Leidenschaft für Spanien, beherrschte die Sprache fließend und wünschte sich schon früh eine spanische Braut. Im Jahr 1856 heiratete er Amalia Felipe Pilar. Die Hochzeit fand am 70. Geburtstag von König Ludwig I. in Madrid statt. Aus der Ehe gingen fünf Kinder hervor: Die Prinzen Ludwig Ferdinand (1859–1949) und Alfons (1862–1933) sowie die Prinzessinnen Isabella (1863–1924), Elvira (1868–1943) und Clara (1874–1941).
Gemälde von Joseph Karl Stieler, o. J.

Prince Adalbert of Bavaria.
Prince Adalbert harboured a real passion for Spain, was fluent in the language and had wanted a Spanish bride from a young age. In 1856 he married Amalia Felipe Pilar. The wedding took place on King Ludwig I's 70th birthday in Madrid. The marriage produced five children: the princes Ludwig Ferdinand (1859–1949) and Alfons (1862–1933) as well as the princesses Isabella (1863–1924), Elvira (1868–1943) and Clara (1874–1941).
Painting by Joseph Karl Stieler, undated.

DAS KÖNIGREICH BAYERN
Prinz Adalbert von Bayern – Adalbertinische Linie

Amalia Felipe Pilar (1834–1905), Gemahlin von Prinz Adalbert von Bayern.
Amalia Felipe war die Tochter des Infanten Franz de Paula von Spanien und seiner Gemahlin Luise, Prinzessin beider Sizilien. Sie begründete die enge Bindung der adalbertinischen Linie des Hauses Wittelsbach an Spanien.
Gemälde eines unbekannten Künstlers, 1856.

Amalia Felipe Pilar (1834–1905), consort of Prince Adalbert of Bavaria.
Amalia Felipe was the daughter of Infante Franz de Paula of Spain and his consort Luise, Princess of the Two Sicilies. She founded the strong bond between the House of Wittelsbach's Adalbert line and Spain.
Painting by an unknown artist, 1856.

DAS KÖNIGREICH BAYERN
Prinz Adalbert von Bayern – Adalbertinische Linie

Taufe von Prinz Ludwig Ferdinand von Bayern (1859–1949) in Madrid im Jahr 1859.
Der spanische Hof wünschte die Geburt und Taufe des ältesten Sohnes des Prinzenpaares im Heimatland der Infantin Amalia.
Gemälde eines unbekannten Künstlers, o. J.

Christening of Prince Ludwig Ferdinand of Bavaria (1859–1949) in Madrid in 1859.
The Spanish court wanted the birth and christening of the royal couple's eldest son to be in the homeland of Infanta Amalia.
Painting by an unknown artist, undated.

DAS KÖNIGREICH BAYERN
Prinz Adalbert von Bayern – Adalbertinische Linie

Königin Isabella II. von Spanien (1830–1904) mit ihren Töchtern Infantin Maria de la Paz (1862–1946) und Infantin Eulalia (1864–1958).
Gemälde von Franz von Lenbach, 1889.

Queen Isabella II of Spain (1830–1904) with her daughters Infanta Maria de la Paz (1862–1946) and Infanta Eulalia (1864–1958).
Painting by Franz von Lenbach, 1889.

Prinz Ludwig Ferdinand von Bayern (1859–1949) in Uniform.
Ludwig Ferdinand absolvierte neben seiner Militärlaufbahn auch ein Medizinstudium, zu dem König Ludwig II. sein Einverständnis geben musste, da sein Vater Prinz Adalbert verstorben war, als sein Sohn noch minderjährig war. Er praktizierte als Facharzt für Chirurgie und Gynäkologie. 1883 heiratete er wie sein Vater eine Spanierin: Infantin Maria de la Paz.
Pastellgemälde von A. Feiks, 1898.

Prince Ludwig Ferdinand of Bavaria (1859–1949) in uniform.
Besides his military career, Ludwig Ferdinand also completed studies in medicine, which King Ludwig II had to give his permission for as his father Prince Adalbert died when his son was still a minor. He practised as a specialist doctor for surgery and gynaecology. In 1883 he married a Spanish woman, like his father: Infanta Maria de la Paz.
Pastel painting by A. Feiks, 1898.

DAS KÖNIGREICH BAYERN
Prinz Adalbert von Bayern – Adalbertinische Linie

Infantin Maria de la Paz von Spanien (1862–1946), Gemahlin des Prinzen Ludwig Ferdinand.
Maria de la Paz engagierte sich vor allem im sozialen Bereich: Sie wurde Vorstand des katholischen Frauenbundes und war nach dem Ersten Weltkrieg in der Mittelstandshilfe tätig. Sie war Mitglied des Dritten Ordens des Hl. Franziskus und setzte sich vorwiegend für das Krankenhauswesen ein.
Pastellgemälde von Franz von Lenbach, um 1889.

Infanta Maria de la Paz of Spain (1862–1946), consort of Prince Ludwig Ferdinand.
Maria de la Paz was committed to social work in particular: she became Chair of the Catholic Women's Association and worked on providing aid to the middle classes after the First World War. She was a member of the Third Order of Saint Francis and was mainly involved in supporting hospitals.
Pastel painting by Franz von Lenbach, c. 1889.

Infantin Maria de la Paz von Spanien mit ihren Kindern Ferdinand Maria (1884–1958), Adalbert (1886–1970) und Maria del Pilar (1891–1987).
Pastellzeichnung von Franz von Lenbach, 1895.

Infanta Maria de la Paz of Spain with her children Ferdinand Maria (1884–1958), Adalbert (1886–1970) and Maria del Pilar (1891–1987).
Pastel drawing by Franz von Lenbach, 1895.

DAS KÖNIGREICH BAYERN
Prinz Adalbert von Bayern – Adalbertinische Linie

Prinzessin Maria de la Paz von Bayern und ihre Mutter Königin Isabella II. von Spanien in einem Garten.
Gemälde eines unbekannten Künstlers, o. J.

Princess Maria de la Paz of Bavaria and her mother Queen Isabella II of Spain in a garden.
Painting by an inknown artist, undated.

Prinzessin Maria del Pilar von Bayern (1891 – 1987).
Maria del Pilar war das dritte und jüngste Kind von Prinz Ludwig Ferdinand von Bayern und Infantin Maria de la Paz. Sie wurde eine erfolgreiche Künstlerin.
Pastellgemälde von Helene von Frauendorfer-Mühlthaler, o. J.

Princess Maria del Pilar of Bavaria (1891 – 1987).
Maria del Pilar was the third and youngest child of Prince Ludwig Ferdinand of Bavaria and Infanta Maria de la Paz. She became a successful artist.
Pastel painting by Helene von Frauendorfer-Mühlthaler, undated.

DAS KÖNIGREICH BAYERN
Prinz Adalbert von Bayern – Adalbertinische Linie

Prinz Konstantin von Bayern (1920–1969) und sein Sohn Prinz Leopold (geb. 1943).
Prinz Konstantin war von 1962 bis 1965 Abgeordneter des Bayerischen Landtags, danach Bundestagsabgeordneter bis zu seinem frühen Tod beim Absturz seines Privatflugzeugs im Juli 1969. Er war der älteste Sohn Prinz Adalberts von Bayern und seiner Gemahlin Auguste, geb. Gräfin Seefried auf Buttenheim.
Fotografie, aufgenommen Anfang der sechziger Jahre des 20. Jahrhunderts.

Prince Konstantin of Bavaria (1920–1969) and his son Prince Leopold (born 1943).
Prince Konstantin was a member of the Bavarian Landtag from 1962 to 1965 and afterwards a member of the Bundestag until his early death in a private plane crash in July 1969. He was the eldest son of Prince Adalbert of Bavaria and his wife Auguste, née Countess Seefried auf Buttenheim.
Photograph, taken at the start of the 1960s.

Prinz Konstantin von Bayern im Kindesalter.
Gemälde von M. v. Bischoffshausen, o. J.

Prince Konstantin of Bavaria as a child.
Painting by M. v. Bischoffshausen, undated.

DAS KÖNIGREICH BAYERN
Prinz Adalbert von Bayern – Adalbertinische Linie

Prinzessin Hella von Bayern (geb. 1921).
Nach einer Verbindung mit Maria Adelgunde von Hohenzollern-Sigmaringen, heiratete Prinz Konstantin von Bayern 1953 in zweiter Ehe Helene von Khevenhüller-Metsch, Tochter von Franz Graf von Khevenhüller-Metsch.
Fotografie, aufgenommen 1940.

Princess Hella of Bavaria (born in 1921).
Following his marriage to Maria Adelgunde of Hohenzollern-Sigmaringen, Prince Konstantin of Bavaria entered a second marriage with Helene of Khevenmüller-Metsch, daughter of Count Franz of Khevenmüller-Metsch, in 1953.
Photograph, taken in 1940.

Prinzessin Hella von Bayern in Tracht.
Fotografie, aufgenommen 1943.

Princess Hella of Bavaria in traditional costume.
Photograph, taken in 1943.

DAS KÖNIGREICH BAYERN
Prinz Adalbert von Bayern – Adalbertinische Linie

Prinzessin Ysabel von Bayern (geb. 1954).
Die Tochter von Prinz Konstantin und seiner zweiten Frau Prinzessin Helene von Bayern wurde in Landshut porträtiert.
Gemälde, Signatur unleserlich, 1970.

Princess Ysabel of Bavaria (born 1954).
This portrait of the daughter of Prince Konstantin and his second wife Princess Helene of Bavaria was painted in Landshut.
Painting, illegible signature, 1970.

King Maximilian II

After the abdication of Ludwig I, Maximilian II was faced with the challenge of stabilizing the Bavarian monarchy considering the 1848 revolution. He did not pursue this goal with an oppressive style of leadership, however, but in the fulfilment of a more balanced political approach. He accepted constitutional reforms such as a democratisation of the state election law, and through the precise weighing and consideration of the facts by experts, he consistently tried to find the right balance.

In 1842, Crown Prince Maximilian married Princess Marie Friederike of Prussia, who quickly attained the general approval of the people. Hohenschwangau Castle and its surrounding mountains became the favourite abode of the couple and their sons Ludwig and Otto, where they enjoyed taking extended walks in the summer months. The family also enjoyed spending holiday time in Berchtesgaden.

Maximilian studied at the Universities of Göttingen and Berlin and once said that he would have been a scientist were he not to have been born into a royal family. This personal leaning also found reflection in his cultural and educational policy: Maximilian generally supported the sciences, appointed famous names such as the historian Leopold von Ranke to Munich University and had a keen sense of enthusiasm for the achievements of modern technology. He wanted Bavaria to become one of the leading industrialised states, and so Maximilian pushed ahead with the construction of the railway network in the way his father did, but also applied himself to finding solutions for the increasingly urgent social issues of the times. He also recognised the potential of a successful integration policy: by encouraging tradition and the national costume he attempted to strengthen a far-reaching, national Bavarian sentiment in every part of the state.

In foreign policy, regarding the German States' battle for supremacy, Maximilian II represented the Trias idea: to prevent itself from being crushed by the major powers of Prussia and Austria, Bavaria should join the other small and medium-sized states in a pact in Germany to create a counterweight. This project never came to fruition, however, as the King was unable to exert sufficient influence on the other Crown Princes, who for their part feared Bavaria would take too strong a position in any such pact. The sudden death of Maximilian in 1864 left the pressing questions which arose for Bavaria out of the rivalry between Prussia and Austria unsolved.

König Maximilian II.

Nach der Abdankung Ludwigs I. sah sich Maximilian II. vor die Herausforderung gestellt, die bayerische Monarchie angesichts der Revolution von 1848 zu stabilisieren. Dieses Ziel verfolgte er jedoch nicht mittels eines restriktiven Führungsstils, sondern in der Erfüllung einer eher ausgleichenden Politik. Er akzeptierte Verfassungsreformen, beispielsweise eine Demokratisierung des Landtagswahlrechts, und versuchte, durch genaues Abwägen und Prüfung der Sachverhalte durch Experten in politischen Entscheidungen stets das rechte Maß zu finden.

1842 heiratete Kronprinz Maximilian Prinzessin Marie Friederike von Preußen. Diese erfreute sich äußerst schnell einer allgemeinen Beliebtheit beim Volk. Der liebste Aufenthaltsort des Paares und seiner Söhne Ludwig und Otto wurden Schloss Hohenschwangau und die umgebende Bergwelt, wo in den Sommermonaten ausgedehnte Wanderungen unternommen wurden. Auch Berchtesgaden avancierte zu einem bevorzugten Ferienort der Familie.

Maximilian hatte an den Universitäten zu Göttingen und Berlin studiert und bemerkte einmal, wäre er nicht in eine Königsfamilie geboren, dann wäre er wohl Wissenschaftler geworden. Diese persönliche Neigung spiegelte sich auch in seiner Kultur- und Bildungspolitik: Maximilian förderte allgemein die Wissenschaften, berief berühmte Namen, u. a. den Historiker Leopold von Ranke, an die Münchner Universität und begeisterte sich für die Errungenschaften der modernen Technik. Bayern sollte nach seinem Willen zu einem der fortschrittlichsten industrialisierten Länder werden. Daher trieb Maximilian wie schon sein Vater den Ausbau der Eisenbahnstrecken voran, bemühte sich aber auch um Lösungsansätze für die immer dringlicher werdenden sozialen Fragen. Ebenso erkannte er das Potenzial einer erfolgreichen Integrationspolitik: Durch die Förderung von Brauchtum und Volkstracht versuchte er, ein übergreifendes bayerisches Nationalgefühl aller Landesteile zu stärken.

Außenpolitisch vertrat Maximilian II. im Ringen um die Vorherrschaft unter den deutschen Staaten die Trias-Idee: Um nicht zwischen den Großmächten Preußen und Österreich aufgerieben zu werden, sollte sich ein Bündnis Bayerns mit den anderen deutschen Klein- und Mittelstaaten als Gegengewicht etablieren. Dieses Vorhaben wurde jedoch nie Wirklichkeit; zu gering war wohl der Einfluss des Königs auf die anderen Fürsten, die ihrerseits eine zu starke Position Bayerns innerhalb dieses Bündnisses fürchteten. Der plötzliche Tod Maximilians 1864 ließ die drängenden Fragen, die für Bayern aus der Rivalität zwischen Preußen und Österreich erwuchsen, ungelöst.

DAS KÖNIGREICH BAYERN
König Maximilian II. von Bayern

Eintrag mit Wappen König Maximilians II. im Bruderschaftsbuch der Corpus-Christi-Bruderschaft bei St. Peter in München.

Entry with the coat of arms of King Maximilian II in the Book of the Brotherhood of the Corpus Christi Brotherhood at St. Peter's Church in Munich.

König Maximilian II. von Bayern als Hubertusritter.
Im Jahr 1848 folgte Kronprinz Maximilian Ludwig I. von Bayern nach dessen Abdankung auf den Thron. In der Tradition seiner Vorgänger ließ sich Maximilian II. in der Tracht eines Ritters des St.-Hubertus-Ordens mit Collane und Ordensstern abbilden. Ähnlich dem St.-Georgs-Ritterorden ist auch der Hubertusritterorden bis heute ein Hausorden der Wittelsbacher.
Gemälde von Wilhelm von Kaulbach, nach 1854.

King Maximilian II of Bavaria as a Knight of St. Hubertus.
In 1848, Crown Prince Maximilian succeeded Ludwig I of Bavaria on the Bavarian throne after Ludwig's abdication. In the tradition of his predecessor, Maximilian II allowed himself to be painted in the costume of a Knight of the Order of St. Hubertus with a collar and star of the Order. Similar to the St. George Order of Knights, the Hubertus Order of Knights remains an Order of the House of Wittelsbach to this day.
Painting by Wilhelm von Kaulbach, after 1854.

DAS KÖNIGREICH BAYERN
König Maximilian II. von Bayern

Kronprinz Maximilian II. von Bayern auf dem Alpsee bei Hohenschwangau. Auf dem Bild füttert der Prinz edle Schwäne, symbolträchtige Tiere, vor dem Hintergrund des Schlosses Hohenschwangau. Tatsächlich wurden eigens weiße und wertvolle schwarze Schwäne im Jahr 1838 von der Königsfamilie in England erworben und auf dem Alpsee ausgesetzt.
Gemälde von Lorenzo Quaglio, 1841.

Crown Prince Maximilian II of Bavaria on Lake Alpsee near Hohenschwangau. The picture shows the Prince feeding the symbolic royal swans before the backdrop of Hohenschwangau Castle. Special white and valuable black swans were actually acquired from the English royal family in 1838, making Lake Alpsee their home.
Painting by Lorenzo Quaglio, 1841.

DAS KÖNIGREICH BAYERN
König Maximilian II. von Bayern

Einzug der Prinzessin Marie von Preußen (1825–1889) als Braut des Kronprinzen Maximilian am 11. Oktober 1842 in der Münchner Ludwigstraße.
Marie, die protestantische Prinzessin, war im überwiegend katholischen Bayern schnell äußerst beliebt. Als Königin engagierte sie sich vor allem sozial, die Gründung des Bayerischen Roten Kreuzes geht u. a. auf sie zurück. Bekannt war sie vor allem auch für ihre Wanderleidenschaft: Als erste Frau bestieg sie zahlreiche Gipfel der bayerischen Alpen.
Lithografie von Gustav Wilhelm Kraus, um 1842.

Procession of Princess Marie of Prussia (1825–1889), bride of Crown Prince Maximilian, on 11 October 1842 on Ludwigstraße, Munich.
Marie, the protestant Princess, quickly became very popular in predominantly Catholic Bavaria. As Queen she dedicated herself to social causes, with, among others, the foundation of the Bavarian Red Cross dating back to her epoch. She was also known for her passion for walking, becoming the first woman to climb many of the peaks in the Bavarian Alps.
Lithograph by Gustav Wilhelm Kraus, c. 1842.

DAS KÖNIGREICH BAYERN
König Maximilian II. von Bayern

Kronprinzessin Marie von Bayern im Kostüm ihres „Achsel-Alpenrosen-Ordens".
Jeder, der mit der Kronprinzessin, der späteren Königin Marie, den Berg Achsel bei Reutte in Tirol bestiegen hatte, erhielt den „Achsel-Alpenrosen-Orden".
Aquarell von Eduard Rietschel, 1844.

Crown Princess Marie of Bavaria in the costume of her "Achsel Alpine Rose Order".
Everyone to climb mount Achsel at Reutte in Tyrol with the Crown Princess, who later became Queen Marie, obtained the "Achsel Alpine Rose" medal.
Watercolour by Eduard Rietschel, 1844.

König Maximilian II., Königin Marie, Kronprinz Ludwig und Prinz Otto von Bayern auf Schloss Hohenschwangau.
Im Jahr 1832 erwarb Kronprinz Maximilian die Ruinen der Burg Schwanstein über dem Alpsee. Angeblich hatte er schon als Jugendlicher davon geträumt, die Burg einst neu zu errichten – und das tat er bis 1855, als sie nun als Schloss Hohenschwangau endlich fertig gestellt war. Fortan war Hohenschwangau die Lieblingsresidenz der Königsfamilie, besonders der beiden Prinzen Ludwig und Otto.
Kolorierte Lithografie von Erich Correns, um 1850.

King Maximilian II, Queen Marie, Crown Prince Ludwig and Prince Otto of Bavaria at Hohenschwangau Castle.
In 1832, Crown Prince Maximilian acquired ownership of the ruins of Schwanstein Castle overlooking the Alpsee lake. He had supposedly dreamt of rebuilding the castle as a youth which he went on to do, culminating in the completion of Hohenschwangau Castle in 1855. Hohenschwangau then became the favourite residence of the royal family, especially the two Princes Ludwig and Otto.
Colour lithograph by Erich Correns, c. 1850.

DAS KÖNIGREICH BAYERN
König Maximilian II. von Bayern

Kronprinz Ludwig und Prinz Otto von Bayern bei Hohenschwangau.
Im Hintergrund sowie im Skizzenbuch des etwa zehnjährigen Ludwig ist das bereits weitgehend fertiggestellte Schloss Hohenschwangau zu sehen.
Aquarell von Friedrich Hohbach, um 1855.

Crown Prince Ludwig and Prince Otto at Hohenschwangau.
The largely complete Hohenschwangau can be seen both in the background and in ten year old Ludwig's sketch book.
Watercolour by Friedrich Hohbach, c. 1855.

Schloss Hohenschwangau von der „Jugend" aus gesehen.
Aus der Perspektive des Aussichtspunkts „Jugend" sind bereits der angebaute Prinzenbau und die Orangerie des Schlosses zu sehen. Im Vordergrund betrachtet Königin Marie von Bayern mit Kronprinz Ludwig und Prinz Otto die Aussicht.
Gemälde von Lorenzo Quaglio, 1856.

Hohenschwangau Castle seen from the perspective of "Youth".
From the perspective of the lookout "Youth" the newly constructed "Prinzenbau" and the castle orangery can already be seen. In the foreground Queen Marie of Bavaria is taking the view with Crown Prince Ludwig and Prince Otto.
Painting by Lorenzo Quaglio, 1856.

DAS KÖNIGREICH BAYERN
König Maximilian II. von Bayern

462 | 463 **König Maximilian II. und Königin Marie von Bayern mit Jagdgesellschaft am Fuße des niederen Straussberg bei Schwangau.** *Gemälde von Philipp Foltz, 1852.*

King Maximilian II and Queen Marie of Bavaria with hunting party at the foot of the Lower Straussberg near Schwangau. *Painting by Philipp Foltz, 1852.*

DAS KÖNIGREICH BAYERN
König Maximilian II. von Bayern

Zeitgenössische Darstellung des Glaspalasts in München.
Der Glaspalast wurde aus Anlass der „Ersten Allgemeinen Deutschen Industrie-Ausstellung" in München 1854 nach Plänen von August von Voit errichtet. Das Gebäude, eine zu dieser Zeit äußerst moderne und wegweisende Konstruktion aus Gusseisenträgern und Glaselementen, befand sich im Norden des Alten Botanischen Gartens. Maximilian II. beabsichtigte, mit der Industrieausstellung und ihrem spektakulären Messegebäude Bayern und München als ernstzunehmende Wirtschaftsstandorte zu etablieren.
Farblithografie von Peter Herwegen, 1854.

Contemporary presentation of the Glass Palace in Munich.
The Glass Palace was built in Munich in 1854 for the "First General German Industrial Exhibition" according to a design by August von Voit. The building, an exceptionally modern and innovative construction at the time, and made from cast iron girders and glass sections, was situated in the northern part of the old Botanical Gardens. With the Industrial Exhibition and its spectacular exhibition buildings, Maximilian II intended to establish Bavaria and Munich as leading centres for business and industry.
Colour lithograph by Peter Herwegen, 1854.

Der Hauptbahnhof in München.
Die moderne Rundbogenhalle wurde von 1847 bis 1849 von Friedrich Bürklein, einem Schüler Friedrich von Gärtners, erbaut. König Ludwig I. wünschte einen repräsentativen Neubau am heutigen Standort, da die älteren Vorgängerbauten zu klein waren und zu weit entfernt von der Innenstadt lagen. Ab 1851 wurde der Bahnhof mit pettenkoferschem Leuchtgas beleuchtet. In den 1880er Jahren erfolgte eine weitere großangelegte Umgestaltung der Bahnhofsgebäude.
Aquarellierte Zeichnung von Gustav Seeberger oder Rudolf Gottgetreu, um 1850.

Munich Central Station.
The modern arched hall was built by Friedrich Bürklein, a scholar of Friedrich von Gärtner, between 1847 and 1849. King Ludwig I wanted an impressive new building at the current site, as the previous buildings were too small and too far away from the city centre. The station was lit with Pettenkofers light gas from 1851 onwards. In the 1880s, the station buildings were subject to further major remodelling.
Watercolour drawing by Gustav Seeberger or Rudolf Gottgetreu, c. 1850

DAS KÖNIGREICH BAYERN
König Maximilian II. von Bayern

Die Königliche Villa auf der Roseninsel im Starnberger See, Ansicht von Norden.
1850 kaufte Maximilian II. die Roseninsel und ließ auf ihr eine königliche Villa, das „Casino", als Sommerhaus errichten. Besonders sein Sohn Ludwig II. liebte die Insel und das Schlösschen, in dem er nur ausgewählte Besucher, u. a. Richard Wagner und die russische Zarin Maria Alexandrowna, empfing.
Aquarell von Franz Jakob Kreuter, 1852.

The Royal Villa on Roseninsel island in Lake Starnberg, viewed from the north.
In 1850, Maximilian II bought the Roseninsel, where he built a royal villa, the "Casino", as a summer retreat. His son Ludwig II especially loved the island and its villa, and welcomed only select visitors to stay there, including Richard Wagner and Russian Tsar Maria Alexandrovna.
Watercolour by Franz Jakob Kreuter, 1852.

Die Königliche Villa in Berchtesgaden.
Max II. hatte den Wunsch, neben dem Königlichen Schloss in Berchtesgaden dort auch eine Sommervilla für sich und seine Familie zu unterhalten. 1853 war die Villa fertiggestellt und seitdem beliebtes Feriendomizil.
Kolorierte Lithographie von Georg Pezolt, 1855.

The royal villa in Berchtesgaden.
In addition to the royal castle in Berchtesgaden, Max II also wanted a summer villa for his personal use and to entertain his family. The villa was completed in 1853 and immediately become a popular holiday home.
Colour lithograph by Georg Pezolt, 1855.

DAS KÖNIGREICH BAYERN
König Maximilian II. von Bayern

Versammlung bedeutender Staatsmänner des 18. und 19. Jahrhunderts. Links: Neben einer Büste von König Max I. Staatsminister Ludwig von der Pfordten, dahinter Freiherr Wiguläus von Kreittmayr. Im Zentrum (v. l. n. r.): Fürst Talleyrand/Frankreich, Graf Montgelas/Bayern, Fürst Hardenberg/Preußen, Fürst Metternich/Österreich. Rechts William Pitt, Earl of Chatham sowie der Nationalökonom Adam Smith. Thematisiert wird der politische und wirtschaftliche Status quo Bayerns zur Regierungszeit Max' II., symbolisert durch die Personen, die ihn herbeigeführt haben. Ein historisches Treffen dieser für Bayern wichtigen Männer, deren Lebensspannen sich über 175 Jahre erstrecken, fand jedoch niemals statt.
Skizze zum im Zweiten Weltkrieg zerstörten Wandgemälde von Engelbert Seibertz im Lesesaal des Maximilianeums in München, 1858.

Gathering of significant statesmen of the 18th and 19th century. Left: adjacent to a bust of King Max I, Minister of State Ludwig von der Pfordten, behind him, Baron Wiguläus von Kreittmayr. In the centre (from left to right): Prince Talleyrand/France, Count Montgelas/Bavaria, Prince Hardenberg/Prussia, Prince Metternich/Austria. Right: William Pitt, Earl of Chatham and State Economist, Adam Smith. Here, the political and economic status quo in Bavaria during the governing era of Max II is taken up, as symbolised by the people who helped bring the era into fruition. No such historic meeting of these men, who played an important role in Bavaria and whose lives spanned over 175 years, ever took place, however.
Study of the mural painting by Engelbert Seibertz, which was destroyed during the Second World War, in the reading room of the Maximilianeum in Munich, 1858.

DAS KÖNIGREICH BAYERN
König Maximilian II. von Bayern

Einführung Alexander von Humboldts in den Kreis der Maximiliansordensträger.
Das Gemälde ehrt lebende und verstorbene Männer aus Wissenschaft und Kunst, denen Maximilian II. seinen Orden verlieh oder verliehen hätte, wären sie noch am Leben gewesen. Darunter waren z. B. Josef von Fraunhofer (4. v. l., im Hintergrund) und Ludwig von Schwanthaler (5. v. r., ganz im Hintergrund). In den illustren Kreis wird Alexander von Humboldt (Mitte, an der Seite Justus von Liebigs) eingeführt. Im Vordergrund, Humboldt begrüßend, der Altphilologe Friedrich von Thiersch und der Dichter Emanuel von Geibel.
Gemälde von Engelbert Seibertz, 1858.

Introduction of Alexander von Humboldt to the members of the Order of Maximilian.
The portrait honours men both alive and dead from the world of art and science to whom Maximilian II awarded his Order – or would have awarded, had they still been alive. These included, for instance, Josef von Fraunhofer (fourth from left, in the background) and Ludwig von Schwanthaler (fifth from right, in the very background). Alexander von Humboldt (centre, to the side of Justus von Liebig) also joins the illustrious group. In the foreground greeting Humboldt are classicist Friedrich von Thiersch and poet Emanuel von Geibel.
Painting by Engelbert Seibertz, 1858.

DAS KÖNIGREICH BAYERN
König Maximilian II. von Bayern

Maximiliansbrücke in München im Zuge der Maximilianstraße.
Von 1857 bis 1863 ließ König Maximilian II. in Verlängerung seines Prachtboulevards, der Maximilianstraße, über die Isar mit der Praterinsel eine zweiteilige Brücke zum gerade im Bau befindlichen Maximilianeum errichten.
Gemälde eines unbekannten Künstlers, o. J.

The Maximilian Bridge in Munich showing the course of Maximilianstraße.
Between 1857 and 1863, a two-part bridge was constructed over the river Isar on the orders of King Maximilian II, which saw his boulevard of splendour, Maximilianstraße, being extended over the Praterinsel and on to the Maximilianeum, then under construction.
Painting by an unknown artist, undated.

Transport des Denkmals für König Maximilian II. über den Königsplatz in München.
Das Denkmal wurde im Oktober 1875 feierlich enthüllt. Kronprinz Rupprecht schenkte den Königsplatz und die Glyptothek 1921 dem bayerischen Staat.
Gemälde von Eugen Adam, 1875.

Aufstellung des Denkmals für König Maximilian II. („Max-Monument") in der Maximilianstraße in München.
Ein Jahr nach dem Tod Maximilians II. wurde ein Denkmal für ihn in Auftrag gegeben, das im Bronzeguss von Ferdinand von Miller ausgeführt und 1875 feierlich aufgerichtet wurde.
Gemälde von Eugen Adam, 1875.

Transportation of the monument for King Maximilian II across Königsplatz in Munich.
The monument was unveiled in a formal ceremony in October 1875. Crown Price Rupprecht gave the Königsplatz and the Glyptothek to the state of Bavaria in 1921.
Poainting by Eugen Adam, 1875

Opening of the monument for King Maximilian II (the "Max Monument") in Maximilianstraße in Munich.
One year after Maximilian II died, a monument was commissioned for him which was made by Ferdinand von Miller in cast bronze and unveiled at a festive ceremony in October 1875.
Painting by Eugen Adam, 1875

King Ludwig II

When discussing Ludwig II it would be unfair to simply talk of the "Fairytale King" and his unforgettable palaces, which even in those days appeared to have come from a completely different time. The 18-year-old Crown Prince was catapulted into the role of King with relatively little time to prepare due to the sudden death of his father. Whilst he had, until then, received a rounded education which also included strict military training, the young Ludwig was ill-prepared to assume the duties of state. The inexperienced King found it hard to impose his will on his established administration – although he initially demonstrated much interest in political decision-making and had been keen to set to work. As King, he continued to pursue the enthusiasm for literature, music and theatre that he had first developed as a youth. In 1864, Ludwig invited his idol Richard Wagner to Munich, who then lived and composed under his patronage. This decision earned the disapproval of both his ministers and the wider population, however, which forced Ludwig to dismiss Wagner from Munich just one year later.

Ludwig's repeated failure to finally establish himself within his administration as a royal decision maker helped cause his initial withdrawal from public life, which was ultimately followed by his retreat from state business. Ludwig also felt that he was in a disadvantageous position in his role as sovereign monarch due to the domination of Prussia within the federation of German states after 1871. He had joined Austria in the war against Prussia only reluctantly in 1866 – after the defeat at Königgrätz, he was forced to enter into a "defensive and offensive alliance" with the victors. It therefore followed that in 1870/71, Bavaria was obliged to provide military support to Prussia in the war against France. In 1871, in the famous "Kaiser letter", on behalf of German Crown Princes Ludwig formally proffered the German imperial crown to Emperor Wilhelm – a personal humiliation which also saw Bavaria relinquishing much of its sovereignty with the foundation of the German Reich.

The ideal of an absolutist monarchy, which Ludwig sorely missed, was instead expressed in his personal idea of an artistic monarchy, which was in turn manifested in the palaces that he built. Inspired by Louis XIV and his times, as well as by the heroes of a medieval world of legends and Far Eastern exotica, Ludwig created a highly symbolically charged artistic oeuvre that reflected his self-image as a monarch in his magical palaces and homes. His unsociable nature, which worsened over time and gradually developed into a personality disorder, made a decisive contribution to Ludwig's withdrawal into his dream world – although he continued to carry out the most important governmental business in writing until the end of his life.

In June 1886, Ludwig II was declared to be unable to govern and discharged of his duties by his administration on the grounds of what was an unjustly diagnosed "mental illness". This episode was preceded by a serious financial crisis which was largely deemed attributable to the construction of Ludwig's expensive palaces, but which was ultimately caused by the king's lost grip on reality. The mysterious death of Ludwig II and his physician, Dr von Gudden, in Lake Starnberg on the evening of 13 June 1886 remains a source of speculation to this day, further adding to the sense of legend that surrounds by far the most famous member of the House of Wittelsbach.

König Ludwig II.

Es würde Ludwig II. kaum gerecht werden, spräche man an dieser Stelle ausschließlich vom „Märchenkönig" und seinen unvergleichlichen Schlossbauten, die schon damals so ganz und gar aus der Zeit gefallen zu sein schienen. Der 18-jährige Kronprinz wurde durch den plötzlichen Tod seines Vaters relativ unvorbereitet in die Rolle des Königs katapultiert. Zwar hatte er bis dahin eine umfassende Bildung erhalten, die auch eine strenge militärische Ausbildung mit einschloss, doch für die Übernahme der Staatsgeschäfte war Ludwig kaum bereit.

So hatte es der unerfahrene König schwer, sich gegen sein etabliertes Ministerium zu behaupten, obwohl er zunächst durchaus Interesse an der politischen Arbeit zeigte und zum Handeln entschlossen war. Gleichzeitig ging er weiterhin seiner jugendlichen Begeisterung für Literatur, Musik und Theater nach. Schon 1864 holte Ludwig sein Idol Richard Wagner nach München, der fortan unter seiner Protektion lebte und komponierte, allerdings nicht ohne das Missfallen der Minister und der Bürger zu erregen; ein Jahr später war Ludwig gezwungen, Wagner wieder aus München zu entlassen.

Ludwigs wiederholtes Scheitern, sich endgültig gegenüber dem Ministerium als königlicher Entscheidungsträger zu etablieren, begünstigte seinen graduellen Rückzug zunächst aus dem öffentlichen Leben und später auch aus den Staatsgeschäften. Zudem sah sich Ludwig nach 1871 in seiner Rolle als souveräner Monarch durch die Vorherrschaft Preußens im Bund der deutschen Staaten beeinträchtigt. Nur widerwillig war er 1866 an der Seite Österreichs in den Krieg gegen Preußen eingetreten; nach der Niederlage bei Königgrätz musste er ein Schutz- und Trutzbündnis mit dem Sieger eingehen. So war Bayern 1870/71 dazu verpflichtet, Preußen im Krieg gegen Frankreich militärisch zu unterstützen. 1871 trug Ludwig II. im Namen der deutschen Fürsten König Wilhelm im berühmten „Kaiserbrief" formell die Deutsche Kaiserkrone an – eine Demütigung für ihn, der mit der Gründung des Deutschen Reichs die Souveränität Bayerns zu großen Teilen aufgeben musste.

Das Ideal eines absoluten Königtums, das Ludwig in der politischen Realität schmerzlich vermisste, verwirklichte er in seiner persönlichen Vorstellung eines Kunstkönigtums, das sich in seinen Schlossbauten manifestierte. Inspiriert von Ludwig XIV. und seiner Zeit, den Helden der mittelalterlichen Sagenwelt und von fernöstlicher Exotik schuf Ludwig in seinen Schlössern und Lusthäusern ein hochgradig symbolisch aufgeladenes Gesamtkunstwerk seines königlichen Selbstverständnisses. Seine über die Jahre immer heftigere Menschenscheu, die sich bis zur Persönlichkeitsstörung entwickelte, trug wesentlich zum Rückzug Ludwigs in seine Traumwelten bei, obwohl er bis zuletzt die nötigsten Regierungsgeschäfte schriftlich erledigte.

Im Juni 1886 erklärte das Ministerium Ludwig II. aufgrund einer zu Unrecht festgestellten „Geisteskrankheit" für abgesetzt. Vorangegangen war eine tiefe Finanzkrise, die vordergründig auf Ludwigs teure Schlossbauten zurückgeführt wurde, ihre tiefere Ursache aber im verloren gegangenen Bezug des Königs zur Realität hatte. Der rätselhafte Tod Ludwigs II. und seines Arztes Dr. von Gudden im Starnberger See am Abend des 13. Juni 1886 sorgt bis heute für allerlei Spekulationen, die wesentlich zur Legendenbildung um den weltweit wohl berühmtesten Wittelsbacher beitrugen.

DAS KÖNIGREICH BAYERN
König Ludwig II. von Bayern

Eintrag mit Wappen König Ludwigs II. im Bruderschaftsbuch der Corpus-Christi-Bruderschaft bei St. Peter in München (datiert 31. Mai 1864).

Entry with the coat of arms of King Ludwig II in the Book of the Brotherhood of the Corpus Christi Brotherhood at St. Peter's Church in Munich (dated 31 May 1864).

König Ludwig II. von Bayern (1845–1886) in Uniform mit der Ordenskette des St.-Hubertus-Ritterordens und dem Stern des St.-Georgs-Ritterordens.
Die Könige von Bayern waren stets auch Großmeister dieser Orden. Nach dem überraschend frühen Tod seines Vaters trat Kronprinz Ludwig 18-jährig die Thronfolge an.
Ölgemälde von Ferdinand von Piloty d. J., 1865.

King Ludwig II of Bavaria (1845–1886) in uniform with the collar of the Knights of the Order of St. Hubertus and the star of the Knights of the Order of St. George.
The Kings of Bavaria were consistently Grand Masters of these Orders as well. Crown Prince Ludwig ascended to the throne aged just 18 after the unexpectedly premature death of his father.
Oil portrait by Ferdinand von Piloty the Younger, 1865.

DAS KÖNIGREICH BAYERN
König Ludwig II. von Bayern

Audienzzimmer der Wohnung König Ludwigs II. in der Münchner Residenz.
Aquarell von Conrad Hoff, 1867/68.

Audience room of King Ludwig II's apartment in the Munich Residenz.
Watercolour by Conrad Hoff, 1867/68.

Der im Zweiten Weltkrieg zerstörte Thronsaal im Festsaalbau der Residenz zu München.
Zwischen den Säulen erkennt man die Statuen der Wittelsbacher Ahnen von Ludwig von Schwanthaler, deren Modelle im Alten Rathaussaal Aufstellung fanden. Anstelle des zerstörten Thronsaals wurde nach 1945 der „Herkulessaal" als Konzertsaal eingebaut.
Stich von Johann Poppel nach einer Federzeichnung von Gustav Seeberger, um 1860.

The Throne Room in the festival hall of the Munich Residenz, subsequently destroyed in the Second World War.
Between the pillars it is possible to see the effigies of the Wittelsbach antecedents of Ludwig von Schwanthaler, whose mockups were exhibited in the former town hall chamber. Taking the place of the destroyed throne room is the "Hercules Hall", built as a concert hall in the post-war era.
Engraving by Johann Poppel based on a pen and ink drawing by Gustav Seeberger, c. 1860.

DAS KÖNIGREICH BAYERN
König Ludwig II. von Bayern

Der ehemalige Wintergarten König Ludwigs II. auf dem Dach der Münchner Residenz, Landschaftsmotiv mit See, Prunkzelt und Himalayagebirge. Hofgartendirektor Carl Effner und der Theatermaler Christian Rank errichteten auf Anweisung Ludwigs II. um 1870 über dem Nordwestflügel des Festsaalbaus der Münchner Residenz einen 70 auf 17 Meter großen Wintergarten. Ein künstlicher See mit Fischerhütte, ein maurischer Kiosk und große austauschbare Panoramabilder sollten zusammen mit der im Garten angesiedelten exotischen Tier- und Pflanzensammlung den König in eine andere Welt versetzen. Der Wintergarten ist nicht mehr erhalten, schon kurz nach dem Tod Ludwigs 1886 wurde der aufwendige Bau wieder abgetragen.
Ölgemälde von Julius Lange, 1871.

King Ludwig II's former winter garden on the roof of the Munich Residenz, a landscape with a lake, ornate tent and Himalaya style mountains. In 1870, on the instruction of Ludwig II, director of the court gardens Carl Effner and theatre painter Christian Rank built a 70 x 17 metre-sized winter garden on the north-west wing of the festival hall of the Munich Residenz. Together with the exotic world of plants and animals depicted in the garden, an artificial lake with fishing huts, a Moorish kiosk and large exchangeable panoramic images were designed to transport the King into another world. The winter garden no longer exists, with the elaborate structure having been dismantled shortly after Ludwig's demise in 1886.
Oil painting by Julius Lange, 1871.

DAS KÖNIGREICH BAYERN
König Ludwig II. von Bayern

König Ludwig II. von Bayern und sein Generalstab.
Auf dem Bild wird die erste große Truppenparade dargestellt, die König Ludwig II. im September 1864 auf dem Marsfeld, dem späteren Oberwiesenfeld, abnahm. Neben dem König der General der Kavallerie, Fürst von Thurn und Taxis, Generaladjutant von Laroche, Kriegsminister von Lutz, Herzog Ludwig in Bayern.
Gemälde von Ludwig Behringer, 1864.

King Ludwig II of Bavaria and his general staff.
The portrait depicts the first major parade of troops led by King Ludwig II in September 1864 on the Marsfeld, later known as the Oberwiesenfeld. Next to the King, the General of the Cavalry, Prince of Thurn and Taxis, Adjutant General von Laroche, Minister of War von Lutz, Duke Ludwig of Bavaria.
Portrait by Ludwig Behringer, 1864.

DAS KÖNIGREICH BAYERN
König Ludwig II. von Bayern

Prozession zur 400-Jahr-Feier der Grundsteinlegung des Doms Zu Unserer Lieben Frau in München.
Ludwig II. hatte anlässlich der neugotischen Ausgestaltung und der Restaurierung des Kirchenraums neue Pfeilerfiguren gestiftet. Bei der Prozession zeigte sich der junge König der Öffentlichkeit.
Aquarell von Friedrich Eibner, 1868.

Procession to commemorate the 400th anniversary of the laying of the foundation stone of the Cathedral of Our Lady in Munich.
Ludwig II donated new column figures on the occasion of the neo-gothic decoration and restoration of the interior of the church. The procession saw the young King presenting himself to the people.
Watercolour by Friedrich Eibner, 1868.

DAS KÖNIGREICH BAYERN
König Ludwig II. von Bayern

„Cosa Rara" in Linderhof.
König Ludwig II. von Bayern ließ seine Lieblingspferde von Friedrich Wilhelm Pfeiffer an ihrem jeweiligen Einsatzort porträtieren.
Gemälde von Friedrich Wilhelm Pfeiffer, o. J.

"Cosa Rara" in Linderhof.
King Ludwig II of Bavaria arranged for his favourite horses to be painted by Friedrich Wilhelm Pfeiffer at their respective stations.
Painting by Friedrich Wilhelm Pfeiffer, undated.

„Wala" vor dem königlichen „Schweizerhaus" bei Hohenschwangau.
Die dunkelbraune, fast schwarze irische Stute galt als ausdauerndes Bergpferd.
Gemälde von Friedrich Wilhelm Pfeiffer, um 1867.

"Wala" before the royal "Schweizerhaus" at Hohenschwangau.
The dark brown, almost black Irish mare was a tenacious mountain horse.
Painting by Friedrich Wilhelm Pfeiffer, c. 1867.

„Woluspa" bei Schloss Berg am Ostufer des Starnberger Sees.
Gemälde von Friedrich Wilhelm Pfeiffer, um 1867.

"Woluspa" at Berg Castle on the eastern bank of Lake Starnberg.
Painting by Friedrich Wilhelm Pfeiffer, c. 1867.

König Ludwig II. von Bayern in bürgerlicher Kleidung zu Pferde.
König Ludwig II. von Bayern war ein begeisterter und kühner Reiter.
Ölgemälde von Feodor Dietz, 1866.

King Ludwig II of Bavaria in bourgeois attire on his horse.
King Ludwig II of Bavaria was an enthusiastic and bold rider.
Oil painting by Feodor Dietz, 1866.

DAS KÖNIGREICH BAYERN
König Ludwig II. von Bayern

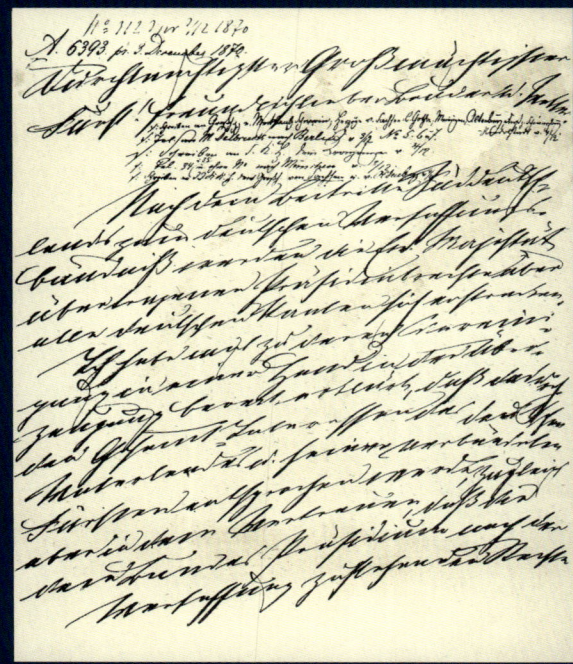 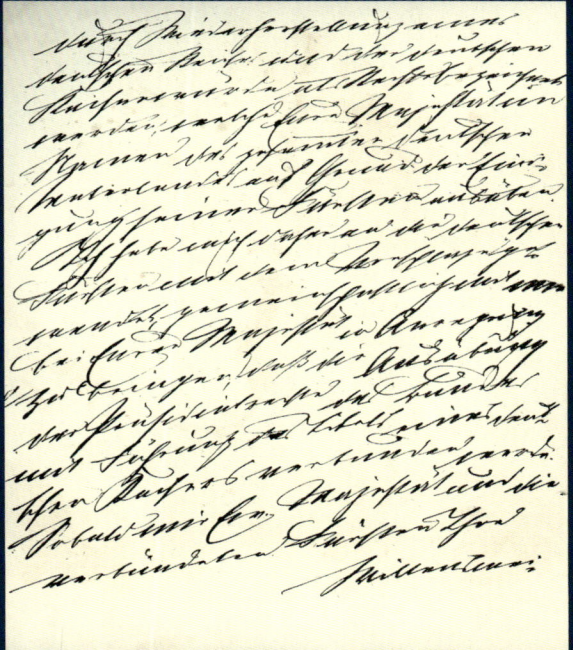 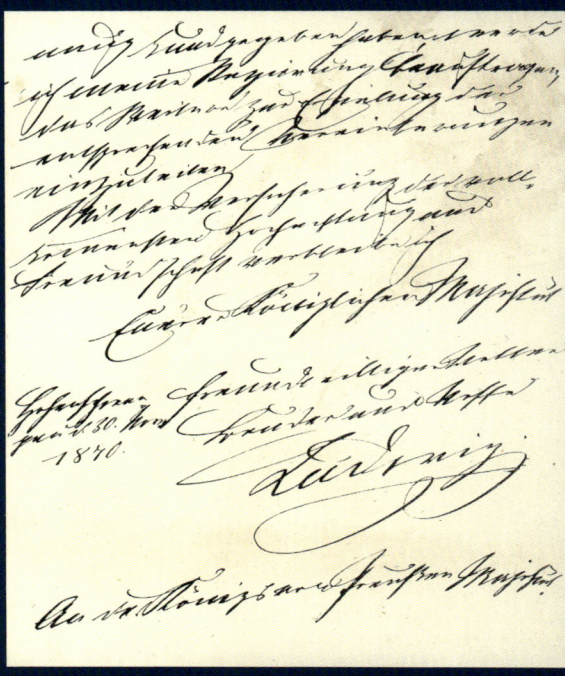

Der „Kaiserbrief" Ludwigs II.
Während des deutsch-französischen Krieges bot Ludwig II. im Namen der deutschen Fürsten König Wilhelm I. von Preußen mit diesem Schreiben die Kaiserkrone an. Ludwig hatte widerwillig dem Anschluss Bayerns an ein neues Deutsches Reich unter der Führung Preußens zugestimmt. Obwohl Bayern einige „Separatrechte" behielt, fühlte Ludwig II. sich in seinem Selbstverständnis als Monarch tief gekränkt.
Handschrift auf Papier, signiert „Ludwig", 30. November 1870.

The "Kaiser Letter" from Ludwig II.
During the Franco-Prussian war, with this letter, Ludwig II proffered the imperial German crown to King Wilhelm I of Prussia on behalf of the German Crown Princes. Ludwig only reluctantly agreed for Bavaria to join a new German Reich under the leadership of Prussia. Although Bavaria maintained some "separate rights" of its own, Ludwig II felt deeply aggrieved in terms of his own conception of his role as monarch.
Handwritten letter on paper, signed "Ludwig", 30 November 1870.

König Ludwig II., König Wilhelm I. von Preußen 1871 die Kaiserkrone darbietend.
Die Szene ist fiktiv; in Wirklichkeit schrieb Ludwig II. nur den sogenannten „Kaiserbrief". Neben Ludwig II. sind folgende deutsche Fürsten zu sehen: König Karl I. von Württemberg, König Johann von Sachsen, Fürst Georg von Schwarzburg-Rudolstadt, Großherzog Friedrich von Baden und Großherzog Ludwig III. von Hessen-Darmstadt.
Ausschnitt eines Freskos von Hermann Wislicenus in der Kaiserpfalz in Goslar, 1882.

King Ludwig II offering Emperor Wilhelm I of Prussia the imperial German crown.
This scene is fictitious, as in reality, only Ludwig II wrote the "Kaiser Letter." The following German Crown Princes can be seen next to King Ludwig II: King Karl I of Württemberg, King Johann of Saxony, Prince Georg of Schwarzburg-Rudolstadt, Grand Duke Friedrich of Baden and Grand Duke Ludwig III of Hesse-Darmstadt.
Detail of a fresco by Hermann Wislicenus in the imperial palace in Goslar, 1882.

DAS KÖNIGREICH BAYERN
König Ludwig II. von Bayern

König Ludwig II. von Bayern mit seiner Verlobten Herzogin Sophie in Bayern (1847–1897).
Die 1867 geschlossene Verlobung zwischen Ludwig und seiner zwei Jahre jüngeren „Tante" Herzogin Sophie wurde noch im selben Jahr wieder gelöst. Sophie und Ludwig verband wohl seit Kindertagen eine innige Freundschaft, doch verschob der König die Hochzeit immer wieder und löste schließlich die Verlobung. Sophie verliebte sich im selben Jahr in den bürgerlichen Edgar Hanfstaengl, heiratete aber 1868 Herzog Ferdinand von Alençon.
Gemälde von Franz Adam, 1866/71.

King Ludwig II of Bavaria with his fiancée Duchess Sophie of Bavaria (1847–1897).
The engagement, announced 1867, between Ludwig and his "aunt", Duchess Sophie, two years his junior, was broken off in the same year. Sophie and Ludwig had enjoyed a close friendship since early childhood, but the King repeatedly delayed the wedding before finally breaking off the engagement. In the same year, Sophie fell in love with the bourgeois Edgar Hanfstaengl, but eventually married Duke Ferdinand von Alençon in 1868.
Painting by Franz Adam, 1866/71.

DAS KÖNIGREICH BAYERN
König Ludwig II. von Bayern

König Ludwig II. landet mit seinem Dampfer „Tristan" in Berg am Starnberger See.
Das kleine Dampfschiff hatte Ludwig II. von seinem Vater, Maximilian II., übernommen; ebenso das im Hintergrund sichtbare Schloss Berg, in dem er im Jahr 1886 festgesetzt werden sollte. Der Name „Tristan" verweist auf Ludwigs Leidenschaft für die altdeutsche Sagenwelt und die Opern Richard Wagners.
Aquarell von Erich Correns, 1867.

King Ludwig II arrives with his steamer "Tristan" at Berg on Lake Starnberg.
Ludwig inherited the small steamer from his father, Maximilian II; the same applies to Berg Castle, visible in the distance, where he was to be detained in 1886. The name "Tristan" is a reference to Ludwig's passion for the world of old German legends and the operas of Richard Wagner.
Watercolour by Erich Correns, 1867.

DAS KÖNIGREICH BAYERN
König Ludwig II. von Bayern

König Ludwig II. von Bayern im Tableau „Lohengrin" im Jahr 1867.
Im Mittelpunkt König Heinrich, daneben Elisabeth, ihr gegenüber Ludwig II. als Heerrufer. Der König ist vermutlich bewusst jünger dargestellt, da er 1861 als Kronprinz das erste Mal „Lohengrin" miterlebte. Im Vordergrund: „Lohengrin besiegt Talramund".
Temperamalerei von Eduard Ille, 1867.

King Ludwig II of Bavaria in the "Lohengrin" tableau in 1867.
In the centre, King Heinrich, next to him Elisabeth, opposite her, Ludwig II as the King's herald. The King appears to be deliberately shown as a younger figure, as in 1861, he was to experience "Lohengrin" as Crown Prince for the first time. In the foreground: "Lohengrin conquers Talramund".
Tempera painting by Eduard Ille, 1867.

Bühnenbildentwurf für den 1. Aufzug „Lohengrins Ankunft" zur Aufführung der Oper am Hof- und Nationaltheater in München.
Malerei von Heinrich Döll, 1868.

Set design for the 1st act, the "Arrival of Lohengrin" for the performance of the opera at the Royal and National Theatre in Munich.
Painting by Heinrich Döll, 1868.

DAS KÖNIGREICH BAYERN
König Ludwig II. von Bayern

Festbankett in der Münchner Residenz anlässlich des Empfangs des frisch vermählten Paares Prinz Leopold von Bayern (1848–1930) und Erzherzogin Gisela (1856–1932) in München, 1873.
Prinz Leopold war der zweite Sohn des späteren Prinzregenten Luitpold und bis nach dem Ersten Weltkrieg Berufssoldat. 1873 heiratete er in Wien Erzherzogin Gisela von Österreich, die zweite Tochter Kaiser Franz Josephs und Kaiserin Elisabeths (Sisi). Dem Paar wurden vier Kinder geboren.
Aquarell von Friedrich Eibner / Wiedemann, 1873.

Festive banquet in the Munich Residenz on the occasion of the reception of the newlywed couple, Prince Leopold of Bavaria (1848–1930) and Archduchess Gisela (1856–1932) in Munich, 1873.
Prince Leopold was the second son of the later Prince Regent Luitpold and a professional soldier until after the First World War. In 1873 he married Archduchess Gisela of Austria, the second daughter of Emperor Franz Joseph and Empress Elisabeth (Sisi), in Vienna. The couple had four children.
Watercolour by Friedrich Eibner / Wiedemann, 1873.

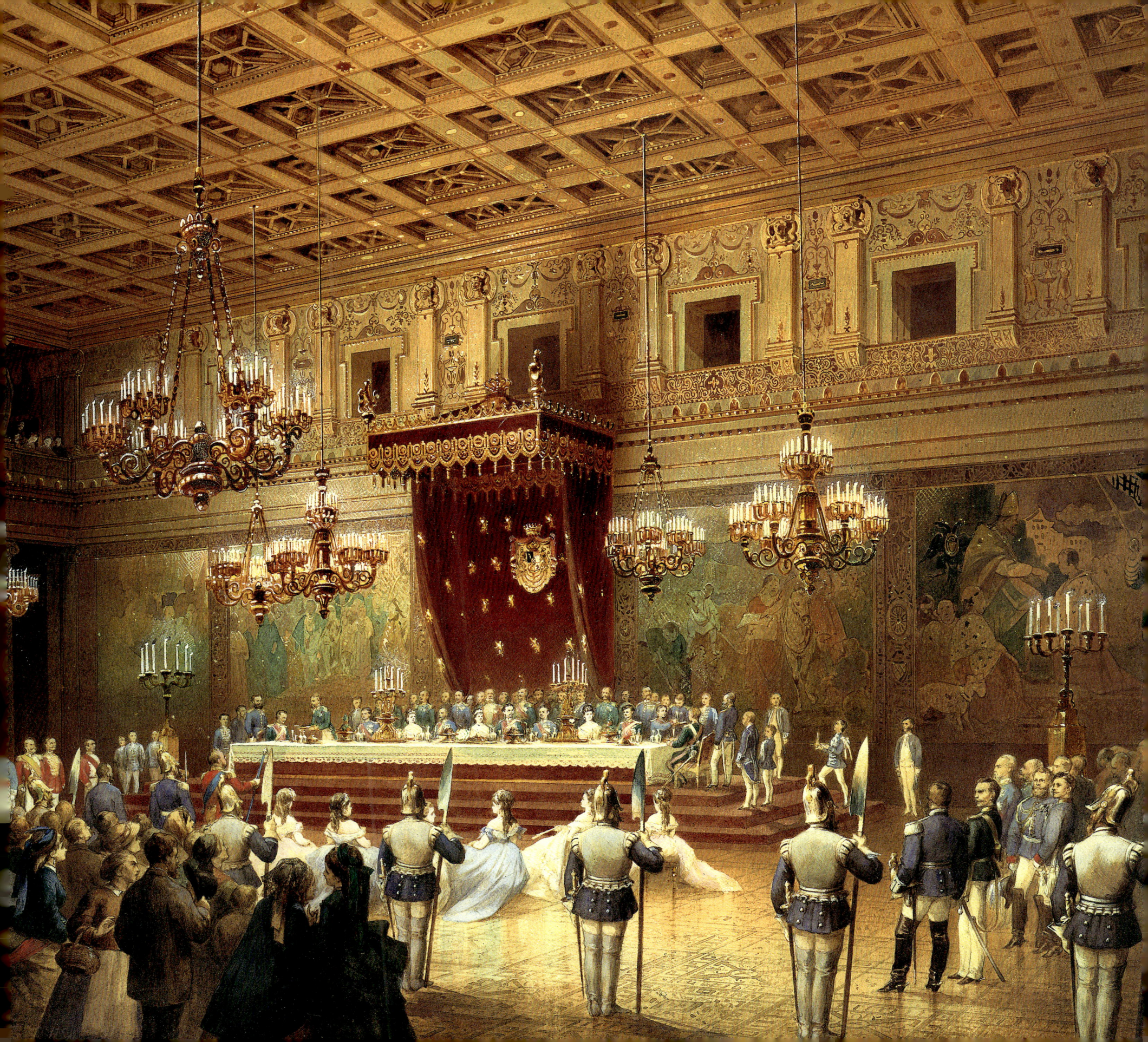

DAS KÖNIGREICH BAYERN
König Ludwig II. von Bayern

Der „Linderhof", ein ehemaliges Jagdhaus König Maximilians II., mit Anbauten König Ludwigs II.
Aus dem ehemaligen, eher schlicht gehaltenen Jagdhaus ließ Ludwig II. in mehreren Phasen das erste seiner prunkvollen Schlösser erstehen. Schloss Linderhof blieb jedoch immer ein eher intimes Refugium. Das Bild zeigt die zweite Erweiterung des Baus 1872. Hinter dem Holzgebäude in alpenländischem Stil entwickelt sich schon der für das spätere Schloss typische luxuriöse Stil des Spätbarock.
Aquarellierte Bleistiftzeichnung von Leopold Rottmann, 1871.

The "Linderhof", a former hunting lodge of King Maximilian II, with extensions by King Ludwig II.
Over several phases, Ludwig II transformed the former rather modest hunting lodge into the first of his ostentatious palaces. Linderhof Palace was always a rather private refuge for the King, however. The picture shows the second extension to the complex in 1872. Behind the wooden building in the Alpine style, we see the luxurious style typical of the late baroque developing in the shape of the later palace.
Watercolour pencil drawing by Leopold Rottmann, 1871.

Schloss Linderhof im Winter.
Mit den Jahren zog Ludwig sich mehr und mehr in die Einsamkeit seiner Schlösser zurück. Die unberührte Berglandschaft um Schloss Linderhof veranlasste ihn zu zahlreichen Ausfahrten in seinen Prunkwägen und Schlitten, insbesondere des Nachts, die bis heute den Mythos des „Märchenkönigs" nähren.
Aquarell von Heinrich Breling, 1881/1882.

Linderhof Palace in the winter.
With each passing year, Ludwig retreated more and more into the solitude of his stately homes. The peaceful mountain scenery surrounding Linderhof Palace prompted the King to take numerous trips in his royal coaches and carriages, particularly during the night, which continued to feed the myths surrounding the "Fairytale King" to this day.
Watercolour by Heinrich Breling, 1881/1882.

DAS KÖNIGREICH BAYERN
König Ludwig II. von Bayern

Die Blaue Grotte bei Schloss Linderhof, illuminiert in blauem Licht. Das Lichtspektrum der blauen Farbe kam dem der Blauen Grotte auf Capri sehr nahe. Sie wurde über mehrere Jahre hinweg von der Firma BASF für Ludwig II. entwickelt. Darüber hinaus wurde die künstliche Blaue Grotte im Linderhofer Schlosspark von dem ersten Elektrokraftwerk der Welt betrieben.
Aquarell von Heinrich Breling, 1881.

The Blue Grotto at Linderhof Palace, illuminated in blue light. The light spectrum of this blue colour came very close to the Blue Grotto on Capri. It was developed for Ludwig II by BASF over the course of several years. The artificial Blue Grotto in Linderhof Palace Park was also home to the first hydroelectric power plant in the world.
Watercolour by Heinrich Breling, 1881.

Die Hundinghütte. Nach dem Vorbild der Wohnstatt Hundings im ersten Akt der Oper „Walküre" von Richard Wagner ließ Ludwig II. sich 1876 die Hundinghütte am Fuß der Kreuzspitze im Ammergebirge einrichten. Heute ist ihr Nachbau im Schlosspark von Linderhof zu besichtigen.
Aquarell von Heinrich Breling, 1882.

The Hunding Hut. Inspired by the home of Hunding in the first act of Richard Wagner's opera "Valkyrie", Ludwig II had the Hunding Hut built for himself at the foot of the Kreuzspitze in the Ammergau Alps in 1876. Its replica can now be visited in Linderhof Palace Park.
Watercolour by Heinrich Breling, 1882.

DAS KÖNIGREICH BAYERN
König Ludwig II. von Bayern

Vorentwurf für Schloss Neuschwanstein, Ansicht von Nordwesten.
1868 begann der König mit ernsthaften Planungen zum Wiederaufbau der Burgruine „Vorder- und Hinterhohenschwangau" auf einem schmalen Höhenrücken über der Pöllatschlucht, in direkter Nachbarschaft zu Schloss Hohenschwangau, das sein Vater Maximilian II. neu errichtet hatte. Der Theatermaler Christian Jank lieferte zahlreiche Entwürfe zur Gestaltung der „altdeutschen Burg".
Gouachemalerei von Christian Jank, 1869.

Artist's draft for Neuschwanstein Castle, view from the north west.
In 1868 the King earnestly began planning the reconstruction of the ruins of the "Vorder- und Hinterhohenschwangau" on a small incline above the Pöllatschlucht gorge and in the direct vicinity of Hohenschwangau Castle, which had been newly built by his father Maximilian II. Theatre painter Christian Jank provided numerous drafts for the design of the "old German castle".
Gouache painting by Christian Jank, 1869.

DAS KÖNIGREICH BAYERN
König Ludwig II. von Bayern

Maurischer Saal im Königshaus auf dem Schachen bei Garmisch-Partenkirchen.
Von 1869 bis 1872 ließ Ludwig II. auf dem Berg Schachen ein von außen eher unscheinbares alpines Holzhaus errichten. Der Besuch der Pariser Weltausstellung 1867 inspirierte ihn dazu, im Inneren des Hauses mit dem Maurischen Saal eine Welt von Tausendundeiner Nacht auferstehen zu lassen.
Gouachemalerei von Peter Herwegen, 1879.

Moorish hall in the royal residence on the Schachen near Garmisch-Partenkirchen.
Between 1869 and 1872, Ludwig II built a rather unprepossessing looking wooden Alpine house on Mount Schachen. His visit to the Paris World Fair in 1867 inspired him to create a Moorish hall, transforming the interior into a world akin to a thousand and one nights.
Gouache painting by Peter Herwegen, 1879.

Die Kreuzigungsgruppe in Oberammergau.
Ludwig II. schenkte der Gemeinde Oberammergau im Jahre 1875 diese monumentale Kreuzigungsgruppe, die zu dieser Zeit das größte in Stein gemeißelte Denkmal der Neuzeit gewesen sein soll. Wegen des enormen Gewichts benützte man zum Transport des Bildwerks von Oberau nach Oberammergau einen eigens konstruierten Dampfwagen. 1871 hatte der König einer Separataufführung der Oberammergauer Festspiele beigewohnt.
Zeichnung eines unbekannten Künstlers, o. J.

The Crucifixion Group in Oberammergau.
In 1875, Ludwig II donated this monument of the Crucifixion Group to the municipality of Oberammergau, which at the time is reputed to have been the biggest stone carved monument to the modern era. Due to its colossal weight, it was necessary to use a specially constructed steam engine to transport the sculpture from Oberau to Oberammergau. In 1871, the King attended a separate performance of the Oberammergau Passion Plays.
Drawing by an unknown artist, undated.

Die Kreuzigungsgruppe in Oberammergau. Kolossalmonument von Professor J. Halbig. (S. 315.)
Geschenk des Königs Ludwig II. von Baiern für Oberammergau.

DAS KÖNIGREICH BAYERN
König Ludwig II. von Bayern

Die Burgruine Falkenstein auf einem Nymphenburg Porzellanteller.
Die Wiedererrichtung der Burg Falkenstein bei Pfronten im Allgäu war Ludwigs viertes großes Schlossbauprojekt, das jedoch nicht mehr zur Ausführung kam. Ludwigs Finanznot und sein unvorhergesehener Tod 1886 kamen der Verwirklichung der Pläne zuvor.
Bemalung von J. von Maßenhausen nach Carl August Lebschée, 1843.

The ruins of Falkenstein Castle depicted on a Nymphenburg porcelain plate.
The reconstruction of Falkenstein Castle at Pfronten in the Allgäu was Ludwig's fourth major castle building project. It did not, however, come to fruition, as Ludwig's financial situation and his unexpected death in 1886 put an end to the plans.
Illustration by J. von Maßenhausen adapted from Carl August Lebschée, 1843.

Entwurf für das königliche Schlafzimmer auf Burg Falkenstein.
Ebenso wie in Linderhof und Herrenchiemsee sollte das Schlafzimmer des Königs das Herzstück des Baus bilden. Die Entwürfe sahen eine Ausführung im byzantinischen Stil vor, die Ludwigs Idealvorstellung des absoluten, gottgegebenen Königtums huldigen sollte. Das Schlafzimmer war in erster Linie also nicht privater Rückzugsort, sondern repräsentativer, symbolisch aufgeladener „Sakralraum".
Aquarell von Max Schultze und August Spieß, 1885.

Artist's draft of the royal bedroom in Falkenstein Castle.
As in Linderhof and Herrenchiemsee Palace, the King's bedroom suite was to be the centrepiece of the building. The plan was to create a Byzantine palace that would pay homage to Ludwig's ideal of the absolutist form of royalty, ordained by God. In this context, the bedroom was less a place of private retreat, than a representative, symbolically laden "sacred room".
Watercolour by Max Schultze and August Spieß, 1885.

DAS KÖNIGREICH BAYERN
König Ludwig II. von Bayern

Schloss Herrenchiemsee.
Ab 1878 ließ Ludwig II. auf der abgelegenen Insel im Chiemsee sein drittes Schloss zu Ehren Ludwigs XIV. von Frankreich errichten. Der Bau im neobarocken Stil sollte nach dem Vorbild von Schloss Versailles bei Paris dem absolutistischen Königtum huldigen; er konnte jedoch niemals ganz fertiggestellt werden. Ganz links im Hintergrund ist ein Teil des im Rohbau ausgeführten Seitenflügels des Schlosses zu sehen, der jedoch 1907 aufgrund zu hoher Instandhaltungskosten abgetragen wurde.
Kolorierter Stich (?) von E. Beer, vor 1907.

Herrenchiemsee Palace.
From 1878, Ludwig II built his third palace on the secluded island in Lake Chiemsee to honour Louis XIV of France. The building, in the neo-Baroque style of the Palace of Versailles near Paris, was to pay homage to the absolutist royalty; it was never fully completed, however. In the background, on the far left, it is possible to see a part of the shell of the castle's side wing, which was demolished in 1907 due to excessively high maintenance costs.
Coloured engraving (?) by E. Beer, before 1907.

DAS KÖNIGREICH BAYERN
König Ludwig II. von Bayern

König Ludwig II. von Bayern im Großen Prunkwagen.
Ludwig II. ließ sich einige Wägen und Schlitten nach seinem Geschmack anfertigen. Mit den livrierten Dienern erschien der sechsspännige Zug des Großen Galawagens im Stil Louis XIV. auf den Straßen Münchens.
Gemälde eines unbekannten Künstlers, o. J.

King Ludwig II of Bavaria in large royal coach.
Ludwig II had his own coaches and carriages built according to his tastes. With its liveried servants, the Gala Carriage in the style of Louis XIV appeared on the streets of Munich drawn by six horses.
Painting by an unknown artist, undated.

Der Stadtwagen König Ludwigs II. von Bayern.
Zeichnung eines unbekannten Künstlers, o. J.

The town coach of King Ludwig II of Bavaria
Drawing by an unknown artist, undated.

Nächtliche Schlittenfahrt König Ludwigs II. von Neuschwanstein über den Schützensteig nach Linderhof.
Ludwigs prächtiger neobarocker Schlitten war angeblich das erste Fahrzeug mit elektrischer Beleuchtung.
Gemälde von R. Wenig, um 1880.

Night-time carriage trip by King Ludwig II from Neuschwanstein to Linderhof via the Schützensteig path.
Ludwig's beautiful neo-Baroque carriage was supposedly the first ever vehicle to be fitted with electric lights.
Painting by R. Wenig, c. 1880.

DAS KÖNIGREICH BAYERN
König Otto I. von Bayern

Schloss Fürstenried, der Aufenthaltsort des wegen „Geisteskrankheit" nicht regierungsfähigen Königs Otto von Bayern.
Titelseite der Zeitung „Bairische Volks-Stimmen" vom 24. August 1890.

Fürstenried Palace, residence of King Otto of Bavaria, who was unable to govern due to "mental illness".
Title page of the "Bairische-Volks-Stimmen" newspaper dating from 24th August, 1890.

Prinz Otto von Bayern, nachmaliger König Otto I. von Bayern (1848–1916).
Nach dem Tod Ludwigs II. im Starnberger See 1886 beerbte ihn sein jüngerer Bruder Otto als rechtmäßiger König. Da Prinz Otto jedoch seit dem jungen Erwachsenenalter Verhaltensauffälligkeiten zeigte, die in eine psychische Erkrankung mündeten, und daher seit 1883 dauerhaft im Schloss Fürstenried untergebracht war, übernahm sein Onkel Luitpold als Prinzregent die Regierungsgeschäfte.
Gemälde von S. Braun, 1871.

Prince Otto of Bavaria, subsequently King Otto I of Bavaria (1848–1916).
When Ludwig II died on Lake Starnberg in 1886, his younger brother Otto succeeded him as monarch. Prince Otto developed a behavioural disorder in young adulthood, which eventually lead to a mental illness. From 1883, he resided in Fürstenried Palace on a permanent basis, with his Uncle Luitpold managing the business of government as Prince Regent.
Painting by S. Braun, 1871.

Prince Regent Luitpold

King Ludwig I showed foresight as he did not forego the education of a future sovereign during the upbringing of his third son: young Luitpold was not only militarily shaped into a soldier, but was also surrounded by intellectual authorities of the era. The circle of his teachers ranged from mathematician von Hagens and natural philosopher Schubert to the German philologist and gymnast Maßmann as well as painter Domenico Quaglio – an outstanding encouragement of the prince who was already artistically talented as a child.

The later Prince Regent originally had little prospect of succeeding to the throne. With the abdication of his father Ludwig I, the title of king passed to Luitpold's oldest brother in 1848, who reigned until 1864 as Maximilian II and passed on the reign to his first-born Ludwig. When Ludwig II was first legally incapacitated on 9 June 1886, Luitpold was appointed administrator, i.e. acting regent – Prince Regent – of Bavaria the following day. Ludwig II's younger brother Otto, the actual legitimate successor to the throne, suffered from a mental-emotional disorder since his childhood and was not able to assume responsibility for governmental affairs, but formally held the title of king. As Ludwig II shortly thereafter died tragically, the royal crisis of 1886 rose to a dramatic worsening, which initially put a strain on the reputation of the Prince Regent, who merely wished to fulfill his duty to the kingdom.

The Prince Regent gave his governmental debut with an example of his conscientiousness and loyalty to duty: he started to pay off the loans which his nephew Ludwig II had taken with several banks as well as diverse accrued invoices with royal resources and without encumbering the government budget. These maxims of performance of one's duties, reliability and above all fairness characterized the following 26 years of his regency. Luitpold received reports several times a day on all procedures within his ministry and had correspondence submitted. Ministers and ministerial advisors were summoned for personal discussion in important affairs, and if the situation required it, the Prince Regent himself presided in the Council of State and Council of Ministers. Following his course of objectivity and compromise, he filled the posts of his ministers with politicians who thought and acted as independently of party interests as possible.

Luitpold stayed in touch with the people during his numerous excursions into the alpine upland, where he indulged in his passion for hunting as often as official duties allowed. His attachment to the homeland also contributed towards his great popularity among the population, which was not a matter of course to him after the royal crisis of 1886.

The changes in Bavaria under Luitpold were considerable. The Prince Regent installed a Ministry of Transport, modernised the army with a newly established aviator battalion, promoted the development of the school and university system and thus facilitated access to education for children of any origin. He opened the doors for women to participate in an academic education at Bavaria's universities and provided the introduction of direct elections of the representatives. Until then, the possibilities to falsify the will of the electorate by the interposition of electoral delegates and an arbitrary arrangement of electoral districts were significant. During his reign Munich evolved into a centre of flourishing modern political and cultural forces.

Prinzregent Luitpold

König Ludwig I. bewies weise Voraussicht, als er auch bei der Erziehung seines dritten Sohnes nicht auf die Bildung eines zukünftigen Herrschers verzichtete: Der junge Luitpold wurde nicht nur militärisch zum Soldaten geformt, sondern war stets auch von geistigen Größen der Zeit umgeben. Der Kreis seiner Lehrer reichte dabei vom Mathematiker von Hagens und dem Naturphilosophen Schubert über den Germanisten und Turner Maßmann bis zum Maler Domenico Quaglio – eine hervorragende Förderung des schon als Kind künstlerisch begabten Prinzen.

Ursprünglich hatte der spätere Prinzregent wenig Aussicht auf den Thron. Mit dem Rücktritt des Vaters Ludwig I. fiel die Königswürde 1848 an den ältesten Bruder Luitpolds, der als Maximilian II. bis 1864 regierte und die Herrschaft an seinen Erstgeborenen, Ludwig, weitergab. Erst als dieser Ludwig II. am 9. Juni 1886 entmündigt wurde, wurde Luitpold am Tag darauf zum Verweser, also zum stellvertretenden Regenten – Prinzregenten – Bayerns ernannt. Ludwigs II. jüngerer Bruder Otto, der eigentlich legitime Thronfolger, litt seit seiner Jugend an einer seelisch-geistigen Erkrankung und war nicht in der Lage, die Regierungsgeschäfte zu übernehmen, erhielt aber formell den Titel des Königs. Da Ludwig II. wenig später tragisch zu Tode kam, erreichte die Königskrise des Jahres 1886 eine dramatische Zuspitzung, die das Ansehen des Regenten, der lediglich seine Pflicht gegenüber dem Königreich erfüllen wollte, zunächst schwer belastete.

Seinen Regierungseinstand gab Luitpold mit einem Beispiel seiner Gewissenhaftigkeit und Pflichttreue: Die Darlehen, die sein Neffe Ludwig II. bei mehreren Banken aufgenommen hatte, begann er ohne Belastung der Staatskasse ebenso mit Mitteln des Krongutes zu begleichen wie diverse unbezahlte Rechnungen. Diese Maxime der Pflichterfüllung, Zuverlässigkeit und vor allem auch Gerechtigkeit stand über den folgenden 26 Jahren seiner Regentschaft. Luitpold ließ sich mehrmals täglich von allen Vorgängen innerhalb seines Ministeriums berichten und den Schriftverkehr vorlegen. Minister und Ministerialreferenten wurden in wichtigen Angelegenheiten zum persönlichen Gespräch einbestellt und wenn es die Situation verlangte, führte der Prinzregent selbst den Vorsitz im Staats- und Ministerrat. Die Posten seiner Minister besetzte er – seiner Linie von Sachlichkeit und Ausgleich folgend – mit Politikern aus der hohen Beamtenschaft, die möglichst unabhängig von Parteiprogrammen und -interessen dachten und handelten.

Volksnah zeigte sich Luitpold bei seinen zahlreichen Ausflügen ins Voralpenland, wo er, so oft es die Amtsgeschäfte zuließen, seiner Jagdleidenschaft frönte. Seine Heimatverbundenheit trug auch zu seiner großen Popularität bei der Bevölkerung bei, die ihm angesichts der Umstände der Regentschaftseinsetzung zunächst keineswegs selbstverständlich zugefallen war.

Die Veränderungen Bayerns waren unter Luitpold beachtlich. Der Prinzregent installierte ein Ministerium für Verkehr, modernisierte die Armee, u. a. mit einem neu gegründeten Fliegerbataillon, förderte den Ausbau des Schul- und Universitätswesens und erleichterte so Kindern jeglicher Herkunft den Zugang zu Bildung. Er öffnete Frauen die Tore zu einer akademischen Bildung an Bayerns Hochschulen und sorgte für die Einführung der direkten Volkswahl der Abgeordneten unter Abschaffung der bis dahin durch die Zwischenschaltung von Wahlmännern und eine willkürliche Wahlkreiseinteilung gegebenen Möglichkeiten zur Verfälschung des Wählerwillens. München entwickelte sich während seiner Regierungszeit zu einem Zentrum aufblühender moderner politischer und kultureller Kräfte.

DAS KÖNIGREICH BAYERN
Prinzregent Luitpold von Bayern

Prinzregent Luitpold von Bayern (1821–1912) in Generalsuniform.
Prinz Luitpold war der dritte Sohn Ludwigs I. und seiner Gemahlin Therese. Nachdem seine älteren Brüder Maximilian und Otto beide einen Königstitel erhielten, war Luitpold eine militärische Laufbahn vorherbestimmt. Nach dem Tod seines Neffen Ludwig II. übernahm er im Alter von 65 Jahren die Regentschaft für dessen regierungsunfähigen Bruder Otto.
Gemälde von Friedrich August von Kaulbach, 1902.

Prince Regent Luitpold of Bavaria (1821–1912) in a General's uniform.
Prince Luitpold was the third son of Ludwig I and his wife Therese. With both of his elder brothers having received the title of king, Luitpold was destined for a military career. After the death of his nephew Ludwig II he took over the regency from his brother Otto, who was unable to govern, at the age of 65.
Painting by Friedrich August von Kaulbach, 1902.

DAS KÖNIGREICH BAYERN
Prinzregent Luitpold von Bayern

Prinz Luitpold von Bayern als junger Artillerieoffizier.
Prinz Luitpold schlug wie sein Onkel, Generalfeldmarschall Prinz Karl von Bayern, die Militärlaufbahn ein. „Das Soldatenleben gefällt mir sehr gut", schrieb er am 5.4.1839 an seinen Vater König Ludwig I.
Gemälde von Joseph Karl Stieler, o. J.

Prince Luitpold of Bavaria as a young artillery officer.
Prince Luitpold followed a military career like his uncle, General Field Marshal Prince Karl of Bavaria. "I like the soldier's life very much", he wrote to his father King Ludwig I on 5/4/1839.
Painting by Joseph Karl Stieler, undated.

Prinz Luitpolds erste Wache in der Dienergasse in München.
Als der junge Prinz Luitpold mehrere Tage vor dem Haus des Artillerie-Generalleutnants Freiherr von Zoller Wache stand, erregte dies Aufsehen beim Volk und bei Hofe. Ferdinand Jodl verewigte diese Szene auf einem „Uhrenbild", welches der „Kanonier" Luitpold 1841 seinem Kommandanten schenkte.
Gemälde von Ferdinand Jodl, um 1840.

Prince Luitpold's first guard duty in the Dienergasse in Munich.
When the young Prince Luitpold stood guard in front of the Artillery General Lieutenant Baron von Zoller's house for several days, it caused a sensation among the people and at courts. Ferdinand Jodl immortalised this scene in a "clock picture" that "Gunner" Luitpold gave to his Commander as a gift in 1841.
Painting by Ferdinand Jodl, c. 1840.

DAS KÖNIGREICH BAYERN
Prinzregent Luitpold von Bayern

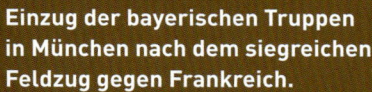

Einzug der bayerischen Truppen in München nach dem siegreichen Feldzug gegen Frankreich.
Prinz Luitpold von Bayern führte als Generalinspekteur der Armee den Einzug der bayerischen Truppen am 16. Juli 1871 in München an.
Gemälde von Ludwig Behringer, 1887.

Arrival of Bavarian troops in Munich after the victorious military campaign against France.
Prince Luitpold of Bavaria led the procession of Bavarian troops into Munich on 16 July 1871 as the Inspector General of the army.
Painting by Ludwig Behringer, 1887.

DAS KÖNIGREICH BAYERN
Prinzregent Luitpold von Bayern

Prinzregent Luitpold von Bayern nimmt die Huldigung der Schäffler an der Münchner Residenz entgegen.
Traditionell warteten die Schäffler mit ihrem Tanz auch dem regierenden Monarchen auf. Ihr Auftritt vor dem Landesherrn fand schon unter Kurfürst Karl Theodor, also nachweisbar seit 1795 statt.
Aquarell von Paul Hey, um 1900.

Prince Regent Luitpold of Bavaria accepts the homage by the coopers at the Munich Residenz.
Traditionally the coopers also attended on the reigning monarch with their dance. Their performance in front of territorial lords already took place under Elector Karl Theodor and has therefore been documented since 1795.
Watercolour by Paul Hey, c. 1900.

Prinzregent Luitpold von Bayern in Jagdkleidung.
Seiner Jagdleidenschaft ging der Prinzregent besonders gern im Voralpenland nach, wo er bei der Bevölkerung besonders beliebt und geachtet war. Sein Auftreten in Tracht oder Jagdanzug wurde zum Symbol seiner Volksnähe, sein Jägerhut zu seinem Markenzeichen. Nach Defreggers Gemälde wurden die Luitpold-Standbilder in Berchtesgaden und in Oberstdorf im Allgäu errichtet.
Ölgemälde von Franz von Defregger, 1888.

Prince Regent Luitpold of Bavaria in hunting attire.
The Prince Regent pursued his passion for hunting in the alpine uplands in particular, where he was extremely popular and respected by the people. His appearance in traditional costume or hunting attire became symbolic of how close he was to the people; his hunting hat became his trademark. The Luitpold statues built in Berchtesgaden and in Oberstdorf were based on Defregger's painting.
Oil painting by Franz von Defregger, 1888.

DAS KÖNIGREICH BAYERN
Prinzregent Luitpold von Bayern

526 | 527

Prinzregent Luitpold von Bayern als Oberbefehlshaber der bayerischen Armee zu Pferd.
Gemälde von Jacobus Leisten, 1911.

Prince Regent Luitpold of Bavaria as Commander in Chief of the Bavarian army on horseback.
Painting by Jacobus Leisten, 1911.

DAS KÖNIGREICH BAYERN
Prinzregent Luitpold von Bayern

Prinzregent Luitpold von Bayern besucht die Baustelle der von ihm gestifteten und nach ihm benannten Brücke in München.
Im Jahr 1891, zu seinem 70. Geburtstag, wurde zunächst die von Luitpold in Verlängerung der Prinzregentenstraße in Auftrag gegebene Stahlbrücke fertiggestellt. Acht Jahre später wurde diese von einem Isarhochwasser so stark unterspült, dass sie als Steinbrücke neu errichtet werden musste. Sie führt bis heute hinauf zum auf der „Luitpold-Terrasse" befindlichen Monument mit dem Friedensengel.
Gemälde von Fritz Martin, 1889.

Prince Regent Luitpold of Bavaria visits the building site of the bridge donated by him and named after him in Munich.
The steel bridge initially commissioned by Luitpold to extend the Prinzregentenstraße was completed in 1891, on his 70th birthday. Eight years later it was so severely eroded by the Isar flooding that it had to be rebuilt as a stone bridge. Today it leads up to the monument with the Friedensengel on the "Luitpold Terrace".
Painting by Fritz Martin, 1889.

DAS KÖNIGREICH BAYERN
Prinzregent Luitpold von Bayern

Prinzregent Luitpold von Bayern bei der Grundsteinlegung des Deutschen Museums, die Kaiser Wilhelm II. am 13.11.1906 vornahm.
Der Prinzregent konnte zur Grundsteinlegung des Deutschen Museums, des Lebensprojekts des Ingenieurs Oskar von Miller, Kaiser Wilhelm II. nach München einladen. Im Vordergrund v. l. n. r.: Prinzessin Therese von Bayern, Prinzregent Luitpold, Kaiserin Auguste Viktoria, Prinz Ludwig (später König Ludwig III.), Kaiser Wilhelm II., und schräg hinter ihm, ein Blatt Papier haltend, Oskar von Miller.
Ausschnitt eines Gemäldes von Georg Waltenberger, um 1906.

Prince Regent Luitpold of Bavaria at the laying of the foundation stone for the German Museum, which Emperor Wilhelm II performed on 13/11/1906.
The Prince Regent was able to invite Emperor Wilhelm II to Munich for the laying of the foundation stone for the German Museum, the life project of engineer Oskar von Miller. In the foreground from left to right: Princess Therese of Bavaria, Prince Regent Luitpold, Empress Auguste Viktoria, Prince Ludwig (later King Ludwig III), Emperor Wilhelm II and diagonally behind him holding a piece of paper, Oskar von Miller.
Painting (detail) by Georg Waltenberger, c. 1906.

DAS KÖNIGREICH BAYERN
Prinzregent Luitpold von Bayern

Prinzregent Luitpold bei der Gratulations-Cour der deutschen Fürsten anlässlich des 60. Regierungsjubiläums von Kaiser Franz Joseph I. in Schönbrunn bei Wien.
V. l. n. r.: Kaiser Franz Joseph von Österreich-Ungarn, Großherzog Friedrich II. von Baden, Fürst Leopold IV. von Lippe-Detmold, König Friedrich August III. von Sachsen, Großherzog Wilhelm Ernst von Sachsen-Weimar, Prinzregent Luitpold von Bayern, Kaiser Wilhelm II., Herzog Friedrich II. von Anhalt, König Wilhelm II. von Württemberg, Großherzog Friedrich August von Oldenburg, Großherzog Friedrich Franz IV. von Mecklenburg-Schwerin, Fürst Georg von Schaumburg-Lippe, Bürgermeister Dr. Burchard von Hamburg.
Gemälde von Franz Matsch, 1908.

Prince Regent Luitpold at the German princes' congratulatory reception on the occasion of the 60th anniversary of the start of the reign of Emperor Franz Joseph I in Schönbrunn near Vienna.
From left to right: Emperor Franz Joseph of Austria-Hungary, Friedrich II, Grand Duke of Baden, Leopold IV, Prince of Lippe-Detmold, King Friedrich August III of Saxony, Wilhelm Ernst, Grand Duke of Saxony-Weimar, Prince Regent Luitpold of Bavaria, Emperor Wilhelm II, Friedrich II, Duke of Anhalt, King Wilhelm II of Württemberg, Friedrich August, Grand Duke of Oldenburg, Friedrich Franz IV, Grand Duke of Mecklenburg-Schwerin, Georg, Prince of Schaumberg-Lippe, Mayor Dr Burchard of Hamburg.
Painting by Franz Matsch, 1908.

DAS KÖNIGREICH BAYERN
Prinzregent Luitpold von Bayern

Prinzregent Luitpold von Bayern mit seinem Adjutanten am Badenburger See im Schlosspark von Nymphenburg.
Es war kein unüblicher Anblick, den bis ins hohe Alter rüstigen Regenten in Begleitung seiner Adjutanten ausgedehnte Spaziergänge unternehmen zu sehen. Oftmals fütterte er dabei Enten und Schwäne.
Gemälde von Max Slevogt, 1908.

Prince Regent Luitpold of Bavaria with his adjutant at Badenburger See lake in Nymphenburg Palace park.
It was not an uncommon sight to see the sprightly Regent taking long walks accompanied by his adjutant even into old age. He often fed the ducks and swans.
Painting by Max Slevogt, 1908.

DAS KÖNIGREICH BAYERN
Prinzregent Luitpold von Bayern

Prinzregent Luitpold von Bayern mit Jägerhut.
Pastellzeichnung von Friedrich August von Kaulbach, 1911.

Prince Regent Luitpold of Bavaria with his hunting hat on.
Pastel drawing by Friedrich August von Kaulbach, 1911.

Prinzregent Luitpold von Bayern mit Jagdgesellschaft zu Pferd.
Gemälde von Alexander von Wagner, um 1900.

Prince Regent Luitpold of Bavaria with a hunting party on horseback.
Painting by Alexander von Wagner, c. 1900.

DAS KÖNIGREICH BAYERN
Prinzregent Luitpold von Bayern

Prinzregent Luitpold von Bayern im Ornat des St. Hubertus-Ritterordens.
Gemälde von Georg Papperitz, um 1900.

Prince Regent Luitpold of Bavaria in the ornate dress of the Order of St. Hubertus Knights.
Painting by Georg Papperitz, c. 1900.

Prinzregent Luitpold am Chiemsee.
Prinzregent Luitpold von Bayern mit seiner Schwester Adelgunde (1823–1914), Herzogin von Modena, am Ufer des Chiemsees. Prinzessin Adelgunde heiratete 1842 Franz von Österreich-Este, Herzog zu Modena. Nach seinem Tod 1875 kehrte sie nach Bayern zurück. Adelgunde pflegte ein enges Verhältnis zu ihrem regierenden Bruder, den sie in allen Angelegenheiten zu unterstützen suchte.
Gemälde von Franz Roubaud, um 1900.

Prince Regent Luitpold at Lake Chiemsee.
Prince Regent Luitpold of Bavaria with his sister Adelgunde (1823–1914), Duchess of Modena, on the banks of Lake Chiemsee. Princess Adelgunde married Franz of Austria-Este, Duke of Modena, in 1842. After his death in 1875 she returned to Bavaria. Adelgunde had a close relationship with her reigning brother, who she tried to support in all matters.
Painting by Franz Roubaud, c. 1900.

DAS KÖNIGREICH BAYERN
Prinz Leopold von Bayern

Prinz Leopold von Bayern (1846–1930) in Jagdkleidung.
Prinz Leopold war der zweite Sohn des Prinzregenten und seiner Gemahlin Augusta Ferdinande. Er wurde von seinem Vater 1905 zum bayerischen Generalfeldmarschall ernannt, nachdem er sich bereits hohe Ehren im bayerischen Heer und als kaiserlicher Armeeinspekteur verdient hatte. Wie sein Vater liebte er die Jagd, er reiste sogar bis in die deutschen Kolonien nach Afrika zur Großwildjagd.
Kreidezeichnung von Jószef Arpád Koppay, o. J.

Prince Leopold of Bavaria (1846–1930) in hunting attire.
Prince Leopold was the second son of the Prince Regent and his wife Augusta Ferdinande. He was appointed as Bavarian General Field Marshal by his father in 1905, after he had already earned the highest honours in the Bavarian army and as an imperial army inspector. Like his father he loved hunting; he even travelled to the German colonies in Africa to hunt big game.
Chalk drawing by Jószef Arpád Koppay, undated.

DAS KÖNIGREICH BAYERN
Prinz Leopold von Bayern

Prinz Leopold von Bayern (1846–1930) in Uniform.
Im Jahr 1913 konnte sich Leopold ins Privatleben zurückziehen. Jedoch wurde er kurze Zeit später für den Einsatz im Ersten Weltkrieg reaktiviert. 1916 ernannte ihn der Kaiser zum königlich-preußischen Generalfeldmarschall und Oberbefehlshaber Ost. Der mittlerweile 70-Jährige verteidigte mit seinen Truppen zunächst erfolgreich die Ostfront und leitete später den geordneten Rückzug aus dem Osten. 1919 traf er unversehrt wieder in München ein.
Gemälde von Franz von Lenbach, 1893.

Prince Leopold of Bavaria (1846–1930) in uniform.
In 1913, Leopold was able to withdraw to a private life. However, shortly afterwards he was reactivated for deployment in the First World War. In 1916 the Emperor appointed him as the royal Prussian General Field Marshal and Commander in Chief of the East. Then 70 years old, he initially successfully defended the east front with his troops and led the orderly retreat from the east later on. He arrived back in Munich unscathed in 1919.
Painting by Franz von Lenbach, 1893.

Prinz Leopold von Bayern als Offizier der reitenden Artillerie.
Schon im Alter von 20 Jahren nahm Leopold an militärischen Gefechten teil. Bald darauf verlieh ihm König Ludwig II. für seine Verdienste im deutsch-französischen Krieg 1870 den Militär-Max-Joseph-Orden. 1891 ernannte ihn Kaiser Wilhelm zum Generalinspekteur der IV. Armeeinspektion des deutschen Heeres.
Vom Offizierskorps des 3. Feldartillerie-Regiments dem Prinzen als ehemaligem Batteriechef der 4. und 6. Feldbatterie gewidmetes Gemälde von Ludwig Putz, nach 1906.

Prince Leopold of Bavaria as Officer of the Horse Artillery.
Leopold took part in military battles at the age of just 20. Soon afterwards King Ludwig II awarded him the Military Order of Max Joseph for his services in the Franco-Prussian War. In 1891 Emperor Wilhelm appointed him Inspector General of the German army's IV Army Inspection.
Painting by Ludwig Putz dedicated to the Prince as a former battery chief of the 4th and 6th Field Battery by the Officer Corp of the 3rd Field Artillery regiment, after 1906.

DAS KÖNIGREICH BAYERN
Prinz Leopold von Bayern

**Bronzeportal „Porta della Morte"
zu St. Peter in Rom.**
Der ältere Sohn von Prinz Leopold, Prinz Georg von Bayern (1880–1943), stiftete als Domherr von St. Peter dieses und ein weiteres Portal, die „Porta dei Sacramenti". Nach einer annullierten Ehe studierte Georg Theologie, wurde 1921 zum Priester geweiht und setzte seine Studien in Rom fort. 1930 stieg er zum Domherrn von St. Peter auf, 1941 zum Apostolischen Protonotar.

**Bronze portal "Porta della Morte"
in St. Peter's Church in Rome.**
The eldest son of Prince Leopold, Prince Georg of Bavaria (1880–1943), donated this and another portal, "Porta dei Sacramenti", as canon of St. Peter's Church. After his annulled marriage, Georg studied theology, was ordained as a priest in 1921 and continued his studies in Rome. In 1930 he was promoted to canon of St. Peter's Church and to pronotary apostolistic in 1941.

DAS KÖNIGREICH BAYERN
Prinzessin Therese von Bayern

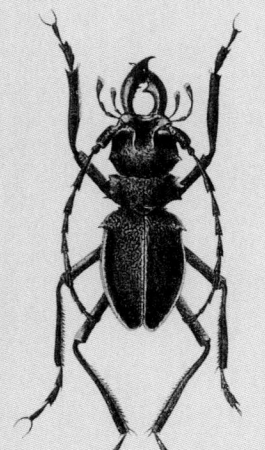

Auswahl der von Prinzessin Therese entdeckten Pflanzen und Tiere.
V. l. n. r.: Wasserhyazinthe (Bolivien), Bockkäfer (Ecuador), Dornheuschrecke (Venezuela), Harnischwels (Kolumbien).

Selection of plants and animals discovered by Princess Therese.
From left to right: water hyacinths (Bolivia), longhorn beetle (Ecuador), groundhopper (Venezuela), Loricariidae (Columbia).

Prinzessin Therese von Bayern (1850–1925), einzige Tochter des Prinzregenten Luitpold.
Prinzessin Therese war das erste weibliche Mitglied der Bayerischen Akademie der Wissenschaften. Auf zahlreichen Forschungsreisen in den Orient und nach Amerika entdeckte sie neue Pflanzen- und Tierarten. Teile ihrer Sammlung sind in den Bayerischen Staatssammlungen für Naturkunde und im Völkerkundemuseum in München ausgestellt.
Kreidezeichnung von Friedrich August von Kaulbach, Geschenk zum 90. Geburtstag Luitpolds, 1911.

Princess Therese of Bavaria (1850–1925), the only daughter of Prince Regent Luitpold.
Princess Therese was the first female member of the Bavarian Academy of Sciences. She discovered new species of plants and animals on numerous research trips to the Orient and America. Parts of her collection are exhibited in the Bavarian State Collection for Natural History and in the Ethnology Museum in Munich.
Chalk drawing by Friedrich August von Kaulbach, a gift for Luitpold's 90th birthday, 1911.

DAS KÖNIGREICH BAYERN
Prinz Arnulf von Bayern

Prinz Arnulf von Bayern (1852–1907).
Prinz Arnulf war wie sein Bruder Leopold ein begeisterter Jäger. 1902 unternahm er eine Forschungsexpedition in das Grenzgebiet von China und der Mongolei. Auf der Rückreise starb er in Venedig an einer Lungenentzündung. Prinzessin Therese veröffentlichte 1907 seine Reisetagebücher.
Gemälde von Hanns Fechner, 1886.

Prince Arnulf of Bavaria (1852–1907).
Like his brother Leopold, Prince Arnulf was a keen hunter. In 1902 he took part in a research expedition in the border region between China and Mongolia. He died of pneumonia in Venice on the return journey. Princess Therese published his travel diaries in 1907.
Painting by Hanns Fechner, 1886.

Ludwig III, the last King of Bavaria

After the death of his father Luitpold in 1912, Ludwig succeeded him as Prince Regent of the Kingdom of Bavaria. Formally, his cousin Otto still held the title of King. However, due to his mental illness he was still unable to exercise the associated governmental duty. This ongoing division of the reign into title and deputy rulership caused the voices to be heard of those who voted for a unified royal dignity in the person of the new Prince Regent. Barely a year passed before a large majority pronounced itself in favour of this proposal in the Landtag. On 5 November 1913, Ludwig III was proclaimed King of Bavaria.

Before his father Luitpold assumed governmental office, a career as an officer had been planned for the young Ludwig. However, a premature end was put to his military ambitions in the Austro-Prussian War of 1866. The severe wound he suffered in the battle against Prussia, which was to hinder his ability to walk throughout his life, led him out of the army and to the University of Munich. There, Ludwig acquired comprehensive legal and economic knowledge. With particular interest he devoted himself to technical advancement and especially to the possibilities of developing Bavaria's hydraulic powers and inland waterway transport.

His constant commitment to the peasantry, which had to cope with major economic and social changes in the second half of the 19th century, was evident in Ludwig's holding the office of Honorary President of the Central Committee of the Agricultural Association from 1868 on. From 1875, the King himself maintained an agricultural business at Leutstetten Palace, where he tested advanced methods of livestock farming and milk processing. Ludwig III always bore his nickname "Millibauer" (dairy farmer) – which stemmed from this and a similar pilot business on Sárvár Estate in Hungary – with humour.

He acquired the high prominence of the politicians of his time, even the respect of the fundamentally republican social democrats, for himself at an early stage for supporting his father in introducing a modern suffrage which matched democratic principles. However, in the summer of 1914 a gruesome caesura blocked the implementation of many of his own social and political plans: the outbreak of the First World War.

Ludwig III hoped that a victorious outcome from the war would form a strong economic and political unit in the centre of Europe. Bavaria was to benefit from an affiliation of Alsace with the Palatinate. The king initially didn't perceive the increasing deterioration of the situation in 1916/17, although his son Rupprecht urged him to see the imperative of an imminent peace agreement. However, his influence would have been limited, as foreign affairs were within the power of the Empire. The longer the war lasted, the more the influence of the Supreme Army Command grew. In spring 1918, only a seperate piece with Russia was accomplished. Still, this was but a brief relief of the German troups at the Western front, which suffered badly from the American entry into the war.

For a long time, the revolutionary mood, that was the result of the growing awareness of the inevitable loss of the war in autumn 1918, was underestimated by Ludwig III and his ministers. His departure from Munich in the night of 7 November 1918 followed an initial warning that reached the King while he was on a walk in the English Garden. After his ministers announced that they could no longer guarantee the safety of the royal family due to the revolutionists marching through the streets, Ludwig III left the city with his wife, who was already terminally ill. Kurt Eisner, a left-wing, socialist member of the Bavarian Landtag and leader of the revolution, had already declared the ruling House of Wittelsbach deposed at a midday rally in the Theresienwiese. In the same night, the politician now proclaimed the "Free State of Bavaria".

Ludwig III., der letzte König von Bayern

Ludwig folgte seinem Vater Luitpold nach dessen Tod im Jahr 1912 als Prinzregent des Königreichs Bayern nach. Formell hielt immer noch sein Vetter Otto den Titel des Königs, konnte die damit verbundenen Regierungsaufgaben jedoch aufgrund seiner psychischen Erkrankung nach wie vor nicht ausüben. Diese andauernde Teilung der Herrscherwürde in Titel und stellvertretende Ausübung ließ nun Stimmen laut werden, die für eine Proklamation des neuen Prinzregenten zum König votierten. Es dauerte kaum ein Jahr, bis sich im Landtag eine große Mehrheit für diesen Vorschlag aussprach: Am 5. November 1913 wurde die Regentschaft offiziell für beendigt erklärt und Ludwig III. zum König von Bayern ausgerufen.

Für den jungen Ludwig war vor dem Regierungsantritt seines Vaters Luitpold die Offizierslaufbahn vorgesehen gewesen. Seinen militärischen Ambitionen wurde im deutsch-deutschen Bundeskrieg von 1866 allerdings ein jähes Ende bereitet: Die schwere Verwundung, die er im Kampf gegen Preußen davontrug und die seinen Gang zeitlebens beeinträchtigen sollte, führte ihn aus der Armee an die Universität Münchens. Ludwig erwarb sich dort umfangreiche juristische und volkswirtschaftliche Kenntnisse. Mit besonderem Interesse widmete er sich dem technischen Fortschritt und speziell den Möglichkeiten zur Erschließung von Bayerns Wasserkräften und Binnenschifffahrtswegen.

Sein steter Einsatz für den Bauernstand, der in der zweiten Hälfte des 19. Jahrhunderts mit großen wirtschaftlichen und gesellschaftlichen Umbrüchen zu kämpfen hatte, zeigte sich im von Ludwig seit 1868 bekleideten Ehrenpräsidentenamt des Zentralkomitees des landwirtschaftlichen Vereins. Auf Schloss Leutstetten unterhielt der König selbst ab 1875 einen landwirtschaftlichen Betrieb, wo er fortschrittliche Methoden der Viehzucht und Milchverwertung erprobte. Seinen von diesem und einem ähnlichen Musterbetrieb auf Gut Sárvár in Ungarn herrührenden Spitznamen „Millibauer" trug Ludwig III. stets mit Humor.

Das hohe Ansehen der Politiker seiner Zeit, selbst seitens der prinzipiell republikanisch gesinnten Sozialdemokraten, erwarb er sich früh durch die Unterstützung seines Vaters bei der Einführung eines modernen, demokratischen Prinzipien entsprechenden Wahlrechts. Der Umsetzung vieler seiner eigenen sozialpolitischen Vorhaben versperrte aber im Sommer des Jahres 1914 eine grausame Zäsur den Weg: Der Erste Weltkrieg brach aus.

Ludwig III. erhoffte sich von einem siegreichen Kriegsausgang die Bildung einer starken wirtschaftlich-politischen Einheit im Zentrum Europas. Bayern sollte von einer Angliederung des Elsass an die Pfalz profitieren. Die zunehmende Verschlimmerung der Lage in den Jahren 1916/17 erkannte der König zunächst nicht – trotz der Mahnungen seines Sohnes Rupprecht über die Notwendigkeit eines baldigen Friedensschlusses. Allerdings wäre sein Einfluss ohnehin sehr beschränkt gewesen, denn Außenpolitik war seit 1871 Sache des Reiches und dort bestimmte, je länger der Krieg dauerte, desto mehr die Oberste Heeresleitung den Kurs. Lediglich ein Separatfriede mit Russland kam im Frühjahr 1918 zustande, doch konnte dies die durch den Kriegseintritt der USA verschärfte Bedrängnis der deutschen Truppen an der Westfront nur vorübergehend erleichtern.

Die revolutionäre Stimmung, die aus der im Herbst 1918 plötzlich zutage tretenden Erkenntnis der militärischen Niederlage resultierte, wurde von Ludwig III. und seinen Ministern unterschätzt. Seiner Abreise aus München in der Nacht vom 7. auf den 8. November 1918 ging eine Warnung voraus, die den König bei einem Spaziergang im Englischen Garten erreichte. Nach der Erklärung seiner Minister, angesichts der durch die Straßen ziehenden Umstürzler nicht weiter für die Sicherheit der königlichen Familie garantieren zu können, verließ Ludwig III. mit seiner todkranken Frau die Stadt. Kurt Eisner, linkssozialistischer Abgeordneter des Bayerischen Landtags und Wortführer der Revolution, hatte das

Awaiting what was to come initially at Wildenwart Palace located in Chiemgau, later at Anif Palace near Salzburg, Ludwig III refused to sign the draft of an abdication that was presented to him. However, he released all officials, officers and soldiers from their oath of allegiance they had made to him. Officially, he never resigned from the office of King of Bavaria and neither chamber of the Landtag pledged itself to the revolution at any time.

After his death at Sárvár Estate in 1921, the remains of the last Bavarian king and his wife Maria Theresa, who had already died in 1919, were transferred to Munich. Under major participation of the people, the couple were laid to rest in the ancestor's grave of the Frauenkirche with all the royal honours.

regierende Haus der Wittelsbacher bei einer mittäglichen Massenkundgebung auf der Theresienwiese bereits für abgesetzt erklärt. Noch in derselben Nacht rief der Politiker nun den „Freistaat Bayern" aus.

Zunächst auf Schloss Wildenwart in Chiemgau, später auf Schloss Anif bei Salzburg der Dinge harrend, lehnte es Ludwig III. ab, den ihm vorgelegten Entwurf einer Abdankung zu unterschreiben, entband aber alle Beamten, Offiziere sowie Soldaten von Ihrem auf ihn geleisteten Treueeid. Offiziell trat er niemals vom bayerischen Königsamt zurück, wie auch beide Kammern des Landtags sich zu keinem Zeitpunkt zur Revolution bekannten.

Nach seinem Tod auf Gut Sárvár im Jahr 1921 wurden die sterblichen Überreste des letzten bayerischen Königs und seiner bereits 1919 verstorbenen Frau Marie Therese nach München überführt. Unter großer Anteilnahme der Bevölkerung wurde das Paar mit allen königlichen Ehren in der Ahnengruft der Frauenkirche zur letzten Ruhe gelegt.

DAS KÖNIGREICH BAYERN
König Ludwig III. von Bayern

Königin Marie Therese von Bayern (1849–1919) im Hermelin.
Am 20. Februar 1868 heirateten Prinz Ludwig und Erzherzogin Marie Therese in Wien. Marie Therese war ursprünglich dem Erzherzog von Österreich-Toskana versprochen, entschied sich jedoch für Ludwig und setzte ihre Heirat gegen alle Widerstände durch. Aus der glücklichen Ehe gingen 13 Kinder hervor, von denen zehn das Erwachsenenalter erreichten.
Ölgemälde von Emil Keck, 1914.

Queen Marie Therese of Bavaria (1849–1919) in ermine.
On 20 February 1868 Prince Ludwig married Archduchess Marie Therese in Vienna. Marie Therese was originally promised to the Archduke of Austria-Tuscany but chose Ludwig and married him despite all the opposition. The happy marriage produced 13 children, ten of which reached adulthood.
Oil painting by Emil Keck, 1914.

König Ludwig III. von Bayern in Uniform.
Prinz Ludwig schlug zwar eine traditionelle Militärkarriere ein, studierte aber gleichzeitig an der Universität in München und wurde später zu einem Fachmann für Landwirtschaft, Infrastruktur- und Energiewesen. 1912 folgte er seinem Vater als Prinzregent nach, 1913 wurde er aufgrund einer Verfassungsänderung zum König proklamiert, obwohl Otto, der eigentliche, jedoch regierungsunfähige Monarch, noch lebte. Die Signatur unten rechts lautet: „nach dem Leben gemalt, München, 5. Dezember 1914, Richard B. Adam."
Ölgemälde von Richard Benno Adam, 1914.

King Ludwig III of Bavaria in uniform.
Although Prince Ludwig pursued a traditional military career, he studied at the University of Munich at the same time and later became an expert in agriculture, infrastructure and energy. In 1912 he succeeded his father as Prince Regent and in 1913 he was proclaimed King as a result of an amendment to the constitution, even though Otto – the actual monarch but who was unable to govern – was still alive. The signature bottom right says: "painted from life, Munich, 5 December 1914, Richard B. Adam."
Oil painting by Richard Benno Adam, 1914.

DAS KÖNIGREICH BAYERN
König Ludwig III. von Bayern

Prinz Ludwig, nachmaliger König Ludwig III. von Bayern, als Knabe.
Der junge Ludwig erhielt eine streng katholische Erziehung. Er verbrachte einen Großteil seiner Kindheit zusammen mit seinen Cousins, Kronprinz Ludwig und Prinz Otto, in Nymphenburg.
Ölgemälde eines unbekannten Künstlers, um 1852.

Prince Ludwig, subsequently King Ludwig II of Bavaria, as a boy.
Young Ludwig had a strict catholic upbringing. He spent the majority of his childhood together with his cousins, Crown Prince Ludwig and Prince Otto, at Nymphenburg.
Oil painting by an unknown artist, c. 1852.

Die Prinzen Leopold und Ludwig von Bayern in Jagdpose.
Gemälde von Friedrich August von Kaulbach, 1860.

Princes Leopold and Ludwig of Bavaria in hunting pose.
Painting by Friedrich August von Kaulbach, 1860.

DAS KÖNIGREICH BAYERN
König Ludwig III. von Bayern

Die Verwundung des Prinzen Ludwig von Bayern am 25. Juli 1866 bei Helmstadt/Unterfranken im Krieg gegen Preußen.
Aufgrund der schweren Verwundung im deutsch-deutschen Krieg 1866, die ihn zeitlebens in seinem Gang beeinträchtigen sollte, musste Prinz Ludwig seine Militärkarriere vorzeitig beenden.
Gemälde von Heinrich Lang, 1873.

The wounding of Prince Ludwig of Bavaria on 25 July 1866 near Helmstadt, Lower Franconia during the war against the Prussians.
Prince Ludwig had to end his military career prematurely as a result of serious wounding during the German-Prussian War in 1866 that was to impair his walking for the rest of his life.
Painting by Heinrich Lang, 1873.

DAS KÖNIGREICH BAYERN
König Ludwig III. von Bayern

Der Hafen von Lindau.
Marie Therese, Erzherzogin von Österreich-Este und dann Gemahlin Prinz Ludwigs von Bayern, des späteren Königs Ludwig III., war u. a. eine begabte Malerin.
Gemälde von Marie Therese von Bayern, 1886.

Lindau harbour.
Marie Therese, Archduchess of Austria-Este and then consort of Prince Ludwig of Bavaria, the later King Ludwig III, was a talented painter, among other things.
Painting by Marie Therese of Bavaria, 1886.

Villa Amsee in Lindau.
Die ersten Ehejahre verbrachten Prinz Ludwig und Prinzessin Marie Therese in der Villa Amsee am Bodensee nahe Lindau. Therese war botanisch interessiert und unterhielt dort ein großes Alpinum.
Gemälde von Marie Therese von Bayern, 1879.

Villa Amsee in Lindau.
Prince Ludwig and Princess Marie Therese spent the first few years of their marriage at Villa Amsee at Lake Constance near Lindau. Therese had an interest in botany and also maintained a large Alpinum there.
Painting by Marie Therese of Bavaria, 1879.

DAS KÖNIGREICH BAYERN
König Ludwig III. von Bayern

Schloss Leutstetten.
Das Schloss und der zugehörige Gutshof von Leutstetten wurden 1875 von Prinz Ludwig, dem nachmaligen König Ludwig III. von Bayern, für sich und seine Familie als Wohnsitz erworben. Ludwig führte dort einen Landwirtschaftsbetrieb nach modernsten Maßstäben. Die Bevölkerung gab ihm daher den durchaus anerkennenden Spitznamen „Millibauer", dem der König stets mit Humor begegnete.
Lithografie eines unbekannten Künstlers, 1. Hälfte des 19. Jahrhunderts.

Leutstetten Castle.
The castle and Leutstetten estate were purchased by Prince Ludwig, later to become King Ludwig III of Bavaria, for himself and his family as a residence in 1875. Ludwig managed the estate and farm using the latest standards of agriculture. The people therefore gave him the nickname "Millibauer" (dairy farmer), which the King always took with humour.
Lithography by an unknown artist, 1st half of the 19th century.

DAS KÖNIGREICH BAYERN
König Ludwig III. von Bayern

Prinz Ludwig von Bayern in Generalsuniform zu Pferd, Manöverszene.
Gemälde von Ludwig Behringer, 1887.

Prince Ludwig of Bavaria in General's uniform on ho manoeuvre scene.
Painting by Ludwig Behring 1887.

DAS KÖNIGREICH BAYERN
König Ludwig III. von Bayern

Porzellanteller, Motiv Wittelsbacherpalais.
Das im Zweiten Weltkrieg zerstörte Wittelsbacherpalais in München war der Stadtwohnsitz des Prinzen Ludwig und seiner Familie.
Stück aus dem anlässlich der goldenen Hochzeit von Ludwig III. und Marie Therese in der Prozellanmanufaktur Nymphenburg gefertigten Bayerischen Königsservice, 1917/18.

Porcelain plate, Wittelsbach Palace motif.
Wittelsbach Palace in Munich, destroyed during the Second World War, was the city residence of Prince Ludwig and his family.
Piece from the Bavarian royal service made at the Nymphenburg porcelain factory on the occasion of Ludwig III and Marie Therese's golden wedding anniversary, 1917/18.

Fischplatte, Motiv Gut Sárvár.
In Sárvár, Ungarn, errichtete König Ludwig III. von Bayern ein land- und forstwirtschaftliches Mustergut mit Pferdezucht und Viehbetrieb. Dort fand die erste Herstellung von Romadurkäse in Ungarn statt.
Königsservice, 1917/18.

Fish platter, Sárvár Estate motif.
King Ludwig III of Bavaria built a model agricultural and forestry estate with horse breeding and cattle farming in Sárvár, Hungary. The first production of Romadur cheese in Hungary took place there.
Royal service, 1917/18.

Porzellanteller, Motiv Residenz Würzburg.
Im barocken Bau der Residenz wurde Ludwigs Vater, Prinzregent Luitpold, geboren. 1914 nahm Ludwig III. an den Feierlichkeiten zur 100-jährigen Zugehörigkeit Würzburgs zum Königreich Bayern in der Residenz teil.
Königsservice, 1917/18.

Porcelain plate, Wurzburg Residence motif.
Ludwig's father, Prince Regent Luitpold, was born in the Residence's baroque building. In 1914 Ludwig III took part in the celebrations at the residence to mark Wurzburg's belonging to the Kingdom of Bavaria for 100 years.
Royal service, 1917/18.

DAS KÖNIGREICH BAYERN
König Ludwig III. von Bayern

Der Yachthafen Starnberg am Starnberger See.
Im Starnberger Yachthafen wurde das ehemalige Prunkschiff Bucentaur der bayerischen Herzöge und Kurfürsten im Trockendock aufbewahrt. Zum Fluten wurde der Georgenbach aufgestaut. Heute stehen der sogenannte „Bucentaur-Stadl" von 1803 und das ehemalige Königliche Schiffsmeisterhaus von 1724 unter Denkmalschutz.
Ölgemälde, Signatur unleserlich, o. J.

Starnberg yacht harbour at Lake Starnberg.
The former Bavarian dukes and electors' bucentaur state barge was kept in dry dock at Starnberg yacht harbour. The Georgenbach river was dammed for flooding. Today the so-called "Bucentaur-Stadl" from 1803 and former royal ship masters' house from 1724 are listed buildings.
Oil painting, illegible signature, undated.

König Ludwig III. von Bayern im Kapitänsanzug als Ehrenkommodore des 1888 gegründeten Königlich Bayerischen Yachtclubs in Starnberg.
Ludwig III. war begeisterter Segler. Er kenterte einmal zum allgemeinen Schrecken mit seiner Jolle vor der Villa Amsee nahe Lindau am Bodensee. Von Leutstetten aus segelte er die Würm aufwärts bis nach Starnberg.
Gemälde von L. Kirschner (?), 1912.

King Ludwig III of Bavaria in Captain's attire as Honorary Commander of the Royal Bavarian Yacht Club founded in 1888 in Starnberg.
Ludwig III was a keen sailor. He once capsized his dinghy in front of the Villa Amsee near Lindau at Lake Constance, much to the horror of everyone. He sailed up the Würm to Starnberg from Leustetten.
Painting by L. Kirschner (?), 1912.

DAS KÖNIGREICH BAYERN
König Ludwig III. von Bayern

Ansicht von Landschaft und Schloss Sárvár (Ungarn).
Marie Therese brachte das Schloss Nádasdy in Sárvár/Ungarn mit in die Ehe. Nach der Revolution 1918 und dem Tod seiner Frau 1919 hielt sich Ludwig III. zeitweise im Exil in Österreich, der Schweiz und auch in Sárvár auf, wo er 1921 starb.
Ölgemälde von Marie Therese von Bayern, 1881.

View of countryside and castle in Sárvár (Hungary).
Marie Therese brought Nádasy Castle in Sárvár/Hungary into the marriage with her. After the revolution in 1918 and the death of his wife in 1919, Ludwig II resided in exile, sometimes in Austria, Switzerland and also in Sárvár, where he died in 1921.
Oil painting by Marie Therese of Bavaria, 1881.

Schloss Wildenwart im Chiemgau.
Als die revolutionären Umbrüche von 1918 die bayerische Hauptstadt erreichten, floh die königliche Familie zunächst nach Schloss Wildenwart im Chiemgau. Königin Marie Therese war zu diesem Zeitpunkt schon schwer krank, sie starb am 3. Februar 1919 auf Schloss Wildenwart. Ihre Töchter wohnten dort weiterhin, auch König Ludwig hielt sich bis zu seinem Tod mehrmals dort auf.
Ölgemälde von Max von Schellerer, o. J.

Wildenwart Castle in Chiemgau.
When the revolutionary upheavals of 1918 reached the Bavarian capital, the royal family initially fled to Wildenwart Castle in Chiemgau. At this time, Queen Marie Therese was already seriously ill; she died on 3 February 1919 at Wildenwart Castle. Her daughters continued to live there; king Ludwig also stayed there several times until his death.
Oil painting by Max von Schellerer, undated.

DAS KÖNIGREICH BAYERN
König Ludwig III. von Bayern

„Kaisermanöver": Seine Majestät erklären dem Prinzen Ludwig von Bayern die feindlichen Stellungen. Die vielgelesene satirische Zeitschrift „Simplicissimus" spielt damit auf das im Gegensatz zum martialischen Gehabe Kaiser Wilhelms II. unmilitärische Auftreten des seit seiner Verwundung 1866 gehbehinderten Prinzen mit seiner schlecht sitzenden Uniform an.
Satirische Zeichnung in der Zeitschrift „Simplicissimus" von Olaf Gulbransson, 1909.

"Kaisermanöver": his Majesty explains the enemy positions to Prince Ludwig of Bavaria. The much-read satirical magazine "Simplicissimus" plays on the unmilitary appearance of the prince with his poorly fitting uniform, who has had difficulty walking since being wounded in 1866, in contrast to Emperor Wilhelm II's warlike posturing.
Satirical drawing in the magazine "Simplicissimus" by Olaf Gulbransson, 1909.

King Ludwig III of Bavaria hands the cardinal biretta to the Papal Nuncio in Munich, Andreas Frühwirth, in the All Saints' Court Church in Munich by order of Pope Benedict XV.
Oil painting by Otto Hierl-Deronco, 1915.

DAS KÖNIGREICH BAYERN
König Ludwig III. von Bayern

„Unschlüssig".
Kurz vor Ende des Ersten Weltkrieges begann die Revolution in Bayern. In Abwesenheit zuverlässiger Truppen und angesichts der kriegsmüden Bevölkerung regte sich kein Widerstand. Die Verwaltung ordnete sich weitgehend widerstandslos der neuen republikanischen Regierung unter. König Ludwig III. dankte nicht ab, entband jedoch Beamte und Soldaten von dem ihm geleisteten Treueid. Die Karikatur thematisiert die allerorts herrschende politische Ungewissheit während und nach den revolutionären Umbrüchen.
Karikatur, Signatur unleserlich, 1918.

"Unschlüssig" (Undecided).
The revolution began in Bavaria just before the end of the First World War. In the absence of any reliable troops and due to people being tired of war, there was no resistance. The administration largely submitted to the new republican government without resistance. King Ludwig III did not abdicate but absolved officials and soldiers from any oath of allegiance to him. The caricature deals with the political uncertainty that prevailed everywhere during and after the revolutionary upheaval.
Caricature, illegible signature, 1918.

Unschlüssig.

The Royal House after the Revolution of 1918

The revolutionary upheaval of November 1918 ended 738 years of Wittelsbach rule in Bavaria. The house of Wittelsbach is nevertheless still present in the years of the Weimar Republic, in the period of National Socialism and in the Federal Republic of Germany in a thoroughly noticeable, albeit different way. Such presence is very closely linked to the three heads of the family who stand for the house after 1918 and/or 1921: Crown Prince Rupprecht (1869–1955), Duke Albrecht (1905–1996) and Duke Franz (born 1933), to whom – because loyalty towards the republican/parliamentary order after 1945 is particularly clearly manifested here – the Princes Adalbert (1886–1970) and Konstantin (1920–1969) can also be added, one as the first ambassador of the Federal Republic of Germany in Spain, the other as a CSU member of the German parliament.

On the one hand, Crown Prince Rupprecht completed the adaptation of the house to the republican order, but on the other he was thoroughly able to imagine a return to monarchy, which should then, however, serve other political priorities: in 1933, committed to the aim of preventing the rise to power of Hitler and the Nazis, and – in the time after 1945 – linked with the hope of ensuring a federal reconstruction of Germany. Unlike some of his fellow aristocrats, he made no attempt at rapprochement with the National Socialists at all, but maintained secret contact with the German resistance, escaped to Italy in 1940 and entered into contact with the Western Allies early on.

Following the death of the Crown Prince in 1955, Albrecht, now bearing the title "Duke of Bavaria", assumed all of his father's rights, yet at the same time marked a decisive change. He was the first head of the house of Wittelsbach not to have an institutional function in the state, but he nonetheless managed to stabilise the presence and charisma of the house in Bavarian society, even to intensify it in places. While in exile in Hungary he and his family fell into the hands of the Gestapo and were then imprisoned in concentration camps at Oranienburg, Flossenbürg and Dachau, without he himself or his sons ever making a big fuss about it after 1945.

Duke Franz of Bavaria: In the tabular curriculum vitae released by the ducal administration, his profession is stated as "Dipl. Kfm." ("business graduate"). In addition to a wide range of charity initiatives, Duke Franz prominently shows a commitment that he not only shares with his grandfather but that leaps to the eye time after time from Duke Albrecht V to Elector Max Emanuel to King Ludwig I, allowing him to be perceived as part of a stable and continuing family tradition, and that signifies a centring of the life of the house of Wittelsbach around the concerns and potentials of art and culture.

Das Königliche Haus nach der Revolution von 1918

Mit der revolutionären Umwälzung vom November 1918 enden 738 Jahre wittelsbachischer Herrschaft in Bayern. Gleichwohl ist das Haus Wittelsbach in den Jahren der Weimarer Republik, in der Zeit des Nationalsozialismus und noch in der Bundesrepublik Deutschland in durchaus bemerkenswerter, wenngleich unterschiedlicher Weise präsent. Solche Präsenz ist aufs Engste verknüpft mit den drei Chefs der Familie, die nach 1918 bzw. 1921 für das Haus stehen: Kronprinz Rupprecht (1869–1955), Herzog Albrecht (1905–1996) und Herzog Franz (geb. 1933), zu denen man – weil hier die Loyalität gegenüber der republikanisch-parlamentarischen Ordnung nach 1945 besonders sinnfällig zum Ausdruck kommt – noch die Prinzen Adalbert (1886–1970) und Konstantin (1920–1969) hinzunehmen wird, den einen als den ersten Botschafter der Bundesrepublik Deutschland in Spanien, den anderen als CSU-Bundestagsabgeordneten.

Kronprinz Rupprecht vollzog einerseits das Arrangement des Hauses mit der republikanischen Ordnung, konnte sich aber andererseits eine Rückkehr zur Monarchie durchaus vorstellen, die dann allerdings im Dienste anderer politischer Prioritäten stehen sollte: 1933 dem Ziel verpflichtet, Hitler und die NS-Herrschaft zu verhindern, in der Zeit nach 1945 verbunden mit der Hoffnung, einen föderativen Neuaufbau Deutschlands zu gewährleisten. Im Gegensatz zu manchen seiner Standesgenossen, frei von jeglicher Annäherung an die Nationalsozialisten, pflegte er geheime Kontakte mit dem deutschen Widerstand, wich 1940 nach Italien aus und nahm frühzeitig Verbindungen mit den Westalliierten auf.

Seit dem Tod des Kronprinzen 1955 mit dem Titel „Herzog von Bayern" ausgestattet, trat Albrecht in sämtliche Rechte seines Vaters ein und markierte dabei doch eine entscheidende Wende. Er war der erste Chef des Hauses Wittelsbach, der ohne eine institutionelle Funktion im Staat war, und dem es gleichwohl gelang, die Ausstrahlung des Hauses in die bayerische Gesellschaft hinein zu stabilisieren, ja in Teilen zu intensivieren. Im ungarischen Exil war er mit seiner Familie in die Hände der Gestapo geraten und dann in KZ-Haft in Oranienburg, Flossenbürg und Dachau, ohne dass er selbst oder seine Söhne davon nach 1945 je großes Aufheben gemacht hätten.

Herzog Franz von Bayern: In dem von der Herzoglichen Verwaltung herausgegebenen tabellarischen Lebenslauf ist als Beruf „Dipl. Kfm." angegeben. Neben vielfältigen caritativen Initiativen tritt bei Herzog Franz ein Engagement in den Vordergrund, das er nicht nur mit seinem Großvater teilt, sondern das ihn als Teil einer stabilen Familien-Kontinuität wahrnehmen lässt, die von Herzog Albrecht V. über Kurfürst Max Emanuel bis zu König Ludwig I. immer wieder ins Auge springt und die eine Zentrierung wittelsbachischer Lebenswege um die Anliegen und Potentiale von Kunst und Kultur als Spezifikum zu erkennen gibt.

DAS KÖNIGLICHE HAUS NACH DER REVOLUTION VON 1918
Prinz Franz von Bayern

**Modell der Yacht „Hengist"
aus dem Besitz von Prinz Franz.**
Prinz Franz absolvierte neben dem Studium eine Bootsbauerlehre bei Rambeck in Percha – sein Gesellenstück war der etwa 5 Meter lange Lugger „Schackerl", benannt nach dem Präsidenten des Königlich Bayerischen Yachtclubs, Geheimrat Kustermann. Kronprinz Rupprecht machte dagegen eine Lehre als Drechsler.

Model of the yacht "Hengist" from the possession of Prince Franz.
In addition to his studies, Prince Franz completed an apprenticeship in boatbuilding with Rambeck in Percha. His journeyman's piece was the roughly 5 metre-long lugger "Schackerl", named after the president of the Royal Bavarian Yacht Club, Privy Councillor Kustermann. In contrast, Crown Prince Rupprecht did an apprenticeship as a turner.

Prinz Franz von Bayern (1875–1957).
Prinz Franz, der dritte Sohn König Ludwigs III., diente im Ersten Weltkrieg als Generalmajor. Nach dem Tod seines Vaters 1921 übernahm er den Besitz in Ungarn, in Bayern hatte er seinen Wohnsitz in Leutstetten.
Ölgemälde von Georg Anderlahn, 1957.

Prince Franz of Bavaria (1875–1957).
Prince Franz, the third son of King Ludwig III, served in the First World War as a major general. After the death of his father in 1921 he took over the estate in Hungary. In Bavaria he resided in Leutstetten.
Oil painting by Georg Anderlahn, 1957.

DAS KÖNIGREICH BAYERN
Prinz Franz von Bayern

Prinzessin Isabella von Croy (1890–1982).
Prinzessin Isabella wurde 1890 auf Schloss L'Hermitage in Belgien geboren. Sie war die Tochter von Herzog Karl Alfred von Croy und seiner Gemahlin Prinzessin Ludmilla von Arenberg. 1912 heiratete sie Prinz Franz von Bayern in Baden bei Wien.
Fotografie, um 1912.

Princess Isabella of Croy (1890–1982).
Princess Isabella was born in 1890 at L'Hermitage Palace in Belgium. She was the daughter of Duke Karl Alfred of Croy and his wife Princess Ludmilla of Arenberg. In 1912 she married Prince Franz of Bavaria in Baden near Vienna.
Photograph, c. 1912.

Prinzessin Isabella von Croy als Vierjährige.
Aquarell von L. Bakst, 1894.

Princess Isabella of Croy as a four-year-old.
Watercolour by L. Bakst, 1894.

DAS KÖNIGREICH BAYERN
Prinz Franz von Bayern

Prinzessin Eleonore von Bayern (1918–2009) im Kindesalter.
Prinzessin Eleonore war nach Adelgunde das vierte Kind von Prinz Franz und Prinzessin Isabella von Bayern. Sie heiratete 1951 Konstantin Graf von Waldburg zu Zeil und Trauchburg.
Kreidezeichnung von Alois Schornböck, 1924.

Princess Eleonore of Bavaria (1918–2009) during childhood.
Princess Eleonore was, after Adelgunde, the fourth child of Prince Franz and Princess Isabella of Bavaria. She married Count Konstantin von Waldburg zu Zeil und Trauchburg in 1951.
Chalk drawing by Alois Schornböck, 1924.

Prinzessin Adelgunde von Bayern (1917–2004) im Kindesalter.
Prinzessin Adelgunde wurde dem Prinzenpaar Franz und Isabella von Bayern als drittes Kind geboren. Im Zweiten Weltkrieg absolvierte sie eine Schwesternausbildung beim Roten Kreuz. 1948 heiratete sie den verwitweten Zdenko Freiherr von Hoenning O'Carroll. Zu dessen neun Kindern aus erster Ehe wurden dem Paar noch fünf weitere geboren.
Kreidezeichnung von Alois Schornböck, 1924.

Princess Adelgunde of Bavaria (1917–2004) during childhood.
Princess Adelgunde was born as the third child to the royal couple Franz and Isabella of Bavaria. During the Second World War she completed training as a nurse with the Red Cross. In 1948 she married the widowed Baron Zdenko von Hoenning O'Carroll. Five more children were born in addition to his nine children from the first marriage.
Chalk drawing by Alois Schornböck, 1924.

DAS KÖNIGLICHE HAUS NACH DER REVOLUTION VON 1918
Prinz Ludwig von Bayern

Prinzessin Irmingard von Bayern (1923–2010) kurz vor ihrer Hochzeit mit Prinz Ludwig von Bayern, 1950.
Prinzessin Irmingard war eine Tochter Kronprinz Rupprechts aus zweiter Ehe. Ihre Jugend verbrachte sie aufgrund der nationalsozialistischen Bedrohung in England und Italien. 1944 wurde sie mit ihrer Familie von der Gestapo in Sippenhaft genommen und nacheinander in den Konzentrationslagern Sachsenhausen, Flossenbürg und Dachau interniert. Nach dem Krieg wirkte sie u. a. als Künstlerin und Schriftstellerin. 1955 erwarb sie die Schlossbrauerei Kaltenberg.
Gemälde von Max Rimböck, 1950.

Princess Irmingard of Bavaria (1923–2010) shortly before her wedding with Prince Ludwig of Bavaria, 1950.
Princess Irmingard was a daughter of Crown Prince Rupprecht from his second marriage. She spent her youth in England and Italy due to the National Socialist threat. In 1944 she was detained with her family by the Gestapo under the aspect of "Sippenhaft" ("kin liability" as a form of collective punishment) and successively interned in the concentration camps at Sachsenhausen, Flossenbürg and Dachau. Among other things, she worked as an artist and author after the war. She acquired the Kaltenberg Castle Brewery in 1955.
Painting by Max Rimböck, 1950.

Prinz Ludwig von Bayern (1913–2008) im Alter von 68 Jahren.
Prinz Ludwig Karl Maria, der älteste Sohn von Prinz Franz von Bayern und Isabella von Croy, verbrachte seine Jugend in München und studierte in Sopron/Ungarn Forstwirtschaft. Im Zweiten Weltkrieg wurde er auf Befehl Hitlers wie alle Prinzen ehemals regierender Häuser vom Wehrdienst ausgeschlossen. 1943 konnte er sich nach Sárvár retten, nach Kriegsende flüchtete er mit den Pferden seines ungarischen Gestüts nach Leutstetten, wo er in der Folge eine bekannte Pferdezucht aufbaute.
Ölgemälde von B. Taznowska, 1981.

Prince Ludwig of Bavaria (1913–2008) at the age of 68 years.
Prince Ludwig Karl Maria, the oldest son of Prince Franz of Bavaria and Isabella of Croy, spent his youth in Munich and studied forestry in Sopron, Hungary. Like all princes of former ruling houses, he was excluded from military service during the Second World War on Hitler's orders. In 1943 he was able to escape to Sárvár. After the end of the war he fled with the horses from his Hungarian stud farm to Leutstetten, where he subsequently established a well-known horse breeding farm.
Oil painting by B. Taznowska, 1981.

DAS KÖNIGLICHE HAUS NACH DER REVOLUTION VON 1918
Prinz Ludwig von Bayern

Kutsche vor Schloss Sárvár.
Prinz Franz gewann zahlreiche Preise bei großen Armeepreisreiten in Wien und Budapest. In Sárvár unterhielt er bis zum Ende des Zweiten Weltkriegs ein Gestüt mit 400 Pferden.
Kohlezeichnung von Eduard Thöny, o. J.

Coach in front of Sárvár Castle.
Prince Franz won numerous prizes at major army prize riding competitions in Vienna and Budapest. In Sárvár he maintained a stud farm with 400 horses up until the end of the Second World War.
Charcoal drawing by Eduard Thöny, undated.

Prinz Ludwig (1913–2008) und seine Schwester Prinzessin Maria (1914–2011), die beiden ältesten Kinder von Prinz Franz und Prinzessin Isabella von Bayern.
Prinzessin Maria Elisabeth heiratete 1937 Prinz Pedro Henrique von Orléans und Bragança. Nach dem Krieg lebte das Paar in Brasilien.
Ölgemälde von Ludwig von Zumbusch, 1916.

Prince Ludwig (1913–2008) and his sister Princess Maria (1914–2011), the two oldest children of Prince Franz and Princess Isabella of Bavaria.
Princess Maria Elisabeth married Prince Pedro Henrique of Orléans and Bragança in 1937. The couple lived in Brazil after the war.
Oil painting by Ludwig von Zumbusch, 1916.

DAS KÖNIGLICHE HAUS NACH DER REVOLUTION VON 1918
Prinz Ludwig von Bayern

Prinz Ludwig von Bayern bei einer Gespannprüfung in Aachen 1951.
Prinz Ludwig von Bayern kam kurz vor Kriegsende im April 1945 mit einem Wagentreck von 16 Gespannen aus Sárvár flüchtend in Leutstetten an. In der Folge nahm er an vielen internationalen Gespannprüfungen teil.
Gemälde von Béla Fluck, um 1951.

Prince Ludwig of Bavaria during a horse and carriage trial in Aachen 1951.
Prince Ludwig of Bavaria came shortly before the end of the war in April 1945 with a wagon trek comprised of 16 teams from Sárvár and arrived in Leutstetten. He subsequently took part in many international horse and carriage trials.
Painting by Béla Fluck, c. 1951.

DAS KÖNIGLICHE HAUS NACH DER REVOLUTION VON 1918
Kronprinz Rupprecht von Bayern

Prinzessin Marie Gabriele von Bayern (1878–1912).
Herzogin Marie Gabriele in Bayern war die vierte Tochter des Augenarztes Herzog Karl Theodor in Bayern und heiratete im Jahr 1900 Prinz Rupprecht von Bayern. Das Ehepaar hatte drei Söhne und eine Tochter. Nur der zweite Sohn Albrecht, das drittgeborene Kind, überlebte das Kindesalter.
Gemälde von Friedrich August von Kaulbach, 1906.

Princess Marie Gabriele of Bavaria (1878–1912).
Duchess Marie Gabriele in Bavaria was the fourth daughter of ophthalmologist Duke Karl Theodor in Bavaria and married Prince Rupprecht of Bavaria in 1900. The married couple had three sons and one daughter. Only the second son, Albrecht, the third child, survived childhood.
Painting by Friedrich August von Kaulbach, 1906.

Prinz Rupprecht von Bayern (1869–1955), ab 1913 Kronprinz, in bayerischer Generalsuniform.
Rupprecht diente sowohl in der Infanterie, Kavallerie als auch der Artillerie der bayerischen Armee. Im Ersten Weltkrieg war er Chef der Heeresgruppe Kronprinz Rupprecht an der Westfront. Die Novemberrevolution von 1918 überraschte ihn im Feld, sodass er sich nach dem Rückzug seiner Truppen inkognito bis nach Bayern durchschlug. Offiziell verzichtete er nie auf seine Rechte als Thronfolger.
Ölgemälde von Carl Blos, 1906.

Prince Rupprecht of Bavaria (1869–1955), from 1913 Crown Prince, in a Bavarian general's uniform.
Rupprecht served in the infantry, cavalry as well as artillery of the Bavarian army. During the First World War he was commander of the "Army Group Crown Prince Rupprecht" on the Western Front. The November Revolution of 1918 surprised him in the field, so that after the retreat of his troops he managed to return to Bavaria incognito. He never officially renounced his rights as successor to the throne.
Oil painting by Carl Blos, 1906.

DAS KÖNIGLICHE HAUS NACH DER REVOLUTION VON 1918
Kronprinz Rupprecht von Bayern

Prinz Rupprecht von Bayern.
Rupprecht wurde als erster Wittelsbacher Prinz auf eine öffentliche Schule, das Maximiliansgymnasium in München, geschickt. Durch seine späteren Studien war er umfangreich gebildet, was ihm bei diplomatischen Reisen in verschiedene europäische Länder zugute kam. Durch die Thronbesteigung seines Vaters, Ludwig III., wurde er 1913 Kronprinz und hatte viele repräsentative Pflichten wahrzunehmen.
Ölgemälde von Franz von Lenbach, um 1880.

Prince Rupprecht of Bavaria.
Rupprecht was the first Wittelsbach prince sent to a public school, the Maximiliansgymnasium secondary school in Munich. Due to his later studies he was comprehensively educated, which benefitted him during his diplomatic travels in various European countries. Because of the accession to the throne by his father, Ludwig III, he became Crown Prince in 1913 and had to exercise many representative duties.
Oil painting by Franz von Lenbach, c. 1880.

DAS KÖNIGLICHE HAUS NACH DER REVOLUTION VON 1918
Kronprinz Rupprecht von Bayern

Prinz Albrecht (1905–1996).
Prinz Albrecht war der zweite Sohn und das einzige überlebende Kind aus der Ehe Rupprechts mit Marie Gabriele.
Fotografie, um 1908.

Prince Albrecht (1905–1996).
Prince Albrecht was the second son and only surviving child from Rupprecht's marriage with Marie Gabriele.
Photograph, c. 1908.

Prinzessin Marie Gabriele (1878–1912).
Büste von Adolf von Hildebrand, einem persönlichen Freund des Kronprinzen Rupprecht, o. J.

Princess Marie Gabriele (1878–1912).
Bust by Adolf von Hildebrand, a personal friend of Crown Prince Rupprecht, undated.

Prinz Rupprecht von Bayern mit seiner ersten Gemahlin Marie Gabriele, geborene Herzogin in Bayern.
Von 1902 bis 1903 begleitete Marie Gabriele ihren Gemahl auf einer Weltreise über Ceylon, China und Japan in die Vereinigten Staaten von Amerika. Auf Java erkrankte die Prinzessin an Malaria. Sie starb aufgrund ihrer angeschlagenen Gesundheit schon 1912, weshalb Rupprecht in zweiter Ehe 1921 Prinzessin Antonia von Luxemburg heiratete.
Fotografie, 1900.

Prince Rupprecht of Bavaria with his first wife Marie Gabriele, born Duchess in Bavaria.
From 1902 to 1903 Marie Gabriele accompanied her husband on a trip around the world via Ceylon, China and Japan to the United States of America. The princess came down with malaria in Java. She passed away in 1912 due to her poor health, which is why in 1921 Rupprecht married Princess Antonia of Luxembourg in his second marriage.
Photograph, 1900.

DAS KÖNIGLICHE HAUS NACH DER REVOLUTION VON 1918
Kronprinz Rupprecht von Bayern

Kronprinz Rupprecht in Uniform.
Kronprinz Rupprecht wahrte während der Weimarer Republik und auch später aufgrund seiner monarchischen Überzeugung und seiner Hoffnungen auf eine Restauration des Königtums in parteipolitischen Fragen Neutralität.
Kohlezeichnung eines unbekannten Künstlers, o. J.

Crown Prince Rupprecht in uniform.
Crown Prince Rupprecht maintained neutrality in party political issues during the Weimar Republic and also later due to his monarchic conviction and his hopes of a restoration of the kingdom.
Charcoal drawing by an unknown artist, undated.

Kronprinz Rupprecht von Bayern mit seinem Generalstabschef General Konrad Krafft von Dellmensingen am 9. Mai 1915.
Im Frühjahr 1915 nahm Kronprinz Rupprecht mit seiner 6. Armee an der Schlacht von La Bassée und Arras („Lorettoschlacht") teil. Am 9. Mai versuchten zahlenmäßig überlegene französische und englische Truppen die deutschen Stellungen zu durchbrechen, wurden unter hohen Verlusten auf beiden Seiten jedoch von den Deutschen, darunter vor allem bayerische Einheiten, zurückgeschlagen.
Ölgemälde von Fritz Reusing, 1916.

Crown Prince Rupprecht of Bavaria with his chief of general staff General Konrad Krafft von Dellmensingen on 9 May 1915.
Crown Prince Rupprecht took part with his 6th Army in the Second Battle of Artois ("Battle of Loretto") in the spring of 1915. Numerically superior French and English troops attempted to break through the German positions on 9 May, but were repulsed by the Germans, among them especially Bavarian units, with high losses on both sides.
Oil painting by Fritz Reusing, 1916.

DAS KÖNIGLICHE HAUS NACH DER REVOLUTION VON 1918
Kronprinz Rupprecht von Bayern

Satirisches Flugblatt auf die Vielzahl der Parteien bei den Wahlen 1919.
Das Flugblatt nimmt die Bayerische Volkspartei als Vertreterin klerikaler und agrarischer Interessen aufs Korn. In ihrem Demonstrationszug sitzt Ludwig III. auf einem Karren mit Milchkannen – Anspielung auf seinen Spitznamen „Millibauer" und Vorwurf einer Parteinahme zugunsten der Bauern. Kritisiert wird auch die den Wähler verwirrende Vielzahl an Parteien. Tatsächlich wurden in der Folge zersplitterte Parlamente und häufig wechselnde Regierungen den großen politischen und wirtschaftlichen Schwierigkeiten nicht Herr, sodass radikale Gruppen mehr und mehr Einfluss gewannen.
Text von Fritz de Crignis, Bilder von Frata, 1919.

Satirical flyer attacking the large number of parties during the election in 1919.
The flyer satirises the Bavarian People's Party as representative of clerical and agrarian interests. In their demonstration march, Ludwig III is sitting on a cart with milk cans – an allusion to his nickname "Millibauer" ("milk farmer") and accusation of partisanship in favour of farmers. The large number of parties confusing voters is also criticised. Subsequently, fragmented parliaments and frequently changing governments were not actually in control of major political and economic difficulties, so that radical groups gained more and more influence.
Text by Fritz de Crignis, illustrations by Frata, 1919.

Die Nationalwahl.
Wen wähle ich?

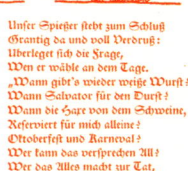

DAS KÖNIGLICHE HAUS NACH DER REVOLUTION VON 1918
Kronprinz Rupprecht von Bayern

Kronprinz Rupprecht von Bayern im Frack mit Ordensband und Stern des Hubertus-Ritterordens.
Ölgemälde von Max Rimböck, 1933.

Crown Prince Rupprecht of Bavaria in tailcoat with ribbon and star of the Chivalric Order of Saint Hubert.
Oil painting by Max Rimböck, 1933.

Kronprinzessin Antonia von Bayern (1899–1954) aus dem Haus Luxemburg.
Antonia von Bayern war die zweite Gemahlin Kronprinz Rupprechts und eine Cousine seiner verstorbenen ersten Gemahlin Marie Gabri Die erste Verlobung der beiden wu Ende 1918 aus politischen Gründ wieder aufgehoben, da sie Luxemb Ansehen bei den Siegermächten d Ersten Weltkriegs geschadet hätte. 1921 konnte die Hochzeit nach ei zweiten Verlobung stattfinden.
Gemälde von Alice Boscowitz, 1928.

DAS KÖNIGLICHE HAUS NACH DER REVOLUTION VON 1918
Kronprinz Rupprecht von Bayern

Prinz Heinrich von Bayern (1922 – 1958) als Knabe.
Prinz Heinrich war der erste Sohn aus der zweiten Ehe Kronprinz Rupprechts mit Antonia von Luxemburg. Ihm folgten noch fünf Töchter: Irmingard, Editha, Hilda, Gabrielle und Sophie.
Gemälde von H. J. Mann, 1928.

Prince Heinrich of Bavaria (1922 – 1958) as a boy.
Prince Heinrich was the first son from Crown Prince Rupprecht's second marriage with Antonia of Luxembourg. He was followed by five daughters: Irmingard, Editha, Hilda, Gabrielle and Sophie.
Painting by H. J. Mann, 1928.

Prinz Heinrich von Bayern mit Flöte.
Während des Zweiten Weltkriegs wohnte Heinrich gemeinsam mit Kronprinz Rupprecht und der übrigen Familie in Florenz. 1943 jedoch wurden seine Schwestern und seine Mutter von der Gestapo verhaftet, ihm selbst und Kronprinz Rupprecht gelang es, in Florenz unterzutauchen. Nach dem Krieg heiratete er Anne Marie de Lustrac. Prinz Heinrich verunglückte 1958 auf einer Andenreise bei einem Verkehrsunfall tödlich.
Gemälde eines unbekannten Künstlers, o. J.

Prince Heinrich of Bavaria with flute.
During the Second World War, Heinrich lived together with Crown Prince Rupprecht and the rest of the family in Florence. But in 1943 his sisters and his mother were arrested by the Gestapo. He himself and Crown Prince Rupprecht managed to go into hiding in Florence. After the war he married Anne Marie de Lustrac. Prince Heinrich was killed in a fatal traffic accident on a journey through the Andes in 1958.
Painting by an unknown artist, undated.

DAS KÖNIGLICHE HAUS NACH DER REVOLUTION VON 1918
Kronprinz Rupprecht von Bayern

Kronprinz Rupprecht von Bayern im Kreis seiner Geschwister.
V. l. n. r.: Prinzessin Helmtrud von Bayern, Herzogin Maria von Kalabrien, Prinz Franz von Bayern, Fürstin Adelgunde von Hohenzollern, Kronprinz Rupprecht, Herzogin Wiltrud von Urach, Gräfin Gundelinde von Preysing-Lichtenegg-Moos.
Fotografie, fünfziger Jahre des 20. Jahrhunderts.

Crown Prince Rupprecht of Bavaria surrounded by his siblings.
From left to right: Princess Helmtrud of Bavaria, Duchess Maria of Calabria, Prince Franz of Bavaria, Princess Adelgunde of Hohenzollern, Crown Prince Rupprecht, Duchess Wiltrud of Urach, Countess Gundelinde of Preysing-Lichtenegg-Moos.
Photograph, 1950s.

Kronprinz Rupprecht von Bayern und sein Bruder Prinz Franz von Bayern im Park von Leutstetten.
Aquarell von Prinzessin Irmingard von Bayern, fünfziger Jahre des 20. Jahrhunderts.

DAS KÖNIGLICHE HAUS NACH DER REVOLUTION VON 1918
Kronprinz Rupprecht von Bayern

Kronprinz Rupprecht von Bayern im Kreis seiner Kinder.
V. l. n. r.: Prinz Heinrich, Prinzessin Editha, Prinzessin Sophie, Prinzessin Hilda, Kronprinz Rupprecht, Prinzessin Gabrielle, Prinzessin Irmingard.
Fotografie, fünfziger Jahre des 20. Jahrhunderts.

Crown Prince Rupprecht of Bavaria surrounded by his children.
From left to right: Prince Heinrich, Princess Editha, Princess Sophie, Princess Hilda, Crown Prince Rupprecht, Princess Gabrielle and Princess Irmingard.
Photograph, 1950s.

Prinzessin Irmingard von Bayern, porträtsitzend im 2. Obergeschoss von Schloss Leutstetten.
Ölgemälde von Max Rimböck, 1950.

Princess Irmingard of Bavaria, sitting for a portrait on the 2nd upper floor of Leutstetten castle.
Oil painting by Max Rimböck, 1950.

DAS KÖNIGLICHE HAUS NACH DER REVOLUTION VON 1918
Kronprinz Rupprecht von Bayern

Der Hubertusbrunnen in München.
Der abgebildete Hirsch wurde von Kronprinz Rupprecht im Perlacher Forst erlegt. Sein Freund, der Bildhauer Adolf von Hildebrand, nahm diesen Hirsch als Modell für den Hubertusbrunnen, der ursprünglich von 1903 bis 1907 am Bayerischen Nationalmuseum errichtet und nach dem Zweiten Weltkrieg an das Ende des Nymphenburger Kanals an der Auffahrtsallee versetzt wurde.
Bronzeplastik von Adolf von Hildebrand, um 1907.

The Saint Hubert Fountain in Munich.
The depicted red deer was shot by Crown Prince Rupprecht in Perlacher Forest. His friend, the sculptor Adolf von Hildebrand, took this deer as a model for the Saint Hubert Fountain, which was originally constructed from 1903 to 1907 at the Bavarian National Museum and was relocated after the Second World War to the end of the Nymphenburg Canal on the Auffahrtsallee.
Bronze sculpture by Adolf von Hildebrand, c. 1907.

Kronprinz Rupprecht von Bayern nach der Jagd.
Zeichnung von Theo Baumgartner, 1955.

Crown Prince Rupprecht of Bavaria after hunting.
Drawing by Theo Baumgartner, 1955.

DAS KÖNIGLICHE HAUS NACH DER REVOLUTION VON 1918
Kronprinz Rupprecht von Bayern

612 | 613

Marionette „Kronprinz Rupprecht".
Anlässlich des 85. Geburtstages des Kronprinzen führte die Künstlergesellschaft Allotria ein Theaterstück mit dieser Marionette auf.

"Crown Prince Rupprecht" marionette.
The artists' society known as "Künstlergesellschaft Allotria" staged a play with this marionette on the occasion of the Crown Prince's 85th birthday.

Der 85. Geburtstag von Kronprinz Rupprecht von Bayern am 18. Mai 1954.
Kronprinz Rupprecht sitzend zusammen mit seinem Sohn Herzog Albrecht und dessen ältestem Sohn Prinz Franz, dahinter v. l. n. r.: Prinz Heinrich (1922–1958), die Prinzen Max Emanuel (*1937, Bruder von Prinz Franz) und Prinz Konstantin (1920–1969), Sohn des Prinzen Adalbert (1886–1970).
Fotografie, 1954.

The 85th birthday of Crown Prince Rupprecht of Bavaria on 18 May 1954.
Crown Prince Rupprecht sitting together with his son Duke Albrecht and his oldest son Prince Franz; standing behind from left to right: Prince Heinrich (1922–1958), Prince Max Emanuel (born 1937, brother of Prince Franz) and Prince Konstantin (1920–1969), son of Prince Adalbert (1886–1970).
Photograph, 1954.

DAS KÖNIGLICHE HAUS NACH DER REVOLUTION VON 1918
Kronprinz Rupprecht von Bayern

Kronprinz Rupprecht von Bayern 1955 beim Staatsbesuch der britischen Königin Elizabeth II. in der Münchner Residenz.
Fotografie, 1955.

Crown Prince Rupprecht of Bavaria in 1955 during a state visit by British Queen Elizabeth II at the Munich Residence.
Photograph, 1955.

Kronprinz Rupprecht im Alter.
Rupprecht, der letzte bayerische Kronprinz, starb hochbetagt am 2. August 1955 in Leutstetten. Auf Anordnung des Ministerpräsidenten Wilhelm Hoegner wurde er wie ein König in München zu Grabe getragen.
Gemälde von Max Rimböck, 1950.

Crown Prince Rupprecht in old age.
Rupprecht, the last Bavarian Crown Prince, died at an old age on 2 August 1955 in Leutstetten. By order of Minister-President Wilhelm Hoegner he was carried to his grave in Munich like a king.
Painting by Max Rimböck, 1950.

DAS KÖNIGLICHE HAUS NACH DER REVOLUTION VON 1918
Herzog Albrecht von Bayern

Prinz Albrecht von Bayern (1905–1996) im Alter von 10 Jahren.
Gemälde von Theodor Bohnenberger, 1915.

Prince Albrecht of Bavaria (1905–1996) at the age of 10 years.
Painting by Theodor Bohnenberger, 1915.

Prinz Albrecht von Bayern als Kind.
Nach dem Tod seiner Mutter wuchs der Prinz (seit 1914 durch den Tod seines älteren Bruders Luitpold Erbprinz), bei seinem Onkel Herzog Ludwig Wilhelm in Bayern auf, da Kronprinz Rupprecht im Ersten Weltkrieg an der Front war. Albrecht studierte später Zoologie und Forstwirtschaft.
Gemälde von Lorenz Vogel, um 1910.

Prince Albrecht of Bavaria as a child.
After the death of his mother, the prince (since 1914 Hereditary Prince due to the death of his older brother Luitpold), grew up with his uncle Duke Ludwig Wilhelm in Bavaria because Crown Prince Rupprecht was on the front during the First World War. Albrecht later studied zoology and forestry.
Painting by Lorenz Vogel, c. 1910.

DAS KÖNIGLICHE HAUS NACH DER REVOLUTION VON 1918
Herzog Albrecht von Bayern

Erbprinzessin (Herzogin) Marita von Bayern (1904–1969).
Maria (Marita) Draskovich von Trakostjan war die erste Gemahlin von Erbprinz, später Herzog Albrecht von Bayern.
Zeichnung von Theo Baumgartner, 1954.

Hereditary Princess (Duchess) Marita of Bavaria (1904–1969).
Maria (Marita) Draskovich of Trakostjan was the first wife of the Hereditary Prince, later Duke Albrecht of Bavaria.
Drawing by Theo Baumgartner, 1954.

Erbprinz Albrecht von Bayern (1905–1996).
Nach dem Tod von Prinz Alfons von Bayern im Jahr 1933 musste Albrecht zunächst repräsentativen Verpflichtungen in Vertretung von Kronprinz Rupprecht nachkommen, zog sich dann aber wie dieser aus Gegnerschaft zu den Nationalsozialisten aus der Öffentlichkeit zurück. 1937 emigrierte er nach Jugoslawien, von dort 1941 nach Ungarn. Von 1914 bis zum Tod seines Vaters 1955 trug er seinen Titel Erbprinz, danach nannte er sich Herzog von Bayern.
Zeichnung von Theo Baumgartner, 1954.

Hereditary Prince Albrecht of Bavaria (1905–1996).
After the death of Prince Alfons of Bavaria in 1933, Albrecht initially had to fulfil representative obligations as a representative of Crown Prince Rupprecht, but then, like Rupprecht, he withdrew from public life out of opposition to the National Socialists. He emigrated to Yugoslavia in 1937, and from there he emigrated to Hungary in 1941. From 1914 until the death of his father in 1955 he bore his title Hereditary Prince, after that he called himself Duke of Bavaria.
Drawing by Theo Baumgartner, 1954.

DAS KÖNIGLICHE HAUS NACH DER REVOLUTION VON 1918
Herzog Albrecht von Bayern

Prinzessin Marie Gabrielle von Bayern (geb. 1931), Tochter von Erbprinz Albrecht von Bayern.
1957 heiratete Marie Gabrielle Fürst Georg von Waldburg zu Zeil und Trauchburg.
Zeichnung von Theo Baumgartner, 1954.

Princess Marie Gabrielle of Bavaria (born 1931), daughter of Hereditary Prince Albrecht of Bavaria.
Marie Gabrielle married Prince Georg von Waldburg zu Zeil und Trauchburg in 1957.
Drawing by Theo Baumgartner, 1954.

Prinzessin Marie Charlotte von Bayern (geb. 1931), die Zwillingsschwester von Prinzessin Marie Gabrielle.
Marie Charlotte heiratete 1955 Fürst Paul von Quadt zu Wykradt und Isny.
Zeichnung von Theo Baumgartner, 1954.

Princess Marie Charlotte of Bavaria (born 1931), the twin sister of Princess Marie Gabrielle.
Marie Charlotte married Prince Paul von Quadt zu Wykradt and Isny in 1957.
Drawing by Theo Baumgartner, 1954.

DAS KÖNIGLICHE HAUS NACH DER REVOLUTION VON 1918
Herzog Albrecht von Bayern

Prinz Franz von Bayern (geb. 1933), der ältere Sohn von Erbprinz Albrecht und Erbprinzessin Marita.
Zeichnung von Theo Baumgartner, 1954/55.

Prince Franz of Bavaria (born 1933), the older son of Hereditary Prince Albrecht and Hereditary Princess Marita.
Drawing by Theo Baumgartner, 1954/55.

Prinz Max von Bayern (geb. 1937), der jüngere Sohn von Erbprinz Albrecht und Erbprinzessin Marita. Kraft Adoption durch seinen Großonkel Herzog Ludwig Wilhelm ist Max Träger des Titels „Herzog in Bayern".
Zeichnung von Theo Baumgartner, 1954/55.

Prince Max of Bavaria (born 1937), the younger son of Hereditary Prince Albrecht and Hereditary Princess Marita. Max bears the title "Duke in Bavaria" by virtue of being adopted by his great-uncle, Duke Ludwig Wilhelm.
Drawing by Theo Baumgartner, 1954/55.

S. Kgl. Hoheit Prinz Franz von Bayern.    S. Kgl. Hoheit Prinz Max v. Bayern.

DAS KÖNIGLICHE HAUS NACH DER REVOLUTION VON 1918
Herzog Albrecht von Bayern

Das Konzentrationslager Sachsenhausen im Winter.
Erbprinz Albrecht wurde mit seiner Familie 1944 in Budapest von der Gestapo verhaftet und nach Deutschland gebracht. Dort wurden sie als „Sonderhäftlinge" in die Konzentrationslager Sachsenhausen, Flossenbürg und zuletzt Dachau verbracht. In Sachsenhausen waren auch die Halbschwestern Albrechts, die Prinzessinnen Irmingard, Editha, Hilda, Gabrielle und Sophie interniert. Sie konnten Kontakt aufnehmen und verbrachten die Haft gemeinsam. Kurz vor Kriegsende wurden sie von Dachau an den Plansee bei Reutte verlegt. Ein Hinrichtungsbefehl wurde nicht mehr vollstreckt, rechtzeitig konnte die Familie von amerikanischen Soldaten der 3. Armee befreit werden. Kronprinzessin Antonia wurde im Konzentrationslager Oranienburg interniert. Sie starb 1953 an den Folgen der dort an ihr vorgenommenen medizinischen Experimente.
Gemälde von Prinzessin Irmingard von Bayern, nach 1945.

Sachsenhausen concentration camp in the winter.
Hereditary Prince Albrecht was arrested with his family in Budapest by the Gestapo in 1944 and brought to Germany. There they were taken as "special detainees" to the concentration camps at Sachsenhausen, Flossenbürg and finally Dachau. Albrecht's half-sisters, Princesses Irmingard, Editha, Hilda, Gabrielle and Sophie, were also interned at Sachsenhausen. They were able to establish contact and spent the imprisonment together. Shortly before the end of the war they were transferred from Dachau to the lake Plansee near Reutte. A death warrant was no longer enforced. The family was able to be liberated just in time by American soldiers of the 3rd Army. Crown Princess Antonia was interned in the concentration camp at Oranienburg. She died in 1953 from the consequences of the medical experiments carried out on her.
Painting by Princess Irmingard of Bavaria, after 1945.

DAS KÖNIGLICHE HAUS NACH DER REVOLUTION VON 1918
Herzog Albrecht von Bayern

„Das jagdliche Vermächtnis Herzog Albrechts von Bayern".
Herzog Albrecht verfasste eine Anzahl wissenschaftlicher Publikationen zum Jagdwesen. Sein Werk wird heute im Jagdmuseum in Berchtesgaden gezeigt.
Paul Parey Zeitschriftenverlag, 1997.

"Duke Albrecht of Bavaria's hunting legacy".
Duke Albrecht authored a number of scientific publications on hunting. His work is exhibited today at the hunting museum in Berchtesgaden.
Paul Parey Zeitschriftenverlag (special interest publishing house), 1997.

Schützenscheibe zu Ehren des 75. Geburtstags Herzog Albrechts von Bayern in der Schießstätte in München-Allach.
Herzog Albrecht war ein begeisterter Jäger und Schütze und selbst Mitglied im Schützenverein München-Allach.
Bemalte Schützenscheibe aus Holz, 1980.

Target in honour of Duke Albrecht of Bavaria's 75th birthday at the shooting range in Munich-Allach.
Duke Albrecht was an enthusiastic hunter and marksman, and was even a member in the Munich-Allach shooting association.
Painted wooden target, 1980.

DAS KÖNIGLICHE HAUS NACH DER REVOLUTION VON 1918
Die Familie heute

Die offizielle Medaille des Hauses Wittelsbach anlässlich des Jubiläums „800 Jahre Wittelsbacher in Bayern". Herzog Albrecht machte zum 800-jährigen Jubiläum des Hauses Wittelsbach eine Zustiftung zur von König Maximilian II. errichteten Maximilianeums-Stiftung für hochbegabte Studenten, um auch Studentinnen aufnehmen zu können.

The official medal of the House of Wittelsbach on the occasion of the anniversary "800 Years of the House of Wittelsbach in Bavaria". For the 800-year anniversary of the House of Wittelsbach, Duke Albrecht made a donation to the Maximilianeum Foundation for gifted male students established by King Maximilian II in order to also be able to accept female students.

DAS KÖNIGLICHE HAUS NACH DER REVOLUTION VON 1918
Die Familie heute

630 | 631

Prinz Adalbert von Bayern, der jüngere Sohn von Prinz Konstantin, mit seiner Familie: Gemahlin Prinzessin Sandra von Bayern mit Tochter Prinzessin Bernadette von Bayern und Sohn Prinz Hubertus von Bayern.

Prince Adalbert of Bavaria, younger son of Prince Konstantin, with his family: wife Princess Sandra of Bavaria with daughter Princess Bernadette of Bavaria and son Prince Hubertus of Bavaria.

Prinz Leopold von Bayern, älterer Sohn von Prinz Konstantin, mit Gemahlin Prinzessin Ursula von Bayern und Familie bei der Hochzeit seiner Tochter Prinzessin Maria Felipa von Bayern.
V. l. n. r.: Prinz Konstantin von Bayern, Prinzessin Maria del Pilar von Bayern, Prinz Manuel von Bayern, Prinzessin Anna von Bayern, Prinz Leopold von Bayern, Prinzessin Ursula von Bayern, Christian Dienst, Prinzessin Maria Felipa, Eltern von Christian Dienst.

Prince Leopold of Bavaria, older son of Prince Konstantin, with wife Princess Ursula of Bavaria and family at the wedding of his daughter Princess Maria Felipa of Bavaria.
From left to right: Prince Konstantin of Bavaria, Princess Maria del Pilar of Bavaria, Prince Manuel of Bavaria, Princess Anna of Bavaria, Prince Leopold of Bavaria, Princess Ursula of Bavaria, Christian Dienst, Princess Maria Felipa and parents of Christian Dienst.

DAS KÖNIGLICHE HAUS NACH DER REVOLUTION VON 1918
Die Familie heute

Prinz Luitpold von Bayern mit Gemahlin Prinzessin Beatrix von Bayern und seiner Mutter Prinzessin Irmingard von Bayern (1923–2010) und Familie.
V. l. n. r.: Prinzessin Beatrix von Bayern, Prinz Ludwig von Bayern, Prinz Ferdinand zur Lippe, Prinzessin Auguste von Bayern, Prinz Heinrich von Bayern, Prinzessin Alice von Bayern, Prinzessin Irmingard von Bayern, Prinz Lukas von Auersperg, Prinz Karl von Bayern, Prinz Luitpold von Bayern.

Prince Luitpold of Bavaria with wife Princess Beatrix of Bavaria and his mother Princess Irmingard of Bavaria (1923–2010) and family.
From left to right: Princess Beatrix of Bavaria, Prince Ludwig of Bavaria, Prince Ferdinand zur Lippe, Princess Auguste of Bavaria, Prince Heinrich of Bavaria, Princess Alice of Bavaria, Princess Irmingard of Bavaria, Prince Lukas von Auersperg, Prince Karl of Bavaria, Prince Luitpold of Bavaria.

Prinz Rasso von Bayern (1926–2011, sitzend), Sohn von Prinz Franz und Neffe von Kronprinz Rupprecht, mit Gemahlin Prinzessin Theresa von Bayern, geb. Erzherzogin von Österreich-Toskana, umringt von ihrer großen Familie.
Die Kinder des Prinzenpaares mit Gemahlin bzw. Gemahl: Gräfin Maria Theresa Kornis von Göncz-Ruszka, geb. Prinzessin von Bayern, Graf Thomas Kornis von Göncz-Ruszka, Pater Florian OSB, Gräfin Elisabeth von Kuefstein, geb. Prinzessin von Bayern, Graf Andreas von Kuefstein, Prinz Wolfgang von Bayern, Freiherrin Benedikta von Freyberg-Eisenberg, geb. Prinzessin von Bayern, Freiherr Rudolf von Freyberg-Eisenberg, Prinz Christoph von Bayern, Prinzessin Gudila von Bayern, geb. Gräfin von Plettenberg-Lenhausen, Prinzessin Gisela von Sachsen-Gessaphe, geb. Prinzessin von Bayern, Prinz Alexander von Sachsen-Gessaphe, Prinz von Sachsen, Herzog zu Sachsen.

Prince Rasso of Bavaria (1926–2011, sitting), son of Prince Franz and nephew of Crown Prince Rupprecht, with wife Princess Theresa of Bavaria, born Archduchess of Austria-Tuscany, surrounded by their large family.
The children of the princely couple with wife or husband: Countess Maria Theresa Kornis of Göncz-Ruszka, born Princess of Bavaria, Count Thomas Kornis of Göncz-Ruszka, Father Florian OSB, Countess Elisabeth of Kuefstein, born Princess of Bavaria, Count Andreas of Kuefstein, Prince Wolfgang of Bavaria, Baroness Benedikta of Freyberg-Eisenberg, born Princess of Bavaria, Baron Rudolf of Freyberg-Eisenberg, Prince Christoph of Bavaria, Princess Gudila of Bavaria, born Countess of Plettenberg-Lenhausen, Princess Gisela of Saxony-Gessaphe, born Princess of Bavaria, Prince Alexander of Saxony-Gessaphe, Prince of Saxony, Duke of Saxony.

DAS KÖNIGLICHE HAUS NACH DER REVOLUTION VON 1918
Die Familie heute

Herzog Max in Bayern mit Gemahlin Herzogin Elizabeth in Bayern, geb. Gräfin Douglas, und ihren Töchtern v. l. n. r.: Prinzessin Sophie von und zu Liechtenstein, geb. Herzogin in Bayern, Herzogin Marie-Caroline von Württemberg, geb. Herzogin in Bayern, Herzogin Helene in Bayern, Elizabeth Terberger, geb. Herzogin in Bayern, und Maria Anna Runow, geb. Herzogin in Bayern.

Duke Max in Bavaria with wife Duchess Elizabeth in Bavaria, born Countess Douglas, and their daughters from left to right: Princess Sophie of Liechtenstein, born Duchess in Bavaria, Duchess Marie-Caroline of Württemberg, born Duchess in Bavaria, Duchess Helene in Bavaria, Elizabeth Terberger, born Duchess in Bavaria, and Maria Anna Runow, born Duchess in Bavaria.

Herzog Max in Bayern mit Gemahlin Herzogin Elizabeth in Bayern, geb. Gräfin Douglas, und ihren Schwiegersöhnen v. l. n. r.: Dr. Daniel Terberger, Herzog Philipp von Württemberg, Dr. Klaus Runow und Erbprinz Alois von und zu Liechtenstein.

Duke Max in Bavaria with wife Duchess Elizabeth in Bavaria, born Countess Douglas, and their sons-in law from left to right: Dr. Daniel Terberger, Duke Philipp of Württemberg, Dr. Klaus Runow and hereditary Prince Alois of Liechtenstein.

DAS KÖNIGLICHE HAUS NACH DER REVOLUTION VON 1918
Die Familie heute

Die Geschwister Herzog Max in Bayern, Herzog Franz von Bayern, Fürstin Marie Gabrielle von Waldburg zu Zeil und Trauchburg und Fürstin Marie Charlotte von Quadt zu Wykradt und Isny, geb. Prinzessinnen von Bayern.

The siblings Duke Max in Bavaria, Duke Franz of Bavaria, Marie Gabrielle, Princess von Waldburg zu Zeil und Trauchburg, and Marie Charlotte, Princess von Quadt zu Wykradt und Isny, born Princesses of Bavaria.

Herzog Franz von Bayern, amtierender Chef des Hauses Wittelsbach.

Duke Franz of Bavaria, current head of the House of Wittelsbach.

EXKURS I: WITTELSBACHER KÖNIGE IN EUROPÄISCHEN LÄNDERN
Béla V. von Ungarn

Wittelsbacher auf europäischen Thronen
Members of the House of Wittelsbach on European thrones

Die Wittelsbacher: Das ist eine seit der Mitte des 11. Jahrhunderts belegbare Familiengeschichte, die sich immer wieder so unauflöslich und innig mit der Geschichte Bayerns vermengt, dass man manchmal geneigt ist, die bayerische und die wittelsbachische Geschichte überhaupt in eins zu setzen. Und doch wäre das ganz falsch: Die Geschichte des Hauses Wittelsbach greift nämlich immer wieder über Bayern hinaus; das sehen wir schon bei den wittelsbachischen Prinzessinnen, die sowohl auf deutsche wie auf europäische Throne gelangten, wobei die Liste der fürstlichen, königlichen und kaiserlichen Ehegatten von König Karl VI. von Frankreich über Wenzel von Böhmen bis zu König Friedrich Wilhelm IV. von Preußen und Kaiser Franz Joseph I. von Österreich reicht. Die internationale Bedeutung des Hauses tritt vielleicht noch deutlicher hervor, wenn wir uns die Abfolge von drei schwedischen Königen, eines ungarischen und eines griechischen Königs, eines Königs von Böhmen und eines Königs von Dänemark, Schweden und Norwegen aus dem Hause Wittelsbach vor Augen führen. Strategisches Kalkül, machtpolitische Ambitionen oder schlicht genealogische Zufälligkeiten mögen dabei in durchaus unterschiedlichen Konstellationen eine Rolle gespielt haben – der europäische Rang des Hauses Wittelsbach war in jedem Fall das Resultat.

The House of Wittelsbach: this is a family history verifiable since the middle of the 11th century which is repeatedly so indissolubly and intimately commingled with the history of Bavaria that one is sometimes inclined to roll the Bavarian and Wittelsbach history into one. And yet that would be completely wrong:
To be precise, the history of the House of Wittelsbach continually transcends Bavaria. We even see this among the Wittelsbach princesses who ascended German as well as European thrones, whereby the list of princely, royal and imperial spouses ranges from King Karl VI of France to Wenceslaus of Bohemia as well as King Friedrich Wilhelm IV of Prussia and Emperor Franz Joseph I of Austria. Perhaps the international importance of the dynasty becomes even more apparent if we visualise the succession of three Swedish kings, a Hungarian and a Greek king, a King of Bohemia and a king of Denmark, Sweden and Norway from the House of Wittelsbach. Strategic calculation, ambitions of power politics or simple genealogical contingencies may have played a role in thoroughly different constellations. At any rate, the European status of the House of Wittelsbach was the result.

Krönung Herzog Ottos III. von Niederbayern (1261–1312) zum König von Ungarn am 6. Dezember 1305.
Als einer der frühesten Wittelsbacher, die ihre Regentschaft in anderen europäischen Territorien antraten, wurde Herzog Otto III. von Niederbayern am 6. Dezember 1305 in Stuhlweissenburg von den Bischöfen von Csanád und Veszprem zum König von Ungarn gekrönt. Als Sohn einer ungarischen Königstochter herrschte er unter dem Namen Béla V. jedoch nur wenige Jahre, politische Konflikte zwangen ihn, um 1308 wieder nach Niederbayern zurückzukehren.
Gemälde von Hans Werl, Ende des 16. / Anfang des 17. Jahrhunderts.

Coronation of Duke Otto III of Lower Bavaria (1261–1312) as King of Hungary on 6 December 1305.
Duke Otto III of Lower Bavaria was crowned King of Hungary on 6 December 1305 in Stuhlweissenburg ("Seat of the White Castle") by the Bishops of Csanád and Veszprem as one of the earliest members of the House of Wittelsbach who acceded to their reign in other European territories. As the son of a Hungarian king's daughter he reigned under the name Béla V, but only a few years. Political conflicts forced him to return to Lower Bavaria around 1308.
Painting by Hans Werl, late 16th / early 17th century.

EXKURS I: WITTELSBACHER KÖNIGE IN EUROPÄISCHEN LÄNDERN
Christoph III. von Dänemark

König Christoph III. von Dänemark, Norwegen und Schweden, Pfalzgraf von Neumarkt (1416–1448).
Christoph III. war das jüngste Kind von Pfalzgraf Johann dem Oberpfälzer (1383–1443) aus der Linie Neunburg-Oberpfalz und dessen erster Gattin Katharina von Pommern-Stolp. Der Bruder seiner Mutter war König Erich von Dänemark – als dieser abgesetzt wurde, berief man Christoph 1438 als Reichsverweser nach Dänemark. 1440 wurde er dort zum König gewählt; er erhielt in der Folge auch die Königreiche von Schweden und Norwegen. Unter seiner Regentschaft erhielt Kopenhagen seine Rechte als Hauptstadt des Königreichs.
Kupferstich eines unbekannten Künstlers, o. J.

King Christoph III of Denmark, Norway and Sweden, Count Palatine of Neumarkt (1416–1448).
Christoph III was the youngest child of Count Palatine Johann of the Upper Palatinate (1383–1443) from the royal line of Neunburg-Upper Palatinate and whose first consort was Katharina of Pomerania-Stolp. His mother's brother was King Eric of Denmark – as Eric was deposed, Christoph was called to Denmark as regent in 1438. There he was chosen as king in 1440; he also subsequently received the kingdoms of Sweden and Norway. Copenhagen received its rights as capital of the kingdom under his reign.
Copperplate engraving by an unknown artist, undated.

Christophorus III Bavarus Rex, Daniæ, Sueciæ, Norvegiæ Vandalorum Gothorum Dux Bavariæ

95

EXKURS I: WITTELSBACHER KÖNIGE IN EUROPÄISCHEN LÄNDERN
Friedrich V. von der Pfalz, König von Böhmen

Doppelporträt des Kurfürsten Friedrich V. von der Pfalz (1596–1632) und seiner Gemahlin Elizabeth Stuart (1596–1662) als König und Königin von Böhmen um 1620.
Der calvinistische Kurfürst und Führer der Protestantischen Union Friedrich V. von der Pfalz wurde nach dem Prager Fenstersturz von 1618 von den böhmischen Ständen zum König erwählt. Durch Annahme der Königskrone forderte Friedrich V. die Habsburger heraus. Seine Regentschaft sollte nur einen Winter währen: In der Schlacht am Weißen Berg brachten ihm sein Vetter Maximilian I. von Bayern und die Truppen des habsburgischen Kaisers eine vernichtende Niederlage bei, die ihn zur Flucht zwang.
Gemälde von Gerrit von Honthorst, 1634.

Double portrait of Elector Friedrich V of the Palatinate (1596–1632) and his consort Elizabeth Stuart (1596–1662) as King and Queen of Bohemia c. 1620.
The Calvinist Elector Friedrich V of the Palatinate, leader of the Protestant Union, was elected by the Bohemian estates as king after the Defenestration of Prague in 1618. Friedrich V provoked the Habsburgs by assuming the royal crown. His regency was only to last one winter: his cousin Maximilian I of Bavaria and the troops of the Habsburg emperor inflicted a crushing defeat in the Battle of White Mountain, which forced him to flee.
Painting by Gerrit von Honthorst, 1634.

EXKURS I: WITTELSBACHER KÖNIGE IN EUROPÄISCHEN LÄNDERN
Karl X. Gustav und Karl XI. von Schweden

König Karl X. Gustav von Schweden (1622–1660).
Karl Gustav war der zweite Sohn des Pfalzgrafen Johann Casimir von Pfalz-Zweibrücken-Kleeburg und dessen Gemahlin Katharina, einer Tochter des Königs Karl IX. von Schweden. 1654 trat er dort die Thronfolge an und begründete somit die Wittelsbachische Herrschaft in Schweden.
Gemälde von Sébastien Bourdon, 1652/53.

King Karl X Gustav of Sweden (1622–1660).
Karl Gustav was the second son of Count Palatine Johann Casimir of Palatinate-Zweibrücken-Kleeburg and his wife Katharina, a daughter of King Karl IX of Sweden. He acceded to the throne there in 1765 and thus established Wittelsbach rule in Sweden.
Painting by Sébastien Bourdon, 1652/53.

König Karl XI. von Schweden (1655–1697), seit 1681 als Karl I. auch Herzog von Pfalz-Zweibrücken.
Der Sohn von König Karl X. Gustav erbte noch minderjährig den Thron. Bis 1672 regierte für ihn seine Mutter Hedwig Eleonore von Holstein-Gottorp, 1675 wurde er zum König von Schweden gekrönt.
Gemälde von David Klöcker Ehrenstrahl, 1676.

King Karl XI of Sweden (1655–1697), since 1681 as Karl I also Duke of Palatinate-Zweibrücken.
The son of King Karl X Gustav inherited the throne while still a minor. His mother, Hedwig Eleonore of Holstein-Gottorp, reined instead of her son until 1672. He was crowned King of Sweden in 1675.
Painting by David Klöcker Ehrenstrahl, 1676.

EXKURS I: WITTELSBACHER KÖNIGE IN EUROPÄISCHEN LÄNDERN
Karl XII. von Schweden

**König Karl XII.
von Schweden (1682–1718).**
Karls Eltern waren König Karl XI. und Ulrike Eleonore, Tochter des dänischen Königs Friedrich III. Da er kinderlos starb, endete mit ihm die Herrschaft der Wittelsbacher über Schweden. Während des Großen Nordischen Krieges um die Vorherrschaft im Ostseeraum eroberte Karl XII. die Stadt Narva durch einen Überraschungsangriff über die zugefrorene Ostsee. Karls Russlandfeldzug endete 1709 mit der Schlacht bei Poltawa, die den Schweden eine vernichtende Niederlage beibrachte.
Zeichnung eines unbekannten Künstlers, o. J.

**King Karl XII
of Sweden (1682–1718).**
Karl's parents were King Karl XI and Ulrike Eleonore, daughter of Danish King Friedrich III. Since he died childless, the Wittelsbach rule over Sweden ended with him. During the Great Northern War for the supremacy in the Baltic Sea region, Karl XII conquered the city of Narva by means of a surprise attack across the frozen Baltic Sea. Karl's Russia campaign ended in 1709 with the Battle of Poltava, which inflicted a crushing defeat on Sweden.
Drawing by an unknown artist, undated.

EXKURS I: WITTELSBACHER KÖNIGE IN EUROPÄISCHEN LÄNDERN
Otto I. von Griechenland

König Otto I. in griechischer Nationaltracht.
Lithografie von Gottlieb Bodmer nach Dietrich Monten, um 1835.

King Otto I in Greek national costume.
Lithography by Gottlieb Bodmer based on Dietrich Monten, c. 1835.

EXKURS II: DER HAUSRITTERORDEN VOM HL. GEORG
St. Georgs-Ritterorden

Der Hausritterorden vom Hl. Georg
Royal Military Order of Saint George

Aus der Nachahmung der geistlichen Orden im Mittelalter entstanden, etablierten sich die weltlichen Ritterorden als fürstliche Stiftungen, die die Loyalität des Adels gegenüber den regierenden Familien sicherstellen bzw. stabilisieren sollten. Als ein europäisches und – seit dem 19. Jahrhundert – weltweites Phänomen werden sie von strenger Ritualisierung, protokollarischem Aufwand und einer konsequenten Hierarchisierung nach unterschiedlichen Graden, Funktionen und Ämtern gekennzeichnet.

Der unbelegten Überlieferung nach wurde der Hausritterorden vom Hl. Georg schon im 12. Jahrhundert gegründet und Ende des 15. Jahrhunderts erneuert. Im Konfessionellen Zeitalter der gegenreformatorischen Politik des bayerischen Herzog- bzw. Kurfürstentums verpflichtet, wurde er am 20. März 1729 von Kurfürst Karl Albrecht auch formell wieder hergestellt; dessen Kaisertum und die damit verbundenen Ambitionen führten zu einer Blütezeit des Ordens. Unter König Ludwig II. modifizierte man den Ordenszweck: Die Verteidigung der katholischen Kirche wurde um die Verpflichtung auf Werke der Barmherzigkeit ergänzt. — Als Hausorden überlebte der Georgi-Orden auch den Umbruch von 1918 und das Ende der Monarchie als Staatsform; heutiger Großmeister ist der Chef des Hauses Wittelsbach, Herzog Franz von Bayern.

Arising from the emulation of religious orders in the Middle Ages, the secular orders of knights became established as royal foundations which were to safeguard or stabilise the loyalty of the nobility towards the ruling families. As a European and – since the 19th century – worldwide phenomenon they are characterised by stringent ritualization, ceremonial extravagance and consistent hierarchism according to varying ranks, functions and offices. According to undocumented tradition, the Royal Military Order of Saint George was founded as early as the 12th century and renewed at the end of the 15th century. Obligated in the denominational era of the Counter-Reformation policy of Bavarian duchies or electorates, it was also formally restored on 20 March 1729 by Elector Karl Albrecht; his empire and the associated ambitions led to a heyday of the order. The purpose of the order was modified under King Ludwig II: the defence of the Catholic Church was supplemented by the obligation to works of compassion. As a dynastic order, the Order of Saint George also survived the upheaval of 1918 and the end of the monarchy as a form of government; the present-day Grand Master is the head of the House of Wittelsbach, Duke Franz of Bavaria.

Ordensritter mit Streitkleid, Wappen und Schwert aus dem Ersten Ordensbuch des Bayerischen Hausritterordens vom Hl. Georg.
Miniatur auf Pergament von Joseph Franz Copisi, 1729.

Knight of the order with battledress, coat of arms and sword from the first order's book of the Bavarian Royal Military Order of Saint George.
Miniature on parchment by Joseph Franz Copisi, 1729.

Ritter in Streittklaid

EXKURS II: DER HAUSRITTERORDEN VOM HL. GEORG
Kurfürst Karl Albrecht

652 | 653

Ordensschild des Ordensgroßmeisters Kurfürst Karl Albrecht mit kurbayerischem Wappen und dem Ordensstern in der Hofkapelle der Münchner Residenz.
Gefertigt von Johann Nikolaus Steinhausen und Johann Georg Saug, Kupfer vergoldet und versilbert, 1729.

Heraldic shield of the order's Grand Master Elector Karl Albrecht with Electorate of Bavaria's coat of arms and heraldic star in the Court Chapel of the Munich Residence.
Made by Johann Nikolaus Steinhausen and Johann Georg Saug, gold-plated and silver-plated copper, 1729.

Kurfürst Karl Albrecht (1697–1745) im Ornat eines Großmeisters des Bayerischen Hausritterordens vom Hl. Georg.
Das großformatige Gemälde zeigt den detailreichen Großmeister-Ornat Karl Albrechts in voller Pracht. Im Hintergrund ist Schloss Nymphenburg im Zustand der 30er Jahre des 18. Jahrhunderts zu sehen.
Ölgemälde F. J. Winter zugeschrieben, dreißiger Jahre des 18. Jahrhunderts.

Elector Karl Albrecht (1697–1745) in the regalia of a Grand Master of the Bavarian Royal Military Order of Saint George.
The large-format painting depicts Karl Albrecht's detailed Grand Master regalia in full splendour. Nymphenburg Palace in the status of the 1730s can be seen in the background.
Oil painting attributed to F. J. Winter, 1730s.

EXKURS II: DER HAUSRITTERORDEN VOM HL. GEORG
Kurfürst Karl Albrecht – Kurfürst Karl Theodor

Kurfürst Karl Albrecht mit blauem Umhang des Georgi-Ritterordens, am Brustpanzer ein Motiv aus der Ordenskollane.

Das Deckenfresko thematisiert die Menschwerdung Jesu, dessen Gnade auch den Zeitgenossen Asams zuteil wird, so vor allem dem gottesfürchtigen Kurfürst, seinem Sohn Kurprinz Maximilian Joseph im Ornat und Kurfürst/Erzbischof Clemens August von Köln.
Deckenfresko von Cosmas Damian Asam in der Kongregationskirche Maria de Victoria, Ingolstadt, 1734.

Elector Karl Albrecht cape of the Order of a motif from the orde on the cuirass.

The ceiling fresco ad incarnation of Jesus, also granted to conte as the Asam Brothers the God-fearing Elec Electoral Prince Max (in regalia) and Elect Clemens August of C
Ceiling fresco by Cosm Asam in the Congrega Maria de Victoria, In 1734.

EXKURS II: DER HAUSRITTERORDEN VOM HL. GEORG
König Maximilian I. Joseph von Bayern – König Ludwig II. von Bayern

Pfalzgraf Maximilian Joseph, nachmaliger König Max I. Joseph, mit seinem Erstgeborenen, dem nachmaligen König Ludwig I.
Der spätere Kurfürst und ab 1806 König von Bayern trägt hier das Gewand des Großpriors des St.-Georgs-Ritterordens.
Miniaturbildnis eines unbekannten Künstlers, 1786.

Count Palatine Maximilian Joseph, future King Max I Joseph, with his firstborn, future King Ludwig I.
The later Elector and (from 1806) King of Bavaria is wearing the robe of the Grand Prior of the Order of Saint George here.
Miniature portrait by an unknown artist, 1786.

König Ludwig II. von Bayern (1845–1886) als Großmeister des Bayerischen Hausritterordens vom Hl. Georg.
Gouache auf Papier, Ferdinand Piloty zugeschrieben, vermutlich 1866/67 aus Anlass des ersten Ordensfestes Ludwigs als Großmeister in Auftrag gegeben.

King Ludwig II of Bavaria (1845–1886) as Grand Master of the Bavarian Royal Military Order of Saint George.
Gouache on paper, attributed to Ferdinand Piloty, presumably commissioned in 1866/67 on the occasion of Ludwig's first Royal Order festivities as Grand Master.

EXKURS II: DER HAUSRITTERORDEN VOM HL. GEORG
König Ludwig II. von Bayern

Kapitelsitzung des Hausritterordens vom Hl. Georg unter dem Vorsitz des Großmeisters König Ludwig II.
Gegenüber dem König sitzt der Großkanzler Graf Arco zu Valley, außerdem sind die Großpriore Prinz Otto, Prinz Luitpold und Prinz Adalbert (rechts) anwesend. Seit 1750 fanden die Kapitelsitzungen im sogenannten Kapitelsaal der Reichen Zimmer der Residenz statt.
Gouachemalerei von Julius Frank und Friedrich Eibner, 1869.

Chapter meeting of the Royal Military Order of Saint George chaired by Grand Master King Ludwig II.
Grand Chancellor Count Arco of Valley is sitting opposite the king. The Grand Priors Prince Otto, Prince Luitpold and Prince Adalbert (right) are also present. Chapter meetings have been held in the so-called "chapter house" of the "Ornate Rooms" in the Residence since 1750.
Gouache painting by Julius Frank and Friedrich Eibner, 1869.

EXKURS II: DER HAUSRITTERORDEN VOM HL. GEORG
König Ludwig II. von Bayern

Ritterschlag in der Alten Hofkapelle.
Das Bildnis zeigt den Ritterschlag durch Ludwig II. beim Ordenshauptfest am 26. April 1880. Die Darstellung ähnelt der des Ritterschlags von 1867, doch erscheint hier die zeremonielle Handlung noch mehr in den Vordergrund gerückt.
Gouachemalerei von Johann Caspar Herterich, 1880.

Knightly accolade in the Old Court Chapel.
The portrait depicts the knightly accolade by Ludwig II at the main Royal Order festivities on 26 April 1880. The portrayal resembles that of the knightly accolade from 1867, yet here the ceremonial act seems to be moved even more in the foreground.
Gouache painting by Johann Caspar Herterich, 1880.

EXKURS II: DER HAUSRITTERORDEN VOM HL. GEORG
Prinzregent Luitpold von Bayern – Prinz Alfons von Bayern

Prinz Alfons von Bayern (1862–1933) als Georgiritter.
Prinz Alfons Maria Franz Clemens war der zweite Sohn von Prinz Adalbert und Amalia Felipe Pilar von Spanien. Als Kavallerieoffizier machte er eine bedeutende Militärkarriere. In späteren Jahren nahm er öffentlichkeitswirksame Ehrenämter an, u. a. das des Protektors des Bayerischen Schützenbundes.
Postkarte, Ende des 19. Jahrhunderts.

Prince Alfons of Bavaria (1862–1933) as a Knight of the Order of Saint Georg.
Prince Alfons Maria Franz Clemens was the second son of Prince Adalbert and Amalia Felipe Pilar of Spain. He had a distinguished military career as a cavalry officer. In later years he assumed publicly effective honorary offices, among others that of the Protector of the Bavarian Shooting Association.
Postcard, end of the 19th century.

Prinzregent Luitpold von Bayern (1821–1912) als Großmeisterstellvertreter des St. Georgs-Ritterordens.
Gemälde von Max Slevogt, 1908.

Prince Regent Luitpold of Bavaria (1821–1912) as Deputy Grand Master of the Order of Saint George.
Painting by Max Slevogt, 1908.

EXKURS II: DER HAUSRITTERORDEN VOM HL. GEORG
König Ludwig III. von Bayern

664 | 665

Königin Marie Therese und König Ludwig III. von Bayern als Groß-meister des St.-Georgs-Ritterordens.
Das Königspaar huldigt Jesus als wahrem „Christkönig".
Hochaltarbild von Maximilian von Schoellerer, Pfarrkirche von Wildenwart/Chiemgau, um 1934.

Queen Marie Therese and King Ludwig III of Bavaria as Grand Master of the Order of Saint George.
The royal couple pays homage to Jesus as the true "Christ the King".
High altar painting by Maximilian von Schoellerer, Parish Church of Wildenwart/Chiemgau, c. 1934.

Anhang

ANHANG
Literaturauswahl

Literaturauswahl

Alberter, Aemilian/Veronika Biebl/ Ernst Fischer: 100 Jahre Pfarrkirche St. Anna in München 1892–1992, Zürich u. a. 1992.

Architektursammlung der Technischen Universität München/Carl von Fischer Gesellschaft (Hrsg.): Carl von Fischer 1782–1820. Gesamtkatalog, München 1983.

Asam, Cosmas Damian: Maria de Victoria, Ingolstadt 1986.

Bartoschek, Gerd: Münchner Biedermeier. Aquarelle aus der Sammlung der Königin Elisabeth von Preußen, München 1991.

Bauchbauer, Wolf et al. (Hrsg.): Pfarr- und Klosterkirche Altomünster. Dokumentation der Innenrestaurierung 1995–2003, Paderborn 2003.

Bäumler, Suzanne/Evamaria Brockhoff/Michael Henker (Hrsg.): Von Kaisers Gnaden. 500 Jahre Pfalz-Neuburg. Katalog zur Bayerischen Landesausstellung 2005 Neuburg a. d. Donau 3. Juni – 16. Oktober 2005, Augsburg 2005.

Dies.: Das Ingolstädter Münster. Zur Schönen Unserer Lieben Frau, Berlin u. a. 2009.

Bayerische Staatsgemäldesammlungen, Neue Pinakothek München (Hrsg.): Spätromantik und Realismus, Gemäldekataloge Bd. V, München 1984.

Bayerische Verwaltung der staatlichen Schlösser, Gärten und Seen (Hrsg.): Der Bayerische Hausritterorden vom Heiligen Georg 1729–1979. Ausstellung in der Residenz München 21. April – 24. Juni 1979, München 1979.

Dies. (Hrsg.): 475 Jahre Fürstentum Pfalz-Neuburg. Ausstellung im Schloß Grünau bei Neuburg an der Donau 20. Juni 1980 – 19. Oktober 1980, München 1980.

Dies. (Hrsg.): Schatzkammer der Residenz München. Amtlicher Führer, München 1992.

Bayerisches Nationalmuseum (Hrsg.): Die Wittelsbacher und das Reich der Mitte. 400 Jahre China und Bayern, München 2009.

Bayerisches Staatsministerium der Finanzen (Hrsg.): Schlösserland Bayern. Staatliche Schlösser, Gärten, Seen und Heilbäder mit Karten des Bayer. Landesvermessungsamts, Bd. 1, München 1987.

Bayern, Adalbert Prinz von: Die Wittelsbacher. Geschichte unserer Familie, München 1979.

Ders.: Der Herzog und die Tänzerin. Die merkwürdige Geschichte Christians IV. von Pfalz-Zweibrücken und seiner Familie, Neustadt a. d. Weinstraße 1966.

Ders.: Erinnerungen 1900–1956, München 1991.

Ders.: Die Herzen der Leuchtenberg. Chronik einer napoleonisch-bayerisch-europäischen Familie, München 1963.

Ders.: Nymphenburg und seine Bewohner, München 1950.

Ders.: Als die Residenz noch Residenz war, München 1967.

Beyer, Professor Dr. Conrad: Ludwig II. König von Bayern. Ein Charakterbild nach Mitteilungen hochstehender und bekannter Persönlichkeiten und nach authentischen Quellen. Des Königs Aufenthalt am Vierwaldstättersee und sein Verkehr mit Josef Kainz, Leipzig 1900.

Blunt, Wilfrid: König Ludwig II. von Bayern, München 1970.

Bodenstedt, Friedrich: Aus meinem Leben. Erinnerungsblätter. Bd. 1 Eines Königs Reise, Leipzig 1879.

Braun-Jäppelt, Barbara: Prinzregent Luitpold von Bayern in seinen Denkmälern, Bamberg 1997.

Brunner, Herbert/Elmar D. Schmid/ Brigitte Langer: Landshut. Burg Trausnitz. Amtlicher Führer, München 2003.

Bußmann, Hadumod: Ich habe mich vor nichts im Leben gefürchtet. Die ungewöhnliche Geschichte der Therese Prinzessin von Bayern 1850–1925, München 2011.

Dau, Daniela: Englischer Garten. Auf Erlebnistour in Münchens Freizeitparadies, München 2011.

Destouches, Ernst von: Geschichte des Königlich Bayerischen Haus-Ritter-Ordens vom Heiligen Georg. Nach urkundlichen Quellen des Ordensarchivs, Bamberg 1890.

Deutsches Historisches Museum (Hrsg.): Bismarck – Preussen, Deutschland und Europa, Berlin 1990.

Dorner, Johann: Herzogin Hedwig und ihr Hofstaat. Das Alltagsleben auf der Burg Burghausen nach Originalquellen des 15. Jahrhunderts, Burghausen 2002.

Dotterweich, Helmut: Das Erbe der Wittelsbacher. Vermächtnis einer europäischen Dynastie, München 1981.

Egg, Erich: Hofkirche in Innsbruck. Grabmal Kaiser Maximilians I., Ried im Innkreis 1988.

Eikelmann, Renate: Von Paris nach Bayern. Das Goldene Rössl und Meisterwerke der französischen Hofkunst um 1400. Bildführer zur Ausstellung in der Stadtgalerie Altötting in Zusammenarbeit mit dem Musée du Louvre und dem Bayerischen Nationalmuseum 21. Juli – 24. September 2006, München 2006.

Dies. (Hrsg.): Die Wittelsbacher und das Reich der Mitte. 400 Jahre China und Bayern. Ausstellungskatalog, München 2009.

Erichsen, Johannes/Katharina Heinemann (Hrsg.): Bayerns Krone 1806. 200 Jahre Königreich Bayern. Begleitbuch zur Ausstellung in der Residenz München veranstaltet von der Bayerischen Verwaltung der staatlichen Schlösser, Gärten und Seen 30. März – 30. Juli 2006, München 2006.

Ders./Michael Henker/Evamaria Brockhoff (Hrsg.): „Vorwärts, vorwärts sollst du schauen …". Geschichte, Politik und Kunst unter Ludwig I., Bd. 8 Katalog zur Ausstellung, München 1986.

Ders./Uwe Puschner (Hrsg.): „Vorwärts, vorwärts sollst du schauen …". Geschichte, Politik und Kunst unter Ludwig I., Bd. 9 Aufsätze, München 1986.

Ders.: Blutenburg. Beiträge zur Geschichte von Schloß und Hofmark Menzing, München 1983.

Ettmayr, Dr. Corbinian: Die Gedächtnis-Kapelle für König Ludwig II. und die Königs-Kapelle im Parke des Schlosses Berg, München 1901.

Faltlhauser, Kurt (Hrsg.): Die Münchner Residenz. Geschichte – Zerstörung – Wiederaufbau, Ostfildern 2006.

Fischer, Ernst/Hans Kratzer (Hrsg.): Unter der Krone. Das Königreich Bayern und sein Erbe, München 2006.

Fischer, Manfred F./Sabine Heym: Ruhmeshalle und Bavaria. Amtlicher Führer, München 1972.

Fried, Pankraz (Hrsg.): Die Chronik des Abtes Konrad von Scheyen (1206–1225) über die Gründung des Klosters Scheyern und die Anfänge des Hauses Wittelsbach. In deutscher Übersetzung mit einem Facsimile-Abdruck und der von Ph. Jaffé besorgten Edition, Weissenhorn 1980.

Gaehtgens, Thomas W.: Anton von Werner. Die Proklamierung des Deutschen Kaiserreiches. Ein Historienbild im Wandel preußischer Politik, Frankfurt a. M. 1990.

Gebhardt, Heinz: Franz Hanfstaengl. Von der Lithographie zur Photographie. Ausstellung im Münchner Stadtmuseum 1. März – 29. April 1984, München 1984.

Glas, Maximilian/Rudolf Dröschel/Renate Wirs: Kristallmuseum Riedenburg (Altmühltal), Braunschweig 1990.

Glaser, Hubert (Hrsg.): Kurfürst Max Emanuel. Bayern und Europa um 1700, Katalog der Ausstellung; im Alten und Neuen Schloß Schleißheim 2. Juli bis 3. Oktober 1976, Bd. II, München 1976.

Ders. (Hrsg.): Die Zeit der frühen Herzöge. Von Otto I. zu Ludwig dem Bayern. Beiträge zur Bayerischen Geschichte und Kunst 1180–1350, Bd. I/1, München u. a. 1980.

Ders. (Hrsg.): Die Zeit der frühen Herzöge. Von Otto I. zu Ludwig dem Bayern. Katalog der Ausstellung auf der Burg Trausnitz in Landshut 14. Juni – 5. Oktober 1980, Bd. I/2, München u. a. 1980.

Ders. (Hrsg.): Krone und Verfassung. König Max I. Joseph und der neue Staat. Beiträge zur Bayerischen Geschichte und Kunst 1799–1825, Bd. III/1, München u. a. 1980.

Ders. (Hrsg.): Krone und Verfassung. König Max I. Joseph und der neue Staat. Katalog der Ausstellung im Völkerkundemuseum in München 11. Juni – 5. Oktober 1980, Bd. III/2, München u. a. 1980.

Ders. (Hrsg.): Quellen und Studien zur Kunstpolitik der Wittelsbacher vom 16. bis zum 18. Jahrhundert, München 1980.

Ders./Hannelore Putz/Maria Glaser (Hrsg.): Das Grabsteinbuch des Ignaz Alois Frey. Ein Zeugnis Freisinger Geschichtsbewusstseins nach 1803, Regensburg 2002.

Goerge, Rudolf: 1250 Jahre Glaube und Leben im Freisinger Land. Ausstellung zur 1250-Jahrfeier des Bistums Freising im Marstall des ehemaligen Prämonstratenserklosters Neustift, Freising 18. Juni – 30. September 1989, Freising 1989.

Götz, Christine/Elfi M. Haller: Prinz-Carl-Palais. Vom Palais Salabert zum Sitz des Bayerischen Ministerpräsidenten, München 1989.

Grasser, Walter: Bayerische Geschichtstaler. Von Ludwig I. und Maximilian II., Rosenheim 1982.

Grimm, Alfred/Isabel Grimm-Stadelmann: Fürsten und Pharaonen. Ägypten in Bayern, Berlin u. a. 2011.

Güse, Ernst-Gerhard/Hans-Jürgen Imiela/Berthold Roland (Hrsg.): Max Slevogt. Gemälde, Aquarelle, Zeichnungen, Stuttgart 1992.

Haasen, Gisela: Schloss Hohenschwangau, München 1999.

Habel, Heinrich: Der Marstallplatz in München. Vorstudien zur archäologischen Untersuchung, München 1993.

Habsburg, Otto: Karl V., Wien u. a. 1971.

Haller, Elfi M./Hans Lehmbruch: Palais Leuchtenberg. Die Geschichte eines Münchner Adelspalais und seines Bauherren, München 1987.

Dies./Gabriele Dischinger/Laurentius Koch: Palais Holnstein. Ein Münchner Adelspalais, München 1988.

Hamann, Brigitte (Hrsg.): Die Habsburger. Ein biographisches Lexikon, Wien u. a. 2001.

Hamberger, Edwin/Angelika Kromas (Hrsg.): Mühldorf a. Inn. Salzburg in Bayern. 935, 1802, 2002. Begleitband zur gleichnamigen Ausstellung vom 8. Juni bis 27. Oktober 2002 im Haberkasten, Mühldorf a. Inn 2002.

Hase-Schmundt, Ulrike von (Hrsg.): Albrecht Adam und seine Familie. Zur Geschichte einer Münchner Künstlerdynastie im 19. und 20. Jahrhundert, München 1981.

Heindl, Hannes: Der letzte Ritterschlag Ludwigs II., München 1980.

Ders.: Marie – Königin von Bayern, München 1989.

Hell, Helmut/Horst Leuchtmann: Orlando di Lasso. Musik der Renaissance am Münchner Fürstenhof. Ausstellung zum 450. Geburtstag 27. Mai – 31. Juli 1982 Bayerische Staatsbibliothek, Wiesbaden 1982.

ANHANG
Literaturauswahl

Heydenreuter, Reinhard: Das Palais Leuchtenberg. Vom Adelssitz zum Finanzministerium, München 2003.

Heym, Sabine: Das Antiquarium der Residenz München, München 2007.

Himmelheber, Georg: Kunst des Biedermeier 1815–1835. Architektur, Malerei, Plastik, Kunsthandwerk, Musik, Dichtung und Mode, München 1988.

Hoffmann, Carl A. et al. (Hrsg.): Als Frieden möglich war. 450 Jahre Augsburger Religionsfrieden. Begleitband zur Ausstellung im Maximilianmuseum Augsburg, Regensburg 2005.

Hofmann, Siegfried/Johannes Meyer: Das Münster zur Schönen Unserer Lieben Frau in Ingolstadt, Ingolstadt 1980.

Hojer, Gerhard: Die Schönheitengalerie König Ludwigs I., München u. a. 2011.

Ders./Elmar D. Schmid: Schleissheim. Neues Schloss und Garten. Amtlicher Führer, München 1989.

Hollweck, Ludwig: 150 Jahre Kaufmanns-Casino e. V. München 1832–1982. Eine Chronik, München 1982.

Hölz, Christoph (Red.): Königliche Träume. Casino und Park auf der Roseninsel im Starnberger See, München 2001.

Huse, Norbert: Kleine Kunstgeschichte Münchens, München 2004.

Immler, Gerhard: Die Wittelsbacher, Darmstadt 2013.

Jahn, Wolfgang/Margot Hamm/Evamaria Brockhoff (Hrsg.): Adel in Bayern. Ritter, Grafen, Industriebarone, Augsburg 2008.

Ders./Evamaria Brockhoff (Hrsg.): Verbündet, verfeindet, verschwägert. Bayern und Österreich. Bayerisch-Oberösterreichische Landesausstellung 2012 27. April – 4. November 2012, Bd. 1: Bayern und Österreich im Mittelalter, Darmstadt 2012.

Kindelbacher, Robert: St. Peter. Kunst und Frömmigkeit, München 2005.

Klemenz, Birgitta (Hrsg.): Kloster Andechs, Zürich u. a. 2005.

Klose, Dietrich O. A.: Ludwig II. König von Bayern. Sein Leben und Wirken auf Medaillen und Münzen. Ausstellung zum 150. Geburtstag, München 1995.

Ders./Franziska Jungmann-Stadler: Königlich Bayerisches Geld. Zahlungsmittel und Finanzen im Königreich Bayern 1806–1918, München 2006.

Koch, Laurentius P.: Ettal. Benediktinerabtei-, Pfarr-, Wallfahrtskirche. Zum 650jährigen Bestehen des Klosters, München u. a. 1980.

Körner, Hans-Michael und Ingrid (Hrsg.): Leopold Prinz von Bayern 1846–1930. Aus den Lebenserinnerungen, Regensburg 1983.

Ders.: Geschichte des Königreiches Bayern, München 2006.

Ders.: Die Wittelsbacher: Vom Mittelalter bis zur Gegenwart, München 2009.

Krückmann, Peter O.: Die Residenzen der Wittelsbacher. Von Landshut und Höchstädt nach München, München 2001.

Kunz-Ott, Hannelore/Andrea Kluge (Hrsg.): 150 Jahre Feldherrnhalle. Lebensraum einer Großstadt. Materialien zu einem Baudenkmal, München 1994.

Lampl, Dr. Lorenz (Hrsg.): Die Klosterkirche Fürstenfeld. Ein Juwel des bayerischen Barock, München 1985.

Langer, Brigitte (Hrsg.): Pracht und Zeremoniell – Die Möbel der Residenz München, München 2002.

Lenz, Angelika/Hans Huber: Die Portrait-Galerie im Nationaltheater, München 1996.

Leutheusser, Ulrike/Hermann Rumschöttel (Hrsg.): Prinzregent Luitpold von Bayern. Ein Wittelsbacher zwischen Tradition und Moderne, München 2012.

Mayerhofer, Johannes: Schleissheim. Eine geschichtliche Federzeichnung aus der bayerischen Hochebene, Bamberg 1890.

Müller-Meininger, Johanna (Hrsg.): Der blau gestreifte Reiter. Gemälde aus dem Münchner Stadtmuseum, München 2000.

Nerdinger, Winfried (Hrsg.): Friedrich von Gärtner. Ein Architektenleben 1791–1847. Mit den Briefen an Johann Martin von Wagner. Ausstellungskataloge des Architekturmuseums der Technischen Universität München und des Münchner Stadtmuseums Nr. 8, München 1992.

Nöhbauer, Hans F.: Auf den Spuren Ludwigs II. Ein Führer zu Schlössern und Museen, Lebens- und Erinnerungsstätten des Märchenkönigs, München 1986.

Nösselt, Hans-Joachim: Ein ältest Orchester 1530–1980. 450 Jahre Bayerisches Hof- und Staatsorchester, München 1985.

Nowald, Inken: Die Nibelungenfresken von Julius Schnorr von Carolsfeld im Königsbau der Münchner Residenz. 1827–1867, Kiel 1978.

Ottomeyer, Hans: Die Kroninsignien des Königreiches Bayern. Mit 31 Schwarzweiß- und 4 Farbbildern, München 1979.

Peltzer, Jörg et al. (Hrsg.): Die Wittelsbacher und die Kurpfalz im Mittelalter. Eine Erfolgsgeschichte?, Regensburg 2013.

Pressler, Christine: Gustav Kraus 1804–1852. Monographie und kritischer Katalog, München 1977.

Rall, Hans/Marga Rall: Die Wittelsbacher in Lebensbildern. Aktualisierte Ausgabe, München 2005.

Ders.: Wittelsbacher Lebensbilder von Kaiser Ludwig bis zur Gegenwart. Führer durch die Münchner Fürstengrüfte, neu bearb. von Gerhard Immler, München 2011.

Riepertinger, Rainhard et al. (Hrsg.): Main und Meer. Katalog zur Bayerischen Landesausstellung 2013, Augsburg 2013.

Rott, Herbert W.: Ludwig I. und die Neue Pinakothek, München 2003.

Rückert, Rainer: Der Schatz vom heiligen Berg Andechs, München 1967.

Rumschöttel, Hermann (Hrsg.): Oberschleißheim. Eine Zeitreise, Oberschleißheim 2010.

Rupprecht, Bernhard: Die Brüder Asam. Sinn und Sinnlichkeit im bayerischen Barock, Regensburg 1980.

Schauss, Dr. Emil von, Schatzmeister des Königl. Hausschatzes, Obermünzmeister und Vorstand des Königl. Bayer. Hauptmünzamtes: Historischer und beschreibender Catalog der Königlich Bayerischen Schatzkammer zu München, München 1879.

Schmid, Alois/Herrmann Rumschöttel (Hrsg.): Wittelsbacherstudien. Festgabe für Herzog Franz von Bayern zum 80. Geburtstag, München 2013.

Schmid, Elmar D./Luisa Hager: Marstallmuseum Schloss Nymphenburg in München. Hofwagenburg und Sattelkammer der bayerischen Herzöge, Kurfürsten und Könige. Amtlicher Führer, München 1992.

Ders.: Schloß Schleißheim. Die barocke Residenz mit Altem Schloß und Schloß Lustheim, München 1980.

Schrott, Ludwig: Herrscher Bayerns. Vom ersten Herzog bis zum letzten König, München 1974.

Schwaiger, Georg (Hrsg.): Das Erzbistum München und Freising im 19. und 20. Jahrhundert, München 1989.

Seidel, Klaus Jürgen (Hrsg.): Das Prinzregenten-Theater in München, Nürnberg 1984.

Slevogt, Max: Prinzregent Luitpold. Aquarelle aus Hohenschwangau, Berlin 1918.

Spengler, Karl: Die Wittelsbacher am Tegernsee, München 1969.

Staatliche Graphische Sammlung München (Hrsg.): Deutsche Künstler um Ludwig I. in Rom. Ausstellung in der Neuen Pinakothek 28. März – 14. Juni 1981, München 1981.

Staatliches Bauamt Regensburg (Hrsg.): Walhalla. Amtlicher Führer, Regensburg 2011.

Stadtmuseum München (Hrsg.): Bayern. Kunst und Kultur. Ausstellung des Freistaates Bayern und der Landeshauptstadt München veranstaltet von den Münchner staatlichen und städtischen Museen, dem Zentralinstitut für Kunstgeschichte und dem Bayerischen Rundfunk, München 1972.

Stiftung Augenklinik Herzog Carl Theodor (Hrsg.): Festschrift zum 100-jährigen Bestehen der Augenklinik Herzog Carl Theodor in München 1995, München 1995.

Svoboda, Karl J.: Prinzessinnen und Favoritinnen. Kurpfälzische Frauengestalten am Mannheimer Hof, Mannheim 1994.

Thoma, Hans: Befreiungshalle in Kelheim. Amtlicher Führer, München 1966.

Traeger, Jörg (Hrsg.): Die Walhalla. Idee, Architektur, Landschaft, Regensburg 1979.

Valentin, Hans E.: Die Wittelsbacher und ihre Künstler in acht Jahrhunderten, München 1980.

Victoria and Albert Museum/ Cooper-Hewitt Museum (Hrsg.): Designs for the Dream King. The Castles and Palaces of Ludwig II. Of Bavaria, New York 1978.

Vogel, Susanne (Hrsg.): Die Wittelsbacher. Herzöge, Kurfürsten, Könige in Bayern von 1180–1918. Biografische Skizzen, München 2012.

Voß, Hiltrud: Klenzes Marstall, München 1987.

Wackernagel, Rudolf H. (Hrsg.): Staats- und Galawagen der Wittelsbacher. Wittelsbach State and Ceremonial Carriages, Bd. 1, Stuttgart 2002.

Wagner, Christoph/Gerald Dagit (Hrsg.): Die Befreiungshalle Kelheim. Geschichte, Mythos, Gegenwart, Regensburg 2013.

Wagner, Richard: Das braune Buch. Tagebuchaufzeichnungen 1865 bis 1882, Zürich 1975.

Weber, Wilhelm: Schloss Karlsberg. Legende und Wirklichkeit. Die Wittelsbacher Schlossbauten im Herzogtum Pfalz-Zweibrücken, Homburg-Saarpfalz 1987.

Weidner, Thomas: Das Siegestor und seine Fragmente, München 1996.

Ders.: Lola Montez oder eine Revolution in München, München 1989.

Wieczorek, Alfried et al. (Hrsg.): Die Wittelsbacher am Rhein. Die Kurpfalz und Europa. Begleitband zur 2 Aus- stellung der Länder Baden-Württemberg, Rheinland-Pfalz und Hessen, Bd. 1 Mittelalter, Regensburg 2013.

Ders. (Hrsg.): Die Wittelsbacher am Rhein. Die Kurpfalz und Europa. Begleitband zur 2. Ausstellung der Länder Baden-Württemberg, Rheinland-Pfalz und Hessen, Bd. 2 Neuzeit, Regensburg 2013.

Ders./Hansjörg Probst/Wieland Koenig (Hrsg.): Lebenslust und Frömmigkeit. Kurfürst Carl Theodor (1724–1799) zwischen Barock und Aufklärung, Bd. 1 Handbuch, Regensburg 1999.

Wild, Joachim: Die Jesuiten in Bayern 1549–1773. Ausstellung des Bayerischen Hauptstaatsarchivs und der Oberdeutschen Provinz der Gesellschaft Jesu, Weißenhorn 1991.

Wilhelm-Bernstein, Daniela (Hrsg.): Berge, Schlösser, Königsträume. Auf den Spuren König Ludwigs II., München 2011.

Witzleben, Hermann von/Ilka von Vignau: Die Herzöge in Bayern. Von der Pfalz zum Tegernsee, München 1976.

Zink, Jochen: Ludwig I. und der Dom zu Speyer, München 1986.

Internetquellen

www.alt-moosburg.de/suchen/historisch_1313.htm
(Zugriff am 26.08.14)

www.bayerisches-nationalmuseum.de/index.php?id=545&tx_paintingdb_pi[detail]=181
Art.: Stifterrelief.
(Zugriff am 26.08.14)

www.bayerische.staatsoper.de/729---service-geschichte-geschichte_oper.html
Art.: Bayerische Staatsoper: Geschichte der Oper in München.
(Zugriff am 26.08.14)

www.bayerische-staatszeitung.de/staatszeitung/unser-bayern/detail ansicht-unser-bayern/artikel/zitherklaenge-gegen-den-schamlosen-bauchtanz.html?tx_felogin_pi1[forgot]=1
Bergmann, Rudolf Maria: Zitherklänge gegen den schamlosen Bauchtanz.
(Zugriff am 01.04.14)

www.bayern-france.info/pdf/Kapitel_3_Beitrag_1_neu.pdf
Malisch, Kurt: Pfalzgraf Wolfgang von Zweibrücken und Neuburg und die französischen Hugenotten. Le comte palatin Wolfgang de Deux-Ponts et Neubourg et les huguenots français.
(Zugriff am 26.08.14)

www.deutsche-biographie.de/sfz70317.html
Heigel, Karl Theodor von: Karl Theodor, Prinz von Baiern.
(Zugriff am 26.08.14)

www.hdbg.de/ludwig-der-bayer/
Art.: Bayerische Landesausstellung 2014. Kaiser Ludwig der Bayer.
(Zugriff am 26.08.14)

www.hdbg.de/parlament/content/persDetail.php?id=2665
Art.: Bayern, Carl Theodor Maximilian Prinz von Bayern.
(Zugriff am 28.02.14)

www.hdbg.de/portraitgalerie/gemaelde-6787.php

ANHANG
Literaturauswahl

Art.: Bildnis des Herzogs Georg des Reichen von Bayern-Landshut.
(Zugriff am 26.08.14)

www.hdbg.de/bavaria2003/de/c_vergro/c05_07/text.htm
Art.: Hausvertrag von Pavia. Ausfertigung für die Pfalzgrafen mit Majestätssiegel Kaiser Ludwigs des Bayern.
(Zugriff am 26.08.14)

www.hdbg.de/frauen/fbd1-5c.htm
Art.: Isabeau de Bavière.
(Zugriff am 26.08.14)

www.hdbg.de/bayern-italien/bayern-italien_storielle_02.php
Skoruppa, Ralf: Der „Bucentaur" im Würmsee.
(Zugriff am 26.08.14)

www.hdbg.eu/koenigreich/web/index.php/themen/index/herrscher_id/7/id/56
Art.: Die königliche Familie in der Zeit Ludwigs III.
(Zugriff am 26.08.14)

www.hdbg.eu/kloster/web/index.php/detail/geschichte?id=KS0003
Lankes, Christian: Altomünster – Die Frauen mit der Krone.
(Zugriff am 26.08.14)

www.hdbg.eu/kloster/web/index.php/detail/geschichte?id=KS0323
Scherr, Laura: Die Augustinereremiten in Ramsau bei Haag – Reformation und Gegenreformation.
(Zugriff am 26.08.14)

www.historisches-lexikon-bayerns.de/artikel/artikel_45034
Burmeister, Enno: Alter Hof, München.
(Zugriff am 26.08.14)

www.historisches-lexikon-bayerns.de/artikel/artikel_45352
Immler, Gerhard: Wittelsbachische Primogeniturordnung, 1506.
(Zugriff am 26.08.14)

www.ingolstadt.de/stadtmuseum/scheuerer/ausstell/ludw7-00.htm
Schönewald, Dr. Beatrix: Herzog Ludwig VII. von Bayern-Ingolstadt. Ausstellung im Stadtmuseum Ingolstadt, 1997.
(Zugriff am 26.08.2014)

www.residenz-muenchen.de/deutsch/museum/ahnen.htm
Art.: Residenzmuseum. Ahnengalerie, Porzellankabinett.
(Zugriff am 26.08.14)

www.residenz-muenchen-blog.de/?p=1655
Quaeitzsch, Christian: Zum Max Emanuel-Jahr, Teil I: Kleiner Sonnenschein? Kindheit und Erziehung eines Kurprinzen im 17. Jh., 2012.
(Zugriff am 26.08.14)

www.schloesser.bayern.de/deutsch/schloss/objekte/kelheim.htm
Art.: Befreiungshalle Kelheim.
(Zugriff am 26.08.14)

www.schloss-benrath.de/entdecken/schloss-und-schlosspark/
Art.: Schloss und Schlosspark.
(Zugriff am 26.08.14)

www.schloss-heidelberg.de/schloss-garten/garten/hortus-palatinus/
Art.: Ein italienischer Garten in Heidelberg. Der Hortus Palatinus.
(Zugriff am 26.08.14)

www.schloss-nymphenburg.de/deutsch/p-burgen/magdalen.htm
Art.: Parkburgen im Schlosspark Nymphenburg. Magdalenenklause.
(Zugriff am 26.08.14)

www.schloss-schwetzingen.de/garten/anlage/moschee/
Art.: Ein Sinnbild für Toleranz. Die Moschee.
(Zugriff am 26.08.14)

Bildquellen

Prolog

19–27 Kloster Scheyern,
Foto: Anton Brandl, München

Kapitel 1

33 **links** Original: Landesmuseum
Mainz, Kath. 2000 Bd. 4, S. 203
(Griff nach der Krone)

33 **rechts** GDKE, Ursula Rudischer
(Landesmuseum Mainz)

34/35 Grundschule Gammelsdorf

36 **links** Bayerische Verwaltung der
staatlichen Schlösser, Gärten und Seen,
München, Residenz München, Ahnengalerie, R.4, *Inv.-Nr. ResMü.Gw0083*

36 **rechts** Kunsthistorisches Museum
der Stadt Wien, *Inv.-Nr. SK XIII 1*

37 Bayerische Verwaltung der
staatlichen Schlösser, Gärten und Seen,
München, *Inv.-Nr. BSV.WA 156*

38 Stadt Nürnberg (Bildarchiv Foto
Marburg)

39 Bayerisches Nationalmuseum,
München, *Inv.-Nr. MA 957,
Foto-Nr. D28710*

40 Münchner Stadtmuseum,
Inv.-Nr. G-P964, Sammlung
Graphik/Plakat/Gemälde

41 Münchner Stadtmuseum,
Inv.-Nr. G-P 958, Sammlung
Graphik/Plakat/Gemälde

42 **links** und 43 Bayerisches Hauptstaatsarchiv, Geheimes Hausarchiv,
München, *Inv.-Nr. 2402/2*

42 **rechts** Bayerisches Hauptstaatsarchiv, München, *Inv.-Nr. 2402/1*

45 Stadtarchiv Ingolstadt,
Graphische Sammlung V/1376

46 Stadtarchiv Ingolstadt, Leihgabe
der Münsterpfarrei Ingolstadt

47 British Library, Foto: akg-images

48 Bayerisches Nationalmuseum,
München, *Inv.-Nr. 936*

49 Heimathaus der Stadt Lauingen,
Foto: mwi

52 Augsburg, Kunstsammlungen
und Museen, *Inv.-Nr. G 2850-52*

53 Bayerische
Staatsgemäldesammlungen,
München, *Inv.-Nr. 3518*,
Foto: Blauel/Gnamm – Artothek

54 Alt-Moosburg.de: Hochaltar
Kastulus Münster Moosburg,
Foto: Karl A. Bauer

55 Blutenburg, Schlosskapelle

57 **links** Bayerische Verwaltung der
staatlichen Schlösser, Gärten und Seen,
München, *Inv.-Nr. ResMüSch. 233*

57 **rechts** Bayerisches
Nationalmuseum, München,
Inv.-Nr. MA 1989, Foto-Nr.: D15368

58/59 Albertina, Wien,
Inv.-Nr. 25247

60 Bayerische
Staatsgemäldesammlungen,
München, *Inv.-Nr. 2444*

61 Bayerische Staatsbibliothek,
Hofbibliothek, Cgm 908, fo. 41

62/63 Bayerisches Hauptstaatsarchiv,
München, Bayerische Landschaft
Urkunden 1506 VII 8

64 Götz Frhr. v. Pölnitz, Denkmale
und Dokumente zur Geschichte der
Ludwig-Maximilians-Universität
Ingolstadt – Landshut – München,
München 1942, Tafel III

65 Universitätsarchiv München, D-V-2

66 **links** und 66 **rechts** Privatbesitz

67 Bayerisches Nationalmuseum,
München, *Inv.-Nr. R 6685*

68 Bayerische Verwaltung der
staatlichen Schlösser, Gärten und
Seen, München, Burg Trausnitz,
Landshut, Söllerstube R.27, *Inv.-Nr.
LaT. G 11*

69 Bayerische
Staatsgemäldesammlungen,
München, Alte Pinakothek,
Foto: Bayer&Mitko – Artothek

70 Bayerische Verwaltung der
staatlichen Schlösser, Gärten und
Seen, München, Burghausen,
Inv.-Nr. Bgh.P0012

71 Bayerische Staatsbibliothek,
Clm. 28812, fol 1r

Kapitel 2

75 **oben links** Bayerisches
Nationalmuseum, München,
Inv.-Nr. D28189, Foto-Nr. D28189

75 **oben rechts** Bayerisches
Nationalmuseum, München,
Inv.-Nr. D28197, Foto-Nr. D28197

75 **unten links** Bayerisches
Nationalmuseum, München,
Inv.-Nr. D28193, Foto-Nr. D28193

75 **unten rechts** Bayerisches
Nationalmuseum, München,
Inv.-Nr. D28192, Foto-Nr. D28192

77 **oben links** Bayerisches
Nationalmuseum, München,
Inv.-Nr. D28191, Foto-Nr. D28191

77 **oben rechts** Bayerisches
Nationalmuseum, München,
Inv.-Nr. D28194, Foto-Nr. D28194

77 **unten links** Bayerisches
Nationalmuseum, München,
Inv.-Nr. D28196, Foto-Nr. D28196

77 **unten rechts** Bayerisches
Nationalmuseum, München,
Inv.-Nr. D28187, Foto-Nr. D28187

78 Bayerische Verwaltung der staatlichen Schlösser, Gärten und Seen, München, Schloss Dachau, Decke, Festsaal

79 Bayerische Verwaltung der staatlichen Schlösser, Gärten und Seen, München, *Inv.-Nr. B I a 59* (WAF)

80 f. Privatbesitz, Foto: Anton Brandl,
München

82 f. Bayerische Staatsbibliothek,
München, 2 L.impr.membr. 63,
fol. 36v - 37 r

84 Bayerisches Nationalmuseum,
München, *Inv.-Nr. MA 1765,
Foto-Nr. D30064*

85 Bayerisches Nationalmuseum,
München, *Inv.-Nr. MA 1766,
Foto-Nr. D30065*

ANHANG
Bildquellen

87 Bayerische Staatsgemäldesammlungen, München, Alte Pinakothek, *Inv.-Nr. 2448*, Foto: Blauel/Gnamm – Artothek

88 Bayerisches Nationalmuseum, München, *Inv.-Nr. R 579*, *Foto-Nr. 58502*

89 Bayerisches Nationalmuseum, München. *Inv.-Nr. G 739*, *Foto-Nr. D30063*

91 Bayerische Staatsgemäldesammlungen, München, Alte Pinakothek, Foto: Bayer&Mitko – Artothek

93 Bayerische Staatsbibliothek, München, Cod. con. 429, fol. 1v

94 Wittelsbacher Ausgleichsfonds, München, Foto: Guido Burkhardt

95 Bayerische Staatsbibliothek, München, Mus.ms. A II

96f. Bayerische Verwaltung der staatlichen Schlösser, Gärten und Seen, München, Foto: Anton Brandl, München

99 Bayerische Staatsbibliothek, München, Rar. 636

101 Staatliche Graphische Sammlung, München, *Inv.-Nr. 44034 Z*

104 Archiv Pfarrei St. Peter, München, Wappenabbildungen aus: ASP vorl. Nr. 4727: Corporis Christi Fraternitas, Liber Cimeliorum No. 2 „Omnes Reges", Lfzt.: 1645-1190

105 Bayerische Staatsgemäldesammlungen, München, Alte Pinakothek, *Inv.-Nr. 1025*

107 Bayerisches Nationalmuseum, München, R 951. Wittelsbacher Familienalbum 1578

109 Bayerische Staatsgemäldesammlungen, München, *Inv.-Nr. 2472*

110 Bayerische Verwaltung der staatlichen Schlösser, Gärten und Seen, München, Residenz München, Steinzimmer, *Inv.-Nr. ResMü.M 140, Kat. 6*

111 Bayerische Verwaltung der staatlichen Schlösser, Gärten und Seen, München, Residenzmuseum, Zimmer der Kirche, *Inv.-Nr. ResMü.P.II.104*

112/113 Bildarchiv Bayerischer Landtag, Foto: Rolf Poss

114/115 Bayerische Staatsgemäldesammlungen, München, *Inv.-Nr. 2309*, Foto: Blauel/Gnamm – Artothek

117 Kloster Scheyern

118/119 Bayerisches Armeemuseum, Ingolstadt, *Inv.-Nr. 0564-2004*

121 Pfarr- und Wallfahrtskirche Maria Ramersdorf, München

123 Kunsthistorisches Museum, Wien, *Inv.-Nr. GG 8034*

125 Bayerisches Nationalmuseum, München, *Inv.-Nr. R 7386*

127 Bayerische Verwaltung der staatlichen Schlösser, Gärten und Seen, München, Neues Schloss Schleißheim, Bayerische Staatsgemäldesammlungen München, *Inv.-Nr. 2569.*

128/129 Heeresgeschichtliches Museum/Militärhistorisches Institut, Arsenal, Wien

Kapitel 3

132 Archiv Pfarrei St. Peter, München, Wappenabbildungen aus: ASP vorl. Nr. 4727: Corporis Christi Fraternitas, Liber Cimeliorum No. 2 „Omnes Reges", Lfzt.: 1645-1190

133 Bayerische Staatsgemäldesammlungen, München, *Inv.-Nr. 2570*

134 Foto: Erzbischöfliches Ordinariat München, Hauptabteilung Kunst (Wolf-Christian von der Mülbe)

135 Kloster Scheyern, Foto: Anton Brandl, München

136 Bayerische Staatsgemäldesammlungen, München, Alte Pinakothek, *Inv.-Nr. 3187*, Foto: bpk, Nicole Wilhelms

137 Kurfürstensaal des ehemaligen Zisterzienserklosters zu Fürstenfeld, heute Fachhochschule zur Ausbildung von Kommissaren für die Schutz- und Kriminalpolizei. Foto: Philipp Schönborn, München

139 Preußischer Kulturbesitz, Foto: bpk.

141 Bayerische Staatsgemäldesammlungen, München, *Inv.-Nr. 7356*

142 Staats- und Stadtbibliothek, Augsburg.

143 Staatliche Graphische Sammlung, München, *Inv.-Nr. 228599 D*

144/145 Wittelsbacher Ausgleichsfonds, München, *Inv.-Nr. B I 363*

147 Staatliche Graphische Sammlung, München, *Inv.-Nr. 228406 D*

149 Bayerische Verwaltung der staatlichen Schlösser, Gärten und Seen, München

152 Archiv Pfarrei St. Peter, München, Wappenabbildungen aus: ASP vorl. Nr. 4727: Corporis Christi Fraternitas, Liber Cimeliorum No. 2 „Omnes Reges", Lfzt.: 1645-1190

153 Bayerische Verwaltung der staatlichen Schlösser, Gärten und Seen, München, Residenz München, *Inv.-Nr. ResMü.G 433*

155 Bayerische Staatsgemäldesammlungen, München, Schloss Nymphenburg, *Inv.-Nr. 7502*

155/157 Bayerische Staatsgemäldesammlungen, München, *Inv.-Nr. 2580*

159 Bayerische Verwaltung der staatlichen Schlösser, Gärten und Seen, München, Miniaturenkabinett R. 62, *Inv.-Nr. ResMü. G 919*

160 Bayerische Verwaltung der staatlichen Schlösser, Gärten und Seen, München, Herrenchiemsee, Ludwig II.-Museum, *Inv.-Nr. 983 (WAF)*

161 Wittelsbacher Ausgleichsfonds, München, *Inv.-Nr. BI a 21*

162 Bayerisches Nationalmuseum, München, *Inv.-Nr. T 3938*

163 Bayerische Verwaltung der staatlichen Schlösser, Gärten und Seen, München, Residenz München, *Inv.-Nr. ResMü. G979*

164 Bayerische Staatsgemäldesammlungen, München, *Inv.-Nr. 2480*

165 Bayerische Verwaltung der staatlichen Schlösser, Gärten und Seen, München, Schloss Nymphenburg, Schlafzimmer, R. 12, *Inv.-Nr. Ny. G 21*

166/167 Münchner Stadtmuseum, *Inv.-Nr. P 1505*, Sammlung Graphik/Plakat/Gemälde

169 Bayerische Verwaltung der staatlichen Schlösser, Gärten und Seen, München, Residenz München, *Inv.-Nr. 1978/212*

170 Benediktinerabtei Ettal

171 Frans Hals Museum, Haarlem

172 Archiv Pfarrei St. Peter, München, Wappenabbildungen aus: ASP vorl. Nr. 4727: Corporis Christi Fraternitas, Liber Cimeliorum No. 2 „Omnes Reges", Lfzt.: 1645-1190

173 Bayerische Verwaltung der staatlichen Schlösser, Gärten und Seen, München, Schloss Nymphenburg, Südflügel, *Inv.-Nr. G 112*

175 Bayerische Staatsgemäldesammlungen, München, Schloss Schleißheim, *Inv.-Nr. 2483*, Foto: bpk

176 Bayerische Verwaltung der staatlichen Schlösser, Gärten und Seen, München, Nymphenburg/Amalienburg, *Inv.-Nr. NyAm.G0025*

177 Bayerische Verwaltung der staatlichen Schlösser, Gärten und Seen, München, Nymphenburg, *Inv.-Nr. Ny.G0189*

179 Bayerische Verwaltung der staatlichen Schlösser, Gärten und Seen, München, Nymphenburg/Amalienburg, *Inv.-Nr. NyAm.G27*

180/181 Historisches Museum Frankfurt, *Inv.-Nr. C01140*, Foto: Horst Ziegenfusz

182/183 Historisches Museum Frankfurt, *Inv.-Nr. C01148*, Foto: Horst Ziegenfusz

184 Archiv Pfarrei St. Peter, München, Wappenabbildungen aus: ASP vorl. Nr. 4727: Corporis Christi Fraternitas, Liber Cimeliorum No. 2 „Omnes Reges", Lfzt.: 1645-1190

185 Wittelsbacher Ausgleichsfonds, München, *Inv.-Nr. B I a 406*

186/187 Münchner Stadtmuseum, *Inv.-Nr. GM-37/i771*

189 Bayerische Verwaltung der staatlichen Schlösser, Gärten und Seen, München, Residenz München, *Inv.-Nr. ResMü.G 57*

191 Bayerische Staatsgemäldesammlungen, München, *Inv.-Nr. 27153*

192/193 Bayerische Verwaltung der staatlichen Schlösser, Gärten und Seen, München, Residenz München, *Inv.-Nr. ResMü.G 36*

194/195 Wittelsbacher Ausgleichsfonds, München, *Inv.-Nr. B I 579*

196 Deutsches Jagd- und Fischereimuseum, München

197 Wittelsbacher Ausgleichsfonds, München, *Inv.-Nr. B I a 72*

198 Bayerische Verwaltung der staatlichen Schlösser, Gärten und Seen, München, Residenz München, *Inv.-Nr. ResMü.G 1241*

199 Bayerische Verwaltung der staatlichen Schlösser, Gärten und Seen, München, Residenz München, *Inv.-Nr. ResMü.G 1242*

200 Bayerische Verwaltung der staatlichen Schlösser, Gärten und Seen, München, Residenz München, Kurfürstenzimmer, *Inv.-Nr. ResMü. G 55*

201 Bayerische Verwaltung der staatlichen Schlösser, Gärten und Seen, München, Schloss Nymphenburg, *Inv.-Nr. Ny.G 11*

202 Münchner Stadtmuseum, *Inv.-Nr. G-IIe/115*, Sammlung Graphik/Plakat/Gemälde

203 Bayerische Verwaltung der staatlichen Schlösser, Gärten und Seen, München, *Inv.-Nr. Res.MüG 168*

205 Kloster Andechs

207 Bayerische Staatsgemäldesammlungen, München, Diözesanmuseum Freising, *Inv.-Nr. 4279*

209 Dombibliothek Freising

211 Bayerische Verwaltung der staatlichen Schlösser, Gärten und Seen, München, Schloss Nymphenburg, *Inv.-Nr. ResMü.G 168*

213 Bayerische Verwaltung der staatlichen Schlösser, Gärten und Seen, München, *Inv.-Nr. Res. Mü.G 440*

214/215 f. Schloss Augustusburg, Brühl

217 Schloss Moos, Graf von und zu Arco-Zinneberg

218/219 Historisches Museum, Frankfurt, *Inv.-Nr. C01139*, Foto: Horst Ziegenfusz

220/221 Schloss Augustusburg, Brühl

222 Schloss Falkenlust, Brühl

223 Museo di Ca Rezzonico, Venedig

225 Diözesanmuseum Freising, *Inv.-Nr. D 77127*

Kapitel 4

229 Bayerisches Nationalmuseum, München, *Inv.-Nr. 3608*

231 oben Bayerisches Nationalmuseum, München, *Inv.-Nr. 3609*

231 unten Bayerisches Nationalmuseum, München, *Inv.-Nr. 3610*

232 Bayerisches Hauptstaatsarchiv, Geheimes Haus, B3 B262v

233 Österreichische Nationalbibliothek, Cod. 2899, fol. 10r

235 Hl.-Geist-Kirche, Heidelberg, Foto: akg-images

239 Badische Landesbibliothek, Karlsruhe, Kat. 2000, S. 285

238 Landesarchiv Baden-Württemberg, Generallandesarchiv Karlsruhe, 67/1057, fol. 41r

239 Universitätsbibliothek Heidelberg, Graphische Sammlung, A 701

240 Österreichische Nationalbibliothek, Cod. 2899, fol. 42r

241 Kurpfälzisches Museum der Stadt Heidelberg, *Inv.-Nr. S 40*

243 links Museum der Stadt Regensburg, *Inv.-Nr. G 1959/3b*

243 rechts Kunsthistorisches Museum, Wien, *Inv.-Nr. GG 8177*, Schloss Ambras

244/245 Bayerische Staatsgemäldesammlungen, München, Foto: Bayer&Mitko – Artothek

246 Bayerische Staatsgemäldesammlungen, München, *Inv.-Nr. 2450*, Foto: Bayer&Mitko – Artothek

247 Bayerische Staatsgemäldesammlungen, Staatsgalerie Flämische Barockmalerei, *Inv.-Nr. 2449*, Foto: bpk

248 Stiftung Preußischer Kulturbesitz, Staatliche Museen zu Berlin, Kupferstichkabinett (798-10)

249 Badische Landesbibliothek, Karlsruhe, *Sig. 42 c 38 RH*

251 Wittelsbacher Ausgleichsfonds, München, *Inv.-Nr. B I a 63*

252 Historisches Museum der Pfalz Speyer, *HM_1932_58*

253 Universitäts- und Landesbibliothek, Darmstadt, Hs 1971, Bd. IV, fol. 139r

255 Universitäts- und Landesbibliothek, Darmstadt, Hs 1971, Bd. V, fol. 172r

256/257 Frans Hals Museum, Haarlem

258/259 Kurpfälzisches Museum der Stadt Heidelberg, *Inv.-Nr. G 1822*

261 Kurpfälzisches Museum der Stadt Heidelberg, *Inv.-Nr. L 323*

262 Reiss-Engelhorn-Museen Mannheim, *Inv.-Nr. O 458*, Foto: Jean Christen

263 Historisches Museum der Pfalz Speyer, *HM_1926_70 (BS_2780)*

265 Musée National des Châteaux de Versailles et de Trianon, Foto: akg-images / Visioars

267 Bayerische Staatsgemäldesammlungen, München, *Inv.-Nr. 402*, Foto: Blauel/Gnamm – Artothek

268 Wittelsbacher Ausgleichsfonds, München, *Inv.-Nr. B I a 66*

269 Bayerische Verwaltung der staatlichen Schlösser, Gärten und Seen, München, *Inv.-Nr. HöS.G 41*

271 links Reiss-Engelhorn-Museen Mannheim, *Inv.-Nr. O 230*, Foto: Jean Christen

271 rechts Reiss-Engelhorn-Museen Mannheim, *Inv.-Nr. O 231*, Foto: Jean Christen

272/273 Privatbesitz, Foto: akg-images

275 Kurpfälzisches Museum Heidelberg, *Inv.-Nr. G 1861*

278 Archiv Pfarrei St. Peter, München, Wappenabbildungen aus: ASP vorl. Nr. 4727: Corporis Christi Fraternitas, Liber Cimeliorum No. 2 „Omnes Reges", Lfzt.: 1645-1190

279 Bayerische Staatsgemäldesammlungen, München, Alte Pinakothek, *Inv.-Nr.181*, Foto: Blauel/Gnamm – Artothek

281 Reiss-Engelhorn-Museen Mannheim, *Inv.-Nr. RMM 1966/2*, Foto: Jean Christen

283 links Kurpfälzisches Museum der Stadt Heidelberg, *Inv.-Nr. G 20*

283 rechts Kurpfälzisches Museum der Stadt Heidelberg, *Inv.-Nr. G 19*

284 Gesellschaft der Freunde Mannheims und der ehemaligen Kurpfalz Mannheimer Altertumsverein von 1859, *Kat. Nr. A 25*, Foto: Jean Christen

285 Reiss-Engelhorn-Museen Mannheim, *Inv.-Nr. A 57,1*, Foto: Jean Christen

287 Kurpfälzisches Museum der Stadt Heidelberg, *Inv.-Nr. G 1642*

288 Albertina, Wien, *Inv.-Nr. 15077*

289 Paris, Elysée-Palast, Stiftung Schloss und Park Benrath

290 Generallandesarchiv Karlsruhe, *Inv.-Nr. 67 Nr. 1057*

291 Reiss-Engelhorn-Museen Mannheim, *Inv.-Nr. Mh 9801*, Foto: Jean Christen

292 Kurpfälzisches Museum, Heidelberg, *Inv.-Nr. GM 120*

293 Bayerisches Nationalmuseum, München, *Inv.-Nr. R 5783*

295 Pfarrei Ramsau bei Haag

296/297 Bayerisches Nationalmuseum, München, *Inv.-Nr. R 5802*

298/299 Staatliche Graphische Sammlung, München, *Inv.-Nr. 32116 Z*

300 Privatbesitz, Foto: Anton Brandl, München

301 Stiftung Karlsberger Hof, Homburg/Saar

302 Bayerische Staatsgemäldesammlungen, München, *Inv.-Nr. 2498*, Foto: Blauel/Gramm – Artothek

303 Kurpfälzisches Museum der Stadt Heidelberg, *Inv.-Nr. E 6033*

305 links Bayerisches Armeemuseum, Ingolstadt, *Inv.-Nr. R 6160*

305 rechts Zweibrücker Kulturgutstiftung Gehrlein-Fuchs

306/307 Stiftung Karlsberger Hof, Homburg/Saar

309 Capitol, Washington

310/311 Stadtmuseum Zweibrücken, *Inv.-Nr. 45*

313–321 Privatbesitz, Foto: Anton Brandl, München

322 Münchner Stadtmuseum, *Inv.-Nr. G-MII/113*, Sammlung Graphik/Plakat/Gemälde

323 Münchner Stadtmuseum, *Inv.-Nr. G-MII/3434*, Sammlung Graphik/Plakat/Gemälde

324 Privatbesitz, Foto: Anton Brandl, München

325 Schloss St. Emmeram, Regensburg, *Inv.-Nr. 2720*

326 Privatbesitz, Foto: Anton Brandl, München

327 Schloss St. Emmeram, Regensburg, *Inv.-Nr. St.E. 4246*

328–331 Privatbesitz, Foto: Anton Brandl, München

333 Allgemeines Krankenhaus, Wien, Foto: akg-images

334 f. Privatbesitz, Foto: Anton Brandl, München

336 f. Schloss Ringberg

Kapitel 5

342 Archiv Pfarrei St. Peter, München, Wappenabbildungen aus: ASP vorl. Nr. 4727: Corporis Christi Fraternitas, Liber Cimeliorum No. 2 „Omnes Reges", Lfzt.: 1645–1190

343 Bayerische Staatsgemäldesammlungen, München, Alte Pinakothek, *Inv.-Nr. 1021*, Foto: Blauel/Gnamm – Artothek

345 Privatbesitz

347 links Hessische Hausstiftung, Schlossmuseum Darmstadt, *Inv.-Nr. DA H 21190*

347 rechts Hessische Hausstiftung, Schlossmuseum Darmstadt, *Inv.-Nr. DA H 21191*

349 und **351** Foto: akg-images

353 Kloster Kaisheim

354/355 Stiftung Preußischer Kulturbesitz – Staatliche Museen zu Berlin, *Inv.-Nr. MV2561*

357 Musée National du Château de Versailles, Foto: bpk

358 Bayerisches Nationalmuseum, München, Foto: akg-images

359 RMN-Grand Palais, Malmaison, Chateaux de Malmaison et Bois-Préau, Foto: bpk, Gérard Blot

360 Münchner Stadtmuseum, *Inv.-Nr. GR-A 89 (Kat. 305)*

361 Münchner Stadtmuseum, *Inv.-Nr. GM 67/257*, Sammlung Graphik/Plakat/Gemälde,

362 Musée National du Château de Versailles, Paris

363 Historisches Museum Regensburg, *Inv.-Nr. K 1979/1*

365 Historisches Museum, Wien, *Inv.-Nr. 132 553*, Foto: akg-images/ De Agostini Pict.Lib.

366 Privatbesitz

366/367 Wittelsbacher Ausgleichsfonds, München, *Inv.-Nr. B II 146/10*

368 Münchner Stadtmuseum, *Inv.-Nr. G-P 1134*, Sammlung Graphik/Plakat/Gemälde

368/369 Privatbesitz

370 Münchner Stadtmuseum, *Inv.-Nr. GR-Z 533*, Sammlung Graphik/Plakat/Gemälde

370/371 Münchner Stadtmuseum, *Inv.-Nr. GR-M 1/1883*, Sammlung Graphik/Plakat/Gemälde

373 Münchner Stadtmuseum, *Inv.-Nr. GM IIa/30*, Sammlung Graphik/Plakat/Gemälde

374 Bayerische Staatsbibliothek, München, *Inv.-Nr. 170686*, Foto: bpk

375 Galerie Koller, Zürich, Foto: Artothek

376 Münchner Stadtmuseum, *Inv.-Nr. GR-M/I 2067*, Sammlung Graphik/Plakat/Gemälde

377 Privatbesitz, Foto: Anton Brandl, München

380 Archiv Pfarrei St. Peter, München, Wappenabbildungen aus: ASP vorl. Nr. 4727: Corporis Christi Fraternitas, Liber Cimeliorum No. 2 „Omnes Reges", Lfzt.: 1645-1190

381 Bayerische Verwaltung der staatlichen Schlösser, Gärten und Seen, München, Schloss Nymphenburg, *Inv.-Nr. B Ia 236 (WAF)*

382 Privatbesitz, Foto: Anton Brandl, München

383 Bayerische Staatsgemäldesammlungen, *Inv.-Nr. L 162*, Foto: Artothek

384 Münchner Stadtmuseum, *Inv.-Nr. GM-IIb/6*, Sammlung Graphik/Plakat/Gemälde

385 Antiquariat Robert Wölfle, München

386/387 Münchner Stadtmuseum, *Inv.-Nr. G-IIIc/8*, Sammlung Graphik/Plakat/Gemälde

389 Wittelsbacher Ausgleichsfonds, München, *Inv.-Nr. B I a 242*

390 f. Privatbesitz, Foto: Anton Brandl, München

392 Staatliche Münzsammlung, München, Foto: Nicolai Kästner

393 Privatbesitz, Foto: Anton Brandl, München

394 Bayerische Staatsgemäldesammlungen, München, *Inv.-Nr. WAF 784*

395 Bayerische Staatsgemäldesammlungen, München, *Inv.-Nr. WAF 142*, Foto: Bayer&Mitko – Artothek

396 Privatbesitz, Foto: Anton Brandl, München

396/397 Münchner Stadtmuseum, *Inv.-Nr. GR-Ic/87*, Sammlung Graphik/Plakat/Gemälde

398 links Münchner Stadtmuseum, *Inv.-Nr. GR-P 2661*, Sammlung Graphik/Plakat/Gemälde

398 rechts Münchner Stadtmuseum, *Inv.-Nr. GR-P 2664*, Sammlung Graphik/Plakat/Gemälde

399 links Privatbesitz

399 rechts König Otto von Griechenland-Museum der Gemeinde Ottobrunn, Prof. Dr. Jan Murken, *Katalog-Abb. 83 a*

400 links Münchner Stadtmuseum, *Inv.-Nr. GR-P 2663*, Sammlung Graphik/Plakat/Gemälde

400 rechts Münchner Stadtmuseum, *Inv.-Nr. GR-32/365*, Sammlung Graphik/Plakat/Gemälde

401 links Münchner Stadtmuseum, *Inv.-Nr. GR-M I/2053*, Sammlung Graphik/Plakat/Gemälde

401 rechts Münchner Stadtmuseum, *Inv.-Nr. GR-Greis I/19*, Sammlung Graphik/Plakat/Gemälde

402/403 Münchner Stadtmuseum, *Inv.-Nr. G-P 1567*, Sammlung Graphik/Plakat/Gemälde

404 Münchner Stadtmuseum, *Inv.-Nr. GM-P 11638*, Sammlung Graphik/Plakat/Gemälde

405 Münchner Stadtmuseum, *Inv.-Nr. GR-P 664*, Sammlung Graphik/Plakat/Gemälde

407 Münchner Stadtmuseum, *Inv.-Nr. 29/1034*

408 Architekturmuseum der Technischen Universität München

409 Museen der Stadt Regensburg, Foto: Jochen Remmer, Artothek

410 Bayerische Staatsbibliothek, München, *Inv.-Nr. Hbks/F 18 o*

411 Haus der Bayerischen Geschichte, Augsburg, Foto: Philipp Massmann, München

412 links Bayerisches Nationalmuseum, München, *Inv.-Nr. L 97/187. 1-2, Foto-Nr. D52005*

412 rechts Bayerisches Nationalmuseum, München, *Inv.-Nr. L 97/186.1-2, Foto-Nr. D76855*

413 Porzellan Manufaktur Nymphenburg, Firmenarchiv

414 Münchner Stadtmuseum, *Inv.-Nr. GR-M II/196*, Sammlung Graphik/Plakat/Gemälde

415 Münchner Stadtmuseum, *Inv.-Nr. G-51/402*, Sammlung Graphik/Plakat/Gemälde

416 Münchner Stadtmuseum, *Inv.-Nr. GR-Z 680*, Sammlung Graphik/Plakat/Gemälde

417 Münchner Stadtmuseum, *Inv.-Nr. P 13682*, Sammlung Graphik/Plakat/Gemälde

418 Bayerische Verwaltung der staatlichen Schlösser, Gärten und Seen, München, Schloss Nymphenburg, Hauptschloss, R.15, *Inv.-Nr. Ny.G 53*

419 Bayerische Verwaltung der staatlichen Schlösser, Gärten und Seen, München, Schloss Nymphenburg, *Inv.-Nr. Ny.G 44*

420 links Bayerisches Nationalmuseum, München, *Inv.-Nr. R 6201*, Foto: Peter Haag-Kirchner, Speyer

420 rechts Bayerisches Nationalmuseum, München, *Inv.-Nr. T 5843, Foto-Nr. D73545*

421 Bayerische Verwaltung der staatlichen Schlösser, Gärten und Seen, München, Schloss Nymphenburg, Maserzimmer, R.16, *Inv.-Nr. Ny.G 58*

422 Foto: Hannes Heindl

423 Bayerische Verwaltung der staatlichen Schlösser, Gärten und Seen, München, Residenz München, *Inv.Nr. Res. Mü G 1275*

425 Bayerische Staatsgemäldesammlungen, Neue Pinakothek, München, *Inv.-Nr. 7935*, Foto: Blauel/Gnamm – Artothek

426/427 Bayerische Staatsgemäldesammlungen, Neue Pinakothek, München, *Inv.-Nr. 352*, Foto: Blauel/Gnamm – Artothek

428 links Bayerisches Armeemuseum, Ingolstadt, *Inv.-Nr. G 625*

428 rechts Stiftung Preußische Schlösser und Gärten, Potsdam-Sanssouci, *Slg.-Nr. 2041*

429 König Otto von Griechenland-Museum der Gemeinde Ottobrunn, Prof. Dr. Jan Murkens, *Katalog-Abb. 76*

430 König Otto von Griechenland-Museum der Gemeinde Ottobrunn, Prof. Dr. Jan Murkens, *Katalog-Abb. 60 a*

431 König Otto von Griechenland-Museum der Gemeinde Ottobrunn, Prof. Dr. Jan Murkens, *Katalog-Abb. 56*

432 BayHStA, GHA, Wittelsbacher Bildersammlung, Prinz Adalbert 5/9 b

433–444 Privatbesitz, Foto: Anton Brandl, München

445–449 Privatbesitz

452 Archiv Pfarrei St. Peter, München, Wappenabbildungen aus: ASP vorl. Nr. 4727: Corporis Christi Fraternitas, Liber Cimeliorum No. 2 „Omnes Reges", Lfzt.: 1645-1190

453 Bayerische Staatsgemäldesammlungen, München, *Inv.-Nr. 5194*, Foto: Bayer&Mitko – Artothek

454/455 Wittelsbacher Ausgleichsfonds, München, *Inv.-Nr. B I 427*

456/457 Münchner Stadtmuseum, *Inv.-Nr. G-P 1579*, Sammlung Graphik/Plakat/Gemälde

458 Geheimes Hausarchiv, Wittelsbacher Bildersammlung, Königin Marie III 6/10

459 Privatbesitz, Hannes Heindl

460 Privatbesitz

461 Stiftung Preußige Schlösser und Gärten, Berlin-Brandenburg, Foto: akg-images

462/463 Wittelsbacher Ausgleichsfonds, München, *Inv.-Nr. B I 426*

464 Münchner Stadtmuseum, *Inv.-Nr. G Z 993*, Sammlung Graphik/Plakat/Gemälde

465 Münchner Stadtmuseum, *Inv.-Nr. G-Z 947*, Sammlung Graphik/Plakat/Gemälde

466 Wittelsbacher Ausgleichsfonds, München, Kgl. Bayer. Familienbibliothek, Artes 15 c (Roseninsel-Album, 1853), Blatt 5.

467 Privatbesitz, Hannes Heindl

469 Stiftung Maximilianeum, München, Foto: Rolf Poss

471 Stiftung Maximilianeum, München, *Inv.-Nr. 61*

472/473 Münchner Stadtmuseum, *Inv.-Nr. GM-31/50*

474 Münchner Stadtmuseum, *Inv.-Nr. GR-P 827*, Sammlung Graphik/Plakat/Gemälde

474/475 Münchner Stadtmuseum, *Inv.-Nr. G-P 824*, Sammlung Graphik/Plakat/Gemälde

478 Archiv Pfarrei St. Peter, München, Wappenabbildungen aus: ASP vorl. Nr. 4727: Corporis Christi Fraternitas, Liber Cimeliorum No. 2 „Omnes Reges", Lfzt.: 1645-1190

479 Historisches Museum der Pfalz, Speyer, Foto: Peter Haag-Kirchner

480 Bayerische Verwaltung der staatlichen Schlösser, Gärten und Seen, München, Neues Schloss Herrenchiemsee, Ludwig II.-Museum, *Inv.-Nr. L. II.-Mus. 545*

481 Bayerische Verwaltung der staatlichen Schlösser, Gärten und Seen, München, *Inv.-Nr. BSV. GNyM0889*

483 Bayerische Verwaltung der staatlichen Schlösser, Gärten und Seen, München, Neues Schloss Herrenchiemsee, Ludwig II.-Museum, *Inv.-Nr. L.II.-Mus. 550 (WAF)*

484/485 Bayerische Verwaltung der staatlichen Schlösser, Gärten und Seen, München, *Inv.-Nr. L.II.-Mus. 8, Kat. 162.*

487 Münchner Stadtmuseum, *Inv.-Nr. GR-37/292*, Sammlung Graphik/Plakat/Gemälde

488 links Bayerische Verwaltung der staatlichen Schlösser, Gärten und Seen, München, Marstallmuseum Schloss Nymphenburg, *Inv.-Nr. W 35* (WAF)

488 oben rechts Bayerische Verwaltung der staatlichen Schlösser, Gärten und Seen, München, Marstallmuseum Schloss Nymphenburg, *Inv.-Nr. W 45, Schmid Kat. 5* (WAF)

488 unten rechts Bayerische Verwaltung der staatlichen Schlösser, Gärten und Seen, München, Marstallmuseum Schloss Nymphenburg, *Inv.-Nr. W 49, Schmid Kat. 22* (WAF)

489 Bayerische Verwaltung der staatlichen Schlösser, Gärten und Seen, München, Marstallmuseum Schloss Nymphenburg, *Inv.-Nr. NyMar.G 149*

490 Politisches Archiv des Auswärtigen Amtes, Berlin, Foto: akg-images

491 Stadt Goslar

493 Stadtmuseum München, *Inv.-Nr. GM A 22*

494/495 Bayerische Verwaltung der staatlichen Schlösser, Gärten und Seen, München, Herrenchiemsee, Ludwig II.-Museum, *Inv.-Nr. L.II.u.d.Kunst 814, L.II.-Mus.102* (WAF)

496 Wittelsbacher Ausgleichsfonds, München, *Inv.-Nr. B I 512*

496/497 Bayerische Verwaltung der staatlichen Schlösser, Gärten und Seen, München, Herrenchiemsee, Ludwig II.-Museum, *Inv.-Nr. L.II., Kat. 153*

498/499 Wittelsbacher Ausgleichsfonds, München, *Inv.-Nr. B II 164*

500 Benediktinerabtei Ettal

501 Bayerische Verwaltung der staatlichen Schlösser, Gärten und Seen, München, Herrenchiemsee, Ludwig II.-Museum, *Inv.-Nr. L. II.-Mus. 126, Kat. 126* (WAF)

502 Bayerische Verwaltung der staatlichen Schlösser, Gärten und Seen, München, Herrenchiemsee, Ludwig II.-Museum, *Inv.-Nr. L. II.-Mus. 296, Kat. 896* (WAF)

503 Bayerische Verwaltung der staatlichen Schlösser, Gärten und Seen, München, Herrenchiemsee, Ludwig II.-Museum, *Inv.-Nr. LII.-Mus. 300*

504/505 Bayerische Verwaltung der staatlichen Schlösser, Gärten und Seen, München, Herrenchiemsee, Ludwig II.-Museum, *Inv.-Nr. LII.-Mus.402, Kat. 197*

506 Bayerische Verwaltung der staatlichen Schlösser, Gärten und Seen, München, Neues Schloss Herrenchiemsee, Ludwig II.-Museum, *Inv.-Nr. L.II.-Mus. 558*

507 Privatbesitz, Hannes Heindl

508 Bayerische Verwaltung der staatlichen Schlösser, Gärten und Seen, München, Residenzmuseum, *Inv.-Nr. ResMü. K II Ny 1508, Kat. IVe*

509 Bayerische Verwaltung der staatlichen Schlösser, Gärten und Seen, München, Herrenchiemsee, Ludwig II.-Museum, *Inv.-Nr. Mus. 519*

510/511 und 512 oben Privatbesitz, Hannes Heindl

512 unten Privatbesitz

513 Bayerische Verwaltung der staatlichen Schlösser, Gärten und Seen, München, Marstallmuseum Schloss Nymphenburg, *Inv.-Nr. G 1186*

514 Privatbesitz, Hannes Heindl

515 Wittelsbacher Ausgleichsfonds, München, *Inv.-Nr. B I a 442*

519 Bayerische Staatsgemäldesammlungen, München, *Inv.-Nr. 8262*

520 Privatbesitz, Foto: Anton Brandl, München

521 Wittelsbacher Ausgleichsfonds, München, *Inv.-Nr. M X c 17*

522/523 Bayerisches Armeemuseum, Ingolstadt, *Inv.-Nr. B 5644*

525 links Münchner Stadtmuseum, *Inv.-Nr. III. c /173 b*

525 rechts Privatbesitz, Foto: Anton Brandl, München

527 Privatbesitz, Johannes Fischer, München

528/529 Münchner Stadtmuseum, *Inv.-Nr. 34/572*

531 Deutsches Museum, München, *Inv.-Nr. 02100*

532/533 Wien Museum, *IN. 37.197*

534/535 Wittelsbacher Ausgleichsfonds, München, *Inv.-Nr. B I 37*

536 Wittelsbacher Ausgleichsfonds, München, *Inv.-Nr. B I a 281*

537 Wittelsbacher Ausgleichsfonds, München, *Inv.-Nr. B I a 218*

538 Wittelsbacher Ausgleichsfonds, München, *Inv.-Nr. B I a 371*

538/539 Heimatmuseum Prien am Chiemsee

541–543 Privatbesitz, Foto: Anton Brandl, München

545 Archivo Fotografico Fabbrica di San Pietro

546 links Bussmann / Neukum-Fichtner, S. 89

546 mittig Bussmann / Neukum-Fichtner, S. 92

546 rechts Bussmann / Neukum-Fichtner, S. 94

547 links Bussmann / Neukum-Fichtner, S. 91

547 rechts Alexander Lockett von Wittelsbach, Privatbesitz, Foto: Anton Brandl, München

549 Wittelsbacher Ausgleichsfonds München, *Inv.-Nr. B I 227*

554–556 Privatbesitz, Foto: Anton Brandl, München

557 Wittelsbacher Ausgleichsfonds, München, *Inv.-Nr. B I a 248*

558/559 Wittelsbacher Ausgleichsfonds, München, *Inv.-Nr. B I 302*

560–562/563 Privatbesitz

564 Bayerisches Armeemuseum, Ingolstadt, *Inv.-Nr. B 5639*

565 Wittelsbacher Ausgleichsfonds, München, Schloss Berchtesgaden, *Inv.-Nr. WAF B I a 251*

566 f. Kunstaktionshaus Neumeister, Sonderaktion „Das Bayerische Königsservice" am 28. Juni 2006, Foto: Christian Mitko

568 f. Königlich Bayerischer Yachtclub, Starnberg, Foto: Anton Brandl, München

570 f. Privatbesitz, Foto: Anton Brandl, München

573 Sammlung Archiv f. Kunst & Geschichte, Foto: akg-images

574/575 Diözesanmuseum Freising, *Inv.-Nr. D 7429*

577 Stadtarchiv München, *Inv.-Nr. REV-330*

Kapitel 6

580–590/591 Privatbesitz, Foto: Anton Brandl, München

592 Wittelsbacher Ausgleichsfonds, München, *Inv.-Nr. B I a 254*

593 Wittelsbacher Ausgleichsfonds, München, *Inv.-Nr. B I a 253*

595 Wittelsbacher Ausgleichsfonds, München, *Inv.-Nr. B I a 231*

596–598 Privatbesitz, Foto: Anton Brandl, München

599 Wittelsbacher Ausgleichsfonds, München, *Inv.-Nr. B I a 215*

601 oben Stadtarchiv München, *Inv.-Nr. ZS-565-1-01*

601 unten Stadtarchiv München, *Inv.-Nr. ZS-565-1-02*

602 Wittelsbacher Ausgleichsfonds, München, *Inv.-Nr. B I a 288*

603–605 Privatbesitz, Foto: Anton Brandl, München

606 Privatbesitz, Foto: Meta Köhler

607 Privatbesitz, Foto: Anton Brandl, München

608 Privatbesitz, Foto: Meta Köhler

609 Privatbesitz, Foto: Anton Brandl, München

611 Landeshauptstadt München, Foto: Anton Brandl, München

611 Privatbesitz

612 Privatbesitz, Foto: Anton Brandl, München

613 Privatbesitz, Foto: Meta Köhler

614 Privatbesitz, Hannes Heindl

615 Privatbesitz, Foto: Anton Brandl, München

616 Privatbesitz

617 Privatbesitz, Foto: Anton Brandl, München

618–623 Privatbesitz

625 Privatbesitz, Foto: Franz Dilger, St. Ottilien

626 „Das jagdliche Vermächtnis Herzog Albrechts von Bayern", Paul Parey Zeitschriftenverlag

627 Kgl. Priv. FSG „Der Bund", Foto: Brigitte G. Hölscher

629 Staatliche Münzsammlung München, Foto: Nicolai Kästner

631–637 Privatbesitz

Exkurs I

639 Bayerische Staatsgemäldesammlungen, München, *Inv.-Nr. 3518*, Foto: Blauel/Gnamm – Artothek

641 Österreichische Nationalbibliothek, Wien

643 links Kurpfälzisches Museum, Heidelberg, Leihgabe: Ministerium für Wissenschaft und Kunst Baden-Württemberg, *Inv.-Nr. L 156*

643 rechts Kurpfälzisches Museum, Heidelberg, Leihgabe: Ministerium für Wissenschaft und Kunst Baden-Württemberg, *Inv.-Nr. L157*

644 Nationalmuseum Stockholm, *Inv.-Nr. NM 2642*

645 Nationalmuseum Stockholm, *Inv.-Nr. NMGrh 459*

647 Nationalmuseum Stockholm, *Inv.-Nr. NMDrh 191*

649 König Otto von Griechenland-Museum der Gemeinde Ottobrunn, Prof. Dr. Jan Murkens, *Katalog-Abb. 43*

Exkurs II

651 Wittelsbacher Ausgleichsfonds, München, Hausritterorden vom Heiligen Georg

652 Wittelsbacher Ausgleichsfonds, München, Residenz München, Alte Hofkapelle

653 Bayerische Verwaltung der staatlichen Schlösser, Gärten und Seen, München, Marstallmuseum Schloss Nymphenburg, *Inv.-Nr. G 112 BSV*

654 Ingolstadt, Kongregationskirche Maria del Victoria, Foto: Georg Pfeilschifter

655 Bayerische Verwaltung der staatlichen Schlösser, Gärten und Seen, Schloss Nymphenburg, *Inv.-Nr. Ny G 17*

656 Wittelsbacher Ausgleichsfonds, München, *Inv.-Nr. B III a 56*

657 Privatbesitz

658/659 Wittelsbacher Ausgleichsfonds, München, *Inv.-Nr. B II 144*

661 Bayerische Verwaltung der staatlichen Schlösser, Gärten und Seen, Ahnengalerie, R 4, *Inv.-Nr. ResMü Gw 22, Seelig Kat. 80*

662 Privatbesitz

663 Bayerische Staatsgemäldesammlungen, München, *Inv.-Nr. 9088*, Foto: Blauel/Gnamm – Artothek

665 Mariae Himmelfahrt, Wildenwart

WITTELSBACH
EDITION

® Marke der
SCHLOSS KALTENBERG KÖNIGLICHE HOLDING UND LIZENZ KG,
Schloßstr. 8, 82269 Geltendorf

© 2014 by Volk Verlag München; Streitfeldstraße 19; 81673 München
Tel.: 0 89/420 79 69 80; Fax: 0 89/420 79 69 86
www.volkverlag.de
Druck: Himmer AG, Augsburg

Der Herausgeber hat sich bemüht, alle Rechteinhaber der Abbildungen
ausfindig zu machen. Berechtigte Ansprüche werden selbstverständlich im
Rahmen der üblichen Vereinbarungen abgegolten.

Die Deutsche Bibliothek verzeichnet diese Publikation in der Deutschen
Nationalbibliografie; detaillierte bibliografische Daten sind im Internet über
http://dnb.ddb.de abrufbar. Alle Rechte, einschließlich derjenigen des auszugs-
weisen Abdrucks sowie der fotomechanischen Wiedergabe, vorbehalten.

ISBN 978-3-86222-136-3